Law and Economics of International Telecommunications

Under the Auspices of the Max Planck Institute for Foreign and International Private Law
edited by Prof. Ernst-Joachim Mestmäcker and Prof. Christoph Engel

Volume 43

Christoph Engel/Kenneth H. Keller (eds.)

# Governance of Global Networks in the Light of Differing Local Values

Nomos Verlagsgesellschaft
Baden-Baden

Die Deutsche Bibliothek – CIP-Einheitsaufnahme
Die Deutsche Bibliothek – CIP Cataloguing-in-Publication-Data

Ein Titeldatensatz für diese Publikation ist bei der
Deutschen Bibliothek erhältlich. (http://www.ddb.de)

A catalogue record for this publication is available from
Die Deutsche Bibliothek. (http://www.ddb.de)

ISBN 3-7890-6703-2

ISSN 0935-0624

1. Auflage 2000

# Foreword

Leviathan or Behemoth, Athens or Orwell, the end of the nation state or political power without limits – these are the contrasting perceptions that different groups have of global networks, and the Internet in particular. Views differ fundamentally not only in the public debate, but among academics, who are no less divided in their judgments and forecasts.

The debate, itself, however, is far from academic. Ultimately, it will affect decisions that nations must take on the policies and governance structures needed to facilitate and regulate high bandwidth communications, encryption, intellectual property protection, e-commerce and even web content. In turn, these policies and structures must be sensitive, as the public surely is, to the potential impact of the Internet on the ability of communities at all levels to maintain or even to enhance local values.

This volume offers a collection of papers that address the governance of global networks from the point of view of its effects on local values. These papers were presented and discussed at a symposium held in June 1999 at Woods Hole, Massachusetts. The papers in a previous volume explored how specific local values might be affected by the global character of electronic networks. The topics covered stretched from pornography and hate speech to broad aspects of culture, from privacy and freedom of information to general issues of democracy. In this volume, the papers deal with governance tools – legal and technical, public and private, and hybrid mixtures of them.

The two volumes, and the symposia which gave rise to them, are part of an endeavor financed by the German American Academic Council and jointly organized by the Computer Sciences and Telecommunication Board of the U.S. National Research Council, Washington, and the Max Planck Project Group on the Law of Common Goods, Bonn. The overall project is directed by a bi-national Steering Committee whose hard work we, as co-chairmen, would like to acknowledge. The members of the Committee are listed in the Appendix. We are also indebted to Herb Lin (senior scientist) and to Nicci Dowd (project assistant) of the Computer Science and Telecommunications Board, and to Joachim Dölken, Dr. Lorenz Müller, and Wolf Osthaus (research associates), Thomas Feldkamp (editorial assistant) and Anja Moosmann (project assistant) of the Max Planck Project Group on the Law of Common Goods.

The views expressed in these papers are those of the authors and do not necessarily represent those of the organizing institutions. A final National Research Council report, drawing in part on these papers, will be published in early 2001, upon completion of the project.

Christoph Engel | Kenneth H. Keller

# Foreword

# Contents

*Bernd Holznagel*

# Responsibility for Harmful and Illegal Content as well as Free Speech on the Internet in the United States of America and Germany

# A. Introduction

We all know that a society's values find an expression in its legal system. Values which are regarded as very important are protected by means of criminal law. This is also the case as far as communication is concerned: The communication of certain content is penalized, as many examples show: defamation, copyright violations, the transmission of child pornography or - especially in Germany a point of concern with regard to our history - the agitation against minorities or the disparagement of victims of national socialist crimes. Communication is forbidden and sanctioned, as far as it excessively threatens the interests of third persons or society as a whole.

Since the Internet makes the worldwide distribution and reception of information for the private citizen much easier than was the case with traditional means of communication, countries encounter the problem of how to defend themselves against forbidden communications content and of how to hold the persons who create and distribute such content liable for their actions. Moreover, in democratic societies, any attempt at regulating communication has to be balanced with the important constitutional rights of freedom of expression and freedom of speech. It is obvious that this balancing attempt can result in varying outcomes in different countries due to differing local values. Conflicts between the different legal systems are the result, as the example of liability for content that is illegal or harmful to minors shows.

Recently, there were two cases in this context with similar factual settings, one in the USA and one in Germany, which gave rise to a controversial discussion not only in legal circles, but also amongst the general public: The verdict of the *Amtsgericht München* (local court in Munich) against the former CompuServe executive Felix Somm and the decision rendered by the Florida Court of Appeals in the matter *Doe v. America Online*.

In the German case, Mr. Somm was accused of being an accomplice to the crime of distributing child pornography, in accordance with statutes which are part of the German Criminal Code (*StGB)* and the "Law against Writings which are Harmful to Minors" (*GjSM))*[1]. At the time of his alleged offenses, Mr. Somm was managing director of CompuServe GmbH Germany, a wholly-owned subsidiary of CompuServe Inc., USA. CompuServe GmbH provided German users with dial-up access to the online service of CompuServe Inc. in the USA. In November 1995, German police notified Mr. Somm of five newsgroups with child pornography content on the servers of CompuServe, Inc. and served on the defendant a list of 282 Usenet newsgroups accessible through CompuServe that supposedly contained pornographic images or could at least be used to place such content. Mr. Somm immediately passed this information to the parent company in the United States, asking it to "delete or block" those news-

* I would like to thank *Daniel Nathrath* for his support in the preparation and the translation of this paper.

1 The court sentenced *Mr. Somm* because he allegedly violated § 184 par. 3 No. 2 StGB and §§ 3 par. 1 No. 2, 1 par. 3, 21 par. 1 No. 2, par. 3 GjSM.

groups. CompuServe, Inc. promptly deleted said information on the newsgroups and blocked access to all 282 newsgroups for users in Germany. The result was a wave of protests by users. Therefore, while the five newsgroups that had contained pornographic material relating to children remained permanently blocked, the other 277 newsgroups were re-opened in February 1996 after CompuServe, Inc. and CompuServe GmbH Germany had provided their members with "child safeguard software". On subsequent checks, German police retrieved individual news postings with "hard pornographic" content from the news servers of CompuServe, Inc. through the network node computer of CompuServe GmbH Germany. Supposedly, it was possible to retrieve these files because the blocking software did not function properly or because the creators of the criminal content somehow avoided the blocking mechanisms. The pornography charges against Mr. Somm related to 13 of the above-mentioned images. And, indeed, the *Amtsgericht München* held Mr. Somm criminally liable for this third-party content. Mr. Somm was given a two-year suspended sentence, three years' probation, and a fine of 100,000 German marks (approximately $ 55,000 as of May 25, 1999).

The outcome in the civil lawsuit *Doe. v. America Online* was entirely different. The plaintiff in this case alleged that AOL had negligently permitted one of its subscribers to disseminate advertisements in AOL chatrooms for a videotape depicting the subscriber having sex with the plaintiff's son, who was a minor. The plaintiff claimed that AOL was negligent for not supervising and filtering the conversations in its chatrooms in a sufficient manner and that AOL therefore was liable in tort for allegedly violating two Florida state statutes that established criminal penalties for participation in the sale or distribution of obscene materials[2]. The suit was dismissed and the dismissal was confirmed on appeal[3], with the courts basing their decision on 47 U.S.C. § 230 (c)(1) - one of the provisions of the so-called Communications Decency Act of 1996 (CDA), which had survived the Supreme Court decision in *Reno v. ACLU*[4]. The court concluded that AOL should not be put in the same shoes as the subscriber who had published his statements.

How are such different outcomes possible? The cases seem to be similar in spite of the fact that one is a criminal case and the other a civil lawsuit. In both cases the Internet provider was not the creator of the allegedly illegal content and had most probably not even known about the existence of this content and about the fact that it was communicated through its infrastructure before being made aware of it. Are the local values in both countries so different? Or is the Somm decision perhaps an expression of an alleged hostility towards new technologies in Germany, where the central position of providers for the functioning of the new medium Internet is not recognized? Or, even worse, are our courts still locked in the tradition of a state where censorship and sur-

2 Fla.St. §§ 847,011(1)(a) and 847,0135(2).

3 1997 WL 374223, at *1, *aff'd, Doe v. America Online, Inc.*, No. 97-2587, 1998 WL 712764 (Fla. Ct. App. Oct. 14, 1998).

4 117 S. Ct. 2329 (1997).

veillance rule, while free speech is not guaranteed[5]? Should providers stop doing business in Germany in order to avoid unforeseeable liability risks? Let us consider the legal traditions which are mirrored in these two decisions.

## B. Protection of Minors as a Common Tradition and Value in the USA and Germany

### I. Goals and Instruments of Youth Protection

The protections of minors is seen as a very significant goal in the USA as well as in Germany. In Germany, it is even constitutionally guaranteed, as Art. 6 par. 2 *Grundgesetz* (Basic Law, abbreviated *GG*) or Art. 5 par. 2 GG shows[6]. In the United States, the Supreme Court has, for instance in the case *Ginsberg v. New York*[7], found that the government has a legitimate interest in protecting the physical and psychological well-being of minors[8]. Thus, it is not surprising that there are several statutes in both countries with the purpose of protecting children and adolescents. It is also typical for both countries that rules exist which attempt to limit the typical dangers originating from the media. In general, we can single out two different goals contained in these rules:

One goal aims at the direct protection of children and adolescents from physical abuse. To achieve this goal, certain types of content are regularly declared illegal, so that the distribution or even possession of writings, videos etc. is prohibited. The basis for this concept is the underlying assumption - and let me stress the word "assumption" - that the possession or distribution of pornographic pictures of children encourages the "producers" of such criminal content to rape, abuse or - as recently demonstrated in spectacular cases in Belgium - even kidnap and murder children for this purpose. One hopes that, if distribution can be stopped, pursuit of the demand for such content will cease and, as a result of that, a corresponding decrease in its production will occur. So the reason for criminally sanctioning the possession and distribution of child pornography is based on the premise that the consumer who accesses such pornographic material, indirectly aids the sexual abuse of children and that the consumer therefore carries responsibility for the existence of the child pornography market and the sexual abuse of children which occurs to feed this market[9]. At the same time, it aims to discourage others from imitating the pictured conduct.

---

5 Some comments in the international media seem to indicate that this was indeed a widespread perception, see, e.g., *Wired*, "German Internet Angst", at: <http://www.wired.com/news/news/email/other/politics/story/12884.html>.

6 See *Engels*, Kinder- und Jugendschutz in der Verfassung, AÖR 122 (1997), 220 ff.; *Schulz*, Jugendschutz bei Tele- und Mediendiensten, MMR 1998, 182, 183.

7 390 U.S. 629 (1968).

8 390 U.S. 629, 640.

9 *Tröndle*, Kommentar zum StGB, 48th edition, München 1997, § 184, Rn. 42; to understand the *ratio legis* of § 184 StGB the reasons given in the government draft of the law are interesting, BT-Drs. 12/3001.

The other goal aims at the avoidance of subjecting children and adolescents to content which could have a negative influence on the development of their personalities in line with their ages. Traditionally, the chosen means of protection are fine-tuned to the special characteristics of the different media. Thus, one can find the total prohibition of distribution as well as *watershed*-rules, which are typical for the television industry and which limit the transmission of films that could harm minors to late-night programs.

Experiments in media-specific youth protection, via procedural elements such as a "government youth protection officer" (*Jugendschutzbeauftragter)* or via technical means such as the V-Chip also now exist.

In the following chapters, I examine the specifically Internet-related statutory sanctions and their constitutionality. I shall try to depict the basic structure of the American law in this field first and then the German legal situation.

## II. Statutory Prohibitions and their Constitutionality

### 1. United States

a) Prohibition of pornographic content relating to children

There is a separate statute in the USA which regulates criminal sanctions for child pornography, called the "Child Pornography Prevention Act" from 1996[10], which added some provisions to the former "Child Pornography Act" and which increased the scope of behavior giving rise to criminal liability. According to these statutes, everyone commits a crime who knowingly, using any means of communication, including computers, possesses, sends, distributes or receives three or more copies of a depiction of sexually explicit behavior with the participation of a minor[11]. The scope of prohibited and sanctioned behavior includes - just as in Germany[12] - also the possession or distribution of depictions which were created by use of computers (e.g., *morphing)* and for which there was no actual physical sexual contact made with minors[13].

10 Child Pornography Prevention Act of 1996, Pub. L. No. 104-208, 110 Stat. 3009-26.

11 18 U.S.C. § 2252. The reason given for this statute is: "Child pornography is often used as part of a method of seducing other children into sexual activity, encourages child sexual abuse, and is a model for sexual behavior."

12 § 184 par. 4 StGB

13 However, it is disputed among legal scholars in the USA whether this expansion of the scope of criminally sanctioned behavior could pass a First Amendment scrutiny. See, e.g., *Esposito*, Regulating the Internet: The New Battle Against Child Pornography, 30 Case W. Res. J. Int'l L. 541, 551; *Loundy*, E-Law: In Case You Had Not Noticed, Child Porn is Already Illegal, 3 No. 4 Cyberspace Law. 11; *Edick,* Regulation of Pornography on the Internet in the United States and the United Kingdom: A Comparative Analysis, 21 B.C. Int'l & Comp. L. Rev. 437, 445; *Wasserman*, Virtual.Child.Porn.com: Defending the Constitutionality of the Criminalization of Computer-Generated Child Pornography by the Child Pornography Prevention Act of 1996 - A Reply to Professor Burke and Other Critics, 35 Harv. J. on Legis. 245 pp; *Burke,* The Criminalization of Virtual Child Pornography: A Constitutional Question, 34 Harv. J. on Legis. 439, 440; Stewart, If This is the Global Community, We Must Be On The Bad Side of Town: International Policing of Child Pornography on the Internet, 20 HOUS. J. INT'L L. 205;. Recently, the U.S. Court of Ap-

b) Initiatives towards online-specific rules for the protection of minors

*aa) The Communications Decency Act (CDA)*

*(1) Criminal sanctions for "indecent" and "patently offensive" speech*

In contrast to the law in Germany, there are currently no statutes in force in the United States which are designed to counter the Internet-specific dangers for the well-being of children and adolescents. However, there have been several initiatives in this direction. In February, 1996, the U.S. Congress passed the Communications Decency Act (CDA) which prohibited the transmission of "indecent or patently offensive" content under certain circumstances.

The CDA made it a crime "to use a telecommunications device to create, or solicit any communication which is obscene, lewd, lascivious, filthy, or indecent with the intent to annoy, abuse, threaten, or harass". Furthermore the CDA made it illegal "to make any obscene or indecent communication knowing the recipient is under eighteen years old, no matter who initiated the communication". The CDA also prohibited people "to use an interactive computer service to (1) send specific minors a communication that depicts or describes sexual or excretory activities or organs in terms patently offensive under contemporary community standards, regardless of who initiated the communication; or (2) display such communication in a manner available to a person under eighteen years of age; or (3) intentionally permit one's telecommunications facility to be used for the acts described above". The potential sanction was up to two years of imprisonment and/or monetary fines. Minutes after the CDA was passed, the American Civil Liberties Union (ACLU) and other organizations filed suit[14] to enjoin enforcement of these provisions. The suit was supported through *briefs amici* by 27 other groups, including the Electronic Frontier Foundation, National Writers' Union, Human Rights Watch etc.

*(2) Standard of scrutiny for governmental speech regulation*

In June, 1996, in *ACLU v. Reno*, the U.S. District Court for the Eastern District of Pennsylvania declared several provisions of the CDA unconstitutional[15] and enjoined the Justice Department from enforcing them[16]. Before we look at the central passages of the verdict, we want to glance briefly at the standard of scrutiny that is applied to state action in the First Amendment area. The First Amendment states, as you all probably know: "Congress shall make no law ... abridging the freedom of speech, or the press".

---

peals for the First Circuit overturned a decision by a lower court which had viewed the Child Pornography Prevention Act as too vague and therefore unconstitutional. The First Circuit Court of Appeals decided that the law neither impinges substantially on protected expression nor is so vague as to offend due process (*U.S. v. Hilton*, No. 98-1513, 1999 U.S. App. LEXIS 1105 (D. Me. Jan. 27, 1999).

14 929 F. Supp. 824, 828 (E.D. Pa. 1996), aff'd., 117 S. Ct. 2329 (1997).

15 This presents a contrast to the law in Germany, where laws can only be declared unconstitutional by the Federal Constitutional Court (*Bundesverfassungsgericht*).

16 ACLU v. Reno, 929 F. Supp. 824, 856, 858 (E.D. Pa. 1996).

The scope of protection generally includes any form of expression, which also means "symbolic conduct" like the burning of a flag. However, according to the Supreme Court, obscene speech is not protected. The test for obscenity was developed in 1973 in the case *Miller v. California*[17] (therefore also called the "Miller Test"). The questions to be examined are: 1) if the average person, applying contemporary community standards, would find that the work, taken as a whole, appeals to a "prurient interest" in sex; (2) if the work depicts or describes sexual conduct in a patently offensive manner; (3) if the work, taken as a whole, lacks substantial literary, artistic, political or scientific value". Material which is merely "sexually explicit", pornographic, indecent or which includes nudity or "dirty words" is not obscene and generally protected by the First Amendment.

Although the words of the First Amendment do not contain any limits to the freedom of expression, such limits were developed by the Supreme Court. The Court applies a balancing test. The central part of this test examines the relationship between the interest the state seeks to protect and the means it intends to use to do so. However, as is typical in American constitutional law, there is no abstract balancing of colliding rights: particular cases are considered instead.

Government action which aims at the content of expression must pass a strict scrutiny test. Action can only be justified if the state can prove that the regulation serves a compelling state interest through narrowly-defined means. These requirements can rarely be met in practice. The Supreme Court has held that content-based regulations of speech are presumptively invalid, because the government shall not have the power to suppress speech on account of its content[18].

If, on the other hand, government regulation does not aim directly at content but affects expression only indirectly, as a by-product of regulating other conduct, a more lenient standard is applied. In general, the government may impose reasonable *time, place and manner* restrictions on speech. Time, place and manner restrictions are reasonable if they are content-neutral, serve significant government interests, are narrowly-defined and not overbroad, and leave open ample alternative opportunities for communication.

Moreover, several general requirements must be met. Because free expression is easily "chilled", the courts sometimes permit laws restraining expression to be challenged "on face value" for vagueness or overbreadth. A facial challenge can be brought by someone whose speech is not constitutionally protected, but who is permitted, in effect, to raise the rights of third parties before the court. Thus, such challenges can be successful even though the law, *had it been properly drawn up*, could have applied constitutionally in the particular instance. A statute is *vague* and, thus, unconstitutional on its surface, if a person of common intelligence could not know what behavior is prohibited. A law is *overbroad* and, thus, unconstitutional on its surface, if it prohibits substantially more expression than is necessary. An overbroad law may, but need not, be vague. Indeed, it might be very clear, but simply encompass too much protected behavior.

---

17 *Miller v. California,* 413 U.S., 24.

18 See *R.A.V. v. City of St. Paul,* 505 U.S. 377 (1992).

### *(3) Constitutional analysis of the CDA*

The Eastern District Court of Pennsylvania found that the CDA was unconstitutional because Sec. 223(a)(1)(B) and 223(a)(2) of the Act were "vague"[19] and therefore *unconstitutional on their surface*[20]. Since the law speaks of "indecent" and "patently offensive", it could not be ruled out that it also affects and prohibits protected communication between adults. However, the court stated that this could not be justified with the protection of minors alone. The three-judge district court panel also stated in this context that, at the time of the decision, there were no technologically or economically feasible means to make content on the Internet accessible only to adults or only to minors. Furthermore, it said that the use of credit cards to prevent access by minors to harmful content is no solution, since non-commercial content providers are affected as well[21]. The court found a verification system employing "adult check"-like passwords to be of questionable success as well, due to the administrative burdens it would place on non-commercial web publishers[22]. Another problem the court noted with the regulatory concept of the CDA was the fact that an estimated 40% or more of Internet content originates from outside the United States, with foreign content being indistinguishable from domestic content, a problem which is aggravated by the use of caching. This makes a distinction between foreign and domestic source material impossible, so that it would be practically impossible to enforce the attacked provisions in practice[23]. Also, the court observed that there is a vast amount of worthwhile material available online that would be banned by the statute, including information about homosexuality, female genital mutilation, prison rape, art - subjects that the government has not shown it has a compelling interest in preventing a 17-year old from accessing.[24]. On June 16, 1997 the U.S. Supreme Court confirmed the District Court's decision[25].

### *bb) COPA*

#### *(1) Regulated behavior*

The failure of the CDA did not lead to the legislature giving up its attempts to introduce Internet-specific rules for the protection of minors. In fall 1998, Congress passed the Child Online Protection Act (COPA)[26], following an initiative by Rep. *Mike Oxley* (R-Ohio) and *Dan Coats* (R-Ind.)[27]. COPA is narrower in scope than the CDA, but is similar in its regulatory approach and is therefore often called "CDA II". Its creators view it

19 *ACLU v. Reno*, 929 F. Supp. 824, 856, 858 (E.D. Pa. 1996).

20 *ib.*, 929 F. Supp. 824, 849 (E.D. Pa. 1996).

21 *ACLU v. Reno*, 929 F. Supp. 824, 846 (E.D. Pa. 1996) (findings 99-100).

22 *ib.*, 929 F. Supp. 824, 846-847 (E.D. Pa. 1996) (findings 103-107).

23 *ib.*, 929 F. Supp. 824, 848 (E.D. Pa. 1996) (findings 118-119).

24 *ACLU v. Reno*, 929 F. Supp. 824, 852-853 (E.D. Pa. 1996) .

25 *Reno v. ACLU*, 117 S. Ct. 2329 (1997).

26 H.R. 3783.

27 This is only one of several attempts of representatives to introduce youth protection rules for the Internet in Congress.

as being tailored to meet the guidelines set down by the Supreme Court in its previously mentioned decision striking several provisions of the CDA, by using a narrower "harmful to minors" standard instead of the "indecency" standard. Moreover, COPA only targeted the commercial distribution of material over the World Wide Web, not chatrooms, e-mail or newsgroups.

The central provision of COPA is Sec. 231:

"(Restriction of Access by Minors to Materials Commercially Distributed by Means of the World Wide Web That are Harmful to Minors): (a) Requirement to Restrict Access

> (1) PROHIBITED CONDUCT – "Whoever knowingly and with knowledge of the character of the material, in interstate or foreign commerce by means of the World Wide Web, makes any communication for commercial purposes that is available to any minor and includes any material that is harmful to minors shall be fined not more than $ 50,000, imprisoned not more than 6 months, or both[28]."

Material is "harmful to minors" according to COPA'S definition, if it, "applying contemporary community standards, is designed to appeal to the prurient interest; depicts or describes any sexual act or conduct in a "patently offensive" manner and lacks serious literary, artistic, political, or scientific value".

In contrast to the CDA, COPA provides good faith affirmative defenses to prosecution which are supposed to reflect current and future Web technology. According to Sec. 231(c) COPA, the content provider does not incur liability from Sec. 231(a) COPA, if he tries in good faith to shield material from minors, which is "harmful to minors" by making access to his content only possible by means of using a credit card[29], a debit card, an adult access code, an adult personal identification number or any other technologically feasible access restriction[30]. Similar to age restrictions for the purchase of potentially harmful printed publications or for access to establishments in a red-light district, only minors, but not adults, shall be prohibited from accessing this online content. However, this so-called "zoning"[31] approach does not intend a complete ban of such content.

---

28 In addition to the criminal penalty of up to $ 50,000, which is, in the case of intentional violations, applied for every single day of a continuing violation, there can also be a civil penalty of up to $ 50,000 for every day of a violation.

29 Taking privacy concerns with regard to age verification systems into account, Sec. 231(d) COPA prohibits content providers from giving out the data they obtain from their customers in the age verification process.

30 Sec. 231(a)(2) und (3) COPA.

31 "Zoning" is now a commonly used term, see for example *Lessig*, What Things Regulate Speech, S. 14, accessible online at: <http://cyber.harvard.edu/works/lessig/what_things.pdf>.

### (2) *Constitutional analysis*

As was the case with the CDA, it only took a very short time after the law was passed until the American Civil Liberties Union (ACLU) and other groups[32] filed suit against the law. On. November 19, 1998, the plaintiffs obtained a temporary restraining order[33] and on February 1, 1999, a preliminary injunction against COPA in United States District Court in Philadelphia[34]. Judge *Reed* came to the result that a fear of criminal sanctions from COPA could, considering the broad applicability of the law, lead to excessive self-censorship. *Reed* stated, "such a chilling effect could result in the censoring of constitutionally protected speech, which constitutes an irreparable harm to the plaintiffs"[35]. The judge expressed personal regret that his decision once again delays the introduction of a carefully improved law for the protection of minors. However, he then added: "...perhaps we do the minors of this country harm if the First Amendment protections, which they will with age inherit fully, are chipped away in the name of their protection". On April 2, 1999, the U.S. Department of Justice appealed the decision of the Philadelphia District Court at the 3rd Circuit Court of Appeals. There, the case is still pending.

Thus, it is still not clear if COPA will withstand constitutional challenge. COPA tries to avoid some of the CDA's problems by using the "harmful to minors" standard instead of the "indecency" standard, introducing good faith defenses, limiting its scope to commercial web sites and not interfering as much with parental educational privileges. However, the majority of legal commentators[36] agrees with the District Court in Philadelphia. They say that COPA would prevent the publication of information such as the "Starr Report", if it was distributed through commercial web sites such as CNN, Yahoo or MSNBC[37]. They see COPA as suffering from the same fundamental flaw as the CDA: The result would be that constitutionally protected speech would be criminalized and the Internet would be reduced to what would be acceptable for a six-year old[38].

---

32 There are 17 plaintiffs altogether, besides the ACLU - for instance The American Booksellers' Foundation for Free Expression, Electronic Frontier Foundation, Condomania, Internet Content Coalition (which has, for example, as its members CBS New Media, The New York Times Electronic Media Company, Time Inc., Cnet, Warner Bros. Online, Playboy Eterprises, MSNBC, Sony Online und ZDNet), Philadelphia Gay News.

33 American Civil Liberties Union Freedom Network, JudgeHalts Enforcement of Internet Censorship Law (Nov. 19, 1998), <http://www.aclu.org/features/f101698a.html>.

34 Judge *Reed* posted the decision on the court's web site, <http://www.paed.uscourts.gov>; see also "First Amendment wins another round online", <http://www.salonmagazine.com/21st/feature/1999/02/02feature.html>.

35 See *Mendels,* Judge Delays Online Pornography Law, New York Times, February 1, 1999, <http://www.nytimes.com/library/tech/99/02/cyber/articles/01copa.html>.

36 See, e.g., *Campbell,* The Child Online Protection Act: Like CDA (Clearly Dead on Arrival)?, 5 No. 2 Multimedia Strategist 1; *Doherty,*<www.obscenity.com>: An analysis of obscenity and indecency regulation on the Internet, 32 Akron L. Rev. 259, 282 (1999); see also the constitutional analysis of the *Center for Democracy and Technology,* Constitutional Analysis of the Oxley Bill - The Child Online Protection Act (H.R. 3783), <http://www.cdt.org/speech/constitutional.html>.

37 *Center for Democracy and Technology,* Constitutional Analysis of the Oxley Bill - The Child Online Protection Act (H.R. 3783), <http://www.cdt.org/speech/constitutional.html>.

38 *Doherty,* <www.obscenity.com>: An analysis of obscenity and indecency regulation on the Inter-

Moreover, they criticize that COPA does not define which community's standard would determine what material "appeals to the prurient interest of children". The traditional U.S. approach, i.e. to determine the standard from the community affected, could not be applied to the Internet[39]. Thus, COPA's enforcement would mean that any commercial communication over the Web would have to follow the standard of the most conservative and restrictive community in the United States [40].

## 2. Germany

### a) Prohibition of pornographic content relating to children and the online-specific youth protection laws

The central provisions in the fight against the distribution of child pornography in Germany are codified in the Federal Criminal Code (*Strafgesetzbuch, abbr. StGB)* in § 184 par. 3 to 5 StGB. This statute imposes criminal sanctions on everyone who distributes, publicly presents or otherwise provides access to child pornography or who creates, receives or keeps child pornography. As you probably noticed, it is significant for the German approach that practically *any* dealing with child pornography is made illegal. With the introduction of the Information and Communication Services Act (*Informations- und Kommunikationsdienstegesetz)* on August 1, 1997, these prohibitions were extended to electronically stored text, pictures or sound files.

In addition to this, the German Internet-specific youth protection law contains several prohibitions, with possible exceptions thereto. It is possible to make an exception to a prohibition if technical access restrictions can prevent the distribution of harmful content to children and adolescents. In this context, we can distinguish between an approach that focuses on the provider and one that focuses on the minors.

The provider-oriented approach is based on the idea of access restriction. This approach, which also finds an expression in COPA can be found, for instance, in Germany in the *Law pertaining to Writings and Media Content which are Harmful to Minors* (*Gesetz über jugendgefährdende Schriften und Medieninhalte,* abbr. *GjSM*).

The instrument used is the creation of an index of writings which can possibly endanger children or adolescents, especially including writings which are indecent or which incite to violence, crimes or racially motivated hate, or which glorify war. § 3 par. 1 GjSM prohibits the distribution, storage or provision of access to a writing[41] which is listed in

net, 32 Akron L. Rev. 259, 282 (1999).

39 *Campbell*, The Child Online Protection Act: Like CDA (Clearly Dead on Arrival)?, 5 No. 2 *Multimedia Strategist* 1.

40 Critics of COPA also point out that the distribution of illegal content over the Internet is already prohibited by the Federal Obscenity Law and the Child Pornography Prevention Act. Therefore, COPA results in double criminal liability for a defendant only because he used a computer. This would imply that a defendant's personal guilt is higher just because the crime was committed over the Internet However, the Internet does not increase the criminal potential; it just makes it easier to commit the crime. See *McCausland,* Regulating Computer Crime after Reno v. ACLU: The Myth of Additional Regulations, 49 *Fla. L. Rev.* 483, 497-498 (1997).

41 This includes sound, picture and storage media.

this index. An exception is made in the statute if through technological means precautions are made to limit distribution within Germany to adults. The statute does not state what kind of technological means must be used. For the so-called media services which are offered to the public and which are not primarily intended for individual use (a distinction made in German federal and state legislation that is rather unclear and not very helpful with regard to the Internet), it is sufficient if technological means are used as a precaution in order for children or adolescents to not "normally" be confronted with harmful content. In general, the distribution of media services which are possibly detrimental to the physical, mental, or emotional well-being of minors is prohibited.

The user-oriented approach is intended for the media services with the potential to harm that have been previously mentioned, as far as they are designed as on-demand services and not offered to the general public (again, this distinction is not clear: I am merely describing the regulatory concept as the legislators designed it). These services are only permitted if precautions are provided by the Internet provider or others which allow the user to block such content[42]. So the decision to block or permit a certain content is left to the legal guardians. This choice of a user-oriented approach can be seen as a parallel to American initiatives to require schools and public libraries to use filtering and rating systems or to require providers to supply their customers with youth protection software. In this case, the German legislator again did not formulate how such blocking is be achieved. The reasons underpinning the law, for instance, do not contain any statement on the question whether systems like PICS are sufficient to fulfill the law's requirements.

### b) Constitutional analysis

#### *aa) Standard of scrutiny for state action limiting the freedom of speech*

Considering the intensity of the discussion about the constitutionality of Internet-specific youth protection laws in the United States, we obviously need to ask ourselves in Germany if the provisions introduced in 1997 do not excessively limit the basic right of freedom of speech. The central provision which contains the standard of scrutiny that we need to answer this question is Art. 5 par. 1 *Grundgesetz* (Basic Law, the German constitution, abbr. *GG*). It reads as follows:

> "Everyone has the right to express his opinion orally, in writing or pictures, to spread his opinion and nobody shall be prevented from obtaining information from freely accessible sources. The freedom of the press and the freedom of reporting through broadcast and film are guaranteed. There is no censorship."

German constitutional law is at least as complicated as American constitutional law. Its complexity was expounded as long ago as Kant. Still, I would like to make an attempt at giving a brief introduction to the concept of scrutiny that is applied using this constitutional norm. We will see some important differences to American law:

---

42 § 8 Para. 3 Media Services State Treaty (Treaty between the German States, *Mediendienste-Staatsvertrag der Länder (MDStV).*

Art. 5 par. 1 sentence 1 GG generally protects *every* expression of a private person's opinion. The use of the term "opinion" serves to make a distinction from the expression of facts. The term "opinion" is characterized through the element of a comment in the context of an intellectual difference of opinions. This means that any kind of opinion is certainly protected by the constitution, be it polemic, provoking or formulated in a repulsive way. The principle is that the state has no right to exclude any opinions from the scope of protection contained in the right to freedom of speech.

However, it cannot be disputed that the expression of an opinion frequently includes the description of facts or is argumentatively based on facts. The knowledge about this leads the German constitutional court (*Bundesverfassungsgericht*) to an approach which includes the description or assertion of such facts in the scope of protection of the basic right. Thus, in a certain manner, even statements of facts are protected as opinions in the sense of Art. 5 par. 1 sentence 1 GG.

At the same time, the necessary connection to the term "opinion" in a narrower sense defines the limits of this indirect protection of factual statements, because facts that are evidently false or have been purposely stated falsely are *not* protected by the basic right to freedom of speech in Germany. The process of forming an opinion, which Art. 5 par. 1 sentence 1 GG seeks to secure, does not require the protection of such statements. Nobody has a right to influence public debates through lies.

Insofar as they satisfy these requirements of the term "opinion", even statements or depictions which are harmful to minors are constitutionally protected behavior which the state cannot regulate easily. Let me stress that while the state cannot regulate this behavior "easily", it can, however, regulate it. The protection of opinions from state action is not absolute. Limitations to freedom of speech in Germany are justified - among other scenarios - if their purpose is the protection of minors. To prevent a misunderstanding: This rule - which can be found in Art. 5 par. 2 GG[43] - does not, for example, take definitions relating to child pornography out of the definition of the term "opinion," thereby causing them to be unprotected. Even those generally belong - in contrast to the American constitutional understanding of "obscene" speech - to the scope of protection of Art. 5 par. 1 sentence 1 GG. Only after we have determined this, can we commence scrutiny of Art. 5 par. 2 GG. Art. 5 par. 2 GG therefore authorizes the state to take certain measures to limit freedom of speech.

This also means a substantive difference to American law. The state needs to fulfill certain requirements whenever it limits basic rights. This is what distinguishes state action that touches basic rights from state measures which do not touch basic rights. Lies can always be prohibited. However, when a basic right is subjected to limitation, one always has to look at the meaning of the basic right being limited. Therefore, for instance, the presence of a danger to minors does not automatically mean that this justifies any state action. Regulation is only constitutional if it is as least as important as the right to freedom of speech in a balance test. This is a question of the importance of a

---

43 The translated text of the norm is: "These Rights find their limits in the rules of general laws, in the statutory provisions for the protection of minors and in the law of personal honor".

particular statute or particular measure being taken because of the statute, in comparison to the basic right to freedom of speech.

This last requirement finds its expression in the constitutional principle of a prohibition of *excessive* regulation (*Übermaßverbot*). This principle means that every state action that limits freedom of speech is scrutinized with regard to the question of whether the state action is absolutely necessary to achieve the intended goal. Under this aspect, the state would be prohibited from passing a statute which blocks adults from accessing material harmful to minors, as long as a measure can be taken which effectively prevents access by minors[44]. Taking television as an example: Since with this medium an instrument is available in the form of prohibiting the transmission of certain content before or after a certain time (e.g., late- night erotic movies), a complete ban on the transmission of programs would be unconstitutional, even if it serves the protection of minors equally well.

Even with measures which are permissible under this test, a further test must be applied: namely, whether the intended goal is out of proportion to the extent of interference with the private citizen's rights. On the one hand, the public interest and the degree of its promotion must be weighed up against the measure and, on the other hand, the affected private rights must be weighed up against the intensity of interference therein.

However, this limitation is not as important in the field of protecting minors because the Basic Law itself ranks the protection of minors very high.

Therefore, we will rarely speak of the state's action being disproportionate to the protection of minors, for instance in a case in which state action severely limits private citizens' rights to freedom of speech but, on the other hand, hardly even has any positive effect. Finally, any state action which causes an interference with basic rights must be definite and certain. This means that the regulation must be formulated so clearly as to ensure that the addressee of the regulation unequivocally understands the behavior desired from him. The requirement of certainty is necessary for the effective legal protection of private citizens, which is guaranteed by Art. 19 par. 4 GG. It makes it possible to control state action. The requirement of certainty is very much comparable to the doctrine of *vagueness* in American law. In contrast to the doctrine of vagueness, the German requirement of certainty demands merely a formal scrutiny with regard to the comprehension of and possibility of compliance with certain regulation.

### *bb) Analysis of the new Internet-specific rules for the protection of minors*

Let us apply these principles to the new online specific rules for the protection of minors and let us question their constitutionality: One could - similarly to the argumentation in *ACLU v. Reno* - say that the use of terms which are widely uncertain and thus open to interpretation (just think about terms such as "pornographic" or "harmful to minors") could violate the requirement of certainty. One could also doubt the feasibility of total bans as an instrument for the effective protection of minors in a global computer

44 BVerfGE 30, 336/348.

network setting. Moreover, one could argue that user-oriented approaches are less restrictive means in comparison to access control systems which place a burden on the provider. Finally, one could argue that these new German laws, just as was done against COPA, cause a "chilling effect", an incentive for self-censorship, which cannot be justified looking at the fundamental significance of the fundamental right of freedom of speech for the democratic process.

Regarding these possible arguments against the new German laws, one might be surprised to find that these arguments were - as far as I can judge - not expressed at all. The constitutionality of these provisions seems to be so self-explanatory to everyone that a controversial discussion about them never even arose. One reason for this is probably that the German legislature has never tried to introduce an absolute ban against indecent content on the Internet, towards which the CDA was leaning. This would have been in contradiction to the regulation used so far in the area of media-specific youth protection. Moreover, in Germany, much trust is generally placed in the provisions for the protection of minors being applied by the authorities with proper respect for the basic right of freedom of speech.

Also, in German society, there is currently no such polarization of the public with regard to moral questions as in the USA, where the issue is being pushed by the "moral right", which leads to liberals feeling called upon to defend freedom rights. Finally, one reason for the fact that there is more of a debate in the USA can be seen in the American tradition of accepting any limitation of the 1$^{st}$ amendment only in exceptional cases like child pornography. The same is true for the balancing test in the field of defamation law, in which personal honor in comparison to freedom of speech is valued higher in Germany than in the U.S.

### 3. Summary

The protection of minors is, without a doubt, traditionally regarded as having a high value in the USA as well as in Germany.

In both countries, a balancing test is used to reach a judgment between the conflicting interests.

Both countries share the point of view that a total ban on child pornography does not violate the basic right of freedom of speech.

However, there are differences with regard to practical questions as far as the assessment of Internet-specific youth protection instruments is concerned. These are - how could it be any different - strongly influenced by the legal cultures of both countries and current conflicts within each country's society.

# C. Liability for Third-Party Content in Germany and the United States

## I. Controversial Liability Situation of Host Providers

In the current discussion concerning free speech on the Internet, a central issue is not only the civil and criminal liability of content providers, which was described above, but also the legal position of intermediaries in the communication process. These are all third persons who contribute to the distribution of third-party content. The situation for mere access providers is quite clear. Access providers only provide the technical infrastructure for connections to the Internet, and do not have any influence on the content transported through their lines. They are comparable to the postal service, which also has no knowledge about the contents of the letters it transports. Thus, the access provider is immune from any liability according to the planned E-Commerce directive of the European Community, the *Teleservices Act (Teledienstegesetz, abbr. TDG)* as part of the *Information and Communication Services Act* in Germany, and the legal situation in the United States[45].

However, the question of liability arises in the case of the so-called host providers, who store third-party content for use by third persons[46]. They have a very central function for the new Internet world, because they provide, either free-of-charge or against payment, web space or bulletin boards for the content providers. In general, the host provider does not have any influence on the content put on its servers by the content provider[47]. However, it can also moderate newsgroups and thereby be involved in the process of putting the content together. These frequently-changing roles are one reason that there is a dispute between placing host providers in the same category as content providers, who are fully responsible for their content, or in the same category as access providers, who are not held responsible for their content. This is also shown by the cases presented in the introduction to this paper and which led to different results.

In the following part, a comparison between the liability situations of host providers in the USA and Germany is made and the implications for the basic right of free speech in this sector are discussed. This leads us back to our original starting point: *Doe v. America Online* and *CompuServe* and *Felix Somm.*

## II. United States

To understand why there was no conviction in the case *Doe v. America Online,* let us consider the development of the rules regarding provider liability in the USA[48].

---

45 § 5 Abs. 3 TDG; § 13 E-Commerce directive.

46 That is the definition in § 5 Abs. 2 TDG.

47 It is somewhat confusing for some that there are companies which perform several of these functions simultaneously. For instance, AOL is at the same time a *content provider* (with its own or purchased content on AOL's own pages), an a*ccess provider* (by providing dial-up access to the Internet to its members) and also a *host provider* (by giving its members the possibility to store their homepages on AOL's servers for access by third persons).

48 The liability for copyright violations by users of Internet services is a special case of liability for

## 1. The Law before the CDA was passed

Before the CDA was passed, there was great uncertainty among American Internet providers about their potential liability for legal violations caused by third persons using their services. Only in two cases were lower courts confronted with this question: *Cubby, Inc. v. CompuServe*[49] and *Stratton Oakmont, Inc. v. Prodigy Servs. Co.*[50] In each case the courts reached different results.

### a) Cubby v. CompuServe

In the case *Cubby v. CompuServe* the issue was a defamation action against the online service CompuServe. CompuServe was running "fora" for different interests as part of its online service, which included electronic bulletin boards, interactive chat services and topic-related databases[51]. One of these fora, which dealt with the topic of journalism, was regulated and controlled by Cameron Communications, Inc. (CCI), an independent contractor. This activity was administered "in accordance with editorial and technical standards established by CompuServe"[52]. In its turn, CCI had contracted with *Don Fitzpatrick Associates of San Francisco* (DFA) for the latter to deliver a daily newsletter for CCI, "Rumorville", which reported about journalism and the activities of journalists. CompuServe had no contractual relationship with DFA and no opportunity to supervise the content of "Rumorville" before DFA uploaded it onto CompuServe's servers, from which it was then immediately accessible by CompuServe's customers[53]. When defamatory statements with regard to *Cubby, Inc.* were published in "Rumorville", *Cubby* sued CompuServe under New York law. CompuServe argued that it had acted as *distributor*, not as *publisher* of the statements and that it could therefore not be held liable for the statements, since it had not known about them[54].

The court pointed out that, although someone who publishes defamatory material in principle incurs the same liability as the one who originally published it, news agencies, bookstores and libraries cannot be held liable if they did not know about the defamatory nature of the material[55]. Furthermore the court stated that it is "deeply rooted in the 1st Amendment" that a distributor cannot be held liable if it had not known the content of

---

which separate legislation has been passed and with which we do not deal in this paper, see the new *Digital Millennium Copyright Act,* summarized at: *Delaney/Kim/Isser,* The Law of the Internet: A Summary of U.S. Internet Caselaw and Legal Developments, 545 PLI/Pat 61, 94ff.

49 *Cubby, Inc. v. CompuServe, Inc.*, 776 F. Supp. 135 (S.D.N.Y. 1991).

50 *Stratton Oakmont, Inc. v. Prodigy Servs. Co*, 1995 WL 323710 (N.Y. Sup. Ct. May 24, 1995).

51 *Cubby, Inc. v. CompuServe, Inc.*, 776 F. Supp. 135, 137 (S.D.N.Y. 1991).

52 *Ibidem.*

53 *Ibidem.*

54 *Cubby, Inc. v. CompuServe, Inc.*, 776 F. Supp. 135, 138 (S.D.N.Y. 1991).

55 *Cubby, Inc. v. CompuServe, Inc.*, 776 F. Supp. 135, 139 (S.D.N.Y. 1991), referring to *Lerman v. Chuckleberry Publishing, Inc.*, 521 F. Supp. 228, 235 (S.D.N.Y. 1981) and *Macaluso v. Mondadori Publishing Co.*, 527 F. Supp. 1017, 1019 (E.D. N.Y. 1981).

the publication[56]. The court came to the result that CompuServe had possessed no more control than a library, bookstore or newsstand over the content of the publications which can be accessed through the firm, and dismissed the suit[57].

b) Stratton Oakmont v. Prodigy

Another court reached a completely opposing result in the case *Stratton Oakmont, Inc. v. Prodigy Services Co.*[58] In this case, an anonymous user of Prodigy's "Money Talk" bulletin board had accused the plaintiff, *Stratton Oakmont, Inc.*, an investment bank, of criminal and fraudulent practices. *Stratton Oakmont* sued *Prodigy* as the company that ran the service on which the statements had appeared. The plaintiff pointed out that Prodigy's Terms of Service included a provision which told users that annoying postings would be removed by Prodigy, should the firm become aware of them[59]. Moreover, Prodigy used software to automatcally search all bulletin board postings for defamatory words and remove them, if found. The court took these facts to distinguish the case from *Cubby v. CompuServe*. The court stated that Prodigy had projected itself to the public, through its Terms of Service and use of screening software, as controlling the bulletin board, while CompuServe had not had comparable control[60]. Thus, the court held that Prodigy was not a *distributor*, but a *publisher* of the statements on the bulletin board. A *publisher*'s liability is stricter than a *distributor*'s, because it is strictly liable even if it does not have knowledge of the illegal content. A *publisher* exercises editoral functions by selecting the material to be published and this editorial activity increases its liability[61]. Just because Prodigy had held itself out as a family-oriented online service and had attempted to gain the benefits of editorial control over third-party content, it had, according to the court, opened itself up to greater liability than CompuServe and therefore had to be held liable as a *publisher*.

## 2. Immunity for Internet Providers, § 230 CDA

a) The law and the intention of Congress

The *Stratton v. Oakmont* decision greatly increased the uncertainty among providers about their potential liability. The strange consequence of the court's argumentation in *Stratton v. Oakmont* was that the provider who made a good-faith effort to remove illegal content from its servers and thereby exercise a certain amount of self-regulation, was subject to stricter liability than the provider who completely abstained from doing anything against illegal content on its servers. Many providers feared unforeseeable liability risks.

---

56 *Cubby, Inc. v. CompuServe, Inc.*, 776 F. Supp. 135, 139 (S.D.N.Y. 1991), the court cited the precedent *Smith v. California*, 361 U.S. 147 (1959).

57 *Cubby, Inc. v. CompuServe, Inc.*, 776 F. Supp. 135, 140 (S.D.N.Y. 1991).

58 *Stratton Oakmont, Inc. v. Prodigy Servs. Co*, 1995 WL 323710 (N.Y. Sup. Ct. May 24, 1995).

59 *Stratton Oakmont, Inc. v. Prodigy Servs. Co*, 1995 WL 323710 *2 (N.Y. Sup. Ct. May 24, 1995).

60 *Stratton Oakmont, Inc. v. Prodigy Servs. Co*, 1995 WL 323710 *4 (N.Y. Sup. Ct. May 24, 1995).

61 *Stratton Oakmont, Inc. v. Prodigy Servs. Co*, 1995 WL 323710 *7 (N.Y. Sup. Ct. May 24, 1995).

The U.S. legislators recognized the legal uncertainty that was created by *Stratton v. Oakmont* and came to the conclusion that this uncertainty was going to be an obstacle to the further development of the Internet. They therefore passed Section 230 as part of the CDA. While the above-mentioned CDA provisions, 47 U.S.C. § 223(a) and 47 U.S.C. § 223(d), which threatened criminal sanctions for the transmission of "indecent" or "patently offensive" material, caused a stricter liability for own content on the Internet, Section 230 went in the opposite direction and limited the liability for third-party content.

The central passage of Section 230 is Section 230(c)(1):

> "No provider or user of an interactive computer service shall be treated as the publisher or speaker of any information provided by another information content provider."

In addition to this, Section 230 (c)(2) contained a direct answer to *Stratton Oakmont*[62]:

> "No provider ... of an interactive computer service shall be held liable on account of any action voluntarily taken in good faith to restrict access to or availability of material that the provider ... considers to be obscene, lewd, lascivious, filthy, excessively violent, harassing, or otherwise questionable."

This clause, labeled "good-samaritan" provision[63], was designed to clarify the point that no provider should be liable because it made a good-faith effort, for instance through the use of computer programs, to remove questionable content from its servers or block access to this content. Finally, Section 230(d)(3) is important:

> "Nothing in this section shall be construed to prevent any State from enforcing any State law that is consistent with this section. No cause of action may be brought and no liability may be imposed under any State or local law that is inconsistent with this section."

The preamble to Section 230 contained the underlying thoughts which prompted Congress to create a far-reaching immunity to providers for third-party content. Interactive computer services - so the preamble - "offer a forum for true diversity of political discourse, unique opportunities for cultural development, and myriad avenues for intellectual activity". These services had flourished to the benefit of all Americans with a minimum of state regulation[64]. Also, the preamble points out that it is "the policy of the

62 The Conference Report to the CDA expressly states that it was designed to overrule *Stratton Oakmont*: "One of the specific purposes of [Section 230] is to overrule *Stratton Oakmont v. Prodigy* and any other similar decisions which have treated such providers and users as publishers or speakers of content that is not their own because they have restricted access to objectionable material. The conferees believe that such decisions create serious obstacles to the important federal policy of empowering parents to determine the content of communications their children receive througth interactive computer services", H.R. Conf. Repl. No. 104-458, 194 (1996).

63 See also *Hein/Davies*, Haftung für fremde Inhalte im Internet nach US-amerikanischem Recht, MMR 1998, 627, 628 (in German).

64 47 U.S.C. §§ 230(a)(3)-(4).

United States...to preserve the vibrant and competitive free market that presently exists for the Internet and other interactive computer services, unfettered by Federal or State regulation"[65].

b) Interpretation of Section 230

*aa) Zeran v. AOL: Confirmation of provider immunity*

Immunity under Section 230(c)(1) requires three elements: (1) that the defendant be a "provider or user of an interactive computer service"; (2) that holding the provider liable would treat the provider as the publisher or speaker of the content at issue and (3) that the information be provided by another information content provider. In the case *Zeran v. America Online, Inc.*[66] a federal court for the first time had to examine and interpret the requirements of Section 230.

The facts of the case were as follows: On April 25, 1995, shortly after the bombing of the Alfred P. Murrah Federal Building in Oklahoma City, an unidentified person posted advertisements on an AOL bulletin board which offered "Naughty Oklahoma T-Shirts" for sale. Interested parties were invited to call Kenneth Zeran, whose private phone number was also given in the ads. Zeran, who had no knowledge of the postings, apparently was the victim of a tasteless joke at his expense. He began to receive abusive phone calls. He could not change his private phone number because he also used it to run a business from his home and his number was well-known to his customers. On the day the anonymous phone calls started, Zeran informed AOL about the incident. An employee assured him that the posting would be removed from AOL's bulletin board, however, he told him that it was not AOL's policy to issue a retraction on the bulletin board. It is unclear when exactly AOL removed the first posting but, during the next four days, there were more anonymous postings with the same content on AOL boards. After another complaint by Zeran, AOL told him that the account from which the postings came would be canceled in the near future. In the meantime, the number of annoying calls continued to increase and, later, things turned even worse for Zeran. On May 1, a radio host of the Oklahoma City radio station KRXO read the text of the first posting on air and told his listeners to call Zeran's number and protest against these ads. This led to a situation in which the abusive phone calls started including death threats and the phone rang around the clock. Zeran had to be put under police protection. Only after Zeran went on Oklahoma media and KRXO issued an "on air" apology to Zeran, the number of abusive calls went down to about 15 per day. On April 23, 1996, Zeran filed suit against AOL. He claimed that AOL had acted negligently by not removing the postings fast enough and by not preventing further postings of the same kind. AOL invoked Section 230 and moved for judgment on the pleadings on the grounds that it was immune from the suit. The United States District Court for the Eastern District of Virginia dismissed the suit[67].

---

65 47 U.S.C. § 230(b)(2).

66 *Zeran v. America Online, Inc*, 958 F. Supp. 1124 (District Court); 129 F. 3d 327 (Court of Appeals) (1997).

67 *Zeran v. America Online, Inc*, 958 F. Supp. 1124.

Zeran argued on appeal before the United States Court of Appeals, Fourth Circuit that the wording of Section 230 did not support the District Court's decision: While it was clear that AOL was a provider and that the content came from a third party, the words of Section 230 did not bar AOL's liability since the words are "...no provider... shall be treated as the *publisher or speaker* of any information provided by another information content provider". Zeran argued that not allowing AOL to be held liable as a publisher or speaker, did not bar liability as a *distributor* as well. He argued that, on the contrary, Congress had only excluded liability as a publisher or speaker in Section 230, and that it had to be understood *e contrario, i.e.* in a way that liability as a distributor needed to be included[68]. Zeran said that AOL had functioned as a distributor, comparable to a library or a newsstand. Zeran stressed that a *distributor* is liable if it has positive knowledge of the illegal third-party content. AOL possessed this knowledge, said Zeran, by way of his repeated complaints to the firm about the postings.

The court did not follow Zeran's argumentation. It stated that AOL was not a *distributor* but a *publisher.* Even if AOL had been a *distributor,* the court said, it should have been even more a reason *not* to hold AOL liable, since holding the firm liable as a *distributor* because it had received notice of the illegal content would, in the end, mean treating AOL just like the real creator of the illegal content[69]. Thus, the court saw the category of *distributor liability* only as a subcategory to *publisher liability*[70]. The court also held up the potential influence of a *notice liability* of providers on *free speech*: If Internet providers became liable as *distributors* as soon as they received notice of potentially illegal content, they would be subject to a permanent, unforeseeable liability risk as soon as they receive a message about a potentially offensive third-party content on their servers - no matter who gave them that notice and no matter what the identity of the third party creating the potentially illegal content. Any such notification would require a thorough and intensive scrutiny of the potentially illegal content and the circumstances of its publication. Moreover, the provider would have to make an assessment of, for instance, the defamatory character of the material and decide very quickly whether or not to remove the content[71]. While this might be feasible for a traditional print publisher, it is already not feasible in the Internet context because of the high number of such postings[72]. Since Internet providers would only be liable for the publication of information, but never for its removal, they would have a natural incentive to remove postings or pages in cases of doubt as soon as they received a notification of illegal content, be this true or not.[73]. Thus, not only *strict liability* as a *publisher*, but also *notice liability* as a *distributor* is seen as having a *chilling effect* on *free speech.*

---

68 *Zeran v. America Online, Inc*, 129 F. 3d 327, 332 (1997).

69 *ib.*, 129 F. 3d 327, 333 (1997).

70 *ib.*, 129 F. 3d 327, 331-332 (1997).

71 *ib.*, 129 F. 3d 327, 333 (1997).

72 The court quotes the case *Auvil v. CBS 60 Minutes,* 800 F. Supp. 928, 931 (E.D. Wash. 1992), in which (for a TV show with audience participation) the court ruled that it is, with regard to *audience participation shows,* impossible for TV stations, "to monitor incoming transmissions and exercise on-the-spot discretionary calls".

73 Concerning this, the court quotes the case *Philadelphia Newspapers, Inc. v. Hepps,* 475 U.S. 767,

The court went on to find that a notice liability would stop providers from taking self-regulation measures, because every attempt by a provider to examine the material on its servers with regard to potential illegality would just lead to increased liability. As a consequence, the court said that, in order to avoid liability, providers would rather not look at the third-party content on their pages at all.[74]

With respect to the intention of Congress in the preamble to Section 230 to encourage self-regulation and to avoid the *chilling effect* on freedom of speech which potential liability would have, the court interpreted Section 230 in *Zeran v. America Online* saying that a provider liability for defamatory statements of third persons should be completely ruled out, and dismissed *Zeran's* suit on appeal.

#### *bb) Blumenthal v. Drudge: Immunity even in the case of financial compensation for illegal content*

In the case *Blumenthal v. Drudge and AOL,*[75] it was confirmed that Section 230 protects providers even then from a liability for third-party content if these third persons are paid by the provider as *independent contractors*. In this case, the Internet columnist Matt Drudge had uploaded an allegedly defamatory statement[76] about Sidney Blumenthal, a well-known former journalist and staff member of the White House. In contrast to the *Zeran case*, Drudge received a monthly fee of around $3,000 for his services to AOL. In the license agreement, AOL had reserved the right to remove any content that violated *AOL's Terms of Service*, however, editorial responsibility and control remained completely with Drudge.

Blumenthal not only sued Drudge, but also AOL, and gave as his reason that AOL was itself the creator of the posting causing the conflict, since it had reserved the right to remove content that violated AOL's *Terms of Service* and since it had paid Drudge for his activities. Blumenthal therefore argued that the information was not "provided by another information content provider".

However, the court came to the result that Drudge was not an *agent* or *employee* of AOL but, rather, an *independent contractor* and that therefore the information *did* originate from a different content provider. In that case, however, the same argumentation as in *Zeran* had to be applied and AOL was freed from any liability, even if it paid for the content in question. Thus, the court dismissed Blumenthal's suit[77].

---

777, 106 S. Ct. 1558, 1564, 89 L.Ed.2d 783 (1986), in which it is pointed out that fears of being eventually liable without fault, have a *chilling effect* towards the basic right of freedom of speech laid down in the 1st amendment.

74 *Zeran v. America Online, Inc*, 129 F. 3d 327, 333 (1997).

75 *Blumenthal v. Drudge and America Online, Inc.*, 992 F. Supp. 44 (D.C.C. 1998).

76 "The DRUDGE REPORT has learned that top GOP operatives who feel there is a double-standard of only reporting Republican shame believe they are holding an ace card: New White House recruit Sidney Blumenthal has a spousal abuse past that has been effectively covered up", *Blumenthal v. Drudge and America Online, Inc.*, 992 F. Supp. 44, 46 (D.C.C. 1998).

77 *Blumenthal v. Drudge and America Online, Inc.*, 992 F. Supp. 44, 50 (D.C.C. 1998).

### cc) *Doe v. America Online, Inc.: Immunity even in the case of evident violation of criminal statutes by third persons*

Now we have established that, at least in the case of insulting or defamatory statements, *Zeran v. AOL* and *Blumenthal v. Drudge and AOL* have made it clear that host provider liability for third-party content is out of the question. However, we now need to determine the situation with clearly illegal content, whose distribution even represents a crime for the content provider according to the Federal Obscenity Law or the Child Pornography Prevention Act.

Shortly after the *Zeran trial,* state and appellate courts in the State of Florida had to deal with this question in the case *Doe v. America Online, Inc.*[78] which we presented in our introduction. Let me just remind you of the facts very briefly: In this case, a mother had sued AOL at the Circuit Court in Palm Beach County as the legal guardian of her underaged son. She claimed that AOL had negligently allowed one of its users, Russell, to solicit a video in AOL chatrooms in which said AOL user was allegedly seen in sexual acts with her son. Although AOL had forbidden its users in its "Terms of Service" and "Rules of the Road" to distribute "unlawful, harmful...obscene...or otherwise objectionable material" via its transmission lines, although it had reserved the right to delete such content, and although AOL had been notified several times of Russell's activities, she said AOL had not taken any steps against Russell. It was not claimed that there was an actual transmission of depictions of her son in sexual activities with Russell. However, the plaintiff claimed that AOL had violated several criminal statutes of the State of Florida[79], which made it a crime to participate in the distribution of child pornography. AOL invoked immunity under Section 230 CDA, and the Circuit Court, Palm Beach County, then dismissed *Jane Doe*'s suit.

*Doe* appealed against this decision and argued at the District Court of Appeal of Florida that Section 230 was not applicable, since she did not try to make AOL liable as *publisher*, but as a *distributor* of child pornography. However, the District Court of Appeal took *Zeran v. AOL* as a *precedent* and pursued the argumentation from that case as to why the provider could not only not be liable as a *publisher*, but also not as a *distributor*. As far as Florida state law came to a different result, 47 U.S.C. § 230(d)(3) was quoted, which rules that there cannot be a responsibility of providers according to state law which is inconsistent with Section 230.

### dd) *Summary*

The interpretation of Section 230 of the CDA in the cases *Zeran v. AOL, Blumenthal v. Drudge and AOL* and *Doe v. AOL* clearly arrives at the total exclusion of providers' liability for third-party content. This immunity applies, regardless whether the provider knew or did not know about the presence of a third party's content on its servers, whether it paid the third party for his services and if it was aware of the illegality of the

---

78 *Doe v. America Online, Inc.,* 1997 WL 374223 *1, *aff'd, Doe v. America Online, Inc.*, No. 97-2587, 1998 WL 712764 (Fla. Ct. App. Oct. 14, 1998).

79 Sections 847.011(1)(a), 847.0135(2), 847.0135, Florida Statutes.

content. Although the reported cases deal with civil lawsuits only, the words of Section 230 do not limit the application of Section 230' to civil cases ("No provider or user of an interactive computer service shall be treated as the publisher or speaker of any information provided by another information content provider."). Thus it can be expected that Section 230 also serves as a bar to the possible criminal prosecution of a provider for content which a third person had put onto its servers.

## III. Germany

### 1. Liability Rule for Host Providers in § 5 TDG

Since August 11, 1997, the liability of host providers is explicitly regulated in § 5 par. 2 TDG. The rule is that host providers are only liable for third-party content, which they store for access by third persons, if they have knowledge of this content and it is technically feasible to prevent its use and they can be reasonably expected to make the use of this content impossible[80]. For this liability, it is sufficient if the provider receives positive knowledge of the content at issue. The provider cannot defend himself by claiming that, although he knew about the content of a web page, he had not believed the content was illegal[81]. The prosecution can destroy a provider's defense that he had not known about the illegal content at all with a "notice". Then he becomes subject to full liability.

The German approach of a *notice liability*, which does not immunize the host provider totally from liability, as is the case in the USA, but which holds it liable if it knows about the content can, incidentally, also be found in the European Commission's proposal for an E-Commerce directive. Art. 14 of the E-Commerce Directive explicitly deals with "hosting". However, the proposal is less strict than the German law, because criminal liability from Art. 14 E-Commerce Directive arises "on condition that the provider does not have actual knowledge that the activity is illegal..."[82]. However, the general concept – *notice liability* – remains unchanged, which means that the Germans are on the same footing as the European Commission.

### 2. Constitutional Analysis

When regulating the responsibility of communication intermediaries, the German legislator - similar to the situation in the United States - has to observe the limits imposed by the constitution on his legislative activity. The activities of the host provider are undoubtedly protected by Art. 5 GG. However, it is not yet clear in the legal discussion, whether it can even invoke Art. 5 par. 1 sentence 2 GG. These communication instruments enjoy particular legal protection, because they create a "marketplace of opinions"

80 Same words: § 5 Abs. 2 MDStV.

81 There is only an exception in the rare case of §17 StGB where, despite serious effort, the provider is unable to discover the illegality of the content.

82 The text of the norm leave leaves the question open as to whether knowledge of the illegality or just knowledge of the content itself is meant.

in a democratic society and therefore guarantee everyone the possibility of being able to freely form an opinion. An argument in favor of this would be that the host provider, as far as it has editorial functions, has a role similar to a publisher or a broadcast station. But even if it just helps with the distribution of third-party content, without exerting any influence on the content, it would have to be viewed in the same manner as, e.g., a movie wholesaler, whose activities are also protected by Art. 5 par. 1 sentence 2 GG.

However, the protected activities of the provider are also subject to the limitations stated in Art. 5 par. 2 GG. This leads to the central question of whether German liability rules are proportionate. One could argue in favor of an unproportionality with the arguments mentioned in *Zeran v. AOL*. Let me summarize them again: The creation of a *chilling effect*, which burdens the communication interests of providers and diminishes plurality of opinions can hardly be disputed[83]. There is a danger that, in a notice liability setting, the provider will, in cases of doubt, lean towards removing the content at issue from its servers without closer scrutiny. On the other hand, we do not wish to neglect the fact that - as the example of child pornography shows - there are significant objectives of legal protection behind norms which give rise to liability.

Moreover, e.g., a traditional print publisher is subject to criminal sanctions according to general principles of accomplice liability if it does not remove illegal content in spite of having received notice of this content. Also, it has to be seen that the host provider has a key position in that it can stop violations of the law. It will regularly be in the best position to delete the content in question from its servers or administer other blocking measures. On the other hand, again, attempting to hold liable content providers resident in other countries is hardly ever successful.

Again, we do not want to go into more detail with our scrutiny, because the constitutionality of § 5 par. 2 TDG has, as is the case with Internet-specific youth protection laws as described above, not yet been seriously doubted. In addition to the reasons for this that have already been mentioned, it can be noted that the chosen liability concept did not go as far as the security community had demanded. The legislation did not impose separate surveillance duties on the providers and neither does it force them to actively look for circumstances which could indicate an illegal activity[84]. Insofar, a broad consensus seems to exist in other European countries as well. The imposition of such duties shall in future be prevented for all E.U. member states by Art. 15 of the proposed E-Commerce Directive. Also, the limitation of notice liability in § 5 par. 2 TDG to cases where it is "possible and it can reasonably be expected" that illegal content be blocked, makes it possible to achieve in each particular case a balance between the underlying purpose for the liability in that case (e.g., protection of minors) and Art. 5 GG (freedom of speech). For instance, the special situation of small providers can be taken into account if an otherwise indicated blocking requirement would exceed their economic capability.

83 The argument that a *notice liability* would lead to providers no longer having an incentive for self-regulation, is not valid for the area pertaining to the protection of minors. There, the use of technical access restrictions or of filter software can provide a justification which bars liability.

84 This was the original demand by the K3 group.

## IV. How to Deal with Different Values and Legal Traditions: the CompuServe Case

### 1. The CompuServeVerdict

Let us now go back to the CompuServe verdict from Germany: The former head of CompuServe Germany was found guilty by the *Amtsgericht München* of wilful distribution of pornographic content, pursuant to § 184 par. 3 No. 2 StGB[85]. The court saw as his criminal act the fact that he provided German customers of CompuServe USA access to the servers of the mother company in the USA over his dial-up access points, via a leased line between CompuServe Germany and CompuServe USA[86]. CompuServe's act of participation in the USA was seen as the provision of access to the Internet, in connection with making data available from its news servers, without having filtered out the violent, bestial and child-pornography content[87]. The accusation was, to make it short - please bear in mind that I am simplifying here - that CompuServe did not block or delete newsgroups from its servers which allegedly clearly seemed to contain violent pornography, child pornography and bestiality, and instead installed a "Cyber Patrol" System which did not function properly. It was for this reason that the *Amtsgericht* convicted the executive of the subsidiary CompuServe GmbH Germany. An exemption from liability according to § 5 par. 3 TDG was explicitly denied. "CompuServe Germany, the accused, had no possibility of controlling the servers of CompuServe USA. However, when looking at the question of what is technologically feasible and what can reasonably be expected, one must not take an isolated look at the subsidiary company, instead, one should focus on the organization as a whole"[88].

### 2. Analysis of the Verdict

In the past few years, there has hardly been a verdict in Germany which would have led to a similarly harsh reaction from the press. Articles about the CompuServe case carried headlines such as "Germany's Internet Angst"[89], "A 'cyber-coup' for Germany's cybercops"[90], "German Net future questioned"[91] or "Efforts to control the Net abuse liberty"[92]. But the decision was also heavily criticized by German legal commentators[93].

---

85 Regarding the violations of the youth protection laws, see AG München MMR 1998, 429 (434 ff.).

86 AG München MMR 1998, 429 (430). An inofficial English version of the verdict can be found under: <http://www.cyber-rights.org/isps/somm-dec.htm> (as of 05/21/99).

87 AG München MMR 1998, 429 (430).

88 AG München MMR 1998, 429 (433).

89 *Wired*, <http://www.wired.com/news/news/email/other/politics/story/12884.html>.

90 *Reuters/FoxNews*, <http://www.foxnews.com/js_index.sml?content=/scitech/wires2/0528/t_rt_0528_12.sml>.

91 *Reuters/CNET*, <http://www.news.com/News/Item/0,4,22544,00.html>.

92 San Jose Mercury News, <http://www.sjmercury.com/columnists/gillmor/docs/dg052998.htm>. "The conviction was alarming for obvious reasons. If this person could be convicted of a crime for allowing users of his online service to gain access to pornography, anyone affiliated with an online

Therefore, let me make one thing clear: The CompuServe verdict of the *Amtsgericht München* was probably, especially in the USA, largely overestimated with regard to its meaning, due to a lack of knowledge of the structure of the German court system and legal tradition. This case is not a precedent in the sense of the common law. This was not the "creation" of law, but just the interpretation of a federal statute by a court - a court from the lowest level. The verdict can be appealed to the *Landgericht München.* Against a verdict by the *Landgericht München,* another appeal to the *Bayerisches Oberstes Landesgericht* would be possible. Moreover, even the district attorney in Munich appealed the verdict *in favor of the plaintiff*, which is possible in a German criminal trial, although it rarely happens. It was widely expected that the verdict will be corrected in the next instance. And, indeed, this happened on November 15, 1999, when the Landgericht München overruled the judgement of the first instance.

However, for our question, this does not make the verdict of the Amtsgericht any less interesting. It may be that everyone agrees that the verdict is wrong, but they do so for completely different reasons:

The U.S. press does not seem to mind Germany's legal approach: Criminal liability of host providers certainly leads to economically unpleasant limitations for those who run such companies. Let me say again, though, that this does not appear to cause consternation to anyone in Germany. I also think that a clear majority of my compatriots sees no problem with expecting a host provider to permanently block incriminated newsgroups - even if it means blocking 282 newsgroups - if they provide fora for child pornography. It is not only since the terrible "Dutroux" affair in Belgium that most Western Europeans see their tolerance end when it comes to child pornography.

However, the options for German district attorneys to act against CompuServe USA were limited. After the company had refused to comply fully with what the authorities in Germany had asked it to do, there was not much they could do. Direct action against the responsible executives of CompuServe USA is not possible until they set foot on German soil. A request for extradition would have failed from the outset because there is no notice liability for Internet providers in the USA.

Obviously, one gains the impression that the prosecution picked the former head of CompuServe Germany because it was unable to sue those it viewed as being principally responsible. Apparently, the district attorneys in Munich were unwilling to accept the unenforceability of German law - namely the absolute ban on child pornography writings – simply on account of the distribution of this content via the Internet.

---

service could suffer the same fate. The damage to Germany, as it seeks to gain a foothold in the emerging Information Age, would be enormous."

93 See, e.g., *Sieber*, Anmerkung zum "CompuServe"-Urteil des AG München vom 28.05.1998, MMR 1998, 429; *Bender,* Bavaria v. Felix Somm: The Pornography Conviction of the Former CompuServe manager, accessible online at: <http://www.digital-law.net/IJCLP/1_1998/ijclp_webdoc_14_1_1998.html>; *Nathrath*, Criminal Liability of Internet Providers in Germany - Conviction of a CompuServe Executive, Journal of Internet Law 11/1998, 1, also accessible online at: <http://www.gcwf.com/articles/journal/jil_nov98_1.html>.

The criticism in my country was directed against this aspect - not against the notice liability of a host provider as a matter of principle. For instance, it was stated that CompuServe Germany was not a host, but an access provider, since the German subsidiary merely provided the access to servers in the USA which belonged to the parent company. Critics said that it is not permissible in criminal law to simply view CompuServe as an entity and thereby attribute an omission by CompuServe USA to the executives of CompuServe Germany.

Others criticized the approach of the *Amtsgericht*, which had apparently viewed the fact that the defendant knew that there was child pornography in *some* newsgroups, as sufficient to satisfy the requirement of notice, although the content in 282 other newsgroups only came up later and it did not even know about that particular content. It is said that one can only be liable for *specific* content of which one has actual knowledge. By the way, this is a criticism I share, and it was also expressed by the prosecution in its appeal in favor of Mr. Somm. For the Landgericht München, the second instance, this was the main argument why the court overruled the judgement of the Amtsgericht München.

Finally, some say that it is neither possible nor can it reasonably be expected from the head of a subsidiary that he force the parent company to act exactly in the manner demanded by the local state law in the country in which the subsidiary is located. This seems to be a reasonable argument when one thinks about the legal confusion that would be present in a company that operates on a worldwide basis.

In any case, much of the criticism in Germany - more or less put into the forms of the dogmatic figures of our criminal law - is directed against the liability of Mr. Somm as representative of American law.

## 3. Summary

Although the CompuServe verdict of the first instance has been overturned, one central difference between German and American law concerning provider liability remains: if a German host provider has knowledge of certain specific illegal content and it can reasonably be expected to block or delete this content, the German provider must take this action, otherwise it renders itself liable. In the USA, on the other hand, a host provider is not liable, even if it knows about the illegal content and leaves it on its servers. This far-reaching immunity from liability is probably caused in some part by the very important position of the basic right of freedom of speech in the American legal system. Since the host provider functions as a communication intermediary and thus can be compared in some respect to a traditional print publisher or wholesaler, this basic right gains significance in the balancing test with other interests. Moreover, it probably plays an important role that the expansion of the Internet and, with it, the "Information Highway", is being pushed worldwide by American companies in particular. These economic realities are another reason to avoid limitations on the economic freedom of AOL or other providers, wherever possible.

This dilemma has - and let me stress this here again - not come up because there is a different position in both countries towards child pornography. It can be assumed that the German authorities informed their American counterparts by way of international cooperation agreements, in order to be able to initiate legal proceedings against the American content providers. At least I hope so!

Behind this controversy are different traditions with respect to how the basic right to freedom of speech is handled, and certainly also economic interests in promoting the American Internet provider industry.

Such a clash of differing legal positions cannot be avoided in a business world where operations are becoming increasingly global. A dispute surrounding the right policy is simultaneously a dispute about the supremacy of legal values and the economic opportunities of national companies. Another example which supports this view is the conflict involving the application of European data protection laws to American companies. As far as one state cannot impose its will on another, a compromise needs to be found. Here, the promotion of understanding differences between legal systems gains great significance. Also, intensified cooperation between the law-enforcement authorities in various countries could be helpful in overcoming misunderstandings. For instance, one should expect that it is possible for German and American prosecutors to support each other when it comes to actions against the creators and distributors of child pornography content. The initiation of such learning processes could then form the basis for a step-by-step evolution of closer cooperation between the respective national legal systems and pragmatic improvements. That this does not have to mean that one has to abandon important national traditions is demonstrated by the European unification process.

# D. Attachment

**Table 1:** Comparison Art. 5 Abs. 1 S. 1 GG and First Amendment

| **Art. 5 Abs. 1 S. 1 GG: Freedom of Opinion** | **First Amendment: Freedom of Speech** |
|---|---|
| **A. Scope of Protection** | **A. Scope of Protection** |
| The term "Opinion":<br>• Element of comment in the context of an intellectual dispute (content neutral)<br>• includes polemc, provoking or disgustingly-formulated expressions<br>• includes facts if they are relevant for an opinion, unless they are evidently untrue or knowingly formulated falsely | Definition of Speech:<br>• Speech includes any kind of expression - not only verbal expression, but also symbolic conduct, e.g., burning of a flag, thus the basic right is also called "Freedom of Expression".<br>Exceptions:<br>• *"Obscenity"* is outside the scope of protection of the 1st amendment according to the Supreme Court. --Test (from Miller v. California (1973)): (1) whether the average person, applying contemporary community standards, would find that the work, taken as a whole, appeals to the prurient interest; (2) whether the work depicts or describes, in a patently offensive way, sexual conduct specifically defined by the applicable state law; (3) whether the work, taken as a whole, lacks serious literary, artistic, political or scientific value from the standpoint of a reasonable person.<br>• *"Fighting words"* are also not protected by the 1st amendment. They are very narrowly defined: They must have a "direct tendency to cause acts of violence by the persons to whom, individually, the remark is addressed" and they must be directed towards an "immediate breach of the peace" They must be more than mere "offensive expression". |

| B. Justification, Art. 5 par. 2 GG | B. Justification |
| --- | --- |
| • general laws (content neutral)<br>• statutory provisions for the protection of minors<br>• Law of personal honor (field of defamation) important: no limitation of the scope of protection by Art. 5 par. 2 GG, but any measure based on Art. 5 par. 2 GG needs to pass an Art. 5 par. 1 sent. 1 GG scrutiny | **1. General distinction**<br><br>• *Content-based restriction*<br>(The state aims to regulate the expression with regard to its content)<br><br>*Strict Scrutiny Test:*<br>The state may not regulate the *content* of speech, unless it can prove that the regulation was necessary to serve a compelling need, this will practically never be the case, so that almost any regulation which aims at the *content* of expression, violates the 1st amendment, unless it belongs to one of the categories which receive no or less protection under the 1st amendment<br><br>• *Content-neutral restriction*<br>(The government action does not aim at the content of the speech, but is a limitation on freedom of speech only indirectly as a "side effect" of the regulation of other behavior)<br><br>*Time, Place and Manner Test:*<br>The state may generally make *reasonable* rules concerning *time, place and manner* of speech. The rules are "reasonable", if they<br>- do not aim at the content of the speech,<br>- serve significant state interests,<br>- are narrowly tailored and<br>- leave open ample alternative opportunities for communication.<br><br>**2. Cases in which content regulation is permitted**<br><br>• *"Commercial Speech"*: Speech, which mainly serves commercial interests, can be subject to content regulation, if this directly and substantially advances a substantial government interest and is narrowly tailored (Example: Restrictions on advertising for Casinos)<br>• *"Defamation":* Defamatory or offensive statements can be sanctioned with civil or criminal sanctions (but: "public figures" cannot demand damages for defamation by private citizens, unless they were done with "actual malice", which has to be proven by the public figure) |

<table>
<tr>
<th>C. General considerations as part of the balancing test and other general requirements</th>
<th>C. General considerations as part of the balancing test and other general requirements</th>
</tr>
<tr>
<td>Requirement of proportionality as expression of the principle that any limitation based on Art. 5 par. 2 GG must itself be measured with Art. 5 par. 1 sent. 1 GG, especially:<br><br>• legitimate purpose<br>• suitability for the desired purpose<br>• necessity<br>• adequacy requirement of certainty, which demands that the regulation is formulated so clearly that the one to whom it is addressed can clearly identify the behavior that is expected from him (purpose: to guarantee the controllability of governmental acts)</td>
<td>• "Overbreadth": A law is "void on its face" if it is "overbroad", which means it also affects the content of speech which may not be regulated. Consequence of the law being void: Even someone whose own statements could be regulated by a properly formulated law (e.g., a pornography distributor) can challenge such a law (Ratio: the "chilling effect", which even an unconstitutional law can have, shall be minimized as soon as possible)<br><br>• "Vagueness": A law is unconstitutional on its face, if a person of common intelligence could not know what behavior is prohibited<br><br>• "Prior Restraints": Prohibition of suppressing certain speech (censorship), unless the government can show that a prior restraint is necessary to prevent direct, immediate, and irreparable harm<br><br>• Least Restrictive Means Test</td>
</tr>
</table>

**Table 2:** Liability of Internet providers in the USA and Germany – Overview

| | **Germany: § 5 TDG** | **E-Commerce Directive** | **USA** |
|---|---|---|---|
| **Own content** | Full responsibility, § 5 par. 1 TDG | Full responsibility (although not expressly stated as it is declaratorily done in the TDG) | Full responsibility, e.g. torts (defamation etc.), criminal liability according to federal (e.g., Child Pornography Prevention Act) and state law |
| **Mere access provision** | No responsibility, § 5 par. 3 TDG | No responsibility, Art. 12 E-Commerce Directive, also no responsibility in the case of automatic, intermediate and transient storage (Art. 12 Abs. 2 E-Commerce Directive) | No responsibility, due to CDA Section 230 (Section 230(c)(1): No provider or user of an interactive computer service shall be treated as the publisher or speaker of any information provided by another information content provider) |
| **Problem: Host provider (hosting of third-party content (e.g., Web space, bulletin boards)** | § 5 par. 2 TDG: Responsibility only if the provider knows about the content, and if it is technologically feasible to block access, and the provider can reasonably be expected to prevent access to the questionable content | Art. 14 E-Commerce Directive: civil liability only if the provider knows that the activity is illegal, or if he is not aware of circumstances from which illegal activity is apparent, criminal liability: similar to § 5 par. 2 TDG, only if there is actual knowledge of the illegality; no criminal or civil liability if the provider, upon obtaining knowledge of illegal activity, acts expeditiously to remove or disable access to the information | **No civil liability (e.g., defamation) or criminal liability due to CDA Section 230 and its interpretation by the courts.** The interpretation of Section 230 of the CDA in the cases Zeran v. AOL, Blumenthal v. Drudge and AOL and Doe v. AOL clearly comes to the result that a liability of providers for third-party content is completely ruled out. This immunity applies, no matter if the provider knew or knew not about the presence of a third party's content on its servers, if it paid the third party for its services and if it was aware of the illegality of the content. Although the reported cases deal with civil lawsuits only, the text of Section 230 does not limit its application to civil cases. |

*Herbert Burkert*

# Privacy - Data Protection

## A German/European Perspective

## Introduction

Bananas, hormones, Hollywood movies and – privacy protection. This is a shorthand description of the current issues in US-European trade relations.

The European Directive on Privacy Protection[1], it is reported, contains a clause according to which the flow of personal data may be interrupted to countries that do not provide adequate protection. The actual wording and the interactions of the regulations concerning the transborder data flow of personal data to third countries are slightly more complex. In policy debates, however, issues tend to get simplified: Will the current regulatory US privacy regime be recognized as adequate? What would have to be done to make it adequate? And what would happen if not?

This paper is not going to provide the answer to this puzzle.

Rather it will recall the history of the data protection concept in Europe, with special emphasis on Germany.

It will then address some of the value issues – as perceived in the European/German context – connected to these legislative approaches.

The third part – a deviation from the chartered course – will briefly offer some speculations on what could be seen as the function and performance of data protection legislation, again from a European/German perspective.

The fourth part addresses the recent "new criticism" of data protection voiced mainly in Germany so far.

The fifth and last part will provide some assumptions on how data protection concepts might react to these challenges (Needless to say: Opinions voiced – if any can be detected and are not attributed to others – are most likely – but not necessarily exclusively – my own).

## 1 The History of a Triumph

### 1.1 The Hesse Act – Setting the Stage

Almost thirty years ago, on September 30, 1970 the ever first data protection law, the Hesse Data Protection Act was passed[2].

This act was about differences between local communities and the state administration, about who should be allowed to buy these new machines, the large computing systems,

---

1 Directive 95/46/EC of the European Parliament and of the Council of 24 October 1995 on the protection of individuals with regard to the processing of personal data and on the free movement of such data.

2 Hessisches Datenschutzgesetz (The Hesse Data Protection Act), Gesetz und Verordnungsblatt I (1970), 625.

and who should decide which programs to run on them, or rather, the act was a follow-up to the law that tried to settle these arguments[3]. The former law addressed the fear of local communities of what they saw as the inherent centralizing power of the machine that would shift their traditional power and influence to the Land [state][4]. That law needed a follow–up because, in that discussion, it had been discovered that the "local community – state administration" conflict was not the only one that needed to be addressed: There was also a conflict between the legislative body and the executive body because of the different use they could make of power-enhancing data processing. The legislature was afraid to be cut off from information if it disappeared in the machines of the executive. There was also the conflict between citizens and the power of the state. The citizens had started to worry about these machines and as to what would happen to their data in these machines, and, of course, these worries added to the more general concerns they were already having as to what would happen to their jobs. Gradually, the concern for confidentiality became an important argument as well[5]. Confidentiality clauses had already been added in the form of administrative regulations to one of the other organizational laws of the Laender, seeking to implement data processing in public administration, the 1968 law of Schleswig Hollstein. The Hesse Law of 1970 was different because for the first time these confidentiality clauses were lifted to the level of a formal law, where they stood side by side with those clauses that addressed the other power conflicts mentioned above.

While the power conflict part of the Hesse law only resurfaced occasionally in the legislation of the other states, the confidentiality part of the law set a legislative program into motion.

The substance of the confidentiality clauses contained in the Hesse Act, however, had been somewhat thin to start with: There was a default confidentiality rule. Exceptions from this rule were possible where other regulations permitted distribution, where there was consent and – what seems to be a very sweeping exception to us today – if processing was necessary. The data subject had an access right, a correction right, the possibility of obtaining an injunction and remedies in case of unlawful processing – and those rights were indeed a breakthrough. Accepted in individual cases under specific circumstances by the administrative courts, these rights had now been put into the clear language of a law.

---

3 Gesetz über die Errichtung der hessischen Zentrale für Datenverarbeitung und kommunale Gebietsrechenzentren (1969) [Law on establishing the data processing center of the State of Hesse and of data processing centers of local communities]. See also Hondius 1975, 35.

4 In the constitutional system of Germany after the war a new emphasis had been put on the executive and rule-making power of the local communities which carried the main burden of executing state and federal laws, as well as their local bye-laws. This role became expressly recognized in the German Basic Law [constitution] in Art.28 II (see also footnote below).

5 This conflict awareness started on the states' level because according to the German constitutional system administrative functions are primarily with the local communities which execute local bye-laws, the law of the states and the federal law, the federal government having only a relatively small administrative infrastructure of its own.

The Act was expressly trial and error legislation: Half of the 17-article law dealt with establishing an independent agency or rather an ombudsman ("Datenschutz-beauftragter") to watch over the application of the law and to gather experience. Citizens had a right to complain to the ombudsman, who would comment on the complaint and pass it on to the appropriate authority, but who had had no decision-making power.

As limited as this first law was, it already set some of the basic elements for future legislation:

First of all, the law influenced German and later European terminology: As "Datenschutzgesetz" (literally translated as "data protection act"), it was a misnomer, since it did not protect data but the rights of persons whose data was being handled. But misnomers tend to have a high survival rate.

This legislation also set some basic themes for the forthcoming legislation in Europe:

- the negative default rule

  The processing of personal data was seen as interference per se that needed legitimization.

- the rights of the data subject

  For the first time, data subjects had a right of access to information relating to them without the need to show any reason as to why they wanted access.

- the omnibus approach

  Although – due to reasons of legislative competence – the Hesse act could not cover the private sector, it set out to regulate *all* of the state public sector (within its competence).

- the establishing of a privacy protection institution

The Hesse Act expresses the regulative philosophy which is very common in Germany and perhaps also in some other European countries: If you establish regulation that seeks to influence behavior, you cannot (exclusively) rely on litigation to establish that behavior as a pattern. Litigation is associated with burdens, particularly when this litigation is supposed to be directed against the state. One needs institutions, an organizational back-up to take care of one's interests, even if this body by way of its own infrastructure is close to the infrastructure of the state[6].

The Hesse Act implicitly answered a number of questions which became the programmatic questions for subsequent legislation in other countries, and the different answers to these questions would account for the variety of data protection models in Europe and beyond:

6 The Hesse Act and many, but not all, subsequent laws in Germany tried to avoid this "state association" by making the agency or commission directly responsible to Parliament.

- Should only electronic processing be addressed?

One leading international firm that preferred to be seen as a national firm wherever it operated, regarded addressing only electronic processing as a discrimination against computing. Rather than trying to stop data protection all over Europe, it argued for extending the rules to at least automated processing, if not manual processing in general[7]. The extent to which non-automated processing was to be included became one of the recurrent themes in privacy protection legislation.

- How to keep data (information) processing in line?

The Hesse law still refrained from a registration approach (an approach that never became very popular in Germany) which would have required the registration of all processing of personal data (with more or less technical detail). Registration was partly discussed as a means of gaining an overview on what was going on in data processing. Partly it was seen as an opportunity to link authorization or licensing processes with registration. The Hesse act refrained from any of these approaches because some questioned whether registration would be feasible on a long term basis. Also, since the Hesse Act only addressed the public sector, registration was not deemed to be necessary in a context that is already heavily organized and recorded.

- Why limit the approach to the public sector?

This was the most difficult question, and certainly in Germany it was the main reason why federal legislation followed Laender legislation so late: If the private sector was to be covered as well – due to the constitutional distribution of legislative competence – this had to come with a federal law. Whether it would come with a federal law (again in the German context) would depend on the outcome of the lobbying struggle surrounding data protection. Behind this struggle was a legal doctrine that was also occasionally used in the political struggle: the doctrine of horizontal effects. According to this doctrine, a right that is primarily seen as a right against the state can also become a right in the private sector if this right reflects an essential element of the social order as such which, in turn, is transformed into the civil law system through the general value clauses of the civil law system. This constitutional law element was not to be underestimated in the political battle because, in Germany, constitutional law is a cherished tool to settle political disputes. At that stage it already became obvious that, regardless of the shape of federal legislation, only a constitutional court decision would end this dispute[8].

---

7 Whether, initially, this extension had been used to show the limits of a regulation that tried to cover information processing is not quite clear. At least those arguing for effective protection were happy to find such an important a partner in business circles.

8 A constitutional court decision - as we shall see - finally came and it did not explicitly address the horizontal effects. But it became sufficiently clear between the lines that the court would apply the doctrine, if necessary, since the basic right to which data protection was connected by the court had already received horizontal recognition. Also by that time it would have become politically impossible to withdraw the private sector from the legislation. What still lingers on as a political problem today is the private sector's occasional demands for a less stringent approach. The European Directive has effaced the difference between public and private, which - as we shall

## 1.2 National Approaches

### 1.2.1 Northern lights

Germany was not the first country with a *national* data protection law. Although there had been a government draft already in the early 1970s, the process had been halted because of the question of whether and how to cover the private sector.

Instead, it was Sweden which passed the first national law in 1973. Sweden had preceded its legislation with the usual careful analysis in committees. Sweden was also a special case because, since the late forties, it had a personal identification number system – that symbol that would eventually start national initiatives on the federal level in Germany. In the sixties, however, it was felt that this identifier would now serve as an integrator for the still largely decentralized files[9]. Sweden was also the most computerized country in the world (on a pro capita basis). Finally, data security played an important role, since it was linked to national security concerns: Centralized registers could easily fall into the hands of foreign powers and thus jeopardize Sweden's neutrality.

This law also finally introduced a concept that would become one of the cornerstones of early European data protection legislation: The central registration of personal data processing information and a licensing procedure, whose public register was open to the scrutiny of citizens and consumers, and used as an enforcement tool for data protection agencies.

Sweden would eventually also become the first country to modify a data protection law in 1979 and 1982, particularly by increasingly limiting registration and licensing requirements.

Swedish legislation was soon followed by other Scandinavian countries: Denmark with a law each for the public and private sectors in 1978 and in the same year Norway; the Danish laws went into force in 1979 and the Norwegian one in 1980. Finland was a latecomer in 1988. All of these laws have since been revised – even before the revision process initiated by the European Directive[10].

### 1.2.2 German perfection

In Germany, legislation at the federal level finally had to be drawn up:

---

show - sort of effaces the the difference between the public and the private sector in defining its application area. And this approach too is occasionally threatened by some commentators - what else - to be challenged in the European Court of Luxembourg.

9 *Hondius* 1975, 44ff.; Flaherty 1989.

10 For a recent comprehensive overview on the state of privacy legislation around the world: Privacy Laws & Business no. 43 (1998), 2 ff.

Following the example of states like Hesse, the federal government in 1971 asked a research group at the University of Regensburg for an expertise on the structure of a possible federal law[11].

This work and later expertise – among them a book which allegedly "invented" the term "informational self-determination"[12] – drew heavily on US writers, particularly on Westin[13] and Miller[14].

This expertise became the basis for a government draft which, as pointed out above, became stalled because of heavy criticism stemming from the private sector. At the same time, however, the federal government continued to bring forward projects to establish and link national data bases. The most important project was linking the states' population register data banks in a coordinated[15] effort, by introducing a general personal identification number. While the administration was in the midst of introducing the identifier, the bill that was supposed to provide the legal basis for its introduction was almost immediately killed – unanimously – in the Legal Committee of the Federal Parliament in May 1976. No progress was the message, without a data protection law at the federal level.

And, indeed, again across party lines, political agreement was reached and in November 1976 the law, covering the public *and* the private sector, was passed[16].

It took another six years and – as with so many political decisions by the legislature in Germany – a Constitutional Court ruling in 1983[17] – before the law was on its way to general acceptance. The substance of this decision will be examined more closely in part 3 below.

This decision started a wave of new revisions to data protection laws, both at the federal and state level. Now, in 1999, we await yet another wave of revisions due to the European Directive.

### 1.2.3 French and other Latin approaches

The origins of data protection in France are – not surprisingly – quite similar. The Minister of the Interior also tried to combine existing files under a general identifier and named the project – as it turned out, a little unwisely – SAFARI (système automatisé

---

11 *Steinmüller/ Lutterbeck/ Mallmann/ Harbort/ Kolb/ Schneider*: Grundfragen des Datenschutzes. Gutachten im Auftrag des Bundesministeriums des Innern. July 1971 (BT-Drucksache VI/3862).

12 *Mallmann* 1976. The term was used on pages 46ff.

13 *Westin* 1970. The text was first translated into German in 1970 (!) in excerpts by IBM: *IBM-Nachrichten* 1970 189ff., 289ff.

14 Miller 1969 and 1971.

15 Again for constitutional law reasons (distribution of power between the states and the federal government) it could not by itself establish a central data bank .

16 BGBl. 1977 I, 201.

17 Decision of the Federal German Constitutional Court Vol. 65 (1983), 1 ff.

pour les fichiers administratifs et le répertoire des individus)[18]. Even more unwisely, the administration tried to keep the project secret, until it was revealed in an article in Le Monde in 1974 entitled: "SAFARI : Chasing French citizens." The writer of that article later became the first president of the French data protection agency, the Commission nationale de l'informatique et des libertés (CNIL). Again, past memories in Europe and Germany came up: The numerical system to be used in the SAFARI project had already been used by the French statistical office for its own use since 1970 and was, in turn, based on a system introduced into the French administration in 1941 [19].

As if this was not enough: in 1973 the administration had started yet another data bank project – more pleasantly named GAMIN (Gestion automatiséee de la médicine infantile) – intended to process personal information on children from their moment of birth, right through the schooling system, mainly in order to keep a check on these children's medical problems and in order to signal "problematic" children. The symbolic context of such a data bank – again against the background of a not too distant history – was even more dramatic.

Both projects helped to push forward the French data protection bill. In 1978, the French law was published and was put into full operation in 1980. The law emphasized the role of the CNIL, which secured a special advisory role in the planning of administrative data systems. It also believed in registration, and it also covered the private sector.

The French example had an impact on other at least partly French-speaking and Latin countries when writing their drafts: Luxembourg directly followed in 1979, Belgium followed with a law only in 1992, Spain also only in 1992 and Portugal in 1991 (with major amendments in 1994).

### 1.2.4 The pragmatists – the UK and the Netherlands

Cautious approaches were taken by the Netherlands, which passed its law after a very long deliberation process in 1988 and which went fully in force in 1990. They introduced "codes of conduct" into their regulatory regime, an approach often quoted – particularly in the current US/European debate – but again rarely analyzed in depth as to their actual impact. The law provides for a closely-knit connection between self-regulation and (more strongly) state supervision. However, under current changes, this model does contain elements which might become more important in the future, particularly since the European Directive has included similar elements in its Directive.

The UK was very cautious in joining the trend. Private members' bills had been introduced (e.g. the Data Surveillance Bill by Kenneth Baker, as early as 1969). A parliamentary committee had been set up, the report of which did at least influence discussions in other Commonwealth countries (Younger Report 1972).

---

18 See *Delahaie/Paoletti* 1987, 20ff.

19 See *Hogrebe* 1976, 164ff. and *Braibant* 1998, 31f.

The basic shift, however, came when, in 1974, the Swedish Data Inspection Board stopped the export of personal data to the UK because of the lack of a data protection law in that country[20] and when the work in the Council of Europe in the late seventies and early eighties (see below) confirmed the tendency that interrupting the flow of personal data to countries without – at that time equivalent protection – would become legitimate.

The UK realized the economic implications and finally passed its data protection law in 1984, which became fully effective in 1997.

### 1.2.5 Wait and See: Italy and Greece

Italy (and Greece) were the wisest: Although they discussed drafts for a considerable time, they simply waited until the Directive had taken form and shaped their national laws accordingly, thus avoiding the need for adaptation to the Directive, which is now faced by the other countries.

## 1.3 The Race for International Solutions: the Council of Europe and the OECD

In the meantime, the international implications had become more and more apparent, not only with the practice of the Swedish Data Inspection Board. It was inherent to data processing that it would become an international issue, because it would achieve its full potential *precisely by* disregarding geographical limitations.

The Council of Europe, an organization to which more than 40 member states belong today, and which has the promotion of the European Convention of Human Rights (1949) as one of its main objectives, set up a special committee in 1971, subsequently passing two resolutions referring to privacy problems in 1973 [21]. It also started work on a special convention: Particularly the second resolution, pertaining to protection of the privacy of individuals vis-à-vis electronic data banks in the private sector, would have lost all credibility had it not led to a broader international consensus[22].

In the mid-seventies, the OECD, via its Data Bank Panel, had also started to scrutinize more closely the privacy problems associated with data banks[23]. The OECD, by the structure of its membership, then became the main forum for exchanges between North America and Europe on privacy legislation, with Asian countries as patient observers[24].

---

20 A detailed description of this case and other Swedish cases can be found at *Ellger* 1990, 287ff.

21 Resolution 73(2) and 73(22).

22 *Hondius* 1975, 66ff.

23 See e.g.: OECD Informatics Studies 10: Policy issues in data protection and privacy. *Proceedings of the OECD seminar 24-26 June 1974.* Paris 1976.

24 See, e.g., its report on the 1977 Vienna Conference on Transborder Data Flows and the Protection of Privacy, published in 1979.

The OECD was able to beat the Council of Europe in producing the final instrument by four months: The OECD Guidelines on the Protection of Privacy and Transborder Data Flows of Personal Data were passed in September 1980, the text of the European Council Convention for the Protection of Individuals with regard to Automated Processing of Personal Data was finalized in January 1981.

Not surprisingly, both texts showed strong similarities since, on the European side, the OECD and Council of Europe delegations had been made up of more or less the same persons. And privacy/data protection had by then already produced its core of international experts that would demonstrate their influence in the drafting of national laws as well as at the international level, a process which was of course assisted by the similarity of the problems faced in industrial countries[25].

Both texts covered the public and private sectors. In principle, both instruments legitimized restrictions on transborder data flows for reasons of differences in the levels of privacy[26]. The European Council instrument, however, had a stronger impact since, once ratified, it required member states to adapt their laws. But, of course, there was no requirement for all member states of the Council of Europe to ratify it[27]. The OECD instrument did include the US, but it was not a binding instrument. And the underlying expectation, certainly by the US, was that if their national companies eventually made some sort of declaration that they would adhere to principles, no national US legislation for (all of) the private sector would be necessary.

## 1.4 The International Latecomer: The European Community/Union

Due to internal differences, but also because of its own regulatory preferences, the European (at that time) Community, at least its "engine" the European Commission, kept its distance.

On the occasion of the 1977 OECD Conference on Transborder Data Flows, Christopher Layton, then a Director in the European Commission, declared that the Community might encourage Member States to arrive at a better harmonization in their national legislation. The Community might recommend them to eventually join a Council of Europe instrument and, perhaps, if the evidence were sufficiently strong, enter a regulation exercise itself[28].

The recommendation to join the Convention of the Council of Europe did come. But it was not enough. Since 1975[29], the European Parliament had constantly admonished the

---

25 See for an assessment of this "convergence" process: *Bennett* 1988 and 1992.

26 No. 17 of the OECD Guidelines and Art. 12 of the Council of Europe Convention.

27 A Directive of the European Union (Community) was even a stronger instrument since it leaves no choice but to change the national legislation (if necessary). This was why at that time already many argued for a Directive in addition to the Convention.

28 *Layton* 1979, 215f.

29 See *Simitis* at. al. Kommentar zum Bundesdatenschutzgesetz, 4.Aufl. Baden-Baden 1992ff., Rn. 153 ff. zu § 1.

Commission to commence preparation of a Directive. It was only when the "Swedish incident" (i.e. the interruption of transborder data flow from Sweden to the UK – an earlier case had involved Germany when it still lacked a federal law) repeated itself within the European market that serious work on an instrument started: The French CNIL had intervened in a planned transfer from France to Italy (the "FIAT" case). Furthermore, the Schengen agreement, although an instrument outside Community law proper but politically associated with the Community, demanded data protection considerations. By then, the European Community had also realized that data protection could become an argument in discussions with the US on more general issues of data flows, at a time when the US had started to emphasize national security interests to embargo certain data flows[30].

Finally, in 1990, the Commission came out with its proposal for a directive[31] which still took another five years to be finalized.

The Directive gave up the separation between the public and private sectors by defining its application area as the area subject to the application of Community law. The Directive incorporated the basic principles and, in regard to other legal technicalities, it made sure that national legislators in the Member States could recognize some of those elements they had introduced into national legislation, such as the internal (company) data protection officer from German law, the Codes of Conduct from Dutch law, or the prohibition of generating negative decisions on individuals solely through automated processes from French law.

The Directive allowed Member States a further three years to adapt their national legislation, which to date – May 1999 – only a minority of the Member States has succeeded in doing.

## 2 Privacy: Values – Approaches in European Legislation

While the previous chapter has attempted to describe the legislative processes and some of the technical legal elements involved in addressing data protection issues, this chapter addresses the underlying values.

### 2.1 Germany: from the protected sphere to informational self determination

In 1983, the German Constitutional Court summarized the underlying value concept of the (German) approach to data protection as follows:

The freedom of the individual to decide for himself is at stake when the individual is uncertain about what is known about him, particularly where what society might view

30 See the OECD Declaration on Transborder Data Flow (Adopted by the Governments of OECD Member countries on 11th April 1985).

31 COM (90) 314.

as deviant behavior is at stake (the chilling effect)[32]. The individual therefore has the right to know and make decisions on the information being processed about him. At the same time, as a social being, the individual cannot avoid becoming the object of information processing. However, limitations to his basic rights must only be accepted in the case of overriding general interest and if that interest is incorporated into a law that follows the basic requirements of clarity and proportionality[33]. To protect these principles, a number of safeguards are required; these safeguards consist of data processing principles (correctness, timeliness, purpose limitation, fairly and lawfully obtained), derived rights (access, correction), and organizational safeguards (independent institutions).

This decision created a strong echo – not only because it had caused a 300 million deutschmarks administrative investment to be stopped short.

The interpretative response to that judgement became an impressive spectacle of the art of legal interpretation: Some commentators interpreted the decision into non-existence, some even started a discourse on the unconstitutionality of constitutional court decisions, while others saw it to be the landmark of the privacy revolution[34].

In my view, there were two elements that made that decision remarkable:

In terms of constitutional politics, the judgement was an amalgamation of liberal and conservative attitudes towards the new information processing technologies. At the same time, it presented a modern view on the pervasiveness of information processing and its impact on the private sphere. The decision managed to leave behind a concept that the Court had developed in previous decisions: the sphere theory or the theory of the private self as a passive onion, i.e. an understanding, according to which the core of one's personality is surrounded by layers, which may only be removed by state intervention if the closer one comes to the innermost layers, the more pervasive the arguments of legitimation become. In contrast with this decision, the Court had introduced a more active, more communication-oriented picture of the informational self in its exchanges in a communication society.

> The controversies this judgement brought (again) to the surface are still not settled, and tend to resurface whenever new measures of data matching or informational control are introduced into parliament, even subsequently to the Directive. But now, these controversies will increasingly be discussed at the European level, and there the European data protection agencies will find a stronger voice via the Working Group of European Data Protection Commissioners established by Art. 29 of the Directive.

The judgement was followed in Germany by a series of sector-specific legislation, which led to a revision of the general data protection law. It shifted the burden of

---

32 Decision page 43.

33 Decision page 44.

34 Analyzing the response in detail: *Donos* 1998, 71ff.

argument to those who sought to limit privacy and it finally confirmed the existence of data protection agencies as necessary elements of data protection regimes.

This activist view to data protection – with all its limitations – had a strong influence on the debate in neighboring countries and eventually on the Directive although, by then, many European countries had already established their specific understanding of data protection.

## 2.2 Other value approaches

Perhaps the closest position to the German active position had been that of the French, where the title of the data protection act of 1978 already presented the core of the value program: "Informatique et *Libertés*" – informatics and freedom rights, meaning that privacy was seen as providing a sort of "mother right" to other rights and liberties.

The UK approach, as we recall from our brief glance into its history, had been mainly trade oriented.

The problem remained as to how best to operationalize this impulse, if it had to be molded into legislation that affected the whole organizational infrastructure of the public and private sectors. In addition, the impression had to be avoided of merely passing symbolic legislation, therefore necessitating the need for a symbol of effective legislation. And, finally, the whole regime – in the best of Thatcherite traditions – had to more or less self-financing.

The legislative scheme that the UK came up with proved to be ingenious. Somewhat simplified, it worked like this: Data processors had to register their processing activities. For this registration they paid a fee, which was in turn used to pay the registrar. The registrar made sure that registrants only performed the activities they had registered: he compared firms' registrations with their actual practices and his action represented the extent of data protection. Of course, not everything could be registered; only such practices could be registered as observed the basic principles. The scheme also limited the powers of the registrars. (One of the big concerns in the discussion on data protection regulation – mainly in Anglo-Saxon countries – had been the question of who controls the controllers).

Finally, if we look at the Directive in terms of what is understood by privacy, we come across, of course, the market freedoms which require the free flow of personal data in the internal market which, in turn, require the harmonization of the rules on privacy protection in Member States. But, already in the first recital, the Directive emphasizes the civil liberties and democratic society elements of the Directive and the second recital combines both elements in the specific economic civil liberty rhetoric of the European Union:

> "(2) Whereas data-processing systems are designed to serve man; whereas they must, whatever the nationality or residence of natural persons, respect their fundamental rights and freedoms, notably the right to privacy, and contribute to economic and social progress, trade expansion and the well-being of individuals;"

Nevertheless, the civil liberty approach addressing the Member States is strong as hardly ever seen before in a European Directive, and the European institutions obviously seek to avoid the impression that civil liberties are but a pretext to improve the internal market conditions for personal data flows.

This stronger emphasis on basic values in more recent approaches is not only due to the European Court of Luxembourg which, by then, had also become more explicit on that matter.

In my view, the change in attitude is also due – with regard to information and communication technology and the social impact of these technologies – to a value competition in which the European Union had started to see itself with the US, and to which we had alluded in the previous chapter.

At the latest since the White Paper on Competition, Employment and Growth (1993), the European Union and its spearhead for these issues – DG XIII– had consciously used the term "information society" to mark a (perceived) difference to the US approach to the "(super) information highway" [35].

The European approach – as the EU perceives itself – is more oriented towards social values than – again as perceived by the EU – the US economic-technological approach. Against this background, European concern for data protection has become but a symbol of the importance of social values. And, because of its symbolic value, it is now more consciously used, not only in the general directive, but also in other areas: In April 1999, for example, the European Parliament ensured that data protection clauses were explicitly introduced into the draft electronic commerce directive and the draft of the directive on electronic signatures at the time these drafts went through their first reading.

This is not the place to examine to what extent this self-image coincides with reality, both with regard to the more "social" approach to the information society, and whether data protection is really such a valid symbol of this approach[36].

What seems obvious, however, is that the "information society and data protection" rhetoric not only served as an element of external differentiation, but also as a term for drumming up internal support for a faster and smoother integration of information and communication technology into society – in the Member States themselves and not just at the European level.

---

35 The term "information society" was, of course, not introduced in the White Paper. With regard to the history of this term see e.g. *Masuda, Yoneij*: The information society as Post-Industrial Society. Washington DC. 2nd printing 1981. *Lyon, David*: The Roots of the Information Society Idea. In: *O'Sullivan, Tim; Jewkes, Yvonne* (eds): The Media Studies Reader. London 1997, 384-402. [From: *Lyon, David*: The information society: issues and illusions. New York 1988] *Bjoern-Andersen, N.; Earl, M.; Holst, O.; Mumford, E.* (eds.): Information Society for richer, for poorer. Amsterdam 1982. Webster 1995. The White Paper had built strongly on the work of the FAST (Forecasting of Science and Technology) Program of the European Community. As to the early beginnings see also *Andersen* et. al. 1982.

36 See instead e.g. *Burkert* 1997b.

This observation invites a digression to attempt a closer look at the functional side of data protection legislation in Europe.

# 3 An Attempt at a Functional Perspective

## 3.1 Function and performance

Behind values there are functional evolutionary processes at work which help these values to take a particular form at a given time in a special social context.

> By function I am referring to what data protection legislation does for the political/legal system. This also implies some assumptions on how this is achieved (performance). I am not addressing the question as to how efficient or how effective this legislation has been in fulfilling these functions. However, there is, although still tentative, increasing policy research in this field[37].

As a test case for my arguments, I would like to use the current German law and the European Directive, as some sort of European digest of data protection[38].

Data protection legislation was required to address two basic problems:

(a) How to ensure the technology's smooth introduction and integration: The process of diffusing the technology into society was somewhat problematic. The technology had connotations that affected personal identity ("Am I a machine?"). And it affected distribution patterns of social and political power and reopened political debates, on which (at least) intermediate comprises had been reached[39].

In addition, its introduction had to be performed against the background of the global value competition ("Cold War" i.e. still East-West and not yet towards the end of the "Cold War" i.e. Europe-US). In this competition "computer power" became a strange idol of convergence because it seemed to hold the promise of mastering the complexities of the market, as well as the complexity of planned economies[40].

We call this the *legitimization task.*

(b) The second problem was how – once introduced – to keep the technology running to the best of its potential. As a technology, it put emphasis on syntactical rather

---

37 Cf. the publications by *Charles Raab* and *Colin Bennett* as, for example, *Raab* et al. 1998.

38 A more detailed attempt had been undertaken in *Burkert* 1996b. For a more recent and slightly different approach that seeks to stay closer to Luhmann's theory of social systems: *Donos* 1998.

39 Basic political problems (employer/employee relationship, consumer/provider, citizen/State; etc.) were allowed to return to the political stage "disguised" as technology problems. Information and communication technology is being discussed as increasing existing power gaps, as inviting redistribution of political and social power. Implementing such technology in economic, social and administrative systems thus requires addressing the legitimacy of these processes by either shifting power balances or re-legitimizing existing power differences.

40 Hence in the sixties the belief on *both* sides that good government was (also) a management problem to be solved by mastering complexity and quantity.

than semantical aspects and, as such, was prone to fallacies that needed sufficient control on semantics so as not to jeopardize the introduction process described under (a).

This task we call the *efficiency task.*

In this introduction and stabilization process, data protection became part of social modernization or, rather, yet another instrument legitimizing modernization. In this process, procedural aspects had to be emphasized: Charismatic elements were not available, and scientific proof and economic success were no longer reliable mechanisms for long term stabilization – although all of these elements were occasionally used in the context of the "privacy problem" [41].

Since science could no longer be used as a long-term, reliable source of legitimization, the political system had to resort to *combining* resources of legitimization:

- emphasizing the democratic *process* over the material merits of the issue,
- *supplementing* (not replacing) the democratic process by expert advice,
- *supplementing* expert advice by elements of direct democracy, and/or "common sense" and/or "the man/woman in the street".

Data protection law incorporated these techniques:

- By being a *law and referring to laws* it represented the collective democratic *process:*

  Therefore, in data protection legislation we find: Processing of personal data is permitted when it is permitted by a law.

- By refering to a contract it emphasized the individual consensual *process*:

  Therefore, in data protection legislation we find: Processing is permitted if there is informed consent, if there is a contract, or if there is a contractual relationship.

- By taking the symbolic institutional approach:

  Therefore, in data protection legislation we find data protection agencies combining elements of the "expert", the ombudsman and, in some committees, representatives of the "people" (in a multitude of variations). Sometimes these elements are combined by giving the data protection agency specific tasks in the law-making *process* (e.g. its opinion on a bill is required.).

Ensuring efficiency, however, is a more difficult task, because it has to be achieved almost behind the backs of users. Users of technology tend to be absorbed by short term benefits rather than taking into account mid or long- term results.

---

41 See the personifications of developments in information and communication technology or the arguments exchanged in the "automation" debate. For this whole process of legitimation see: *Laufer*, 1990.

The protection of data processing from the fallacies of its users demands ensuring the *semantic quality* of the process, that is

- optimal representation of information by data in terms of exactness and timeliness
- safeguarding its context as far as possible.

The search for optimal representation is expressed in the data quality principles of the data protection laws.

Context is dependent on purpose. Purpose limitation, one of the key concepts of data protection laws, helps to guarantee context.

The optimization of external quality also necessitates the possibility of external quality control: Therefore, processing must operate under the constant possibility of access by the data subject (subject verification). External institutional verification processes (data protection agencies) further add to efficiency.

This analysis may be extended to other elements of data protection laws. For example, data protection agencies also provide legitimacy competition (among themselves; with the courts; with the "law abiding" administration; with self-regulating mechanisms).

The purpose of such an approach is not to completely deny the "value" side of data protection. It is only to contribute to an explanation as to why, as a legislative program, data protection has apparently been so successful, at least if one looks at the spread of the concept across national boundaries.

Nor is the performance of data protection legislation uncontested (as we shall see below). However, much of this criticism will confirm that what is seen as not being performed (or not sufficiently) is modernization, if we regard modernization as a process of managing paradox requirements[42].

> For example, as regards rule-making for information systems in public administrations, data protection regulations are a necessary but not a sufficient condition: It is, in particular, their transparency elements that are in need of further extension toward more general structural transparency. At that stage then, terms as such «privacy» or «access to information» or «freedom of information» legislation will turn into historical labels rather than functional descriptions: What is needed is a *comprehensive* framework for information processes in public sector information systems.

I do not wish to give the impression that I am pursuing a sort of intentionist approach, arguing that, while politicians preached human and civil rights, they intended to establish an ever more perfect system of personal data handling. I would argue, however, that regardless of the intention, some of the systemic necessities have received a greater chance of success against the oddities of complex social interactions, and that these needs found their way into legislation that tried to ensure at least symbolic protection, as well as credibility among those who worked with the "machine", not to mention, of course, that not all interested parties tend to have the same impact in the legislative process.

---

42 Cf. *van der Loo, Hans; van Reijen, Willem*: Modernisierung. Projekt und Paradox. München 1992.

### 3.2 What makes Us different from Them?

It has also not been the purpose of this diversion to subsume all elements of data protection laws to the function/performance paradigm. There are elements that stand by themselves, that explain themselves, if at all, by local rites, historic collective memory, or just obstinate cultural relicts. But this is the advantage of the functional approach: it sharpens one's view to differences in *values:* If we assume that the functional requirements of data protection are more or less the same across societies that have reached a certain stage of economic and technological development, then the differences in historic residues should become more apparent.

As an example of such differences between the US and the European/German approach, the stronger impact of history may then be explained in particular to the experience in Europe with totalitarian regimes.

This experience has a two-fold effect: On the one side, there is a strong distrust in the growing surveillance potential of public institutions and, at the same time, there is an almost paternal belief that relief from such institutions can only come from other institutions that are somewhat related to "public administration."

## 4 The Crisis of Data Protection

Whatever their reach, the performances of data protection laws bear in themselves the roots of disintegration. These disintegrating processes were perhaps realized from the outset, but they had not necessarily been voiced very prominently, for fear of jeopardizing the rule-making process. Now, with the Directive passed and ever more Eastern European countries accepting data protection as a principle, these frictions are coming into the open and characterize the current phase of data protection, certainly in Germany.

Being able to make privacy an issue in the American/European relationship, listening to a US rhetoric that is largely a rhetoric of defense (US enterprises seeking a "safe harbor"), seeing data protection accepted internationally in a UN declaration, with even China giving it a thought by means of an already very active Hong Kong data protection commissioner: Data protection has traveled a long way and it has arrived as a phenomenon.

With data protection having been achieved at the European Union level, criticism can now be voiced more openly without the risk of being accused of kicking an ailing value[43].

In Germany, this critical self-assessment is now coming from the former proponents of data protection, while, of course, in the ancient critics' camp of the constitutional court decision, the fire had always been kept burning.

---

43 From recent publications the situation in the US still seems to be different: While *Whitaker* 1999 claims the end of privacy, Etzioni goes into considerable length to justify why he is giving privacy a critical assessment (*Etzioni* 1999, 5ff.).

The "new criticism"[44] targets:

- the internal differentiation of data protection,
- the bureaucratization of data protection,
- the apparent incapability of data protection legislation to meet the challenges of technology (i.e.: the Internet),
- the incompleteness of data protection as a regulatory concept.

## 4.1 Internal differentiation of data protection

While national legislatures are still preparing to make their data protection laws compatible with the European Union Directive – in Germany's case, for example, this will be the third major revision of its national law – it is no longer just omnibus laws that make up the data protection landscape. We are also faced with a multitude of what are being called "sector-specific data protection laws". These special laws are either separate laws, or clauses built into other laws, which address data protection issues in areas like national security, policing, health and social security, public registers, etc. These regulations seek to apply the general data protection principles to their specific contexts although, even in these more specific contexts, they cannot avoid leaving areas of discretion.

This has been an almost logical development: If the rights of the data subject are to be limited and if this has to be done by law, as we remember from the basic assumptions of informational self-determination, then it will be laws which introduce sector-specific considerations. However, sufficient room must also be left there in order to retain flexibility for individual cases unless information systems are prescribed in full detail.

With this approach, problem by problem, issue by issue, legislators tend to lose sight of the overall picture. Legislative techniques of reference and cross-reference add to complexity. One ends up with a highly differentiated system of rules, if system is still the right word, which still leaves much discretion to the courts and even broader discretion (or a broader margin of appreciation) to the administration: complexity without the benefit of predictability. With this approach, not only the demand for clarity is omitted, a demand that had once been an integral part of data protection, but it is also becoming more and more difficult to obtain an overall view of the extent and limits of data protection, if one is not to take a more sinister view, seeing legislatures as merely "nodding" to the complex demands of the "expert" administration.

The role of the sector-specific legislation in the public sector is taken over in the private sector by the contract approach: The creation of consent as the all-exonerating instrument. Data protection clauses have become part of numerous contracts, privacy

44 See e.g.: Die Landesbeauftragten für den Datenschutz: 20 Jahre Datenschutz - Individualismus oder Gemeinschaftssinn. Düsseldorf 1998.

policies appear on websites. Not all of these clauses meet the requirements of data protection principles, not all of them meet the requirements of consent or even informed consent.

In most cases, however, challenging these classes of consent or non-consent in the private sector means activating the courts, which , indeed, is occasionally being done by competitors, rarely by consumer associations, and even less frequently by individuals and almost never – because this is not foreseen in the regulatory systems in Europe – by the data protection agencies. So data protection in the private sector has been reduced to a consumer protection issue and is going to share its fate.

> This does not exclude occasional eruptions of protest, not unlike the Lotus market place reaction in the US. But, usually, these eruptions need argumentative support from the data protection agencies and, in these cases, privacy concerns tend to get mixed with other concerns or resentments, in which case data protection issues are just the catalyst. In Germany this was the case when banks changed their general contract provisions to introduce a very limited right to give (positive) credit information to requesting third parties, and when the German Railway Corporation (which although privatized is still regarded as a public sector institution) started a campaign (that was ill fated right from the beginning) to market a card that would have combined credit card and rail card functions. In both cases, there had already been a pre-existing feeling of discontent with regard to the services offered by these institutions and to which data protection added legitimacy. And, in both cases, an explicit act of consent was necessary on behalf of the "consumers" to introduce the scheme.

## 4.2 The bureaucratization of data protection

While more tradition-inclined jurists are finally discovering the attractions of privacy legislation (the recent Annual Conference of German Jurists even dedicated a whole session to the issue[45]) and while some of them are falling back into ancient dreams of codifying information as such, a sort of Codex Iuris Informationis, (this already being another signifier of decay in legal discussion) there are increasing doubts about the effectiveness of data protection regulation, and in particular of data protection agencies.

These doubts are raised when one is reading through the annual (and increasingly only biannual) reports of these agencies. Occasionally, they convey the feeling that these institutions regard themselves as being judged by the amount of pages they produce in these reports. With their diminishing role as an authoritative registration agency, with automated processing becoming a banality, many of these agencies have difficulties adjusting to the new demands placed upon them.

---

45 To do justice to *the* social institution of German law, it should be noted that this had already been the second occasion: At an annual conference exactly 25 years ago, data protection had also been the subject of a session.

These agencies seem to shift uneasily between the image of data protection bureaucratization[46] and an ombudsman role. Doubts are reinforced in both roles when one compares the demands they made themselves in their reports and the changes they actually initiated through their intervention.

> Occasionally, this general impression is modified by the particular personality of a commissioner; above all if he or she knows how to make use of the mass media, or by the explicit political understanding of his/her role or the role of the agency, as is the case with, e.g., the French Commission.

This somewhat dissatisfying impression may be part of the role these institutions had to play in current data protection concepts as described in the functional analysis above. This may change with the Directive and its implementation, which has given these agencies a more eminent role. However, at the current stage, dissatisfaction is not only an appropriate term to describe how these agencies are seen from the outside; it also reflects to a large extent the image they have of themselves.

## 4.3 The challenge of the Internet

The Internet poses a double challenge to data protection regulations. There is the obvious technical challenge, but there is also the more fundamental challenge to regulatory concepts in general, of which the Internet is only one example.

Current data protection regulations address – with the exception of a few attempts recently to extend past wordings to current and future problems[47] – previous generation technology: the arrival of the personal computer, distributed processing, online data banks and highly formalized electronic data interchange.

The technology of the day is – of course – characterized by increasing network connectivity, high speed transmissions, the ubiquity of information processing, for which the Internet has become the catchword.

Data protection regulation is no longer capable of meeting the technical challenges of recording e.g. information consumption behavior in increasing detail with a decreasing chance of the user becoming aware of this monitoring. Data protection regulation cannot stay ahead of technical developments and is not even able to follow them at an acceptable distance.

> Independently from the Internet there are also challenges to the more traditional forms of processing through techniques such as data mining, which finally seem

---

46 See e.g. *Trute* 1998, 828f.

47 In Germany e.g.: Federal Act Establishing the General Conditions for Information and Communication Services - Information and Communication Services Act - (Informations- und Kommunikationsdienste-Gesetz - IuKDG) August 1, 1997. Or, on the level of the European Union, the activities e.g. the Privacy Directive Working Party: Recommendation 1/99 on Invisible and Automatic Processing of Personal Data on the Internet Performed by Software and Hardware.

to give justification to the idea that one should never throw any data away because one might need it one day[48]. The concept provides the strongest challenge yet to the purpose limitation principle.

The criticism of data protection regulation in view of the Internet also echoes some of the more fundamental criticism of regulation in general:

- Data protection regulation is no longer capable of getting a hold on the responsible keeper: Organizational entities disappear and reconfigure constantly in the era of virtual international corporate but also public sector institutions.
- Data protection - even where it is regionally organized as on the EU level – cannot meet the challenges of global data flows.
- Data protection regulation is not fine-tuned to the economic mechanisms of the use of information and communication technology today.

## 4.4 The need for complementation

As indicated above, looking at its implementation history in Germany, it is surprising (or perhaps not) that data protection as a concept seems to have been so successfully adopted by the public sector. There are occasional skirmishes, particularly concerning the right of access by individuals, and occasional conflicts with data sharing across agencies. While particularly the latter type of conflict is one perceived from the outside, access by an individual is more or less the only problem seen from the inside, because it threatens the administration with transparency. We briefly addressed this observation in the previous part when we looked into the functional concept of these rules in the public sector, and indeed, what the introduction of data protection into the public administration certainly achieved is to confirm the administration in its view on administrative secrecy. There have been, and there still are, many examples where the administration uses data protection arguments to block access to potentially compromising material.

There are more and more signs that data protection needs complementation by freedom of information regulations. While the European history of freedom of information will be dealt with in a different paper, it is obvious that European legislators have only recently realized the interrelation between data protection and access legislation.

A peculiar example is France, where both laws were passed within a few weeks of each other and where it took a turf conflict lasting several years between the two agencies administering these laws and which had to be settled by the Conseil d' Etat to realize that indeed these laws were related.

Now, more and more European countries have legislation of both types and the Directive was forced to make clarifications in its recitals due to the Scandinavian

48 Very instructive for the privacy problems of data mining: *Ann Cavoukian, Ph.D* (Information and Privacy Commissioner/Ontario): Data Mining: Staking a Claim on Your Privacy. January 1998.

(mainly Swedish) concerns about access. Judging from a recent Green paper, the EU might even be moving towards a *Directive* on access to government information.

What is becoming obvious in the process is that:

- data protection legislation already contains structural elements of access as well as ones pertaining to individual rights;
- data protection and freedom of information complement each other and where one of the elements is missing the other has to be introduced to strike the proper balance;
- both types of legislation need harmonization to avoid lacunae and overlaps, as well as conflicts between supervising agencies.

# 5 From Here to Where?

## 5.1 Discussing Remedies

Overspecialization of data protection regulations, bureaucratization, technological challenges and the need to balance them with access principles may, of course, be read as signs that the data protection concept is as vital as ever, as a digest of sociopolitical conflicts only waiting for their solutions.

### 5.1.1 Technology

One source for solutions may be provided by technology itself.

The "technological solutions to technological problems" debate already surfaced at a very early stage in privacy debates, but was more or less rejected or channeled into the data security debate, because

- law makers doubted in principle that technological problems could be solved with even more technology,
- of the lack of availability of a technology that would both guarantee (or at least help to guarantee) anonymity and identifiability of the anonymous.

Now, with "privacy-enhancing technologies"[49], a whole new era of organizational and technological solutions seem possible.

### 5.1.2 Trying out new approaches – learning from the US?

Right from the outset, the concept of data protection in Europe was not a merely European affair. American international companies and their subsidiaries, even if they regarded themselves to be European companies, conveyed the American view on

---

49 For more detail: *Burkert* 1997.

regulation and on privacy regulation in particular. European companies could point to those companies and issue warnings about their own international competitiveness. The first hearing of the European Parliament had a strong observer delegation from the US. The Council of Europe Convention had received special wording to provide for the unlikely event that the US would join. And, of course, the discourse on how to draft the Directive was a discourse that involved the US from the beginning. Therefore, it is not surprising that then and now it contains some US reflections – now that the European point has been made by the Directive – more strongly into European reconsideration of privacy. Some of these concepts, in my view, have a chance, and others do not.

Among those which are more strongly re-introduced are those favoring more subtle approaches involving the regulated entities themselves. Among these approaches, those might have a better chance that seek to combine regulation by independent agencies with self-regulation. For data protection, one will have to wait and see how such current approaches are being perceived – in mid-term – in other areas like telecommunications.

Significantly less attention (although that may not remain this way) had been given to the perception of privacy rights as a property right that can become subject to transactions and could thus become marketable.

Rather early in the debate, the European approach seemed to have focused on privacy as a – basically – inalienable *liberty* right, comparable perhaps to the personality right element in some European copyright regimes.

### 5.1.3 A new system of information regulation?

Data protection – as already mentioned – is increasingly seen as too narrow an approach to the role of information in our societies. Freedom of information regulation is progressing in Europe. Increasingly, the interaction between freedom of information and data protection is being realized. However, in contrast to data protection as it is seen now, freedom of information regulation lacks – should we add "still"? – direct impact on the private sector. The civil procedure law instrument of discovery (which might have helped to introduce freedom of information in the US) is alien to many of the civil procedure systems in Europe. Currently, most of the (non-personal) information requests the private sector is facing are channeled via the public sector: There is a public law duty to provide information to an agency and that agency might be required to pass on the information to an information requester. But limited rights to information are already – and have been for a long time – also part of the civil law systems in Europe[50] and we might face a similar development as with data protection: As to information requests, the importance of the separation line between the public and the private sector may diminish.

In Germany, the country of the "world champions of systematization" (the words of the Swiss jurist Jean Nicolas Druey)[51], more recent reflections go even one step further:

50 See e.g. *Druey* 1983.

51 *Druey* 1995.

integrating all aspects of information-related regulation. This goes beyond merely creating a new codex of information law; it would also involve a new methodology to examine information conflicts.

## 5.2 A lingering doubt

The deepest challenge, beyond all remedies, however, seems to be that there is an inherent "relativity" element in data protection that seems to come to the surface when the data protection principle is explicitly set against other social and political demands like, e.g., the need for security.

This demand to provide even more security than there is in the pre-digital world has its effects on all sorts of regulatory activities of information and communication technology, and particularly on privacy protection. Against this background, the Internet, for example, poses a double threat to the concept of privacy protection: While we cannot trust the system to observe our privacy, we cannot allow the system to provide privacy to others since we can no longer (or not yet) trust our social senses. So, even if privacy protection addresses the Internet, it will remain in a double-bind situation: The same parliament that allows pseudonyms and cryptography for the enhancement of privacy on the Net[52] postulates to identify the person behind each and every e-mail[53].

While privacy still ranks very highly among the concerns of German and other European citizens, and while it is still one of the main concerns, for example, in electronic commerce, whenever it is confronted with a concrete value conflict, privacy rapidly seems to lose its appeal. So, in spite of our esteem for privacy, we Europeans live with dark doubts and we are involved, and even actively participate, in a change of values that seems to contradict our esteem: We have a high regard for privacy indeed, but when faced with other needs like security, or when lured by the logic of efficiency, or even only for reasons of convenience, again and again, we are willing to sacrifice this very same privacy, perhaps not always at once, but certainly step by step.

And no one can express this, our willingness, better than those we elect: The legislator, the executor of our ambiguous attitude towards privacy, has become the greatest threat to privacy protection legislation today.

---

52 See e.g. *the European Parliament, Report* A4-0189/98: Resolution on the communication from the Commission to the Council, the European Parliament, the Economic and Social Committee and the Committee of the Regions on ensuring security and trust in electronic telecommunication - towards a European framework for digital signatures and encryption (COM(97)0503 - C4-0648/97): " 7. Emphasizes, however, the potential benefits offered by the new communication technologies on strengthening European civil society through the development of a European and global public space, and therefore calls on the Commission to inform it of any observations relating to abuse of communications systems, especially through interception, for the purposes of illegitimate surveillance of citizens and individuals in the EU;"

53 *European Parliament*: Draft Joint Action, adopted by the Council on the basis of Article K.3 of the Treaty on European Union, to combat child pornography on the Internet (10850/5/98 - C4-0674/98 - 98/0917(CNS)):"Amendment 16) Article 3 (-1)(new) -1. to ensure that the identity of persons who have set up an electronic mail (e-mail) address can be ascertained; [...]"

## References:

*Bennett, Colin J.* , Different Processes, One Result: The Convergence of Data Protection Policy in Europe and the United States. In: *Governance: An International Journal of Policy and Administration*, Vol. 1, No. 4, Oct. 1988, 415 - 441.

*Bennett, Colin J.*, Regulating Privacy. Ithaka, London 1992.

*Braibant, Guy,* Données personnelles et société de l'information. Rapport au Premier ministre. Paris 1998.

*Burkert, Herbert*, Data-protection legislation and the modernization of public administration. In: *International Review of Administrative Sciences* 62 (1996) 4, 557-568.

*Burkert, Herbert*, Privacy Enhancing Technologies.: Typology, Critique, Vision. In: Agre, Philip E.; Rotenberg, Marc (eds.): Technology and Privacy: The New Landscape. *MIT-Press*. Cambridge 1997, 125-142.

*Burkert, Herbert*, Involving the Citizens: The Normative Model of the Information and Communication Citizen. In: Kubicek, Herbert; Dutton, William H.; Williams, Robin (eds.): The Social Shaping of Information Superhighways. Frankfurt/New York 1997, 211-220.

*Delahaie, Henri / Paoletti, Félix,* Informatique et libertés. Paris 1987.

*Donos, Pelopidas Konstantinos*, Datenschutz - Prinzipien und Ziele. Frankfurt 1998.

*Druey, Jean Nicolas*, Privatrecht als Recht der Kommunikation. In: *Schweizer Juristen Zeitschrift* 1983,185-196.

*Druey, Jean Nicolas*, Information als Gegenstand des Rechts. Entwurf einer Grundlegung. Zürich 1995.

*Ellger, R.*, Der Datenschutz im grenzüberschreitenden Datenverkehr. Baden-Baden 1990.

*Etzioni, Amitai*, The Limits of Privacy. New York 1999.

*Flaherty, D.H.*, Protecting Privacy in Surveillance Societies. Chapel Hill. London 1989.

*Hogrebe, Edmund F.*, Verwaltungsautomation und Datenschutz in Frankreich. Berlin 1976.

*Hondius, Frits W.*, Emerging Data Protection in Europe. Amsterdam, Oxford, New York 1975.

*Laufer, R.*, The Question of the Legitimacy of Computers: An Epistemological Point of View. In: *Report from Namur: Landscapes for an Information Society*. New York 1990, 31-61.

*Layton, Christopher*, Protection of Privacy - Future Prospects at the European Communities Level. In: *OECD: Transborder Data Flows and The Protection of Privacy*. Paris 1979, 213-216.

*Mallmann, Christoph*, Datenschutz in Verwaltungsinformationssysteme. München 1976.

*Miller, Arthur R.*, The Assault on Privacy: Computers, Data Banks and Dossiers. Ann Arbor 1971.

*Miller, Arthur R.*, Computer and Privacy. In: Michigan Law Review 67 (1969), 1162-1246.

*Raab, Charles / Bennett, Colin, J. / Gellman, Robert M./ Waters, Nigel*, Application of a methodology designed to assess the adequacy of the level of protection of individuals with regard to processing personal data. Test of the method on several categories of transfer. Final Report. September 1998.

*Tinnefeld, Marie-Theres / Ehmann, Eugen*, Einführung in das Datenschutzrecht. 2.Aufl. München 1994.

*Trute, Hans-Heinrich*, Der Schutz personenbezogener Informationen in der Informationsgesellschaft. In: *Juristenzeitung* 1998, 823- 831.

*Trute, Hans-Heinrich*, Öffentlich-rechtliche Rahmenbedingungen einer Informationsordnung. In: *Veröffentlichungen der Vereinigung der Deutschen Staatsrechtslehrer* 57 (1998), 216-273.

*Webster, Frank*, Theories of the Information Society. London 1995.

*Westin, Alan F.*, Privacy and Freedom, 6th ed., New York 1970.

*Whitaker, Reg*, The End of Privacy. New York 1999.

*Robert Gellman*

# Privacy and Harmonization



What is privacy? Mining the academic literature on privacy requires a tour through journals of law, philosophy, sociology, political science, and psychology, but the trip will not find consensus anywhere[1]. Every field and every scholar offers different concepts, analyses, objectives, and definitions.

Much of the development of privacy as a legal right has taken place in law journals, and this may account for some of the fundamental confusion. Perhaps the most famous definition comes from the 1890 Harvard Law Review article by Louis Brandeis and Samuel Warren[2]. They describe privacy as the right to be "let alone", but it is far from clear what this phrase means[3]. In the mid-1960s, Professor Alan Westin suggested that the core value of the right of individual privacy was the right of the individual to decide for himself, with only extraordinary exceptions to meet the interests of society, when and on what terms his acts should be revealed to the general public[4]. What does either notion mean to an individual whose medical records have been sent, without notice or consent,

1 For a summary of privacy literature, see *Priscilla M. Regan*, Legislating Privacy 24-41 (1995).

2 The Right to Privacy, 4 *Harvard Law Review* 193 (1980).

3 Professor Paul Schwartz calls the right to be let alone "an incomplete paradigm in the computer age." Privacy and participation: Personal Information and Private Sector Regulation in the United States, 80 *Iowa Law Review* 553, 558 (1995).

4 *Alan F. Westin*, Privacy and Freedom 42 (1967).

by the individual's health plan to an outcomes researcher hired by the individual's employer seeking to hold down the cost of health insurance? How do we translate broad theories of privacy into meaningful rules for record keepers and rights for data subjects?

American case law offers no help in solving definitional problems. A review of American constitutional law cases finds that the right to privacy is an element in many decisions. Although the word privacy does not appear anywhere in the U.S. Constitution, the courts have nevertheless found the right to privacy provides a constitutional basis for a woman's right to have an abortion, the right to be free from unreasonable governmental searches and seizures, the right against self-incrimination, the right to assemble and speak, the right to educate children, and many other disparate rights, including the right not to have soldiers quartered in a private home. The courts have distilled privacy rights into two broad categories, those that affect personal autonomy and those that involve informational privacy interests[5]. That is mildly helpful for purposes of analysis, but it does not address definitions.

Because privacy is a term that reflects so many personal and cultural values, it is not clear that it will ever be possible to agree on a definition of privacy. I choose instead to avoid the broader definitional issue by using an approach to *information privacy* that has been accepted all around the world. The Europeans have contributed the notion of data protection, a most useful phrase for discussing some aspects of privacy. Data protection refers to the rules that regulate the collection, maintenance, use, and disclosure of personal information. We can discuss data protection without slogging through the broader and more difficult privacy definitional problem. We can do this successfully because there is, remarkably, an international consensus on the policy objectives of data protection. Admittedly, focusing on information privacy issues that are inherent in data protection omits other important and fundamental privacy concerns, but that may be the price for a more coherent discussion.

## 1. Fair Information Practices

Fair information practices were invented by an advisory committee established in 1972 by the Secretary of U.S. Department of Health, Education & Welfare to study the effects of the application of computer technology to record keeping about people[6]. Although the advisory committee's attention was focused on automated record keeping systems maintained by government agencies, the principles of fair information practices have more universal application.

---

5 See, e.g., Whalen v. Roe, 429 U.S. 589, 598-600 (1977).

6 See Secretary's Advisory Committee on automated Personal Data Systems, Records, Computers, and the Rights of Citizens (1973). Similar ideas were put forward at the same time in Great Britain by the Committee on Privacy, known more popularly as the *Younger Committee*. Privacy scholars are unable to determine which committee's work came first or whether one committee influenced the other. See *Colin J. Bennett*, Regulating Privacy 99 (1992).

The first law that implemented fair information practices was the Privacy Act of 1974 [7], a law that was taken nearly verbatim from recommendations of the HEW advisory committee. In the following years, fair information practices swept the privacy world, forming the basis for data protection laws and policy statements around the world. The international policy convergence around fair information practices is rather extraordinary. Despite the vast differences in language, legal traditions and institutions, and cultural and social values from country to country, data protection laws invariably reflect the same basic policies[8].

Fair information practices can be expressed in different ways. Statements may include as few as four principles or as many as ten or more. Regardless of how the policies are expressed, the content is virtually identical. One version of fair information practices follows:

1) The Principle of *Openness*, which provides that the existence of record-keeping systems and databanks containing data about individuals be publicly known, along with a description of main purpose and uses of the data.
2) The Principle of *Individual Participation*, which provides that each individual should have a right to see any data about himself or herself and to correct or remove any data that is not timely, accurate, relevant, or complete.
3) The Principle of *Collection Limitation*, which provides that there should be limits to the collection of personal data, that data should be collected by lawful and fair means, and that data should be collected, where appropriate, with the knowledge or consent of the subject.
4) The Principle of *Data Quality*, which provides that personal data should be relevant to the purposes for which they are to be used, and should be accurate, complete, and timely.
5) The Principle of *Finality*, which provides that there must be limits to the uses and disclosure of personal data, that the data should be used only for purposes specified at the time of collection, and that data should not be otherwise disclosed without the consent of the data subject or other legal authority.
6) The Principle of *Security*, which provides that personal data should be protected by reasonable security safeguards against such risks as loss, unauthorized access, destruction, use, modification, or disclosure.
7) The Principle of *Accountability*, which provides that record keepers should be accountable for complying with fair information practices.

---

7 5 U.S.C. §552a (1994).

8 See *Colin J. Bennett*, Regulating Privacy 95-115 (1992). Perhaps the most important and most influential policy statement came in 1980 from the Organization for Economic Cooperation and Development. *Guidelines on the Protection of Privacy and Transborder Flows of Personal Data*, 1981 I.L.M. 422, O.E.C.D. Doc. No. C(80)58 final.

As a device for organizing a discussion or for outlining a privacy statute, fair information practices are extremely useful[9]. They make international harmonization a much simpler task because of the fundamental agreement on broad policy objectives. However, simpler does not mean simple, and the complex realities of the modern world make the application of fair information practices a significant challenge.

Fair information practices are not self-executing. Indeed, they may be applied in a variety of ways through different institutions. In Europe, independent data protection authorities are mainly responsible for oversight and enforcement of fair information practices[10]. In the United States, which does not have any broadly applicable fair information practice requirements except for federal agencies, enforcement of the occasional privacy laws that exist usually comes through lawsuits brought by aggrieved individuals[11]. Oversight or enforcement by government agencies is rare[12].

Different implementations of fair information practices are important because record keepers and record subjects often have different needs. While the same broad policies may be applicable to all records containing personal information, the implementation of those policies may differ significantly from system to system. Compare, for example, disclosure policies for health records with policies for pizza delivery records. Health records have many users who can legitimately argue for access without the specific authorization of the patient. In order to meet other social, economic, and health needs, we may allow access to health records by public health authorities, health researchers, fraud and abuse investigators, accreditation agencies, and even law enforcement under some circumstances. For the pizza delivery records, there may not be a need to allow for any non-consensual disclosures because there are no overriding societal needs that justify disclosure without consent. In both cases, we have outlined a policy implementing the principle of finality (disclosure limitation), but the substance of the policies differs considerably. Applying the same fair information practice principle to the same records in other countries will produce different rules because the economic, social, and cultural needs of nations can differ significantly. Policies may be identical, but outcomes are not.

## 2. A Failure of Distinctions

Making distinctions on which to base privacy rules is a growing challenge because of changes occurring elsewhere in the world. For example, in the United States, we have

---

9 Critics of fair information practices have begun to emerge. See, e.g., *Gary T. Marx*, Ethics for the New Surveillance. In: Visions of Privacy: Policy Choices for the Digital Age 39-67 (*Colin J. Bennett & Rebecca Grant*, eds., 1999).

10 Independent supervisory authorities are required under Article 28 of the EU data protection directive. Council Directive 95/46/EC on the Protection of Individuals With Regard to the Processing of Personal Data and on the Free Movement of Such Data, 1995 O.J. (L 281) 31.

11 See *Robert Gellman*, Does Privacy Law Work? In: Technology and Privacy: The New Landscape (*Philip E. Agre & Marc Rotenberg*, eds., 1997).

12 See *Robert Gellman*, Fragmented, Incomplete, and Discontinuous: The Failure of Federal Privacy Proposals and Institutions, 6 *Software Law Journal* 199 (1993).

traditionally had different regulatory structures for local telephone companies, long distance companies, cable television, Internet providers, and other telecommunications entities. Because of ongoing changes in telecommunications, these traditional distinctions between institutions no longer necessarily make sense. The issues here are much broader than just privacy, but the privacy aspects are complex enough.

Different laws regulate the privacy of communications in different contexts. A telephone call is entitled to one form of legal protection against interception while an electronic mail message has a different form of protection. Records that reflect viewing habits of cable television subscribers receive some federal legal protection for privacy[13], but records of satellite television viewing habits do not. It may be easy to suggest that all telecommunications records should be governed by the same privacy rules, but the requirements of users vary widely and the traditions from existing policies cannot be ignored. Changing policies will likely result in improved protections for some records and reduced protections for others, and that can create enormously complex political problems. It is sobering to remember that it took Congress 40 years before it finally passed a law regulating wiretapping in 1968 [14].

Other types of traditional distinctions also no longer have clear value for privacy regulatory purposes. Consider Experian, a large, multinational company with English owners and extensive operations in the United States. In the United States, Experian is principally known as a credit reporting company, an activity regulated under federal law[15]. It also has interests in consumer marketing companies, individual reference service operations, and other personal information intensive activities. Most marketing records are not regulated for privacy, but some state motor vehicle records are subject to the rules set out in the federal Driver's Privacy Protection Act[16]. The company is a member of various American trade associations, including Associated Credit Bureaus, Software and Information Industry Association, Direct Marketing Association, and the Individual Reference Services Group. Each of these associations has its own industry privacy policy. Experian has its own company privacy code as well. Experian also operates in Canada, Europe, and elsewhere around the world.

From any perspective, applying privacy rules to a company like Experian is a challenge. In the United States, privacy laws offer spotty coverage, and major differences in requirements can be found among different types of records. The same information may be regulated in one context, but not in another. Occasional state laws add geographic complexity. Industry self-regulatory activities raise the same types of jurisdictional conflicts as do the statutory protections. Even determining which national privacy laws apply may be complex because computer networks allow data to be stored and accessed from locations around the world. Neither Experian itself nor its governmental regulators can always be certain which laws apply to which data. Experian customers in the United

---

13 18 U.S.C. §2710 (1994).

14 *Priscilla M. Regan*, Legislating Privacy 109-143 (1995).

15 Fair Credit Reporting Act, 15 U.S.C. §1681 et seq.

16 18 U.S.C.§2721 (1994).

States can exercise opt-out rights under several federal laws as well as several industry self-regulatory codes. Data subjects in other countries have a different set of choices. Educated consumers are likely to find the array of options for this one company alone to be bewildering. Even if harmonizing of laws and self-regulatory standards were a practical political reality, different implementations of fair information practices would still be necessary for different types of records. The problems that information conglomerates like Experian present would not disappear.

The Experian case begins to hint at how traditional distinctions between national and international are under pressure in many ways[17]. Routine consumer transactions can easily have a nexus in five or more countries, as consumers, merchants, manufacturers, website, credit card companies, and other parties to a single transaction can all be located in different political jurisdictions. Worse, the parties to a transaction may not even know who the other parties are or in what country they reside. When the fundamental elements to transactions are obscure or even unknowable, agreeing on privacy rules is even harder.

Other basic distinctions are just as hard to sustain today. Is it possible to distinguish between online and offline activities for purposes of privacy regulation? The United States recently passed a law designed to protect information collected online from children under 13 [18]. For organizations that maintain information about children from both online and offline sources, the law may require that each item of information be tagged for its source because some information may be regulated while the same information obtained offline or even online from a parent may not be controlled. A magazine subscription ordered online may have a different set of rules than a subscription taken over the telephone or though snail mail. Information collected and passed on to others – e.g., an address collected from an online order for a product – may become regulated information in the hands of a fulfillment company that fills orders and of shipping companies that deliver them.

Another traditional distinction – the line between public sector and private sectors – can be just as difficult to identify today. The point can be made most clearly by considering which sector presents a greater threat to privacy. In the 1970s, federal agencies were at the forefront of the mainframe computer era. The combination of government law enforcement and investigative powers together with ever-increasing computer capabilities offered the prospect of an Orwellian future. Regular congressional hearings and privacy studies were responses to the perceived threat of technology and government.

The government is no less of a threat today. But the private sector has grown, and it is easy to make the case for the private sector as the biggest threat in the United States. Private companies today collect, compile, and resell as much personal information as they can. Every transaction that includes a name, address, telephone number, credit card

---

17 See *Robert Gellman*, Can Privacy Be Regulated Effectively on a National Level? Thoughts on the Possible Need for International Privacy Rules, 41 *Villanova Law Review* 129 (1996).

18 Children's Online Privacy Protection Act of 1998, title XIII, Omnibus Consolidated and Emergency Supplemental Appropriations Act, 1999, *Public Law* 105-277, 112 Stat. 2681, (Oct. 21, 1998).

number, or other identifier, likely results in a new addition to a database or mailing list without notice and without consent. Telephone calls to an 800 or 900 number automatically result in the called party obtaining the name and address of the caller. Much of the demand for personal data is driven by the relentless appetite of marketers for information to use to further the sale of goods and services. Marketers sell lists sorted by income, family size, credit history, ethnic origin, race, religion, and other personal and demographic characteristics. Other private companies offer their vast collections of public and private information about individuals to clients that include lawyers, insurance companies, and employers.

A good example of the greatly expanding insistence by the private sector for personal information can be found at most American supermarkets[19]. Ten years ago, records of individual supermarket purchases did not exist. However, frequent shopper programs today force most customers to trade personal information for discounts. Customers are not getting bigger discounts, but they have to share personal data to get items on sale. The result is that the supermarkets are able to build and maintain detailed, long-term customer profiles that they can exploit without any statutory restriction at all. Supermarkets know if individual customers are buying red meat, fat free foods, cigarettes, beer, baby food, organic vegetables, condoms, or Preparation H. It may only be a matter of time before individuals are held accountable for their supermarket purchases in employment, child custody fights, insurance applications, or even political campaigns.

So who really presents the greatest threat to privacy? The reality is that it is harder to distinguish between private and public sector record keepers. Some examples will illustrate the point.

Consider this promotional description of an American company from the individual reference service industry:

Database Technologies, Inc. (DBT) [is a] national provider of on-line database services and related reports to law enforcement and other governmental agencies, law firms, insurance fraud investigation companies, and other qualified entities. DBT has developed proprietary software which contains unique algorithms and utilizes advanced microprocessor-based technology to locate, cross reference and retrieve public records from multiple data sources. DBT acquires data from both governmental and commercial sources and then formats the data for use with its products. DBT allows its restricted customer base to access its system from desktop computers and generate reports, which are delivered in an organized, comprehensive and easy to read format. DBT simultaneously accesses over 1,000 data sources containing billions of records as if they were part of a single database in preparing the computer-generated reports[20].

---

19 *Robert O'Harrow Jr.*, Bargains at a Price: Shoppers' Privacy Cards Let Supermarkets Collect Data, *Washington Post*, Dec. 31, 1998 at page A01.

20 <http://irsg.org/html/irsg_members.htm>. The description is on the website of the trade association for so-called *individual reference service* companies.

The sources of information include publicly available government records. Federal and state agencies do not have to create their own government-wide databases because they can purchase the data from the private sector. This company advertises on its website that its customers include over 1400 law enforcement agencies[21].

The interplay between the government and the private sector is also illustrated by a recent incident involving the sale of digital photographs from state motor vehicle departments to a private firm. The firm developed a system for providing a driver's photograph at the point of sale so that a clerk could verify the identity of the customer. Three states (Florida, South Carolina, and Colorado) agreed to provide the photos to the company. The sales of the photographs were authorized by special legislation, but the public was unaware until the Washington Post broke the story in January 1999 [22]. Drivers licenses have become general identification documents throughout the United States, but the proposed sale of photographs would have been the first large scale sale of information by motor vehicle departments for private sector fraud prevention purposes. Once the public learned about the sale of photos, the reaction in all three states was highly negative. In each state, the politicians who had earlier approved the sale changed course, and the effort collapsed because of public opposition.

A last example of the potential for interrelationships between public and private information activities comes from another failed attempt to establish a new channel for the sharing of information. While the private sector initiated the drivers photo sale, federal banking agencies developed and tried to implement the *Know Your Customer* program.

At the end of 1998, four federal banking regulatory agencies jointly proposed a set of regulations called the *Know Your Customer* rules. The Federal Deposit Insurance Corporation (FDIC) proposal was representative[23]. The FDIC wanted each bank to develop a program designed to determine the identity of its customers; determine its customers' sources of funds; determine the normal and expected transactions of its customers; monitor account activity for transactions that are inconsistent with those normal and expected transactions; and report any customer transactions determined to be suspicious, in accordance with the FDIC's existing suspicious activity reporting regulation. In effect, the federal government wanted banks to conduct active monitoring of bank customers and to report anyone doing anything out of the ordinary.

The *Know Your Customer* proposal drew immediate attention from the Internet community and from others. Comments opposed to the proposed rules began to pour into the banking agencies almost immediately. By the time the comment period ended, the FDIC received over 254,000 comments, a huge public reaction to otherwise obscure banking regulations. Only 105 commenters favored the regulations. The

---

21 <www.dbt.com>.

22 See *Robert O'Harrow, Jr.*, Posing a Privacy Problem? Driver's-License Photos Used in Anti-Fraud Database, *Washington Post*, Jan. 22, 1999, Page A01.

23 63 Federal Register 67529-67536 (Dec. 7, 1998).

public outcry prompted the Senate to unanimously oppose the Know Your Customer rules[24]. In light of the overwhelming public opposition, the banking agencies withdrew their proposal[25].

The public response to the *Know Your Customer* and the drivers photo efforts is evidence that generalized public concerns about privacy have finally developed some political force. For present purposes, however, the point is that the relationships between government and private sector record keepers are growing. Each camp collects data and shares it with the other in ever-increasing ways. *Know Your Customer* was merely an extension of an existing program that requires banks to report customer activities to the government. The distinction between the private and public sectors in this arena is disappearing, and one consequence is that narrow solutions to privacy concerns may be less useful than they appeared to be in the past.

### 3. Responses

The European response to privacy is omnibus laws requiring record keepers, public and private, to comply with fair information practices. The omnibus approach has some attractions despite some of the difficulties identified above. Of course, the commercial market for personal information is not as advanced in Europe as in the United States, and some of the regulatory problems that result from greater institutionalized use of personal records have yet to emerge. Europe has done no better than anyone else in figuring out how to apply rules to electronic commerce transactions, and differences in this area can be found in the laws of the member states regarding Internet activities[26].

The United States approach of so-called sectoral laws is hopelessly inadequate. It offers a random collection of privacy laws that offer inconsistent protections for some records and no protections at all for other records. For example, health, employment, insurance, and marketing records are largely unrelated for privacy anywhere in the United States, but we do have state and federal laws protecting the privacy of video rental records because a particular scandal resulted in narrow privacy legislation. Politically, however, the likelihood that the United States would pass a European-style omnibus privacy law is extremely small, and passing sectoral laws can be tortuous. Health privacy legislation has been actively before the Congress for many years, but the prospect for enactment remains highly uncertain.

No magic bullet for addressing privacy concerns is likely to be found. Nevertheless, some approaches may help with some aspects of the problem.

---

24 145 Congressional Record S2358 (Mar. 5, 1999)

25 See, e.g., 64 Federal Register 14845 (Mar. 29, 1999).

26 See generally European Commission, On-line Services and Data Protection and Privacy (1998, Volume II, Directorate General Internal Market and Financial Services.

a) *Anonymity*

Many schemes have been proposed to permit consumers to interact with merchants or over the Internet and remain anonymous[27]. None has met with great success so far, and it remains to be seen if any will find a market. The governments that have been fighting the unrestricted use of encryption will not welcome the prospect of greater anonymity with any more enthusiasm. Nevertheless, some privacy needs can be met if consumers have the ability to engage in anonymous transactions. Anonymity will never provide a complete solution to privacy concerns because so many activities are necessarily identifiable, but it may still have some value.

b) *Technical Responses and Consumer Choices*

Some argue that information policy rules can be implemented through the technology itself[28]. A network can be structured so that enforcement of some rules comes at the network level so that individual participants cannot vary or evade the rules. Networks can also be directed to support customization of rules to suit the needs of individual participants. An example in the privacy realm is the Platform for Privacy Preferences, or P3P [29]. P3P enables Web sites to describe their privacy practices in a formal way, and this allows users to exercise their own preferences. With P3P, users learn about a website's privacy practices and make decisions about acceptability in an automated fashion. Acceptable sites can be readily accessed, and sites with divergent practices are flagged for decision. Of course, consumer choices can also be accommodated through non-technical or administrative means. The same computers that collect and maintain reams of personal data can also be used to implement choices on a case-by-case basis. A traditional privacy choice is whether a consumer's information can be disclosed for marketing. Allowing consumers to opt-in or opt-out of secondary uses is only one type of choice that could be offered. Other choices could involve the data retention policies, dispute resolution mechanisms, and even choice of applicable law.

It remains to be seen if schemes like P3P will succeed in the marketplace. They suffer from a level of complexity that may tax those with a casual interest in privacy. Without more objective standards, merchants may easily be able to bribe or wheedle customers in waiving privacy rights in order to obtain discounts or other attractive features. Further, technical solutions embedded in the network also raise the prospect that the network itself will become the embodiment of Big Brother, and that unacceptable actions and thoughts will not be processed[30].

---

27 For a useful discussion of privacy-enhancing technologies, see *Herbert Burkert*, Privacy-Enhancing Technologies: Typology, Critique, Vision. In: Technology and Privacy: The New Landscape (*Philip E. Agre & Marc Rotenberg*, eds., 1997).

28 See *Joel R. Reidenberg*, Lex Informatica: The Formulation of Information Policy Rules Through Technology, 76 *Texas Law Review* 553 (1997).

29 For more specifics on P3P, see the Worldwide Web Consortium website at See <http://www.w3.org/P3P/>.

30 See, e.g., *George Orwell*, The Principles of Newspeak in the appendix to 1984 (1949) ("The

c) *Goals and Process*

One of the most important ideas to emerge from the European data protection movement is the *independent* supervisory authority. The structure and powers of data protection agencies vary enormously in Europe and around the world, but the two most important features are a degree of independence from the governments that created them and a singular focus on privacy[31]. Data protection agencies have frequently proved to have an influence that extends far beyond their formal authority. Professor David Flaherty's pioneering review of the early years of data protection concluded that a law is not enough. An agency charged with its implementation is essential[32].

Even in the absence of a regulatory law, a data protection agency can serve a useful role both for consumers and record keepers. The uncertainties of privacy requirements – whether legal or self-regulatory – will be a feature of any data protection regime. An agency can, merely by exercising its moral authority, persuade record keepers to do the right thing and can persuade consumers to accept reasonable practices. A data protection agency can serve as the oil that makes the creaky mechanism of privacy function better.

What are the policies that a data protection agency should be charged with implementing? The answer here is simple: Fair Information Practices. The world has already come to agreement on the broad policies, and many nations have already enacted fair information practices into law. In the United States, where such a law remains highly unlikely, most players still accept fair information practices as a reasonable set of objectives. Major disagreements emerge as soon as implementation is proposed, but a privacy agency armed with a general set of fair information practice goals can help to minimize those disagreements.

A data protection agency is not a comprehensive solution to ongoing privacy policy problems. No simple, one-dimensional solutions will be found. A data protection agency is another mechanism that offers the hope for a resolution of some of the problems.

---

purpose of Newspeak was not only to provide a medium of expression for the world-view...of [English Socialism], but to make all other modes of thought impossible."]

31 Some data protection authorities also have responsibilities for freedom of information laws.

32 *David Flaherty*, Protecting Privacy in Surveillance Societies 381 (1989).

*Joachim Wieland*

# Freedom of Information*



* I thank my assistant Ms. Petra Helbig for her assistance in preparing this article.

## A. Introduction

Freedom of information is closely related to freedom of expression. Both freedoms together establish a marketplace of ideas, which is fundamental not only for the development of a free personality, but also for a democratic government. Without freedom of information, freedom of expression is useless. Article 19 Universal Declaration of Human Rights (1948) acknowledges this fact by including the freedom to seek, receive and impart information and ideas through any media and regardless of frontiers in the right to freedom of opinion and expression. The same concept is expressed in Article 19 Subsection 2 of the International Covenant on Civil and Political Rights (1966). Freedom of information seems to be a global notion. But, on closer examination, this freedom, like others, is influenced by local values in terms of its legal meaning. I will therefore try to give you an impression of the German and European interpretation of that global concept of freedom of information.

## B. Analysis of German and European Law

To begin with, I would like to present a brief analysis of German and European law relating to the freedom of information.

### I. Article 5 Subsection 1 1st Sentence German Basic Law

The legal basis for freedom of information in Germany is Article 5 Subsection 1 1st Sentence of the German Constitution, the Basic Law (BL). Article 5 Subsections 1 and 2 read as follows:

> „(1) Everyone shall have the right to express and disseminate his opinion freely by speech, writing and pictures and to inform himself freely from generally accessible sources. Freedom of the press and freedom of reporting by means of broadcasts and films are guaranteed. There shall be no censorship.
>
> (2) These rights are limited by the provisions of general laws, the provision of law for the protection of youth and by the right to inviolability of personal honour."

The wording of Article 5 grants the right to obtain information and to use the appropriate means to obtain access to information (like antennae). „Source" stands for any person or thing containing information (e.g. newspapers, files, letters, broadcasts) and therefore also includes papers and files of administrative agencies[1]. Article 5 BL reduces the freedom of information to „generally accessible" sources. „General accessibility" is only understood in a technical sense, while it does not depend and may not be made depending on legality[2]. Hence Article 5 BL grants access to all information

---

1 *Schmidt-Jortzig*, in: *Kirchhof / Isensee* (eds.), Handbuch des Staatsrechts, Vol. VI, § 141 [30]; *Schulze-Fielitz*, in: *Dreier* (ed.), Grundgesetz, Kommentar, Art. 5 I, II [57].

2 BVerfGE 27, 71 (83); 33, 52 (65); Herzog, in: *Maunz / Dürig* (eds.), Grundgesetz, Kommentar, Art. 5 I, II [89]; *Schulze-Fielitz*, in: Dreier (ed.), Grundgesetz, Kommentar, Art. 5 I, II [58]; *Wendt*,

which is technically adapted and intended to inform the public[3]. While this definition includes mass media and the Internet[4], it excludes files and papers of administrative agencies or administrative guidelines, because they are not intended to inform the public[5]. Consequently, freedom of information is not guaranteed for information held by the State. This restrictive access to information held by the State was confirmed by the Federal Constitutional Court, which continually rules that the State is not obliged to render information or make information generally accessible[6].

As far as the remaining sources are concerned that clear the hurdle of general accessibility, Article 5 Subsection 2 BL contains three conditions under which restrictions may be justified. The most important justifications are provisions of general laws that allow restrictions on freedom of expression as well as on freedom of information. But what are „general" laws? The answer of the Federal Constitutional Court is somehow cryptic: „General" is a law, which does not aim at the restriction of freedom of expression or information but which does protect a value more important than freedom of expression or information[7]. The uncertainty about the meaning of „general" goes back to the 1920s and the Constitution of Weimar[8]. If one follows the first - formal - part of the definition, the State has no right to ban Nazi propaganda[9]. The Federal Constitutional Court - putting more emphasis on the second part of the definition - did not declare laws banning Nazi propaganda or penalising the denial of the holocaust unconstitutional[10]. These laws intend to protect values more important than freedom of expression and information. This interpretation of the German constitution has to be seen as a reaction to our history. As a consequence, freedom of expression and information is subject to stronger restrictions by the provisions of general laws in Germany than in the USA.

---

in: *v. Münch / Kunig* (eds.), Grundgesetz, Kommentar, Art. 5 [23].

3 BVerfGE 27, 71 (81); 33, 52 (65); 90, 27 (32); *Herzog*, in: *Maunz / Dürig* (eds.), Grundgesetz, Kommentar, Art. 5 I, II [89]; *Jarass*, in: *Jarass / Pieroth* (eds.), Grundgesetz, Kommentar, Art. 5 [ 13]; *Schulze-Fielitz*, in: *Dreier* (ed.), Grundgesetz, Kommentar, Art. 5 I, II [58].

4 BVerfGE 27, 71 (83); 90, 27 (32); *Herzog*, in: *Maunz / Dürig* (eds.), Grundgesetz, Kommentar, Art. 5 I, II [91]; *Mecklenburg, Zeitschrift für Urheber und Medienrecht* 1997, 525 (536). It also includes new media techniques: *Bethge*, in: *Sachs* (ed.), Grundgesetz, Kommentar, Art. 5 Rn. 54; *Degenhardt*, in: *Dolzer* (ed.), Bonner Kommentar zum Grundgesetz, Art. 5 I, II [228].

5 BVerwGE 47, 247 (252); 61, 15 (22); especially pertaining to secret and confidential information: BVerfGE 57, 250 (270); 66, 116 (137); 71, 206 (220).

6 BVerfGE 28, 175 (188); 57, 250 (270); 66, 116 (137).

7 BVerfGE 7, 198 (209); 50, 234 (240); 59, 231 (263); 62, 230 (243); 71, 162 (175); 71, 206 (214); 95, 220 (235).

8 *Bethge*, in: *Sachs* (ed.), Grundgesetz, Kommentar, Art. 5 [136]; *Herzog*, in: *Maunz / Dürig* (eds.), Grundgesetz, Kommentar, Art. 5 I, II [249]; *Schulze-Fielitz*, in: *Dreier* (ed.), Grundgesetz, Kommentar, Art. 5 I, II [107].

9 *Bethge*, in: Sachs (ed.), Grundgesetz, Kommentar, Art. 5 [142]; *Schulze-Fielitz*, in: *Dreier* (ed.), Grundgesetz, Kommentar, Art. 5 I, II [108].

10 BVerfGE 90, 241 (246); 77, 240 (250).

Furthermore, pornography and violence are banned - rather theoretically than practically – from broadcasts, papers etc. by the provisions of the youth protection law[11]. The right to inviolability of personal honour has been discussed during the last ten years following decisions of the Federal Constitutional Court[12]. One of these decisions dealt with the slogan „Soldiers are murderers“[13]. The Court ruled that this expression is protected by freedom of information and does not violate the honour of German soldiers. This decision was severely criticized[14].

Last, but not least, Article 5 Subsection 1 BL establishes the prohibition of censorship. This prohibition is understood to forbid only formal censorship before publication, and not fines or other punishments for publication[15]. On the whole, Article 5 BL allows the legislators to restrict freedom of information as well as freedom of expression in the interest of other values deemed to be more important than those freedoms. The extent of permissible freedom enjoyed by the general population is very much dependent upon the decisions of the judiciary.

### II. Article 10 European Convention on Human Rights

The European Convention on Human Rights (ECHR) was signed in Rome on November 4, 1950 and entered into force on September 3, 1953. Germany - among many other European States - ratified the Convention in 1954, thereby transforming it into German law. The ECHR is not considered to be part of constitutional law. As a statute, it does not prevail over later statutes according to the rule „lex posterior derogat legi priori„. Still, the Federal Constitutional Court takes its provisions into consideration when interpreting the freedoms guaranteed by the Basic Law[16]. Moreover, Germany is obliged by international law to grant everyone within its jurisdiction the rights and freedoms defined in the Convention. The European Court of Human Rights in Strasbourg may be invoked by every German citizen (or every citizen of another member State of the Convention). It exerts compulsory jurisdiction.

In our context, the provisions of Article 10 ECHR are relevant:

> „(1) Everyone has the right to freedom of expression. This right shall include freedom to hold opinions and to receive and impart information and

---

11 BVerfGE 87, 209 (230); 30, 336 (347); *Schulze-Fielitz*, in: *Dreier* (ed.), Grundgesetz, Kommentar, Art. 5 I, II [116]; *Wendt*, in: v. *Münch / Kunig* (eds.), Grundgesetz, Kommentar, Art. 5 [79].

12 BVerfGE 93, 266 (290); 90, 241 (247); 82, 272 (280); 61, 1 (7); 66, 116 (151); 54, 129 (136); 24, 278 (282); 12, 113 (124).

13 BVerfGE 93, 266.

14 *Zuck, Juristenzeitung* 1996, 364; *Mager, Juristische Ausbildung* 1996, 405 (408); *Otto, Juristische Ausbildung* 1997, 139 (142); *Hufen, Juristische Schulung* 1996, 738 (740).

15 BVerfGE 87, 209 (230); 83, 130 (155); 33, 52 (71); 47, 198 (236); *Bethge*, in: *Sachs* (ed.), Grundgesetz, Kommentar, Art. 5 [131]; *Jarass*, in: *Jarass / Pieroth* (eds.), Grundgesetz, Kommentar, Art. 5 [52]; *Schulze-Fielitz*, in: *Dreier* (ed.), Grundgesetz, Kommentar, Art. 5 I, II [ 139]; dissenting opinion: *Hoffmann-Riem*, in: *Wassermann* (ed.) Alternativkommentar zum Grundgesetz, Art. 5 I, II [78].

16 BVerfGE 74, 358 (370); 35, 311 (320).

ideas without interference by public authority and regardless of frontiers. This Article shall not prevent States from requiring the licensing of broadcasting, television or cinema enterprises.

(2) The exercise of these freedoms, since it carries with it duties and responsibilities, may be subject to such formalities, conditions, restrictions or penalties as are prescribed by law and are necessary in a democratic society, in the interests of national security, territorial integrity or public safety, for the prevention of disorder or crime, for the protection of health or morals, for the protection of the reputation or rights of others, preventing the disclosure of information received in confidence or for maintaining the authority and impartiality of the judiciary."

The text itself suggests that there are far more conditions and restrictions than freedom guaranteed. But, as a basic freedom of communication, Article 10 ECHR protects amongst others information traffic in the new media, especially the exchange of information in the Internet. In one of its leading cases[17] the Court in Strasbourg stressed the importance of freedom of expression. According to the Court, Article 10 ECHR constitutes one of the essential foundations of a democratic society, one of the basic conditions for its progress and for the development of every man and woman. That implies that Article 10 is applicable not only to 'information' or 'ideas' that are favourably received or regarded as inoffensive but also to those that offend, shock or disturb the State or any sector of the population. Such are the demands of that pluralism, tolerance and broad mindedness, without which there is no 'democratic society'. This description resembles the American concept of a free marketplace of ideas[18].

Article 10 ECHR does not protect access to information. This was stressed by the Court in 1987, when it dealt with the case of an applicant who demanded access to confidential information in government files, on the basis of which he believed he had been denied a job[19].

Article 10 ECHR imposes the general duty on member States not to obstruct access to information which is available[20]. The States are only obliged to grant access to information which is already available[21]. Moreover, the Court acknowledges a margin of appreciation to the States whether interference with the freedom of expression is „necessary in a democratic society". It is for the State to show that there is a pressing social need for the interference. In this context, the issue of proportionality of the interference to its objective has come to play a prominent part in freedom of information cases[22].

17 Handyside vs. UK - EGMR, EuGRZ 1977, 38.

18 McIntire vs. Ohio elections comm'n, 514 U.S. 334 (1995); Rosenberger, vs., University of Va, 515 U.S. 819 (1995); Milkovich vs. Lorain Journal Co., 497 U.S. 1 (1990); Denver Area Educational Telecommunications Consortium Inc. at all vs. F.C.C., 518 U.S. 727 (1996).

19 Atkinson vs. U.K., D 133 66/87, *Decisions and Reports* 67, 244, 249.

20 Leander vs. S, GH 116, 29 [74]; Gaskin vs. UK, GH 160, 21, [51].

21 *Frowein*, in: *Frowein / Peukert*, EMRK-Kommentar, 1996, Art. 10 Rn. 13.

22 *Lingens, Europäische Grundrechte-Zeitschrift* 1986, 424 (429, [47]); *Oberschlick, Europäische*

## III. Sections 29, 30 Federal Law on Administrative Procedure

German administrative law is dominated by the principle of secrecy of administrative procedures as opposed to the U.S. tradition[23] that places high regard on freedom of information and that grants free access to information[24]. There is no general right to access to records in German Public Law. But there are several specific provisions regulating access to records[25]. The adoption of Sections 29 and 30 of the Federal Law on Administrative Procedure (FLAP) in 1977 marks a significant step from secrecy to a higher degree of transparency in public administration[26]. They establish the so-called principle of limited publicity of administrative records[27], which is the result of a long and controversial debate[28].

Sections 29 and 30 read as follows:

> Section 29: Access to Records by Participants
>
> „(1) Each agency is to make the records of an administrative procedure available for access to its participants to the extent that knowledge of their contents is necessary for the enforcement or defense of the legal interests of such participants. Sentence 1 is inapplicable until the closing of an administrative procedure in respect of drafts for a decision or preparatory work directly related to such decisions. In case of a representation according to sec. 17 and 18 of this Law, solely the representative is entitled to access to records.
>
> (2) An agency may deny access to records as far as such would either affect the proper fulfilment of its functions, or the disclosure of facts contained therein would endanger the vital interests of the Federal State or of any of the Laender, or because the proceedings are to be kept secret by statutory requirement or by virtue of their character, in particular by reason of the legitimate interests of a participant or those of a third party.
>
> (3) The records are made available at the premises of the agency keeping them.
> In particular cases, the records can be made available at the premises of

---

*Grundrechte-Zeitschrift 1991,* 216 (222, [64]).

23 *Scherer,* Verwaltung und Öffentlichkeit, 1978, p. 13, 17.

24 The Freedom of Information Act, Title 5 USC § 552; *Gurlit,* Akteneinsicht in den vereinigten Staaten, in: *Winter* (ed.), Öffentlichkeit von Umweltinformationen, 1990, p. 511-552.

25 OVG Münster, *Neue Juristische Wochenschrift* 1998, 3659; *Bieber,* Die öffentliche Verwaltung 1991, 857.

26 *Bonk,* in: *Stelkens / Bonk / Sachs* (eds.), Verwaltungsverfahrensgesetz, 1998, § 29 Vor I; *Burmeister / Winter,* Akteneinsicht in der Bundesrepublik, in: *Winter* (ed.), Öffentlichkeit von Umweltinformationen, 1990, p. 88.

27 Amtliche Begründung p. 52; *Clausen,* in: *Knack,* Verwaltungsverfahrensgesetz, 1998, § 29 [2.3]; *Hoffmann,* Neue Justiz 1991, 450.

28 For more details: *Scherer,* Verwaltung und Öffentlichkeit, 1978, p. 17.

another agency or those of a diplomatic or consular representation of the Federal Republic of Germany abroad; further exceptions may be granted by the agency keeping the records."

Section 30: Secrecy

„The agency must not disclose any of the participants' secrets, in particular those secrets concerning their personal affairs or their trade and business secrets, without being authorized by them in advance."

Before I start to explain this regulation in detail, I would like to specify the object of the right to information granted in Section 29 FLAP. „Record„ means every information written on paper in administrative procedures, consequently it does not cover computerized information[29]. Access to computerized personal information is regulated in the Federal Privacy Act and the Privacy Acts of the Laender (federal states).

The right of access to records is restricted in four aspects that are typical of the German approach to access to information held by the State. Firstly, as regards the personal scope of application: Only the participants of specific proceedings are entitled to inspect the records[30]. Secondly, as regards the duration of its availability: Access is solely granted during the course of the proceedings[31]. Thirdly, as regards the extent of access: The right of access only covers those records or parts of them that are kept for the same proceedings[32]. And, fourthly, records are only made available on the condition that the requesting participant will require the information for the enforcement or the defense of a proper legal interest. A merely legitimate interest is not sufficient[33]. If these conditions are fulfilled, the agency concerned must grant access to the records.

However, if one of the exceptions of Section 29 Subsection 2 is applicable, access then becomes a question of the agency's discretion. The exceptions describe reasons to withhold records from the parties, but there is no obligation for the agency to do so. In any case, the agency has to weigh the interests of all participants concerned. There are three groups of exceptions: The first one refers to the agency's interests in respect of the proper fulfilment of its functions, the second one refers to the protection of vital national interests or of the vital interests of the Laender and the third one grants privacy in personal and commercial aspects. This enumeration is conclusive. The application of any of the exceptions is open to judicial review[34].

---

29 *Bonk*, in: *Stelkens / Bonk / Sachs* (eds.), Verwaltungsverfahrensgesetz, 1998, § 29 [9].

30 KG, *Zeitschrift für Wirtschaftsrecht und Insolvenzpraxis* 1986, 1614 (1616).

31 OVG Koblenz, Neue *Zeitschrift für Verwaltungsrecht* 1992, 384; BVerwG, *Deutsches Verwaltungsblatt* 1984, 55.

32 KG, *Zeitschrift für Wirtschaftsrecht und Insolvenzpraxis* 1986, 1614 (1616).

33 VG Gießen, *Neue Zeitschrift für Verwaltungsrecht* 1992, 401; VGH München, *Neue Juristische Wochenschrift* 1989, 2643.

34 *Bonk*, in: *Stelkens / Bonk / Sachs* (eds.), Verwaltungsverfahrensgesetz, 1998, § 29 [51].

The right of access to records is derived from the principles of human dignity and the rule of law. According to precedents of the Federal Constitutional Court[35], the principle of human dignity requires that citizens are not objects, but subjects of administrative proceedings[36]. Thereby the right of access to records is an expression of fair trial and a special feature of the due process of law. Simultaneously, it enhances the transparency of administrative proceedings. The right to access corresponds with an agency's duty to keep records completely and truthfully[37].

Access to records does not include the forwarding of copies, but is limited to the right to read the records and to copy them in writing[38]. Further possibilities - as for example the forwarding of records to an attorney or the provision of copies - are at the discretion of agencies[39]. Only in the case of copies being forwarded do fees become payable.

Section 30 FLAP establishes the participants' right to secrecy. The agency must not disclose participants' secrets, in particular secrets concerning privacy or industrial, business or trade secrets without authorization. The right to privacy, which has a constitutional foundation, is thus set down in Section 30 FLAP. The provision is also meant to establish and improve a so-called „confidential relationship" between citizens and the public administration. Notwithstanding its text, Section 30 not only applies to participants' secrets, but also to the secrets of third persons, knowledge of which has been gained by the agency during proceedings. The provision is also applicable prior to the opening of the proceedings and after their subsequent closure. As an expression of a constitutionally derived principle, Section 30 FLAP is applicable to all agencies' actions[40].

Secrets comprise personal data, as well as medical files or industrial or trade and business secrets[41]. An authorization of disclosure requires either the concerned person's consent, a specific legal provision or an agency's decision after weighing all interests concerned. As a rule, the constitutional foundation of the right to privacy requires a narrow interpretation of authorization reasons[42]. The expediency of administrative co-operation does not justify the disclosure of secrets[43].

---

35 BVerfGE 9, 89 (95); 27, 1 (6); 28, 386 (391); 50, 166 (175); 72, 105 (116); 87, 209 (228).

36 VGH München, *Neue Zeitschrift für Verwaltungsrecht* 1990, 775 (777); VGH München, *Neue Juristische Wochenschrift* 1988, 1615; *Bonk*, in: *Stelkens / Bonk / Sachs* (eds.), Verwaltungsverfahrensgesetz, 1998, § 29 [4].

37 *Bonk*, in: *Stelkens / Bonk / Sachs* (eds.), Verwaltungsverfahrensgesetz, 1998, § 29 [5].

38 *Bonk*, in: *Stelkens / Bonk / Sachs* (eds.), Verwaltungsverfahrensgesetz, 1998, § 29 [73].

39 *Bonk*, in: *Stelkens / Bonk / Sachs* (eds.), Verwaltungsverfahrensgesetz, 1998, § 29 [74, 76].

40 *Bonk*, in: *Stelkens / Bonk / Sachs* (eds.), Verwaltungsverfahrensgesetz, 1998, § 30 [6].

41 KG, *Zeitschrift für Wirtschaftsrecht und Insolvenzpraxis* 1986, 1615 (1616).

42 Papier, NJW 1985, 12; *Bonk*, in: *Stelkens / Bonk / Sachs* (eds.), Verwaltungsverfahrensgesetz, 1998, § 30 [20].

43 *Bonk*, in: *Stelkens / Bonk / Sachs* (eds.), Verwaltungsverfahrensgesetz, 1998, § 30 [23].

Additional rights to access records, that is, access beyond the limits of formal administrative proceedings, are at agency discretion[44]. Section 29 FLAP is not applicable.

## IV. Section 30 Tax Code

Freedom of information is even more restricted in German tax law than in the general law on administrative proceedings. A decision as to whether access to documents in fiscal administrative proceedings is granted to a participant in those proceedings is at the discretion of the fiscal agency. The tax code does not include a right of access to these documents equivalent to Section 29 FLAP[45]. It only stipulates that the interested party is to be heard before a fiscal decision is made. The German Parliament (Bundestag) stated several reasons for this restriction on the freedom of information. Besides protection of the investigation by the fiscal administration, data protection played an important role[46].

This provides us yet another example of the strong position confidentiality enjoys in German law. Especially in the field of taxation, where it is laid down in Section 30 of the German Tax Code, the protection of personal data is seen as an essential guarantee to compensate the taxpayer for his obligation to reveal his financial position[47]. Although the confidentiality of fiscal data is not mentioned in the German constitution, it is thought to be protected by Article 1 Subsection 1 and Article 2 Subsection 1 BL[48]. The Federal Constitutional Court has interpreted these articles as a right to privacy[49]. Thus, personal data is protected against unrestricted collection, storage, use or transmission by public authorities[50].

## V. European Law

Unlike the restrictive German approach to freedom of information, European Union law has strengthened the principle of freedom of information for approximately the last five years, both at European and at national level. This development was stimulated by the fact that several European states had established free access to information. In Sweden, such a right has existed since 1766 and the other Scandinavian countries followed this

---

44 OVG Münster, *Neue Juristische Wochenschrift* 1998, 3659 (3660); OVG Koblenz, *Neue Zeitschrift für Verwaltungsrecht* 1992, 384; OVG Münster, *Neue Juristische Wochenschrift* 1989, 544; BVerwGE 61, 15 (22); *Bonk*, in: *Stelkens / Bonk / Sachs* (eds.), Verwaltungsverfahrensgesetz, 1998, § 19 [18].

45 *Dißars, Neue Zeitschrift für Verwaltungsrecht* 1997, 481 (481).

46 *Bundestags-Drucksache* 7/4292, p. 24.

47 *Tipke*, Die Steuerrechtsordnung, 1993, p. 236.

48 BVerfGE 65, 1 (45); 67, 100 (142).

49 BVerfGE 27, 1.

50 BVerfGE 65, 1 (45).

example after the Second World War[51]. Other European countries started to introduce similar regulations from the end of the seventies[52]. Meanwhile, most European countries guarantee a right of access to information held by the State[53].

The starting point of the discussion on freedom of information in the European Union was the declaration accompanying the European Union Treaty[54]. The heads of state considered transparency of the decision-making process as an essential component to strengthening the democratic nature of European institutions. Therefore, the Commission was asked to develop a program to grant citizens the right of access to internal documents[55].

### 1. Internal Codes

#### *a. Common Code of Conduct*

In December 1993, the Council and the Commission created a public right of access to internal documents in a common Code of Conduct[56]. In addition to the active information policy of the Union (which implied the use of all technical means in all official languages to distribute information about the European Union) this right was meant to improve transparency, to increase people's interest in Community activities and to ensure more openness in political matters. The Code of Conduct was adopted by the Council in December 1993 by Council Decision 93/731/EC and by the Commission in February 1994 [57].

The right to information provided by the Code is not limited to groups with particular interests, but granted to any person or corporation. The term "documents" in the Code refers to all kinds of papers in the possession of the Council or the Commission. In addition, computerized information is considered to be a document to which access should be allowed (Art. 1 Subsection 2 Common Code of Conduct).

There are several exceptions to the general right of access. Reasons for the rejection of the application are the protection of public and private interests, such as business secrets, as well as financial interests of the Community and the confidentiality of internal proceedings of the Council or the Commission (Art. 4 Common Code of Conduct). Access to internal documents initially requires a written application by the citizen specifying the required document. The application is then examined by the institution and is either granted or rejected (Art. 2 Common Code of Conduct). In the

---

51 *Schwan*, Amtsgeheimnis oder Aktenöffentlichkeit?, München 1984, p. 121; *Österdal, European Law Review* 23 (1998), 336; *Petrén, Verwaltungsarchiv* 1958, 323.

52 FIDE (Fédération Internationale de Droit Européen) - XVIII Congrès FIDE-Stockholm 3 - 6 Juin 1998, Vol. III: Le Citoyen, L'Administration et le Droit Européen.

53 See *Nolte*, Die Öffentliche Verwaltung 1999, 363 (364).

54 Bulletin der Bundesregierung, 12. 2.1992, p.180.

55 O.J. C 156/5, 8.6.1993; O.J. C 166/4, 2.6.1993.

56 O.J. L 340/43, 31.12.1993.

57 O.J. L 46/58, 18.2.1994.

case of access being granted, citizens are allowed to inspect the documents at the premises of the Commission or they may ask for a copy of the document, which will be sent to them at their expense (Art. 3 Subsection 1 Common Code of Conduct). In the case of rejection, the citizen is informed and has the right to reapply. If the second application is also rejected, the citizen has the right to either inform the ombudsman (Article 195 EC-Treaty) or to appeal to the European Court of Justice (Article 230 EC-Treaty).(Art. 7 Subsection 3 Common Code of Conduct)

In addition to the common Code of Conduct of 1993, the Council later declared the right of access to its minutes in its Code of Conduct of 1995 [58]. This kind of access was not granted in the Common Code of 1993 due to the confidentiality of the debates[59].

*b. Jurisdiction*

One of the reasons for denying access to internal documents according to Art. 4 Subsection 2 of Council Decision 93/731/EC was given as the confidentiality of the proceedings of the Council[60]. The decision to deny access under Art. 4 Subsection 2 is at the discretion of the Council. This means that the Council, when exercising its discretion, must balance citizens' interests in gaining access to documents genuinely against any interest of the Council itself in maintaining confidentiality concerning its deliberations[61]. In Carvel vs. Council a restrictive practice of the Council was judged as an abuse of said discretion and the refusal to grant access was annulled by the Court of First Instance[62].

2. Primary Law

*a. The Treaty of Amsterdam*

The right to information is now included in primary European law, in the Treaty of Amsterdam (Article 255). According to Article 255 of the Treaty of Amsterdam, every citizen of the European Union has the right of access to internal documents of the European Parliament, the Commission and the Council. As restrictions of this right, the Treaty mentions public and private interests. The principles and rules for the protection of these interests are fixed by the Council in accordance with the procedure laid down in Article 251. Every institution of the Union is obliged to establish special rules in their standing orders.

---

58 Published in *Revue Europe*, Nov. 1995, n° 347.

59 See also: *Dreher, Europäische Zeitschrift für Wirtschaftsrecht* 1996, 487; Lafay, *Revue Trimestrielle du Droit Européen*, 1997, p. 43

60 O. J. L 340/43, 31.12.1993.

61 See also: *Campbell, International and comparative law quarterly,* 1997, 174 - 180.

62 Carvel and Guardian newspapers vs. Council 19.10.1995, case T-194/94, EuGHE 1995, II - 2765.

### *b. Access according to Articles 85, 86 EC Treaty*

A special right of access to information is granted by a Commission Notice of 1997 [63]. In this notice, the Commission established internal procedural rules for the handling of requests for access to files in cases pursuant to Articles 85 and 86 of the EC Treaty, after several decisions of the Court of First Instance had urged the Commission to do so[64]. Access to files is considered to be one of the procedural safeguards designed to ensure effective exercise of the right to be heard. Because of this, the right of access to internal documents is not granted to everyone interested in the matter, but limited to those companies involved in the proceedings of the Commission. Plaintiffs in these proceedings do not have these rights.

The addressees of the notice receive access to all documents making up the „file" of the Commission, apart from the documents concerning business secrets, internal Commission papers and other confidential information, in order to be able to express their views on the conclusions reached by the Commission. The notice distinguishes between non-communicable documents and communicable documents[65]. The companies and the Commission decide which documents they regard as business secrets or confidential files. Confidential - and therefore non-communicable - documents of companies, which serve as a basis for the decision, have to be delivered in a reasonably coherent non-confidential version.

In addition to these rights, it can be considered Union policy to inform its citizens actively by publishing all kinds of documents using every kind of media (including the Internet)[66]. To ensure access to the information published by the Union, several technical norms are to be harmonized and general rules about copyrights and related rights will have to be developed.

### 3. Secondary Law and its impact on national (esp. German) law: The Federal Law on Information about the Environment

The generous information policy of the European Union not only influences primary law and internal codes; it has also had initial effects on secondary European law, as can be seen in Council Directive 313/90/EEC of June 7th, 1990 [67]. The transformation of this directive into national law may lead to a new information policy taking possession of German law, which might have an impact on the restrictive German approach to freedom of information.

---

63 O.J. C 23/3, 23.1.1997.

64 Cases: Solvay vs. Commission, EuGHE 1995, II-1775; 1995, II-1847; 1995, II-1901.

65 O.J. C 23/3, 23.1.1997.

66 *See Preston*, Openness and the European Union Institutions, Conference of Stockholm 27/28.6.1996; notice of the Commission „transparency in the Community„ O.J. C 166/4, 2.6. 1993; decision of the Council to publish statistical material, O.J. L 52/1, 17.2.1997.

67 O.J. L 158/56, 23.06.1990.

In order to implement Council Directive 313/90/EEC of June 7, 1990, on the freedom of access to information on the environment[68] the Federal Law on Information about the Environment (FLIE) came into force on July 16, 1994 [69]. FLIE might be characterized as a sectoral change in the German regulation of access to information, which is completely determined by European law[70]. These regulations replace the principle of official secrecy which, traditionally, is a fundamental principle of German administrative law, by the principle of publicity whenever the European aim of environmental protection is concerned. Publicity is guaranteed by introducing a right of access to information to any person named in Section 4 Subsection 1 FLIE. According to the first sentence of Section 4 Subsection 1 FLIE, public authorities are obliged to make information relating to the environment available to any person or corporation at his or her request without his or her having to prove an interest.

According to Section 1 FLIE, the main object of the law is to ensure freedom of access to and dissemination of information on the environment held by public authorities. It also seeks to set out the basic terms and conditions under which such information should be made available[71]. The background of this aim is the recognition of the necessity to diminish the deficits of execution in environmental law by introducing a concept of expanded publicity[72]. With regard to the deficient instruments of parliamentary and judicial control in questions of environmental law, the right of free access to information on the environment can be considered as an administrative control instrument. The public becomes the guardian of environmental law[73]. The main aim of providing access to information can be characterized as a decentralized and more effective control of administrative duties by means of the general public[74].

Public authorities that are required to make information available all count as administrative agencies[75]. Access must be granted by agencies at national, regional or local[76] level[77] with responsibilities and possessing information relating to the environment[78] with the exception of bodies acting in judicial[79] or legislative[80] capacity and with the exception of the highest agencies of the Federal State and the Laender[81].

---

68 OJ L 158/56, 23.06.1990; *Scherzberg, Deutsches Verwaltungsblatt* 1994, 733 (733).

69 *Meyer-Rutz*, Das neue Umweltinformationsgesetz, 1995.

70 *Hatje*, Europarecht 1998, 734 (736); *Wegener*, in: *Schomerus / Schrader / Wegener* (eds.), UIG, Kommentar, 1995, § 1 [18]; *Theuer, Neue Zeitschrift für Verwaltungsrecht* 1996, 326 (326).

71 *Wegener*, in: *Schomerus / Schrader / Wegener* (eds.), UIG, Kommentar, 1995, § 1 [1].

72 *Wegener*, in: *Schomerus / Schrader / Wegener* (eds.), UIG, Kommentar, 1995, § 1 [16 et].

73 *Scherzberg, Deutsches Verwaltungsblatt* 1994, 733 (734).

74 *Hatje*, Europarecht 1998, 734 (736); *Wegener*, in: *Schomerus / Schrader / Wegener* (eds.), UIG, Kommentar, 1995, § 1 [16,17].

75 *Theuer, Neue Zeitschrift für Verwaltungsrecht* 1996, 326 (327).

76 *Faber, Deutsches Verwaltungsblatt* 1995, 722 (723).

77 *Schomerus*, in: *Schomerus / Schrader / Wegener* (eds.), UIG, Kommentar, 1995, § 2 [3].

78 § 3 Subsection 1 FLIE; see: *Schomerus*, in: *Schomerus / Schrader / Wegener* (eds.), UIG, Kommentar, 1995, § 3 [10].

79 § 3 Subsection 1 No. 3 FLIE; see: *Schomerus*, in: *Schomerus / Schrader / Wegener* (eds.), UIG,

In order to avoid the danger of bypassing the right to free access by delegating public duties to private responsibility[82], FLIE also binds private bodies that take over public responsibilities for the environment and which are under the control of administrative agencies[83].

The right of free access to information about the environment is divided into three categories[84]: Data about the state of environmental sectors[85], data about activities or measures which cause or may cause a deterioration of this state (e.g. emissions) [86], and data about activities or measures, which serve the protection of the environment[87]. The right of free access to information extends only to information which is already in possession of the previously cited public authorities. Agencies are not required to solicit inquiries for further information[88]. The method of granting access remains at the discretion of the agency[89].

The right of free access to information is restricted in many ways[90]. Several restrictions are based on the protection of public interests. A request must be refused where it affects the confidentiality of public authority proceedings, international relations and national defense[91], public security[92], as well as matters which are, or have been, *sub judice*, or under inquiry, or which are the subject of preliminary investigative proceedings[93] or material supplied by a third party without that party being under a legal obligation to do so[94].

---

Kommentar, 1995, § 3 [34].

80 § 3 Subsection 1 No. 1 FLIE; see: *Schomerus*, in: *Schomerus / Schrader / Wegener* (eds.), UIG, Kommentar, 1995, § 3 [19].

81 § 3 Subsection 1 No. 1 FLIE; see: *Schomerus*, in: *Schomerus / Schrader / Wegener* (eds.), UIG, Kommentar, 1995, § 3 [21].

82 *Scherzberg, Deutsches Verwaltungsblatt* 1994, 733 (735); Theuer, *Neue Zeitschrift für Verwaltungsrecht* 1996, 326 (328).

83 *Faber, Deutsches Verwaltungsblatt* 1995, 722 (725).

84 *Theuer, Neue Zeitschrift für Verwaltungsrecht* 1996, 326 (328).

85 § 3 Subsection 2 No. 1 FLIE; see *Theuer, Neue Zeitschrift für Verwaltungsrecht* 1996, 326 (329); *Schomerus*, in: *Schomerus / Schrader / Wegener* (eds.), 1995, § 3 Rd. 70.

86 § 3 Subsection 2 No. 2 FLIE; *Theuer, Neue Zeitschrift für Verwaltungsrecht* 1996, 326 (329); *Schomerus*, in: *Schomerus / Schrader / Wegener* (eds.), UIG, Kommentar, 1995, § 3 [89].

87 § 3 Subsection 2 No. 3 FLIE; *Theuer, Neue Zeitschrift für Verwaltungsrecht* 1996, 326 (330); *Schomerus, in: Schomerus / Schrader / Wegener* (eds.), UIG, Kommentar, 1995, § 3 [98].

88 *Wegener*, in: *Schomerus / Schrader / Wegener* (eds.), UIG, 1995, Kommentar, 1995, § 4 [12].

89 BVerwGE 102, 282; *Röger, Deutsches Verwaltungsblatt* 1997, 885; *Scherzberg, Deutsches Verwaltungsblatt* 1994, 733 (736); *Theuer, Neue Zeitschrift für Verwaltungsrecht* 1996, 326 (332); *Wegener*, in: *Schomerus / Schrader / Wegener* (eds.), UIG, Kommentar, 1995, § 4 [16].

90 *Theuer, Neue Zeitschrift für Verwaltungsrecht* 1996, 326 (330).

91 *Scherzberg, Deutsches Verwaltungsblatt* 1994, 733 (738); *Schrader*, in: *Schomerus / Schrader / Wegener* (eds.), UIG, Kommentar, 1995, § 7 [7-9].

92 § 7 Subsection 1 No. 1 FLIE "a weighty danger for public security": *Scherzberg, Deutsches Verwaltungsblatt* 1994, 733 (738); *Schrader*, in: *Schomerus / Schrader / Wegener* (eds.), UIG, Kommentar, 1995, § 7 [11].

93 § 7 Subseciton 1 No. 2. FLIE, see: EuGH, *Neue Zeitschrift für Verwaltungsrecht* 1998, 945; *Müller / Heuer, Neue Zeitschrift für Verwaltungsrecht* 1997, 330 (332); *Scherzberg, Deutsches Verwaltungsblatt* 1994, 733 (738); *Schrader*, in: *Schomerus / Schrader / Wegener* (eds.), UIG,

A request must also be refused if it involves unfinished documents, data or internal communications,[95] or if the request is improper[96]. In addition, a request must be refused if the access to information is involved with danger for environmental goods or for the fulfilment of the aim of protecting the environment[97]. Other restrictions serve the protection of private interests. A request is to be refused, where it affects the confidentiality of personal data or files[98] or if it violates the right to privacy[99]. A request must also be refused if it violates commercial and industrial confidentiality[100] or intellectual property[101] or if it infringes the confidentiality of fiscal or statistical data.

To obtain the information, interested persons must formulate a precise[102] and reasonable request[103]. The agency is required to make a decision regarding the request within two months[104]. It may charge for supplying the information, but such charges may not be unreasonable[105].

---

Kommentar, 1995, § 7 [12- 18]; *Theuer, Neue Zeitschrift für Verwaltungsrecht* 1996, 326 (330).

94 § 7 Subsection 4 FLIE, comp.: *Fluck, Neue Zeitschrift für Verwaltungsrecht* 1994, 1048 (1049); *Schrader*, in: *Schomerus / Schrader / Wegener* (eds.), UIG, Kommentar, 1995, § 7 [35].

95 § 7 Subsection 2 FLIE; *Schrader*, in: *Schomerus / Schrader / Wegener* (eds.), UIG, Kommentar, 1995, § 7 [25].

96 § 7 Subsection 3 FLIE; *Schrader*, in: *Schomerus / Schrader / Wegener* (eds.), UIG, Kommentar, 1995, § 7 [30].

97 § 7 Subsection 1 No. 3 FLIE; *Schrader*, in: *Schomerus / Schrader / Wegener* (eds.), UIG, Kommentar, 1995, § 7 [19-24]; compare: CD 90/313/ EEC, Art. 3 Subsection 2 7th sec.:" material, the disclosure of which would make it more likely that the environment to which such material related would be damaged."

98 § 8 Subsection 1 No. 1 FLIE. For further information comp.: *Schrader*, in: *Schomerus / Schrader / Wegener* (eds.), UIG, Kommentar, 1995, § 8 [4].

99 *Scherzberg, Deutsches Verwaltungsblatt* 1994, 733 (740); *Schrader*, in: *Schomerus / Schrader / Wegener* (eds.), UIG, Kommentar, 1995, § 8 [7]; *Theuer, Neue Zeitschrift für Verwaltungsrecht* 1996, 326 (331).

100 § 8 Subsection 1 S. 2 FLIE. For details comp.: *Fluck, Neue Zeitschrift für Verwaltungsrecht* 1994, 1048 (1052); *Scherzberg, Deutsches Verwaltungsblatt* 1994, 733 (741); *Schomerus, Zeitschrift für Umweltrecht* 1994, 226 (228); *Schrader*, in: *Schomerus / Schrader / Wegener* (eds.), UIG, Kommentar, 1995, § 8 [19].

101 § 8 Subsection 1 No. 2 FLIE *Fluck, Neue Zeitschrift für Verwaltungsrecht* 1994, 1048 (1050); *Müller / Heuer, Neue Zeitschrift für Verwaltungsrecht* 1997, 330 (333); *Scherzberg, Deutsches Verwaltungsblatt* 1994, 733 (741); *Schrader*, in: *Schomerus / Schrader / Wegener* (eds.), UIG, Kommentar, 1995, § 8 [13].

102 *Schomerus*, in: *Schomerus / Schrader / Wegener* (eds.), UIG, Kommentar, 1995, § 5 [10].

103 § 5 Subsection 1 FLIE *Schomerus, Zeitschrift für Umweltrecht* 1994, 226 (226).

104 § 5 Subsection 2 FLIE.

105 To the question of the conformity of § 10 FLIE with Article 5 CD 90/313/EEC: "Member States may make a charge for supplying the information, but such charge may not exceed a reasonable cost."; compare *Faber, Deutsches Verwaltungsblatt* 1995, 722 (728); *Scherzberg, Deutsches Verwaltungsblatt* 1994, 733 (744); *Schomerus*, in: *Schomerus / Schrader / Wegener* (eds.), UIG, Kommentar, 1995, § 10 [1-32, 55]; *Schrader, Zeitschrift für Umweltrecht* 1994, 221.

## C. Different approaches concerning access to information held by the State

### I. German Tradition: The Denial of Access

Although both, the U.S. and Germany acknowledge the importance of freedom of communication for a democratic system, they have a different approach to freedom of information. As the analysis of the German legal rules has shown, access to administrative records does not aim at democratic control through publicity. German law does not guarantee an unlimited access to agency records; it generally reduces access to agency files by imposing the following conditions: administrative proceedings - participant - qualified interest in the information. Thus, official secrecy is the rule and access to information held by the State becomes the exception[106].

The strictly limited access to files is not only a consequence of the constitutional demands on data protection. It is rather proof of a completely different understanding of administration itself. The dominance of official secrecy has its roots in absolutism and bureaucracy. Absolutism accepts the governor as a father-figure in the role of a guardian[107]. This implies the right to keep information to himself. Official secrecy has also become a fundamental element of bureaucracy. Speaking in the terms of Max Weber, bureaucracy tends to increase its power by excluding the public and by keeping its knowledge secret[108]. Thus, the historical background of the German administrative system explains the continued limited access to agency files.

The law does not accept a general interest in access to documents; it only grants insight into documents if a person can prove a specific interest in the information contained therein. So far, legal interests in particular are held to be such specific interests. The above limitations to the right to information illustrate that the German concept of access to information held by the State is that of enabling a person to defend his or her rights in administrative or legal proceedings[109]. Thus, the interest of an individual to information is reduced to that of legal defense only[110].

In German law, access to information does not serve the purpose of democratic control. The right to information only meets the demands of the constitutional guarantees to be heard in legal proceedings (rechtliches Gehör) and to be treated fairly in administrative proceedings[111]. The democratic aspect, the control of executive, is seen as an exclusive

---

106 *Scherer, Juristenzeitung* 1979, 389 (389); *Bleyl*, Datenschutz und Datensicherung 1998, 32 (32).

107 *Gurlit*, Die Verwaltungsöffentlichkeit im Umweltrecht, 1989, p. 33.

108 *Weber*, Wirtschaft und Gesellschaft, 1990, p. 572.

109 *Gurlit*, Die Verwaltungsöffentlichkeit im Umweltrecht, 1989, p. 214; *Scherer*, Verwaltung und Öffentlichkeit, 1978, p. 20; *Schröder*, *Die Verwaltung* 4 (1971), 301 (316); *Fehling / Schneider*, in: *Bernhardt / Beyerlin* (eds.), Reports on German Public Law, 1990, p. 167 (172); *Kahl*, in: *Haratsch / Kugelmann / Repkewitz* (eds.), Herausforderungen an das Recht der Informationsgesellschaft, 1996, p. 9 (16); *Bieber*, Die Öffentliche Verwaltung 1991, 857 (857, 859); *Bleyl, Datenschutz und Datensicherung* 1998, 32 (32); *Hatje*, Europarecht 1998, 734 (737).

110 *Gurlit*, Die Verwaltungsöffentlichkeit im Umweltrecht, 1989, p. 214.

111 *Reinhardt, Die Verwaltung* 30 (1997), 161 (166).

task of the legislature (general inspections) and the judiciary (investigation into specific cases)[112]. Publicity as a means of democratic control plays an important role in the inspection of the legislature and judiciary, but not of the executive.

The question is, whether the legislature and judiciary can guarantee an effective control of the administrative system on their own. In view of the specialisation and complexity of administrative decisions this seems rather doubtful[113]. Given these doubts there is a strong tendency to establish publicity as a second means of controlling the executive[114]. The understanding of democratic control seems to undergo a fundamental change. This process has already led to a new generation of legal regulations concerning access to information. The constitution of the state of Brandenburg might prepare/pave the way for this new understanding and can be called the trendsetter for this development. Its Article 21 Subsection 4 contains a generally unlimited right to access to information held by the state[115].

## II. The European Approach: Access to Information as an Implementation Tool of the Law

In general, the European Union follows a more generous approach concerning access to information. It presents itself as a transparent institution, open to public inspection. Article 255 EC Treaty gives evidence of this policy. It grants access to documents of the European Parliament, the Council and the Commission.

Besides this general policy, access to information is also used as an instrument to improve the implementation of EC law. The prominent example for this strategy is Council Directive 90/313/EEC of June 1990 on the freedom of information on the environment[116].

This directive attempts to compensate the Commission for its lack of executive competence that results form the fact that the Commission does not have subordinate agencies, which could supervise the implementation of European environmental law. Thus, in the field of environmental law, implementation falls under the responsibility of the member states and their executive. Although member states are obliged to take all necessary precautions to achieve the targets named in the EC Treaty (Article 10 EC-Treaty), European environmental policy is often especially neglected. The EC Treaty does not provide the Commission with efficient instruments to control the implementation of EC environmental law. The Commission is limited to its powers to

---

112 *Erichsen, Neue Zeitschrift für Verwaltungsrecht* 1992, 409 (418).

113 *Erichsen, Neue Zeitschrift für Verwaltungsrecht* 1992, 409 (418).

114 Not one of the authors mentioned above favours the traditional system of official secrecy. Limits to publicity are only demanded on account of the right to privacy.

115 „Anyone has the right to inspect files and other official documents of the authorities and the administration of the State and the communities according to the law, as long as there are no predominant public or private interests.

116 O.J. L 158/56, 23.06.1990.

initiate an action against a member state for failure to fulfil EC obligations before the European Court of Justice (Article 226 EC-Treaty) and to request information (Article 284 EC-Treaty). These instruments are fairly complex and need a lot of time. This leads to a lack of implementation which is meant to be compensated by the installation of an indirect control by EU citizens[117]. By granting them access to information, the directive instrumentalises EU citizens to establish an indirect influence on the implementation of the environmental law[118]. The directive is seen as the key to a more intensive control of the administration by the public. The citizens are supposed to act as „guardians" of the correct implementation of national and European environmental law[119].

So far, EC Directive 90/313/EC on the freedom of information about the environment is the only example of an indirect control of the implementation of EC law in support of the Commission. From my point of view, this strategy resembles two instruments that were created by the European Court of Justice to increase the efficiency of the implementation of EC law: The direct application of EC directives and the right to damages for the failure of member States to implement EC directives properly and in time.

## D. Intellectual Property

To understand the German concept of freedom of information in relation to private persons one also has to take into account intellectual property.

At first sight, the development of German copyright law seems to be contradictory to freedom of information. But, by taking a closer look at the matter, it becomes obvious that the high level of protection afforded to intellectual property and that is to be maintained, is also meant to ensure the development of an information society by creating a legal framework on copyright that increases the legal certainty for authors as well as for consumers[120]. The fact that the right of making intellectual property available to the information society is still and will remain a monopoly of the authors, is due to the origins of copyright law and the concept of intellectual property.

The concept of intellectual property in Germany was influenced by the theories of natural law[121]. The theory of intellectual property gives the author an original and

---

117 In great detail: *Masing*, Die Mobilisierung des Bürgers für die Durchsetzung des Rechts, 1997, p. 21; *Demmke* in: *Hegele / Röger* (eds.), Umweltschutz durch Umweltinformation, 1993, p. 34, 40; *Wegener* in: *Schomerus / Schrader / Wegener* (eds.), UIG, Kommentar, 1995, p. 54.

118 *Reinhardt, Die Verwaltung* 30 (1997), 161 (164).

119 *Hatje*, Europarecht 1998, 734 (735).

120 *Stögmüller*, Gewerblicher Rechtsschutz und Urheberrecht International 1995, S. 855; COM (97), 628 final, O.J. C 108/6, 7.4.1998.

121 *Stögmüller*, Gewerblicher Rechtsschutz und Urheberrecht International 1995, S. 855; COM (97), 628 final, O.J. C 108/6, 7.4.1998.

exclusive right to his work which has been placed under the protection of property right in general[122].

The protection of intellectual property is regulated by the German copyright law (UrhG). German copyright law tries to counterbalance the interests of authors with those of consumers, who are to achieve full access to the authors' works as part of their cultural identity. On the other hand, the interests of the authors lie in determinining who acquires access to their works and - in order to make their livelihood - in receiving an appropriate remuneration for the use of their works. Making authors' works available by state intervention would thus be as inadmissible[123] as forcing them to tolerate the distribution of their works without adequate remuneration[124].

The legislative aims of the copyright law are challenged by the development of the information society with its rapidly evolving information technology. Accordingly, the world today is at the threshold of the era of digital culture that will ultimately replace the culture of printing[125]. As far as copyright law is concerned, some of the innovative aspects of this information technology are the ability to accurately access any part of a work without the need to buy it, to provide interactive communication and to reproduce it without loss of quality.

The capabilities of the information technology correspond to the fundamental needs of the information society which is granted maximum use of the information on offer.

But the innovative aspects of these technologies simultaneously endanger the authors' interests. Intellectual property, as a property right, is obliged to consider social welfare aspects. To a certain extent, authors who deal with their intellectual property, must take the interests of the community into their considerations. Since protection is crucial to intellectual creation[126], one notices on the one hand a contradiction between granting a high level of protection to the intellectual property on the one hand, and the negative affects such protection will have on access to the information as a common good on the other hand.

As the territorial principle is prevalent in international copyright law[127], the German government is aware of the danger of overregulation possibly leading to an exit of providers and global competitive disadvantages[128]. Nevertheless, German law does not decrease the protection of the intellectual property achieved, but maintains the status quo[129]. It finds a social welfare loss due to underutilization of information more

---

122 *Fechner*, Geistiges Eigentum und Verfassung, 1999, S. 71.

123 *Rehbinder*, Urheberrecht, 1998, p. 80.

124 *Rehbinder*, Urheberrecht, 1998, p. 83.

125 *Bundestags-Drucksache* 13/8110, p. 10.

126 COM (97) 628 final; O.J. C 108/7, 7.4.1998.

127 *Rehbinder*, Urheberrecht, 1998, p. 355.

128 *Bundestags-Drucksache* 13/8110, p. 11.

129 *Bundestags-Drucksache* 13/8110, p. 10.

acceptable than to accede to a social welfare loss due to underproduction [130]. In order to transfer this high level of protection to digital innovations, the discussion in Germany circles around leaving the process of discovering and solving conflicts that may arise from the digital revolution either to the courts or to the legislator[131]. Furthermore, important voices in politics and literature have come to the conclusion that the existing copyright legislation will be able to adapt to the new challenges. To some extent, the German discussion is influenced by EC initiatives concerning copyright law and intellectual property.

On the whole, the EC's ideas concerning intellectual property coincide with the German concept. The EC has adopted several directives in order to harmonize certain aspects of copyright and related rights, e.g. Council Directive 91/250/EEC of May 14, 1991 [132] on the legal protection of computer programs, Council Directive 93/98/EEC of October 29, 1993 [133] on harmonizing the terms of protection of copyright and related rights and Council Directive 96/9/EC of March 11, 1996 [134] on the legal protection of databases. But these directives only apply to particular aspects of the intellectual property and copyright. After having published two greenbooks in 1995 [135] and in 1996 [136], embracing the information society and its impact on copyright and related rights as a whole, the Commission has finally made a proposal for a European Parliament and Council Directive on the harmonization of certain aspects of copyright and related rights in the Information Society[137] in 1998, which includes - in opposition to its title - a comprising concept of copyright[138]. The Commission emphasizes the defense of the authors' rights against abusive on-line use of their works. It proposes harmonization in the following fields[139].

First it deals with the right of reproduction (Article 2). The exclusive right to authorize or prohibit direct or indirect, temporary or permanent reproduction by any means and in any form, in whole or in part shall be granted to the authors. It also refers to the right of communication to the public, including the right of making works or other subject matters available (Article 3). These rights shall also be granted exclusively to the authors. The right of distributing the work (Article 4) in any form is also granted to the authors. This right will only be exhausted with the first transfer of ownership of the

---

130 *Bundestags-Drucksache* 13/8110, p. 10.

131 *Bundestags-Drucksache* 13/8110, p. 10.

132 O.J. L 122/42, 14.5.1991.

133 O.J. L 290/9, 29.10.1993.

134 O.J. L 77/20, 11.3.1996.

135 COM (95) 382 final.

136 COM (96) 568 final.

137 COM (97) 628 final; O.J. C 108/6, 7.4.1998.

138 *Dietz, Zeitschrift für Urheber- und Medienrecht* 1998, 438.

139 See hereto *Reinbothe, Zeitschrift für Urheber- und Medienrecht* 1998, 429; *Flechsig, Zeitschrift für Urheber- und Medienrecht* 1998, 139.

object that is made by the rightholder or with his consent and takes place within the Member States of the EC.

The main exceptions to the restricted acts set out in these articles are mentioned in Article 5. Limitations to the exclusive rights of the authors in the fields of reproduction and of making their works available to the public are provided for the sole purpose of illustration for teaching and scientific research, for the benefit of visually or hearing-impaired persons, for the use of excerpts in connection with the reporting of current events and for the purposes of public security and a proper performance of an administrative or judicial proceeding. The prevailing part of these exceptions only requires the indication of the source the information is taken from and the absence of commercial purposes[140].

The harmonization does not include the reproduction for private use and for non-commercial ends (Art. 5 Subsection 2 b). The delay in harmonizing this field is due to the different legal traditions in the Member States, especially the different remuneration schemes[141]. To the Commission, a harmonization of this field was not urgent as the differences mentioned with respect to analogous private reproduction, do not have a significant impact on the development of the information society, as they soon will be replaced by digital private reproduction. The advantage of the digitalization will then probably be the possibility of controlling the private use of information with the help of digital footprints. Digital footprints will prove the use made of the works, with the effect that private reproduction can become part of the exclusive right of the authors. Therefore, the development of digital reproduction must first be closely observed.

## E. Conclusions

While most European countries and the European Union itself have recognized that the existence of informed public opinion constitutes an essential part of any democratic system and have therefore established the right of access to information held by the state following the U.S. model, Germany has not (yet) joined this general democracy-strengthening development. The fact that Germany remains one of the few European countries that still follows a restrictive information policy, brings up the question as to whether this tradition is suitable in a modern society or whether we should rid ourselves of a policy that some criticize as a „relict of an authoritarian state,,[142]. The time has come to reconsider our tradition that official secrecy should be the general rule, that access to information held by the state should be the rare exception, and that such access should only granted if it is necessary to defend one's rights in legal or administrative proceedings. Although I must admit that important values such as the interests of the

140 Most of these exceptions are also laid down in the copyright law (UrhG); e.g. § 45 UrhG (public security and administrative or judicial proceedings), § 46 UrhG (illustration for teaching and scientific research), §§ 48-50 UrhG (report of current events).

141 COM (97), 628 final, O.J. C 108/8 Art. 1 Nr. 26, 21.1.1998.

142 *Schwan*, Amtsgeheimnis oder Aktenöffentlichkeit?, 1984, p. 95.

government and administrative agencies in keeping their proceedings secret, intellectual property or the protection of personal data may justify a restriction on access to information, I am deeply convinced that a more liberal information policy will lead to more transparency and a more effective supervision of the operations of public authorities by the public. A right of access to information held by the state is not expressly written down in our constitution. It is only restrictively granted by simple law. But the basis for such a right may be seen in the democratic principle. It may not be a requirement of the democratic principle, but it surely strengthens and enhances the status of democracy.

Recent developments show that Germany is on its way to catching up with the current status of European information policy. We can notice the increasing importance of informal cooperation between agencies and citizens. All in all, we are witnessing a fundamental change in how relations between the administration and the citizen are viewed. The relationship is shifting from one of subordination to one of increased populism[143]. These subtle developments show that we might be standing at the dawn of a new information policy. First indications of this daring thesis are several initiatives at 'Bund' and 'Laender' level to establish a right of access to information[144]. While most of these initiatives still lack sufficient political support, Brandenburg has managed to achieve a breakthrough. It has created a general right of access to information in its constitution[145] and has passed a corresponding law fulfilling this obligation[146].

Though it will be a long way before freedom of information will become a local value in Germany that is fundamental not only in theory but also in practice, these examples may be seen as the heralds of a new era of information policy. Global networks have initiated this new trend and will probably accelerate its development.

143 *Nolte*, Die Öffentliche Verwaltung 1999, 363 (364).

144 *Bundestags-Drucksache* 13/8432; 12/7568, 12/6323, 12/5694, Schlußbericht der Gemeinsamen Verfassungskommission, 05.11.1993, *Bundestags-Drucksache* 12/6000, p.60; *Hamburger Bürgschaft-Drucksache* 15/1355, *Berliner Abgeordnetenhaus-Drucksache* 13/1623; *Berliner Abgeordnetenhaus-Drucksache* 11/958.

145 Art. 21 Subsection 4 BbgLVerf, see above.

146 *Gesetz- und Verordnungsblatt* I, p. 46; see *Partsch, Neue Juristische Wochenschrift* 1998, 2559.

*Jacques Arlandis*

# The Clerk, the Merchant and the Politician

## Introduction

This briefing paper addresses an infrequently dealt with subject, one that may be called the "new elite in the Cyberworld". As at the time of the Renaissance, physical movement and virtual movement are now facilitated by new economic infrastructures. This enhances the possibility of creating a "new community" or new communities for a more or less extensive group of decision makers, politicians and experts. The idea of forming one or more communities is admittedly conceivable but for what purpose? by which methods? and with what results?

The problem concerned by the present paper, however, is more limited: it is a question of linking the question of the role of the elites to that of the governance of a socio-economic and social-technical system which, out of laziness or ease, is called the "Information Society". Within this already wide-ranging question, we shall single out a still more limited problematic issue, that of the efficacy of a dialogue between the industrial, the political and the academic elites, each of them identified as the Merchant, the Politician and the Clerk.

### *Is this issue relevant?*

Some time ago, the question of power games could have been based on an examination of interaction among three communities made of up industry leaders, politicians and journalists. In this triangle, it seems that the journalist has gradually been replaced by the expert or the intellectual. For about a decade, the media as the "fourth power" have been losing their legitimacy. The intellectual (today an academic, tomorrow perhaps an artist), in turn, is recovering ground lost since the collapse of ideologies by rebuilding his social capability on that of "imparting form", in the strongest sense of the term, to the decision process. If, moreover, one accepts the common thesis of an ongoing industrial revolution (of digital technologies) and a major impact on the social order, the question concerning the steering of a change of this nature then assumes full legitimacy. Neither the least technological determinism, nor the least economic determinism - that of the market - cannot in itself justify the idea of a social Darwinism. The players have something to say. The elites would like to have their say. But not at any price. The information revolution, advocated in their respective rhetorics by the clerks, the merchants and the politicians, is running the risk of being called into question. This is exacerbated by the inequality in access to information, the frustration of reinforced solitude or even the removal of the right to produce one's own information and communication, at the very moment when technology should make the democratisation of access or production possible. The information revolution would hardly have had its first effects when it would find itself in the thrall of a counter-revolution. Our problem matter is thus justified.

*Do we have any legitimacy whatsoever for dealing with it?*

The expert is asked to "tell us what is important". Insofar as a question of this nature is concerned, his ex-ante legitimacy is established, but only in the way a contact is established. Unless referenced, it remains rather tenuous. As the problem put forward is a relatively new one, the reference cannot be exclusively academic; it must be based on a practice and observation of this practice. These could derive inspiration from numerous case studies, one of which - a major one - is governance of the Internet; by virtue of the fact that the academic community is obliged to share the power (the "joystick", if one wished to continue in this sense of "governance = steering" with the merchants (electronic) and the politicians (more or less visionary) one has a view from the interior of the process, should one happen to be a player involved in the change. Ex-ante legitimacy is not enough, however. As in the best cybernetic systems, there must be a feedback loop; we shall revert to this at the conclusion of our analysis when we draw up a number of recommendations.

*What plan shall we pursue for dealing with this kind of question?*

What we will call « the Triad » along these lines, i.e. the community of merchants, clerks and politicians, will prove to be a workable community if we can assess its potential usefulness. In other words, we will assume that it could be a useful « rouage » of the Information Society every time we can assess a kind of « value added » to solve social and economic problems.

Such an approach requires :

- To identify the stakes, both economic and social, related to the deployment of the Internet
- To justify arrengements where the triad can proved to be a useful mechanism. for governance

To identify the stakes itself requires :

1.1 to understand the paradigme on which the governance of the Internet will have to operate

1.2 to assess the very schemes for such governance

To justify the triad as a useful arrengement we will need :

2.1 to identify specific tasks to be usefully performed by the triad

2.2 to describe the value of bridging three diffferent cognitive models and behaviours

The conclusion will finally draw attention on the key issues for making such an arrangement workable.

## 1 Some key elements of the Internet paradigme

It is not our purpose to discuss all socio-econonomic issues related to the Internet development. We would just like to enlight problematic points which are relevant to tackle governance as an issue.

### 1.1 Paradigme on which the Internet governance will have to operate

Internet modifies basically three interlinked orders :

- The technical order
- The economic order
- The social order

Although this paper in not focused on technical issues, it is worth to recall major technical challenges Internet is now facing.

To break with an economy in which only mediocre products are in abundance and to succeed in switching to an only nascent market economy, the Internet system must cope with three major technological changes. The first is to define priority categories and guarantee end-to-end quality. The second is to enhance the service through a massive image irruption. This changeover to high rates, in conjunction with a demand context that points in favour of focusing content on existing linguistic and socio-cultural areas, will thus lead to polycentric development of the Internet, which constitutes the third major technical change. The speed and the spread of these technical changes are depending on the requirements the economic sphere would address to the Internet.

*Economic tensions*

In appearance, the Internet represents the triumph of the Schumpeter vision: a huge wave of innovation carries start-ups to the peaks, and veritable empires are built up in important segments of the market. This is the triumph of property rights (real or virtual). At the same time, however, the Internet calls intellectual property rights into question; contents are recopied or pirated; software offered in the form of freeware or shareware; an economy featuring free or shared goods and services is being established that is poles apart from the Schumpeter model, based on the prospect of exclusive use and of which the best illustration is the patents system. From the very start, the Internet undertakes the dismantling of the intellectual property system and offers unrestricted dissemination of information and a sharing of cultural capital. It thus contributes to calling into question established positions and to ensuring improved social fluidity. It also implements social co-operative mechanisms, accelerating the creation and dissemination of innovation beyond the screens that business firms are naturally seeking to install.

Even though it seems to be dominated by Schumpeterian monopolies, the Internet could serve as a fantastic accelerator of social fluidity and as a catalyst for the dissolution of established positions, especially with the backing of a political desire to use it as a means of reducing inequality and of bringing about a permanent redistribution of knowledge and skills.

The new activities and productivity increases that the Internet could generate will thus comprise a local or regional (in the sense of world regions) component and will constitute an essential growth factor. As demonstrated by endogenous growth theories, certain investments may enable a country to widen the gap. Public powers have a part to play in promoting these infrastructures, since private incentives at both R&D and deployment level are inadequate. This has been well understood by the USA, which provides active support for the emergence of tomorrow's infrastructures around the "information highways" theme. To be found in Europe is a seemingly wider view that accentuates technical and social experimentation aimed at bringing about consensus on new technologies.

In the clash between Europeans and Americans, the United States appears to be in a position of force. The fine balance between macro-economic policy and micro-economic incentives, between market initiative and the moderate but skilful use of public financing and policies, have made for the emergence of a race of innovative players who now occupy an upstage position.

*Social implications*

The main question is knowing whether the economic sphere will impose its undivided domination on the social and political spheres.

Will the arrival of merchants completely dash the hopes of men of knowledge of seizing power, transferring the reins to the owners of proprietary rights exploiting traditional capital or informational property?

Even though it seems to be dominated by Schumpeterian monopolies, the Internet could serve as a fantastic accelerator of social fluidity and as a catalyst for the dissolution of established positions, especially with the backing of a political desire to use it as a means of reducing inequality and of bringing about a permanent redistribution of knowledge and skills.

Unlike the hierarchical model of dissemination through traditional media, a model that has always agreed to outside or self-censorship, the refusal of any form of social control over the exchange of information throws doubt over unanimously accepted norms and opens Pandora's box. If it had to be total, transparency would make the individual subject to domination and, with the help of third-party knowledge of individual habits (cookies) would destroy the balance between the private sphere and the public sphere.

Will the global community instituted by the Internet not limit itself to a stratum of intellectuals (in the broadest sense of the term) over which it would establish or strengthen domination? The egalitarianism displayed would then be confined to an aristocracy such as dreamed of by Plato in his Republic. It would in that case in fact amount to an attempt to seize power by a new social stratum, administrators of informational property, possessors of know-how and benevolent organisers ensuring its circulation and dissemination.

## 1.2 Schemes of the Internet governance

The Internet universe is subjected to contradictory forces between anarchistic Utopia and excessive commercialisation. This conflict is, in fact, one of the growth drivers.

Current exchanges take place in highly turbulent environments and will do so in the future. The endless stream of innovations, the dynamism of financial capital and network economy, the "globalisation" of the interdependence of a variety of players with multiple, and often conflicting, interests work in favour of heterogeneous representation venues for electronic exchanges.

Theses exchanges intermingle the problems of container and content; rich in ideology, projects for social or political change interfere with far more prosaic sectoral arrangements such as those called for by the practical and technical demands of co-ordination.

In such a context Internet governance raise, according to us, three specific questions.

*What will be the significant institutional mechanisms of the near future?*

It is clear that any response to the above depends on the identification of the issues. Today, the Information Society in Europe is facing the opening up of telecommunications markets, competition, expansion of the Internet, emergence of electronic commerce, defence of it's own cultural products, problems related to the competitive practice of industry (products and services), and the question of social appropriation of information and communication technology . Today, these challenges are linked to a form of 'governing' characterised by the inclusion of at least three levels of political decision-making (national, regional and global); by the hesitant practice of subsidiarity (Union vs member states); and the practice of representativeness (Union vs international authorities - WTO, ITU, forums such as Global Business Dialogue…).

In the near future, competition will be in place and from this point of view at least, the sector will be calmer; the Internet will have contributed more locally in terms of community links whilst also having accentuated certain social stratifications (not only in access to information but also in the production of information); electronic commerce will have benefited from the Euro zone, but will also have suffered due to the slowness of political harmonisation; the capacity of Europeans for techno-economic and social innovations will have been put to the test… All this will require reorientation and even delays due to an institutional mechanism, which, as yet, is hardly emerging.

*What forms of regulation should we expect ?*

The ICT sector, which, from an orthodox economic point of view, is not a homogeneous one, will certainly require specific regulations in its interpretation of the varied economic issues (via frictions, the balance of power, business culture and work organisation). 'Regulation' refers to the definition of rules which will enable supply and demand to 'keep their place'. This definition may be presented in three generic forms : the market, the law, the standard; in other words, an economic regulation, a legal regulation and an industrial regulation; each of these forms could be related to a doctrine, itself a result of the balance of power, compromise and even the effects of exceptional leadership.

The balance between these three modes is not fixed, its details have not been defined once and for all. This is another dimension of 'governing', that it can characterise the form and equilibrium of the socio-economic challenges linked to the growth of the Information Society.

*What will be the best allocation of resources and the right mechanisms for redistribution?*

The final point which may inform the question of 'governing' is more in relation to the effects of public policy. We know that previously, some people have expected the ICT to contribute significantly in meeting the challenges of growth, employment, innovation and social well-being (and this in varying degrees, owing to the nature of the social groups who hold such expectations). We know that the analysis of such effects is currently varied. In the future, it is possible that these expectations will become demands and that tangible results will be requested; it is equally possible that there will be pressure from the Information Society to fight all forms of economic and social counter-productivity. An even more radical hypothesis is that it could also be that a social demand 'emerges' for the abandonment, albeit partial, of productivist dogma. The question of resource allocation (in particular public resources dedicated to research, human resources, and investment) and of redistribution (access to public services, information and training) will continue to be asked, even from within the framework of the Information Society.

## 2 The « Triad », a useful mechanism for governing the Information Society

*Institutional mechanisms, forms of regulation, allocation and destribution of resources* are at the same time technical and political issues for the governance of the Information Society. And they should be addressed simultanously on these two dimensions.

We are calling here to think in term of a new (or renewed) coalition to address them properly.

What we call « the Triad » along these lines, i.e. the community of merchants, clerks and politicians, will prove to be a workable community if we can assess its potential usefulness. In other words, we will assume that it could be a useful « rouage » of the Information Society governance every time we can assess a kind of « value added » to solve social and economic problems.

We have a very instrumental vision of the case. Therefore we will first try to identify « governance tasks » for which we a priori assume the usefullness of such an arrengement. Then, we will justify it by discussing te kind of value that one may expect from it.

## 2.1 Tasks that could be usefully performed by the « Triad »

The essence of global governance is cooperation, comprising governments, economic actors and civil society entities.

Collective action is all the more important in that it masters three fundamental problems: the ambiguity, efficacy and strategic uncertainty of regulation phenomena. To reduce and maintain control over ambiguity constitutes the quest of common representations, considered correct, of the principles and methods of regulation. The problem of efficacy is an instrumental problem: do the resources and means of regulation enable the desired objectives to be attained?

Hence, the identification of two major processes : representation and deliberation.

*Representation, a first collective problem to be solved*

Today, representations of the phenomena of regulation appear to be complex, problematic (projects seemingly doubtful of their own success), precarious and highly debatable.

In a context of intense ambiguity, an initial option is to allow the production and dissemination of representations to go their own way, for example, in the field of protection of private life. In the absence of an effective framework for debating problems, goals and means, representations are proliferating.

There are those who hope that the "effective work of time" will select the most robust of the representations. Such libertarian measures have their attraction: their ambivalence (non decision/decision) may allow certain categories to put up with the uncertainty surrounding them and others to put the locks on markets and networks.

The second option consists of rapid interventionism ensured by unilateral decisions by the representations, such as universal free trade (this will bring to mind, for example, the attempt to impose the MIA, multilateral investment agreement). Hegemonic decision attracts powerful players or those planning to become so.

*Deliberation, the second key issue*

Obviously, Internet governance will require to enhance the deliberation process.

An argument then becomes a communication process aimed at ensuring the switch from something that is collectively problematic to something that is collectively valid, it being understood that it may very well not be demonstrated that collective validity may comprise contradictions and that it is independent of the truth.

Two models clash: in the dissociation model (transmission and exchange), the private character is the personalisation of the receiver, the public character of the communication to which everyone has access; the consubstantiality model (as early as Aristotle) where deliberation is the expression of public activity, whereas the private aspect lies in domestic activity

What is essential for the rhetoric, be it new or old, is the function of deliberation within uncertain situation ; to acertain extent, rhetoric could provide a theory for decision process.

On which domain, these two processes should be focused ?

According to our observations, three domains should be primarily addressed through the representation and the deliberation processes :

- The relationship between public and private spheres
- The dialogue between decision makers and the public opinion
- The use of cultural diversity

*Governing the frontier between Public and private sphere*

In the information age, it is the link between private and public that deserves attention.

The public area is tending to become increasingly complex and to engage in functions lying outside the public domain. It is also tending to extend to the business sector in a dual direction: from inside to outside (intervention in the social and cultural environment) and from outside to inside (management sharing)

There is a new public area, far more heterogeneous than the earlier one, both from the point of view of the players and the activities that make it up (not a mere enlargement of the bourgeois public area).

When all is said and done, the public area seems to survive by fragmenting into partial areas, but as this change is based on improved exercising of domination and a greater degree of inequality of participation, it may seem to hide profound unity behind this fragmentation.

*Informing the public opinion*

Information management is not merely an incidental aspect of democracy but a constituent component. In the previous order (pre-Internet), the three types of discourse (politicians, journalists, public opinion) constitute a system linking the three elements of democratic legitimacy: politics, information and communication

Accelerating complexity obliges Society to abandon the differentiation between power and truth (Luhman)

Lumières' ideal translates into technocratic regulation of society: the citizen is not omni-skilled and the complexity of the social organisation is increasing; control of information is thus necessary

The concept of public opinion will have taken on another sense: no longer a question of opinion formed (ideally) on the basis of reason but of a segmented mass of private ideas which express divided (possibly conflicting) interests. According to Luc Ferry, current public policy excludes on the one hand, mass political communication in the form of barroom talk and, on the other, political communication by the elites in the form of an exchange of confidential information.

The idea of separation between the irrationality of beliefs and the rationality of knowledge should be replaced by the idea of opposition between the long paths pursued by some and the short paths pursued by others, the latter seemingly irrational in the eyes of the former. The triad could usefully match these two orders, without presuppositions, in order to be used within representaion and deliberation processes.

*Making value out the cultural diversity*

Cultural diversity has often be presented as an asset for Europe. We will assume that, in the information age, cultural diversity is more than the confrontation of national identities and cultures. It is also a question of cross-fertilization between professional cultures. Europe as a unique experience in multi-actor, multi-level and multi-jurisdictional governance. How far this experience can be transformed into an asset is a question that deserves scrutiny.

In such a context, the game of this triad may appear in itself complex as the groups of players are not necessarily homogenous (the question of correct typology remains pertinent), in as much as new mediating players are appearing or could quickly appear. However the plateform here should in itself sufficiently robust so as to support the valuation process we are pledging for.

## 2.2 Bridging different cognitions and behaviours

Once identified the processes and the domain which could beneficiate from the use of the « triad » as a plateform for collective action, in the Internet governance context, we need now to suggest why and how the players should collaborate, mixing related interests and cognition and behavioural models.

*Merchants, Politicians and Clerks: related interests*

Today, merchants often give the impression that it is they who hold the cards and run the game. However, they are aware that they are at once powerful and vulnerable (Microsoft) and naturally look to influence political compromises.

An initial alliance is happening between the Merchants and the Politicians. For example, the Global Business Dialogue has been set up on the initiative of the European Commission although I doubt that this type of alliance can respond fully to the challenges posed by the emergence of the Cyberworld.

Furthermore, the politician has taken care to create a parallel structure, the Global Social Dialogue (which does not yet have a web site) and which causes us to wonder whether it is merely a concession to civil society from which we should not expect any real counter power.

For their part, the clerks can neither remain isolated nor accept the assertive role sometimes offered to them by the Politician.

'The entry of technology into the binary order marks the exit of thought from the same binary order'. This calls to mind the Clerks expression of complexity whereby 'and' replaces 'or', where one thing and its opposite become equally possible or the logical conclusion and topological fractal replace exclusion and hierarchy in an intellectual movement which seems to be the opposite of the social one. In order to resolve this contradiction, the clerk must choose (although this is not exclusive) whether to enter the social arena or to modulate and reformulate his thoughts on direct contact with the Merchant and the Politician. He certainly risks losing his independence but, having taken such a risk, he could gain in social efficiency without resorting to being shut up once again in his ivory cybertower.

The thesis here defended is that these alliances in twos do not correspond to current necessities, that they cause inefficiency and are even dangerous. If they were to be joined in a 'Triad', they would produce more effective rhetoric and action whilst avoiding the ill-suited promethean myth and social rejection and furthermore, taking on daily difficulties subject to a rhythm largely unknown to the virtual criteria of the Cyberworld

*From cognitions to rhetoric, from rhetoric to action*

The credo of the clerks is 'complexity', whereas that of the merchants is 'simplicity'. The politicians don't have a credo, other than possibly 'compromise'. But no single credo can claim to 'govern' the Cyberworld alone. Such claims are an illusion which do not stand up to social reality. It will therefore be necessary to create a composite form of governance: amongst themselves and with society.

Furthermore, no machine which the New Man can produce, perfected seperately one from another, will triumph. Irony, chance and necessity will serve, among other things, to curb the best mechanics (markets run by powerful Merchants, regulation run by powerful Politicians, culture defined by powerful Nobel prizes winner).

And still, the question of social control by the elites remains. Today, this issue is revisited under the auspices of capacities supplied by information technology and communications networks. What is new is that this control is first made possible through a long process of development of new powers and actions.

## Conclusion

With regard to the millenium agenda, there is a question which is often raised pertaining to 'the New Man' or even 'the New Civilisation'. However, the man who will make this civilisation will not be 'naturally' cyberdocile (the dream of the merchants), nor a cybercitizen (the desire of some politicians), nor cybercultivated (the humanist ideal of the clerks).

The elites are therefore faced with a double necessity : to explain and to submit themselves to a minimum standard of social control. This double objective encompasses both a moral duty and economic interests. The 'Triad', that is to say a political platform which would associate and confront the Clerk, the Merchant and the Politician, could prove to be an important factor in forming a new governance adapted to the demands of the Information Society and the Cyberworld.

The plateform we have advocated for, should combine major processess (representation and deliberation), first rank concerns (public/private spheres, public opinion, cultural diversity).

Now that the Cyberworld has arrived and the neccessity for a global order for the Information Society, 'thought in action' may be the justification for a « triad » which combines the three preceeding credos (complexity, simplicity and compromise) on an equal basis and without naiveity, giving them a 'just' social dimension in respect of shared values perhaps based on a revisited 'universalism'.

**Bibliography**

*Attali, J.*, Dictionnaire du XXI siècle, Fayard, 1998

*Bautier , R.,* De la rhétorique à la communication, PUG, 1994

*Gerstlé, J .*, La communication et la dualité public/privé, *Revue Française de Sciences politiques*, vol 27, 1987

*Grewlich, K.W.*, Governance in the Global Information Society, Forthcoming, 1999

*Izraelewicz, E.*, Un « autre Davos » à Davos, *Option finance*, n°533, 1999

*Laswell H.D.*, Democracy through public opinion, Banta , 1941

*Moeglin, P.*, Histoire d'une fiction, le satellite éducatif, *Culture tehnique*, n°24, 1992

*Padioleau, J.*, Les régulations flexibles des échanges électroniques: une pragmatique prospective, Rapport de la Fondation IDATE, 1999

*Trow, G.W.*, Within the context of no context, *Atlantic Monthly Press*, 1997

*Turpin, E.,* La firme et le net, Hermes, 1999

*Vittet-Philippe, P.,* The Governace of the Global Digital Economy, CSIS, 1998

*Jeffrey Abramson*

# Democracy and Global Communications



Let me begin by summarizing a familiar teaching about size and democracy in Western political philosophy from Aristotle to Rousseau. Starting from a definition of democracy as a regime in which citizens "rule and are ruled in turn," Aristotle argued that self-government is possible only when citizens feel a sense of involvement in, and responsibility for, the common good. The common good, Aristotle continued, is more than the sum of individual self-interests. It is the good that people distinctively experience when they view living in a particular place as indispensable to the persons they are or wish to become. Aristotle thought these intense, identity-creating ties were possible only in small-scale political units that fostered shared values and experiences. By contrast, when great numbers of persons conduct politics across large distances, they typically take away only a weak and watery sense of engagement with others in a common way of life[1].

Emphasizing the way political participation transforms and elevates individual interests, Rousseau criticized representative institutions as a weak, fall-back version of democracy necessitated only by the large size of modern nation-states. Even in well-functioning representative governments, the average person never becomes a citizen for Rousseau, never undergoes the transformative moral growth that comes from participating directly in the meetings and debates, the dialogues and deliberations that educate each about the views, interests and needs of others[2].

---

1 *Aristotle*, The Politics (Oxford: *Oxford University Press.* 1995), Books I and III generally.

2 *Jean-Jacques Rousseau*, The Social Contract, Book III, ch. 15.

Not all classical philosophers shared this indictment of large size as the enemy of democratic ideals. Making a virtue of the reach of Rome, stoics reasoned that the sheer expanse of the republic allowed for the discovery of universal values and the transcendental principles of natural law. More recently, the American founders theorized that large republics were less likely to fall prey to a tyranny of the majority, since a numerous and geographically dispersed people would embody a plurality of shifting factions checking the dominance of any one party[3].

James Madison, an architect of the U.S. Constitution, also pointed out that local communities are often closed and parochial enclaves that achieve cohesion only by exiling dissenters and shutting borders to outside influences.

Still, the notion that democracy works best at the local level, among a population small and homogeneous enough to share cultural projects and moral values, has remained a strong theme in modern political theory. Contrasting the centralizing results of the French Revolution with the federalist system of the U.S. Constitution, French philosopher Alexis de Tocqueville concluded that a mass of scattered individuals, no matter how free one at a time, are collectively powerless to oppose the dictates of a central government. Tocqueville credited American democracy with maintaining the power of local institutions over important matters such as education and criminal justice. He also stressed the dependence of democracy on the vitality of civil society and on the local and voluntary associations that first "rub off that private selfishness which is the rust of society"[4].

I begin with this brief review of democratic theory because it locates the fundamental political issues raised by global communications networks. On the one hand, the universal reach of computer and telecommunications technologies weakens the capacity of sovereign governments to police the cultural and information boundaries of their own territories, or to respond effectively to transnational corporations who frequently control the information networks. On the other hand, global networks promise to open up closed and dictatorial regimes to outside influences, precisely because borders are increasingly porous to the on-line march of "1's and 0's." To this extent, the globalization of communications promises democratic results in ways not foreseen by classical political theory.

Moreover, even as the Internet globalizes communication, it also is localizing it, by providing accessible platforms for grassroots community organizing. The proliferation of independent web sites "housing" diverse cultural and ethnic groups is evidence that the Internet is decentralizing control over the content of communication, especially in comparison to the highly centralizing impact of broadcasting on programming supply. At least before the spread of cable delivery systems, broadcast programming was mostly national in its reach, each network aiming at the same mass audience to the exclusion of programs geared to minority cultures. The content of internet programs by contrast is

---

3 *Hamilton, Madison and Jay,* The Federalist Papers, No. 10.

4 *Alexis de Tocqueville,* Democracy in America (New York: Vintage Books, 1961), vol. 1, p. 295.

already far more diverse. Moreover, the interactivity and lower entry cots of online communication promises to break the passivity of television watching, where ordinary citizens are consumers, rarely makers of television programs.

With these introductory remarks as background, let me turn to consider more specifically the potential political impact of global communications on American politics.

## 1. New Communications Networks as Additional Governance Tools for Traditional Political Institutions

Not surprisingly, formal governmental institutions as well as leading political parties have been busy over the past few years establishing a web presence. One important legal principle driving the emergence of online government is that government information is a public asset that ought to be available to the people free of charge, rather than through commercial services only.

In the United States, the federal Office of Management and Budget (OMB) issued a policy directive in 1993 designed to expand public access to government services; President Clinton signed a law in May, 1995 codifying most of these policies[5].

Vice President Al Gore has touted the movement of government information onto the Internet as vital to the "reinvention" of a government that "works better and costs less."[6] The most visible sign of this reinvented government is the number of federal Web sites through which citizens can access a staggering volume of free information. Examples of web sites established by the Executive Branch include:

- The "Welcome to the White House" web site (http:\\www.whitehouse.gov), which offers virtual tours of the White House, links to the home pages of each federal agency, access to White House press releases, and e-mail to the President, Vice President and the First Lady. Approximately a quarter of a million Americans subscribe electronically to White House press releases every day. This obviously carries the art of direct mail campaigning and communication to a new level and shows the ways in which formal governmental institutions can use the Internet to bypass communication through the media and even through political parties to communicate directly to individual Americans.
- FedWorld. The Commerce Department's "FedWorld" web site (http:\\www.fedworld.gov) gives the public access to information on federal jobs, small business administration, directives from the Federal Aviation Administration on airworthiness of planes, automobile crash test results, and so on. On average, some 7,500 persons sign on to FedWorld every day.

---

5 OMB Circular A-130, Management of Federal Information Resources, and the Paperwork Reduction Act of 1995, Pub. L. 104-13.

6 "Creating a Government that Works Better and Costs Less: Reengineering Through Information Technology," Accompanying Report of the National Performance Review (September, 1993).

- The Internal Revenue Service (IRS) maintains a web site (http:\\www.irs.ustreas.gov) which offers official electronic versions of tax forms and instruction booklets. In the two weeks before federal taxes were due on April 15, 1995, more than 200,000 tax forms and booklets were downloaded.

Similar web sites exist for the legislative and judicial branches of the federal government. For instance, the House of Representatives web site (http:\\www.house.gov) includes access to "Thomas" (http:\\www.thomas.loc.gov), an online search engine that permits users to follow bills pending in the House, and an Internet Law Library that provides free access to virtually every basic document of U.S. Law. Information about the federal judiciary can be retrieved from its web site (http:\\www.uscourts.gov).

As of this writing, it is difficult to make predictions about the political impact of federal government on the web. Clearly, geographical remoteness is no longer the obstacle it once was to retrieving documents, say, from The Library of Congress in Washington, D.C. The cost of retrieving that information is also plummeting quickly, at least once the entry costs of buying equipment and subscribing to an Internet provider have been met (even here public libraries are beginning to provide some limited Internet access free of charge). In sum, government on the Internet accomplishes a stunning democratization of information's accessibility. If thoughtful ways are designed to subsidize the access of lower income groups to this new abundance of information, then the Internet will indeed work to close the traditional information gap between rich and poor.

Less desirable political consequences are imaginable. Conceivably, the information gap between rich and poor could widen, if commercial networks come to dominate the Internet or if basic computer literacy skills are not taught in the public schools. Additionally, government on the Internet is in a position to manage the news about its own operations, bypassing independent media outlets and delivering information directly to citizens. Privacy concerns also abound, insofar as the Internet permits government to monitor electronically the concerns of citizens, and to compile vast data bases about citizens in anticipation of the next election.

In the United States, one of the more exciting political consequences of new communications has been the reinvigoration of civic ties and civic associations at the local level. Given all the hoopla about global networking, commentators frequently miss the Internet's support for local networking. Local governments rarely have access to broadcast television for delivering services or information to residents. Cable television began to help matters, as cities and towns successfully negotiated to have cable operators set aside one or more channels for public access programming available to local, civic groups. But these public access channels never attracted much of an audience. The hope now is that online exchanges of information can become an important medium of community conversation.

Starting with the pioneering "FreeNets" in Cleveland, Santa Monica, Seattle, Charlotte, and elsewhere, community activists have used computer networking as a way not only to improve delivery of basic city services (e.g. by offering electronic building permits in Cleveland) but also to restore substance to participatory democracy by sustaining deliberative conversation among ordinary citizens themselves (e.g., a discussion of how to help the homeless of Santa Monica find jobs). The Seattle Community Network's founder, Doug Schuler, claims that some 300 computer-oriented community networks now serve half a million registered users. Schuler estimates that 200 more networks were gearing up to start as of 1997 [7].

The Cleveland FreeNet is the oldest and largest of the civic computer networks[8]. Begun in 1986, it now boasts 160,000 registered users. But scores of local communities now have their own networks, including the Mobile (Alabama) FreeNet; Bridgeport (Connecticut) OnLine; the Sun Coast (Tampa/St. Petersburg, Florida) FreeNet; the Panhandle (northern Idaho) FreeNet; PraireNet (east-central Illinois) BRAIN (Baton Rouge, Louisiana); Big Sky Telegraph (rural Montana); Minnesota E-Democracy; the LaPlaza Telecommunity (Taos, New Mexico); Philadelphia (Pennsylvania) Neighborhoods OnLine; SENDIT (Fargo, North Dakota); and the Ozark Regional Information OnLine Net (southwest Missouri) [9].

The political significance of these local community online networks should be judged in light of the research of political scientist Robert Putnam and others about declining social capital in the United States. "Social capital" refers to the myriad of ways in which joining the parent-teacher organization, singing in the church choir, or even bowling in a league bring people together around a shared purpose, a joint enterprise, a common good. Putnam argues that political democracy is dependent on the creation of social capital in civil society through membership in voluntary associations and community groups. Given his findings that social capital has been declining in the United States since the end of World War II, the emergence of new forms of voluntary association and local community groups on the Internet is a promising development[10].

Consider, for instance, the Public Electronic Network (PEN) in Santa Monica (http:\\www.ci.santa-monica.ca.us/pen). All city organizations are online and a Santa Monica resident is promised an answer to any legitimate query about government services within forty-eight hours, via e-mail. The network also permits residents to "attend" meetings of city commissions or school committees and to download transcripts of the proceedings.

In Berkeley and Oakland, California, a grassroots group known as "Safe Streets Now" uses online technologies to mobilize residents to identify and to close down drug houses in their neighborhoods. In Dayton, Ohio, isolated neighborhoods have established computer bulletin boards to bring their problems to the attention of city government. In East Brooklyn, New York, the online Nehemiah Project concentrates on building

---

7 *Doug Schuler*, New Community Networks: Wired for Change (Boston: Addison Wesley, 1996), preface, p. 25.7.

8 Telnet: *<freenet-in-a.cwru.edu>*.

9 *Schuler*, New Community Networks, Appendix C.

10 *Robert Putnam*, Bowling Alone: America's Declining Social Capital, *Journal of Democracy* (January 1995), 65-78.

affordable housing. In Boston, the Dudley Street Neighborhood Initiative holds online "meetings" of community activists, bank loan officers, supermarket executives, and zoning board officials about economic investment in the inner-city minority community of Roxbury.

The Internet did not create these local community groups but it supports them by providing cheap and effective ways of mobilizing constituents, soliciting contributions, and holding conferences. As of this writing, it is still too early to tell whether virtual meetings can replace face-to-face contact as a way of fostering civic attachments and social capital. But alcoholics have spontaneously formed a group on the Seattle Community Network; afterschool clubs conduct business online in Cleveland; and the Lesbian Gay Bisexual Transgender Community meets regularly in the La Plaza telecommunity. When Elly, a longtime regular on the online virtual community WELL ("Whole Earth 'Lectronic Link) fell ill in the Himalayas with a dangerous liver ailment, word of her illness was posted on the WELL. Regulars, including doctors and travel agents, mobilized quickly to fly her home, where she was treated and cured[11]. These are just some of the ways in which isolated individuals "find" one another and enter into genuine, unscripted dialogue on, and action through, the Internet. If Tocqueville was right to stress the importance of voluntary associations to the spirit of democracy in the United States, then the proliferation of such associations on the web is a positive development.

But there are also dangers. Fragmentation of the body politic looms when single-issue constituencies cocooned in their own chat rooms talk only among "their own kind." Genuine community requires affirmation of the diversity that makes for vibrant, rich democracy and it is important to design computer networks so that people enter into conversation with fellow citizens who think differently, or at least think about different issues. Another danger is illustrated by the Boston-based Firefly Network, which claims two million registered viewers (http:\\www.firefly.com). Firefly employs filtering software that tracks the likes and dislikes of members –movies they enjoyed, restaurants they loathed. Firefly uses this information benignly to make recommendations about new movies and restaurants pegged to the particular tastes of the individual member. But it is not difficult to imagine more sinister, "Big Brother" uses of such monitoring technology.

## 2. Informal versus Formal Power Structures

On June 7, 1998, the Cable News Network (CNN) premiered a news magazine show entitled "Newsstand." The program was a collaborative effort of CNN and Time magazine, both media outlets owned by the giant Time Warner Corporation. On this premiere show, CNN charged that in 1970 the U.S. Army deliberately dropped sarin, a nerve gas, to kill American defectors in Laos during the Vietnam War. Within days of the broadcast, Tom Marzullo, a former member of U.S. Special Operations Forces in Vietnam, was on the Internet with a full and telling rebuttal. Marzullo, who had been

---

11 *Dinty W. Moore*, The Emperor's Virtual Clothes: The Naked Truth About Internet Culture (Chapel Hill, NC: Algonquin Books, 1995), 87-88.

outraged by earlier CNN stories about the work of special forces in Vietnam, had learned of CNN's interest in Operation Tailwind even before the show aired. Using little more than his personal computer, online data bases and e-mail, he independently researched Operation Tailwind, searching both official archives and also the memory of retired Special Forces veterans whom he reached via e-mail.

With this preparation, Marzullo was ready with his Internet rebuttal days after the CNN story on Operation Tailwind finally aired. Retired Major General Perry M. Smith, a military adviser to CNN who in fact had not been consulted prior to the show's airing, "credits his Internet advisers" with persuading him to resign his position with CNN to protest the show's accuracy. Smith's resignation helped spread an "internet uprising of retired Special Forces veterans." A flurry of e-mails and internet postings in short order persuasively established that the CNN story was highly inaccurate and the product of shoddy research. Within a month, Marzullo's internet campaign succeeded in "humbling a worldwide news outfit" and Time Warner publicly retracted its story and apologized to the veterans[12].

It is too early to say whether the CNN episode is an isolated sign of citizen empowerment or a sign of dramatic power transfer from big conglomerates to makeshift groups of watchful citizens. But the story well-illustrates the difference between interactive and passive technologies. With radio and television, citizens are mostly passive receivers of programming and rarely the programmers themselves. Online communications changes the paradigm by decentralizing control over the media of communications and by permitting the likes of a Tom Marzullo to see the initiative to talk back.

In an informal way, the communications revolution also seems to be paving the way for experiments with direct democracy in the United States. In the 1970s, producers of quiz shows on cable television pioneered uses of the interactive capacity of cable networks to invite participation from home viewers, who only had to press a button on a cable box in order to "vote" for one choice rather than another. Not long afterwards, fledgling trials of electronic town meetings were held in various American cities. The official town meeting would be aired over a local cable public access channel and home viewers would be invited (unofficially) to vote on proposals. Where viewers had interactive cable, they could vote through the television box; otherwise they could telephone their votes into a central computer.

By the 1980s, it became customary for the national networks to follow the Presidential debates with an instant telephone plebiscite declaring the winner. The telephone polls were notoriously unscientific and without screening for repeat callers but the experiments demonstrated the capacity of central computers to handle and tally millions of calls nearly instantly.

In the 1992 presidential campaign, third party candidate Ross Perot gave national prominence to debates over direct versus representative democracy when he campaigned on the promise to govern through informal electronic meetings of citizens as well as through the formal representative institutions. Tapping into long-standing anti-elite American

---

12 *Vincent Caroll*, Rout of CNN Not Over Yet, *Denver Rocky Mountain News*, July 21, 1998, p.F1.

populism, Perot argued that representative democracy was becoming obsolete in an age where people could electronically vote on issues themselves, and without even leaving their homes. Insofar as obstacles of numbers, distance or time once made it impossible to gather masses of citizens together to debate and decide issues, Perot argued that computer technology had vanquished the practical obstacles do direct democracy. Perot never went so far as to suggest actually changing the constitutional structures of government – he simply promised to convene electronic town meetings or to hold electronic plebiscites frequently as an informal way of soliciting popular input into his proposals.

Perot was rightly criticized for leaving unanswered a host of practical questions, such as how to prevent persons from voting more than once, what to do about persons without access to the necessary online services, or how to prevent special interests from stacking the virtual assemblies ( for instance, upon hearing that a special open forum on gun control would be held on May 26 of this year in Lyle, Illinois, the Illinois Rifle Association posted a notice on its web page urging members residing in Lyle to attend the forum.)

Deeper debates over Perot's "electronic town hall" proposals raised normative and not just practical questions: even if we could design a workable scheme for holding electronic referenda, should we reconfigure democratic institutions along plebiscitary lines? Those who favor using online services to conduct electronic plebiscites argue that the more directly people get to decide public policies for themselves, the more democratic the government. As political scientist Ted Becker argued early on, in urging Hawaii authorities to use new communications technologies to submit proposed changes in the state constitution to a virtual assembly of the people (as well to the legally required state Constitutional Convention), "public opinion ought to be the law of the land" in a democracy[13].

Those who balk at various schemes for "electrifying democracy" suggest that plebiscitary procedures have historically given the show of democracy without its substance. Instant voting from the home is likely to rush judgment and rip from persons an immediate and therefore unstable expression of opinion. The problem here is that so many schemes for electronic updates of democracy short-circuit the deliberations and meetings, the debates and considerations of opposing views that alone give democratic substance to the act of registering an opinion on an issue. This brings us back to Aristotle's central teaching about democracy, that it requires instilling in citizens a concern for, and a familiarity with, the views of others. When electrified versions of direct democracy are touted as ways to permit individuals, isolated in their own homes, to respond to prefabricated policy choices, while avoiding the meetings and conversations that alone permit these individuals to locate their interests within a public context, then the communications revolution threatens democracy with the historic ills of faction and balkanization – different interests competing for power with no sense of community or a common good. Instant responses become an end in themselves, civic education a lost good.

---

13 *Ted Becker and Christa Slaton*, Hawaii Televote: Measuring Public Opinion on Complex Policy Issues, *Political Science* 33, no. 1 (July 1981): 52-65.

In sum, critics of plebiscitary visions of direct democracy argue that home-centered electronic voting is likely to duplicate all the problems of current public opinion polls. Polling may very well empower public opinion in a democracy, but the problem is that the people polled are giving only their instant responses to the question – without time for reflection and without opportunity to deliberate with others about the common good.

Responding to these criticisms, friends of electronic democracy agree that public opinion polling is a misleading way of consulting the considered views of the people. What is needed, argues political scientist James Fishkin, is a new model he calls "deliberative polling." The key feature of a deliberative poll is that citizens voice their opinion to the pollster only after being given relevant information, as well as time to reflect and to deliberate with others on the material provided. Fishkin faults the formal institutions of American democracy as well as political parties, candidates running for office, and the media covering politics for defaulting on their obligations to provide meaningful courses of civic education to the people. He finds campaigns, and media coverage of those campaigns, to be particularly bankrupt when it comes to civic education, with the media covering only the gossip, the salacious, and the "horse-race" aspects of who is winning and losing. Into this vacuum, Fishkin urges spontaneous groups of citizens to step, harnessing the networking power of computer technologies to provide citizens with relevant policy information and outlets for communicating among themselves about government policies. Pollsters in particular should revamp their technique to facilitate these deliberations, delaying their poll until "citizen juries" have heard the evidence and deliberated about it.

One experiment with "citizen juries" deliberating online occurred in 1996 on the commercial Web site PoliticsUSA (since joined with the rival ElectionLine to become PoliticsNow [http:\\www.politicsnow.com]). In January 1996, while the federal government was enduring one of a series of shutdowns due to Congressional inability to pass a federal budget, members of a PoliticsUSA chat room spontaneously decided to form a "virtual" Budget Committee and to develop a balanced budget of their own. They defined their mission as agreeing on a plan to balance the federal budget within seven years. Of course, members of this virtual budget committee knew that they would not have to live with the consequences of their decisions and hence it is difficult to assess the realism of this experiment. Still, the real Congressional budget committee would do well to imitate the educational odyssey of the virtual committee. Realizing that educating themselves about budget matters was the priority, the virtual committee invited a federal budget analyst from Price Waterhouse to chair their mock sessions. The chairman used online data services to supply each committee member with analysis and data from the actual Congressional Budget Office's "Economic and Budget Outlook." Further experts were brought in to answer technical questions when needed, and two weeks were set aside for discussion. During these two weeks, consensus emerged to take some budget items (principally Social Security) off the budget-cutting table, while keeping others (for example, defense spending) on the chopping block. In the end, conversation, though "often long and frequently contentious" began to change the preconceptions and preferences of the 40 to 50 regular members of the virtual committee. Basically, a bipartisan consensus developed to marry the Clinton administration proposals for cutting the defense budget with Republican Congress calls to scale back several entitlement programs, including Medicaid. Their plan as finally adopted would have balanced the federal budget in five years, according to then available figures from the Congressional Budget Office[14].

Large numbers of Americans did not flock to the PoliticsUSA web site to discuss the federal budget, and those who did were probably not a representative sample of the American population. But, as opposed to the traditional public opinion poll, the experiment did model a way to retrieve the more considered policy judgments Americans might make once if given adequate information resources and a forum for debating that information.

When the G-8 economic submit takes place in Toronto in June, 1999, summit leaders have agreed to hold an online, shadow conversation with as many as 5,000 persons worldwide on a first-come, first-served basis (http:\\www.g8oline.com). The gesture, of course, is largely symbolic and it seems unlikely that online participants will have access to the actual ongoing summit conversations. But who knows what effects on the real conference the holding of a worldwide shadow conference may have, especially since the shadow conference will be supported by an arsenal of academic resources according to planners (http:www.g7.utoronoto.ca and http:\\www.ecollege.com)

## 3. Sovereignty in a Networked World

Michael Nelson, director of Technology Policy for the Federal Communications Commission has observed that "the growth of global information networks, the power of the transnational corporations that run them, and the creation of a truly global electronic market will mean that national governments will no longer be able to exercise many of their prerogatives under the concepts of sovereignty."[15]

Traditionally, sovereign governments could effectively control matters such as citizen's telecommunications options, the content of national culture, or movement of ideas, labor and capital across national boundaries. But the prerogatives of territorial-based sovereigns is in decline today. Consider, for instance, the telecommunications market in Sweden, one of the first nations to open up its telephone market fully to foreign competition. Today, USWest "is among the companies connecting Swedish government offices to each other and the rest of the world." Likewise, the Swedish foreign ministry has its phone service provided by a Singapore concern[16].

---

14 *Michael Cornfield and F. Christopher Arterton*, "Is This for Real?" Democratic Politics and the Internet. In: Institute for Information Studies, *The Internet as Paradigm: 1997 Annual Review of the Institute for Information Studies*, pp 93-98.

15 *Michael R. Nelson*, Sovereignty in the Networked World. In: *The Emerging Internet: 1998 Annual Review of the Institute for Information Studies*: 7.

16 Id at 8.

More dramatically, Internet users throughout the world frequently connect to the Internet using a telecommunications network located outside the borders of their country and beyond the control of national government. This makes it easier for political dissidents to communicate free from oppression. But it also makes it easier for international criminal or terrorist groups to escape traditional law enforcement techniques available to sovereigns, for instance, wiretapping.

Even when sovereigns respond, as the U.S. government did with the proposed merger of British Telecom with MCI by insisting that the new foreign-owned company enter into an agreement ensuring that American law enforcement would retain ability to wiretap the networks of the merged company, the response may prove impotent.

Growth in encryption technology makes it difficult for law enforcement agencies to decipher even the traffic they do intercept. Here, again, the U.S. government has been trying to prohibit the export of strong encryption technologies but it is a difficult policy to enforce.

All this adds up to a future where sovereign governments will have less control over the information flowing to its citizens. Chinese dissidents in Tiananmen Square already were able to use fax machines to send messages around the world; Zapista guerrillas in Mexico have used the Internet to end-run government restrictions on their communications with the outside world. Cell-phones have provided ethnic Albanians in Kosovo with one of the few ways of sending news in the current crisis.

Global networks are also likely to weaken the ability of sovereigns to control the content of national culture. In part, this is an old story, harking back to Hollywood's alleged hegemony over entertainment and the eclipse of indigenous cultures by American-style videos and music. Since the Internet is poised to deliver an inexhaustible supply of American cultural products everywhere, the complaint is bound to grow that diverse, national cultures are being replaced by one mega-culture controlled by a handful of foreign conglomerates.

This certainly is a possibility. But it is worth noting a less bleak cultural future. As opposed to a centralizing medium such as broadcast television, where the high costs of producing and distributing programming made centralization of supply the norm, the Internet and cable television are emerging as decentralizing media, where the costs of producing and distributing programming are relatively minimal[17]. The result in the United States to date has been more, not less varied programming – a Hispanic channel, a Black Entertainment network, web pages and chat rooms and information about every possible ethnic or religious culture. Arguably, then, new communications technologies may support the efforts of diverse cultural groups to support their autonomy, especially since it gives geographically dispersed members of the group access to programming and resources they do not currently have.

---

17 *Nelson*, Sovereignty in a Networked World, p. 9.

## 4. Conclusion

In Rankin Inlet, a Canadian Inuit settlement "800 miles from everything," more than one in five residents now has an e-mail account[18]. In Brazzaville, Congo, a district hospital with only 40 outdated books in its library now hooks up through HealthNet to the National Library of Medicine in Washington, D.C. Hospital doctors also used HealthNet to treat the outbreak of the deadly Ebola virus in early 1995. In 1994, a Canadian company set up the first Internet connection in Mongolia. In Kathmandu, Nepal, the International Centre for Integrated Mountain Development has developed an Internet-based network to promote a sound mountain ecosystem in the Hindu Kush-Himalayan region. When the environmental group Greenpeace wanted to mobilize public opinion quickly against Shell Oil plans to dispose of the Brent Spar oil platform in the North Sea, it turned to the Internet to reach members everywhere instantly and at relatively low cost.

Clearly, dramatic change is afoot in the world. But just as no one could have forecast the impact the Cold War would have on world politics when Winston Churchill first announced it in his famous "Iron Curtain" speech, so no pundit today is wise enough to predict whither politics in the age of global communications. Will the privacy-invading, monitoring and homogenizing features of computer networks yet produce the government of Big Brother predicted by George Orwell in his antiutopia of 1984? Or will the future bear out the techno-optimism of former Citicorp chairman Walter Wriston who argues that Orwell needs to be stood on his head, that "instead of ...Big Brother watching the citizen,...the citizen is watching Big Brother and so the virus of freedom, for which there is no antidote, is spread by myriad electronic networks to the four corners of the world."[19]

As basic a political feature of our world as the territorial-based sovereign nation is changing under impact of global communications. But are national powers devolving downward onto smaller, ethnic powers or upward to international institutions? And if international institutions do emerge, will they be formal structures akin to the United Nations or informal nongovernmental organizations (NGOs) akin to the Red Cross? The excitement of our moment in history is to know that dramatic change is upon us but that the direction of change is not predetermined but lies open to our own efforts and aspirations.

---

18 *Ken MacQueen*, Surfing the World from the Frozen North, *Ottawa Citizen*, February 23, 1997.

19 *Walter Wriston*, The Nationhood Lectures: The Twilight of Sovereignty, *RSA Journal* (August/September 1992): 567.

*Hans-Heinrich Trute*

# The Impact of Global Networks on Political Institutions and Democracy

It is a fairly common occurrence that the supposed globality of information infrastructures seduces us into the assumption of a global society of communication which evens national structures as cultural resources, regulation aims and means and thus fundamentally transforms the nation state and the "Westphalian" system of states. It is quite obvious that this would create serious problems for a theory of democracy. Democracy has always been connected with spatial categories, with the inclusion/exclusion of persons, the affiliation to "Moral Territories"[1] and thus finally related to a national political-administrative system[2]. Then it would be consequent to look for new concepts of a transnational democracy, or to utter a general skepticism on the survival of an old European institution.

We may, however, doubt whether the dedifferentiating and leveling effect of global information infrastructures can be formulated in this way. The investigations often suffer from an empirical deficit. They sometimes assume a change of customs of communication on a worldwide level, which at least for the time being - cannot be observed from a German point of view. Furthermore they suffer from an overestimation of the effects of the new information infrastructures by mistaking different technical possibilities of communication for different and considerably far-reaching effects of the communications means themselves. Moreover, they are not free of a technical determinism without sufficiently taking into account the social embedding of technical infrastructures.

This is why comments on the effects of global nets on political institutions and democracy are highly speculative. Surely, the (existing) architecture of the nets - exemplarily that of the Internet - may, due to their globality, their decentral character, the loss of meaning of time, the small costs of the acquisition and provision of information, the individualization of use, be set into more or less convincing parallels to political institutions, democracy, as well as the possibilities of its modification. Here again, we cannot fail to see that these characteristics may change, because technology is integrated in social practices. The structures of action are often very stable, traditional and supported by the constitution. Therefore, adaptations to technical structures are, per se, no less probable than the accommodation of technical structures to existing social practices of action that fundamental transformations would not have to be expected.

Notwithstanding this skeptical keynote, the following part will seek the possible consequences of global networks for the corresponding national political-administrative system (I), discuss their influence on a normative concept for the public (II) and then consider the problem of denationalization against the background of the global networks (III).

---

1 *D. Jacobson,* New Frontiers: Territory, Social Spaces, and the State Sociological Forum, Vol.12. No 1. (1997), 121, 125 ff.

2 *D. Jacobson,* 123.

## I. The Effects of Global Networks on the Political-Administrative System

### 1. Global Networks as an Information Resource

Free access to information is a decisive condition of democracy, for the formation of opinions by individuals and society as a whole. The German Federal Constitutional Court has always stressed the constitutive connection between freedom of information, freedom of expression, the right to privacy and democracy for the German constitutional order[3]. In doing so, it has attributed a special role and freedom to the institutions responsible for the collection and supply of information, particularly to the modern mass media At the same time, it has related those to the functioning democracy and thus bound them to obligations. Regardless of the problems pertaining to the concept of a "useful" freedom, the constitutive connection of democracy and information is stressed in this manner, as it may be found elsewhere, especially in the normative theories of democracy.

In this sense, the Internet is undoubtedly a democratic medium, because it dramatically changes the possibilities of the individual to obtain information. It is a gigantic resource of information. Its potential lies not only in the mere quantity of information, but in the lack of selectivity of information, the individuality of access, the small costs of information, the missing spatial, factual and temporary delimitations and the opportunity to put information into the Net oneself at equally small cost. Assuredly, these advantages have their own shady side which, among others, may be due to the overload of information, the lack of sufficiently transparent search engines and the threat of information being drowned by the noise of the Net. The development of the Net may lead to an information resource without the "grace of forgetting" to which past, present and future are therefore equally valid. However, there is no doubt that global nets offers immense information opportunities, chances of an essentially uncensored notice and unfiltered reception. Information asymmetries may therefore be evened out, and the action options of individuals, groups, and associations of the civil society may be improved. In this sense, global networks such as the Internet improve the possibility of informed participation and open the political process to the extent to which they are made use of for political purposes.

### 2. Transformation to a Direct Democracy?

From the point of view of a normative theory of democracy which is intended to enhance, if not maximize, participation[4], there can hardly be any doubt that, with their

---

3 BVerfGE 27, 70, 81.

4 *M. G. Schmidt*, Demokratietheorien, 2nd ed. 1997, 170 ff.

information capacity, global networks are able to considerably improve the preconditions for democratic participation via, for instance, the possibility of obtaining specific information on single matters, the creation of platforms and the participation in decisions, as well as the possibility of *televoting*. The *plebiscite de tous les jours* seems to be within reach. The point of view always being formulated as a counterargument, i.e. that information and expenditures of direct democracies in territorial states would call for a representative democracy as the only realistic form, seems to be technically more or less outdated. From this perspective global networks appear as egalitarian, participative and communitary media of information and communication, as electronic marketplaces of free speech[5]. The possibilities of the Internet seem to further the realization of a new, virtually Athenian era of democracy and visions of a growing individualized and at the same time global communication society[6]. In this respect, they come close to strongly normative theories of democracy, for which the representative form is only a weak variant of *true* democracy, which is characterized by the extension of the circle of eligible voters and the participation of voting citizens in the discussion, will-making and decision processes[7].

In the light of reflections on the theories of democracy, one cannot deny that, even in the age of the Internet, the criticism of the referendum democracy as a form of direct democracy has not suffered a loss of its relevance. First of all, the decision costs of such a form of direct democracy are high, regardless of the marginalization of the information costs by the Internet. This applies especially with regard to complex decision problems[8]. Seen from the point of view of efficiency which, for a more complex theory of democracy, must be balanced against the aspect of participation, forms of direct democracy as *alternatives* to the representative democracy hardly seem to be promising. Moreover, they enact a simple zero-sum decision mechanism, which may cause high external costs. If every procedural rule deviating from the principle of unanimity causes external costs for those who do not, or not to the same extent, take advantages out of a collective decision by the other collective members[9], then these costs are especially high in procedures of direct democracy because they are not moderated by the possibility of compromise, negotiation and package solutions. While, in representative forms of democracy, it is already difficult to reconcile the increasing plurality of interests with the votes tending to simple alternatives in a majority democracy and to reproduce this plurality in such a way as to prevent the distortion of preferences in decisions[10] that contradict the interests of a majority, this applies more

---

5 *Th. Zittel*, Über die Demokratie in der vernetzten Gesellschaft, *Aus Politik und Zeitgeschichte* B 42/97, 23 – 29.

6 *Depenheuer*, 669 ff.

7 *M. G. Schmidt*, 171-172.

8 *M. G. Schmidt*, 261-262. Problems of knowledge are discussed by *G. Sartori*, 127 ff.

9 *G. Sartori*, 127 ff.

10 A. *Benz*, Postparlamentarische Demokratie? In: M. *Greven* (Ed.), Demokratie - eine Kultur des Westens? 1998, 201, 203.

strongly to forms of direct democracy. Thirdly, these tend to lead to a fragmented decision-making practise. It is just the small cognitive resources of direct democratic procedures that cause the fragmented treatment of problems, which can in no way be overcome by the Internet and its possibilities *as such*. Information is not knowledge, nor does more information necessarily guarantee the rationality of decisions.

## 3. Increase in Responsiveness Via New Forms of Participation

These skeptical notes on direct electronic democracy as an alternative to representative forms of democracy do not apply to the possibilities of increasing the responsiveness of representative forms of democracy by global networks. The reduction of information costs and costs of participation make new forms of political communication probable. Their realization, however, seems to be different for political institutions according to their level in the federal system, not least due to constitutional reasons.

As far as the federal level is concerned, political institutions, the federal parliament (Bundestag), parliamentary groups, delegates and political parties increasingly use the Internet as a medium of information and (limited) communication. But, again, some reservations are called for[11]. On the one hand, only a small number of members of the Bundestag use the possibility of network communication. On the other hand, they often provide information but seldom make communication offers. Even if they do so, they are seldom taken up by users[12]. According to current examinations, no changes are in sight.

This may be quite different at the local level. Since offers of necessary information are relevant for political decisions, the discussion of matters in the run-up to decisions, the set-up of platforms of representatives, administration and citizens, as far as committees supported by rights that already exist to initiate rule-making at the local level, partially give rise to new forms and intensities of, above all, local public communication and participation. They in no way replace forms of representative constitution of the democratic procedure, but nevertheless they strengthen the participative elements[13]. The approaches to be conceived in Germany at the local level are to be taken less as forms of direct democracy in the sense of a referendum democracy, than as the changed roles

---

11 *Stradtmann,* Deutschland auf dem Weg in die elektronische Demokratie? 1998; *D. Schiller,* Parlamente Online: Zum Strukturwandel parlamentarischer Öffentlichkeit im Internet-Zeitalter, in: *W. Gellner/F.v. Korff* (Ed.), Demokratie und Internet, 1998, 127 ff.

12 *Stradtmann* Fn. 11; *Tauss/Kollbeck*, Der vernetzte Politiker, in: *Leggewie/Maar*, Internet&Politik, 1998, 277, 283 ff.

13 *Kubicek et. al.*, Jahrbuch für Telekommunikation und Gesellschaft, 1999; G-8 Goverment Online Publication on Democracy and Online Services, URL <http://www.statskontort.se/gol-democracy/forward.htm>; especially the contributions therein of C. *Guidi*, Bologna "civic network" service: Telematics for Citizens, Business, and the Third Sector, and *E. Maragall/A. Pont/T. Serra/J. Carreras*, Citizens' Participation through Internet, City of Barcelona.

of public and private actors in the execution of their tasks. Procedural innovations which were already discussed during the 1970s reform debate receive a higher chance of realization through the potentials of the networks. In this sense, *Klaus Lenk* speaks of a connection of citizens' participation with modern citizen and quality-oriented management methods such as citizen panels, user and public questions, complaint management[14], as far as improved direct decision procedures.

The existing experiments suggest that, to a great extent - at least in Europe, and especially in Germany - the forms depend on institutional effort by public actors, and that only to a small extent do they occur spontaneously and from the bottom upwards. Visions of a marketplace of ideas and opinions, where everybody communicates with everybody, easily fail to see that even a participatory democracy whose shape has been hardly formed, has an inherent organizational problem. "Electronic democracy" needs conceptional efforts and procedural innovations by different actors, which is easily forgotten in the naive belief in the democratic potential of technology.

## 4. Transformation of Individual Preferences in Collective Interests

Modern societies are characterized by a high extent of interest plurality, a significant complexity of the public tasks and a multiplication of decision options. The parliamentary majority democracy succeeds less in reducing the interest structures to simple alternatives of a majority vote. The danger that decisions contradict the preferences of a majority of voters, is thus increasing[15]. The economic theory of a rational option recommends, among others, in this respect the restriction of the scope of collective decisions, the introduction of direct democratic procedures and the option of unhindered migration[16].

Even at first sight it is evident that the Internet has, or may have, an effect on some of these solutions. Thus the scope and the restriction of collective decisions may not directly, but at any rate through the effects of the deterritorialization, which are increased by the Internet, come naturally. At least the decentralization of political decision-making and direct democratic procedures are facilitated. This may be an argument for strengthened voice-options in the long term.

---

14 *K. Lenk*, "Electronic Democracy" , 248, 253 ff.

15 *Buchanan/Tullock,* The Calculus of Consent. Logical Foundation of Constitutional Democracy, 1962.

16 *P. Bernholz/F. Breyer,* Grundlagen der politischen Ökonomie, Vol. 2, Ökonomische Theorie der Politik, 1994; *M. G. Schmidt,* 194.

## 5. The Loss (of meaning) of Intermediaries through Global Networks

Due to the increased possibilities of participation and, above all, the changed forms of participation, pressure is put on existing intermediaries. But, at the same time, complaints arise with respect to consequences as far as the reliability of information, the relevance of information and the formation of an informed public is concerned.

No doubt, for any theory of democracy, intermediaries are decisive political institutions. They mediate between the demonstrators and the institutions of democratic decision-making, set topics on the political agenda, prepare the personal selection and focus the discussion of public matters. It is not only the theory of the civil society which has, again and again, pointed out the importance of intermediary institutions.

The comparative research relating to democracy can make it plausible that direct democratic procedures generally diminish the significance of classical political intermediaries like, for example, the political parties. Nevertheless, it appears to me that this development is neither inevitable, nor even generally probable. On the contrary, this might not at least be dependent on the constitutional design of the relevant political-administrative system. Thus, in the USA, with the institutional form of a presidential majority democracy and a well-developed political culture at local and community level, the communication forms made possible by the Internet can more easily form the weakly marked party structures, as is the case in the European, especially German, distinctively neocorporatist tradition of democracy[17].

A strong and partially narrowed representative concept of democracy, like that in Germany, can certainly experience an opening-up with regard to direct democratic elements. This will exercise significant pressure on the classic intermediaries, as it primarily will on the parties. But even the changes that can be observed today, at least in the public field, cannot get along without action groups that promote topics, focus discussions and thereby reduce the decision costs for the participants. They do not necessarily have to be political parties; societies, citizens' associations, pressure groups, etc. can all serve this purpose. At the most, this could lead to a decrease in the cohesive forces of parties, in favor of temporary and factual commitment to single questions, hence a tendency towards *single issue groups*. The parties are, however, not excluded from making use of the networks[18] and thus developing new forms of temporary ties and voting[19]. The development in the parties which can be observed in Germany towards a direct democratic process at least points in this direction. Moreover, empirical

---

17 *Leggewie/Bieber*, From Voice to Vote? – Neue Informations- und Kommunikationstechnologien in der komplexen Demokratie, in: *Kubicek* et. al., *Multimedia @ Verwaltung, Jahrbuch Telekommunikation und Gesellschaft* 1999, 257, 259.

18 *Chr. Müller*, Parteien im Internet, in: *Gellner/v. Korff*, 157 ff.

19 *Leggewie*, Demokratie auf der Datenautobahn oder: Wie weit geht die Zivilisierung des Cyberspace? In: *Leggewie/Maar* (Ed.), *Politik @ Internet*, 1998, 15, 30 ff; see also *R. Werle*, The Impact of Information Networks on the Structure of Political Systems, 13-14

studies concerning online-communication in the last election campaign for the Bundestag merely show a development of online offers by the parties which, at any rate, can be interpreted as approaches to a new arena of election campaign communication. Compared with classical media, they are characterized by a considerably far-reaching inclusion of actors which, until now, have been rather marginalized and can be interpreted as complementary arenas of media publicity which, in essence, are also used by the previous intermediaries like, for example, the parties, societies, pressure groups, etc.

Nevertheless, faced with information overload, the problem of trusted institutions is still there. Whether the function of intermediaries will change, new forms of intermediaries will be created or a shift to users will occur and thus the formation of skills through education and professional training will be secured, remains open for the time being.

The thesis of a loss in the meaning of intermediaries therefore calls for a differentiation. No doubt, the possibilities of their circumvention might be manyfold due to the architecture of the nets and the possibilities of communication thus opened-up. On the other hand, the intermediaries might possibly open themselves to other tasks and new trusted institutions may develop.

## II. The Impact of Global Networks on the Concept of the Public

Democracy constitutes itself through and via the public. A normative concept of democracy has the task of mediating the interests of society and the political-administrative system (mediation function), ensuring the transparency of topics, political procedures and power structures (transparency function), in a normatively more ambitious concept of deliberative democracy also the formation of preferences and their rationalization in a public discourse (validation function). To the extent by which public communication can be exercised in a deliberate way and public opinion can be expressed which the public perceives as convincing, publicity offers the possibility of orientation and integration (function of orientation).

The characteristics of a normatively ambitious public conception are the *equality and reciprocity* of the communicative relations, the *principal openness* towards topics and contributions, and an adequate capacity for their treatment, finally the *deliberative orientation* of communications as well as the *claim of the inclusion of all*[20]. To what extent publicity fulfills or can fulfill the functions which are attributed to it in a strongly normative model is finally an open question that carries different answers according to

---

20 *B. Peters*, Der Sinn von Öffentlichkeit in: *Neidhardt* (Ed.), Öffentlichkeit, öffentliche Meinung, soziale Bewegungen, KZfSS 1999, 42, 46 ff; *Hellmann*, Integration durch Öffentlichkeit. Zur Selbstbeobachtung der modernen Gesellschaft, *Berliner Journal für Soziologie*, 1997, 37, 41 ff.

the competing conceptions of the public. Doubted by representatives of realistic and functionalist theories, admitted even by representatives of normative theories, there might be a long line of fundamental structural restrictions which, above all, relate to the equality of chances of power-sharing/participation, to the openness towards topics and contributions, and to deliberate potentials. Whether this calls for a reduction of the demands of the normative model, which nevertheless finds some normative support in the constitution, especially the freedom of communication, but also in the constitution of the representative system of democracy and in the self-description of democratic societies as an important element of legitimacy, may be left open here. In parts, they could even be reformulated, for example, within the framework of system-theoretic models which would like to conceive publicity as a social system of self-observation of society[21].

## 1. Global Networks and Mass Media

The German constitutional and political discussion is quite instructive, precisely in regard to mass media and the reaction of the Internet on the normative embedding of electronic mass media. It can only be understood against the background of the so-called positive broadcasting order developed by the Federal Constitutional Court from the objective dimensions of Art. 5 § 1, s. 2 of the Constitution of the Federal Republic of Germany, which - entirely in the sense of an ambitious normative model of publicity and its significance for the formation of individual and public opinion - would like to secure a variety of opinion, comprehensive information and cultural variety through normative demands against the providers[22] and considerably far-reaching, constitutionally secured aims of a free information regulation. Against the background of historical experience and the functional determination of electronic media, a complex system of requirements to equal opportunities for the access, pluralism and openness for persons and topics is laid down.

From a realistic point of view, this model is faced with the same doubts concerning its foundation as normatively ambitious models of the public. Notwithstanding the question of whether this model can be maintained any longer, in view of the privatization and commercialization of the media sector with the simultaneous extension of transmission capacities[23], it is just the Internet, due to its interactive

---

21 *Neidhardt*, Öffentlichkeit, öffentliche Meinung, soziale Bewegung, in: *Neidhardt*, 7 ff; *J. Gerhards*, Politische Öffentlichkeit. Ein system- und akteurstheoretischer Bestimmungsversuch, in; *Neidhardt*, 72.

22 BVerfGE 57, 295, 320-321; 73, 118, 157-158; 74, 297, 324.

23 *Trute*, Öffentlich-rechtliche Rahmenbedingungen einer Informationsordnung, VVDStRL 57 (1998), 216, 232 ff.

potential, that is taken as an argument for the abandonment of the complex regulatory framework of the positive radio rules. Behind this lies the assumption that there would no longer be a need for compensatory demands, for the very reason that equal individual access to the public would be given in both roles, i.e. as producer and recipient of information, on the global level and that thereby the electronic media in such an important partial sector would come close to the structures of a conversation, such as to make further precautions to protect the public unnecessary.

However, this mistakes the function of mass media, as well as the structure of the Internet, and how the two are connected is the subject of insufficient definition. Mass media are the medial system of self-observation of a functionally differentiated society. The media recount and inform about subsystems of society and themselves and, as such, they find themselves observed by these subsystems. The public as a social system serves like a mirror and at the same time produces the fiction of a commonly shared reality. This function cannot be reproduced in a conversation model. Apart from the limits in factual and temporary respect, this only leads to noise, but not the reflective structure of mass media public. In an extreme case, everyone communicates with everyone about something different: everybody speaks and nobody hears! The increased interactivity of new media will therefore not displace the classic system of mass media.

The type of public made possible by the Internet is often overestimated. In this regard, one has to recognize that "the" Internet comprises very different configurations of communication which cannot, as a rule, be understood as mass communication, least of all is the Internet itself a mass medium[24]. But even if one, for example, considers the World Wide Web as a mass medium, it is, at any rate as far as its effects are concerned, a different communication form to that of traditional mass media. While it is true that anybody can see and read everything, everybody actually sees and reads something different. Computer networks do not work as mass media, even if they are subjected to heavy use. Notwithstanding the fact that there are also mass media forms, not least in the network offers of classic electronic or print media, the real innovation lies in the formation of communication forms between mass and individual communication. In this sense, one may speak of a "multi-faceted mass medium" or - better still - of a hybrid medium[25], which allows one to change between communication configurations. According to the corresponding communication modus there will be a different extent of individuality, interactivity and mediality, without having displaced the function of

---

24 *P. Rössler*, Wirkungsmodelle: die digitale Herausforderung, in: same author (Ed.), Online-Kommunikation, 1998, 17, 19 ff.

25 *Kubicek*, Das Internet auf dem Weg zum Massenmedium? – ein Versuch, Lehren aus der Geschichte alter und anderer neuer Medien zu ziehen, in: *Werle/Lang* (Ed.), Modell Internet?, 1997, 213, 223 ff; *Höflich*, Zwischen massenmedialer und technisch vermittelter interpersonaler Kommunikation – der Computer als Hybridmedium und was die Menschen damit machen, in: *K. Beck/G. Vowe* (Ed.), Computernetze – ein Medium öffentlicher Kommunikation? 1997, 85 ff.

mass media. Already, in so far as a substitution of the functions of mass media or their dissolutions by individual communication can be expected; more plausible is the thesis of an intensified formation and use of complementary forms of communication configurations, especially forms of group communication.

## 2. Transformation of the Public

This reserved estimate of the impact on the mass media system, however, does not mean to say that online-media will not cause a transformation of the public. It is already the thesis of the complementarity that points at effects, namely the expansion of new communication configurations. To the extent to which they deal with political topics, a new form of political public arises here, at least partially.

It is obvious that the Internet is a global information resource which can avoid the selectivity of the mass media public. Together with an openness towards new topics and contributions, not least given the small prerequisites for the installation of information systems, inequalities and asymmetries in communication circumstances in the form of exclusions, the distribution of knowledge and the influence of social stratification and political power structures on the communication circumstances, can be softened. Equally, differentiation and stratification of the public can rather diminish in tendency, at least in the long run. For the time being, it might be argued that existing user potentials and profiles rather point to an increase in the information and participation asymmetries that already exist. The rather small number of users in comparison with the classic media, who, moreover, show a significant stratification in the dimensions of sex, age, education and income, currently leads rather to a "net world doubling of the real inequality"[26]. But this may be a temporary situation, according to the assertions of the information networks and their users.

Even if the design of the present political system has an essential significance, the use of networks by public interest groups and issue-related communication platforms can be observed. They show a considerably far-reaching pluralization of the public which, in the significantly corporative system of the Federal Republic, may represent a certain opening. They may be altogether more flexible and more temporary. They show, however, the transformation of the electronically-mediated public which can increase the public reaching deliberative potentials[27].

---

26 GfK Medienforschung, Online-Monitor. Strukturerhebung der Online-Nutzer <http://www.gfk.cube.net/ website/mefo/onmowa.htm>. *H. Scherer*, Partizipation für alle? Die Veränderung des Politikprozesses durch Internet, in: *Rössler* (Ed.), Online-Communication, 1998, 171, 176 ff.

27 Vgl. *Holtz-Bucha,* Fragmentierung der Gesellschaft durch das Internet? in: *Gellner/v. Korff*, 219 ff; see *Ruhrmann/Nieland*, Interaktives Fernsehen, 1997, 201 ff.

Certainly it will not rarely be a matter of the rise of fragmented public which will favor fragmentation tendencies being observed in the existing mass media system. To be sure, the public has always been fragmented, overlapping, and, only in parts, has it enjoyed a commonly shared reality. For the time being, this development may be interpreted as pluralization and the opening of an otherwise more closed public forum, without being immediately interpreted as a threat to integration and the decay of the ideal of republican publicity. Thus, one may speak less of a new form of publicity than of an increased responsiveness[28] and thus rather of a conveyance of new resources of legitimacy.

### 3. Modification of Political Communication

To be sure, on the part of the citizens, global networks not only modify their ability to participate and their access to publicity, but also increase the possibility of public relations in the political-administrative system. This may manifest itself in the provision of information, but also in strategic communication, with the aim of receiving approval. Thus, the scope of political actors is increased and the losses of competence in setting agenda topics by the political-administrative system[29] always deplored, in view of the autonomy of the electronic mass medium. Moreover, also from the point of view of *computer-mediated political communication,* it may above all be favorable to those who would otherwise have had more burdensome access because of the control of and dependency of resources on the access to publicity.

Of course, this depends on the general structural conditions of the media system. The scarcity of attention that awards a premium to the real or presumed novelty as news is dropped in the networks, does not structure the attention of the public in the Internet, so that in so far the chance increases of being drowned by the noise of information in the Net. Here again, we see that online-media cannot take over the functions of traditional media and that their substitution would therefore also in the future be rather unlikely.

## III. Denationalization and Global Networks

A severe challenge to any concept of democracy is the denationalization of societal subsystems which are not countered by a mere scaling up of the institutions of the nation state on an international level. Denationalization includes not only a transnational intensification of communication and trading connections and a

---

28 *D. Herzog*, Responsivität, in: *Jarren/Sarcinelli/Saxer* (Ed.), politische Kommunikation in der demokratischen Gesellschaft, 1998, 298.

29 *Zipfel,* Online-Medien und politische Kommunikation im demokratischen System, in: *L. Hagen* (Ed.), Online-Medien als Quellen politischer Information, 1998, 20, 34 ff.

differentiation of societal subsystems on a transnational, partly even global scale. In the economic system, a relative dematerialization of the economy, control of complexity without precedence and acceleration of economic transactions can be observed. Border-crossing communication and actions free themselves from their local attachment; their borders become functionally defined instead of territorially: from territory *to space*. "Transactions", as Ruggie says, "take place in national facilities, which may *be housed* in New York, Tokyo and European financial centers, but they are considered to *take place* in non-territorial space"[30]. In contrast to popular theses on globalization, the scope of the denationalization of societal subsystems is, however, an open case and the findings remain at least ambivalent, even for the economic system[31]. Notwithstanding the scope in particular, here lies a central legitimating problem for the modern democracy and its connection with the nation state. As the capacity of the nation state to influence communication and actions in denationalized subsystems decreases, the legitimacy of the nation state may also decrease.

In the sense of a complex theory of democracy, state action is not only regarded as being democratically legitimate if all citizens have equal possibilities of participation in decision-making processes which enable them to present their interests authentically and if the decision-making processes and the acts of representatives are transparent, understandable and controllable. What is more, effective solutions to problems must be found which are acceptable as such to the citizens. So the principle of effectiveness steps alongside the mediation of interests between the governed and the governing, political equality, publicity and responsibility. Thus legitimacy must also be secured on the output side of the political system[32]. Denationalization causes a serious problem for both the input and output sides of democracy, because it leads to a diminishing congruity between the circle of participants in a decision and that of those being concerned by the decision. On the other hand, it may lead to an incongruity of the scope of the regulations and those thus concerned. Even if these problems have not been caused by global networks, they are certainly intensified by them.

## 1. The Impact of Global Networks on Governance in a Denationalized Context

A reaction to this may be a territorial reorganization of the political-administrative system in the sense of the formation of local, regional, national, supra- and transnational

30 *Ruggie, Constructing the World Polity,* 1998, 174.

31 *Zürn*, Regieren jenseits des Nationalstaates, 1998, 65 ff; *Dahrendorf*, Anmerkungen zur Globalisierung, in: *U. Beck*, Perspektiven der Weltgesellschaft, 1998, 41 ff. For the system of science *Stichweh*, Science in the System of World Society, Social Science Information, 35 (1996), 327, 333 ff.

32 *Scharpf*, Versuch über Demokratie im verhandelnden Staat, in : *R. Czada/M. G. Schmidt* (Ed.), Verhandlungsdemokratie, Interessenvermittlung, Regierbarkeit, 1993, 25, 27.

territorial organization units, which show a differentiation into multilevel systems of governance, the decision-making and legitimating processes of which are indeed anything else but constructed in a satisfying way, as a glance at the comparatively quite well-structured multilevel system of the European Union shows. So, where is the place of sovereignty? How can democratically legitimated control be institutionalized and participation be organized in these multidimensional systems?

This is not the place to discuss the problems of democracy in denationalized contexts in detail[33]. Apart from the incongruity of the participation in decisions and being concerned by the decision, we can mention deficits - discussed manifold in the European example - of a common identity as a precondition of a common weal orientation. Equally, there is a regular lack of sufficiently institutionalized discussion and deliberation platforms, which from the perspective of normatively more ambitious models of democracy are prerequisites of legitimate decisions. It is only very limited that a transnational public is perceptible as a forum of deliberation and control. This applies already for the European area, but even more so for other transnational contexts. Furthermore, democracy calls for an adequate and equal representation of the persons concerned with the regulations. At best, in the contexts of international regulation, indirect representation connections exist that are mediated by the nation state. Due to the intransparency of intergovernmental negotiation systems, their control is rather weak. Moreover, once taken, decisions are difficult to revise later. These examples of democracy problems in multilevel governance concepts beyond the nation state cannot be eliminated through simple institutional reforms, least of all through a simple transfer of the nation state model to a global state model. The increase in the capability of legitimization of international organizations, as it can be found for instance in concepts of the cosmopolitical democracy, could just as little describe promising changes as proposals to delimit the tasks and instruments of supra- and transnational institutions for the nation state by sparing its autonomy. More convincing are those concepts which intensify the various forms of interest mediation, and which consequently admit administrative, societal and functional forms beside territorial ones and, furthermore, aim at intensifying transparency and access to the negotiation arenas[34].

For the time being, the models discussed above are speculative in their concepts but, above all, in the probability of their implementation. Thus, it is even more difficult to discuss the influence of global networks on these problems beyond a speculative level. As a rule, these problems are older than the global networks; in any case older than the Internet. It is interesting to see that the intense discussion surrounding democracy concepts in multilevel systems of governance seldom refers to global networks as a source for locating solutions to problems. The proposals for solution have thus been developed independently. However, it is certain that global networks will increase the possibilities of deterritorialization and thus the need for solutions, too. Not least, it is

33 *Zürn*, 236 ff.

34 *Zürn*, 347 ff.

the global networks themselves which are a case of transnational regulation. Of course, the decisive question will be, whether the global networks can also contribute to the solution of the described deficits. Depending on the way in which they influence the national forms of public and democratic institutions, they might in principle also act in transnational contexts and thus influence the concept of transnational democracy.

Two dimensions could primarily be suitable in this connection. On the one hand, the potential of the Internet lies in its information being independent of space and time, and thus in the possibility of significantly increasing the transparency of international regimes, as it happens factually at present through the informational behavior of international organizations. Additionally, the chance of institutionalization and the work of transnational interests/pressure groups and NGOs will probably be significantly increased. The elements of a civil society in a transnational democracy may at any rate experience a significant intensification through the global networks and thereby also gain influence on the behavior of national representatives in transnational or global institutions or regulation. Insofar, the Internet can thus support a transparency of sovereign action for the control of functional elites[35] in institutionalizing a transnational public. Of course, objections can be raised by the argument that the Internet would probably sooner give rise to issue-dependent forms of the public, which are in no way based on equality of access and the possibilities of expression which are stratified even more. Surely one can argue with good reason that one has to deal here with phenomena that are at long last communicative, without a power developing and a delimiting effect being created for society as a whole. This assumption, which has indeed been supported by an empirical analysis of present user behavior, suggests a rather marginal role by the global communication infrastructures for the development of a concept of transnational democracy. But a certain image of media held by the general public serves as an ideal blue print which is oriented at the national state models of democracy. Just as multilevel concepts of transnational regulation do not allow for a simple transfer of nation state models, does so little speak against an incremental building of institutions of public deliberation and control. But, finally, it seems that the impact of global networks on solving the problems of democracy in a denationalized context is, for the time being, of minor importance. Once again, one may conclude that the problems associated with building adequate institutions will not be solved by the inherent qualities of technologies.

## 2. Legal Instruments in a Denationalized Context

Notwithstanding all losses of effect being diagnosed, the law continues to be the central instrument of guidance of constitutional states. Global networks seem to add new

35 *Marschall,* Das Internet als globaler Raum öffentlicher medialer Kommunikation? In: *Donges/Jarren/Schatz* (Ed.) Globalisierung der Medien?, 1999, 151, 159.

deficits to those already known in the national context[36]. The regulation of transnational transactions meets the territorial borders of the law, thereby restricting the congruity of regulation and the field of action affected by it, and thus the legitimacy of democratic decisions with respect to their effectiveness. The implementation of legal norms can run aground on the architecture of global networks. Intensified possibilities of choice are opened up and the system competition surrounding the legal order is thereby intensified: *the Internet as a source of regulatory arbitrage*[37]. And this does not, or at any rate not primarily, concern the physical migration of subjects which is influenced by the Internet least of all, but rather by the law of citizenship and the rights, duties and opened alternatives connected therewith. Due to the dramatic reduction of costs associated with overcoming space and time, global networks facilitate rather the avoidance of actions of other legal orders which are estimated as being adequate. This applies above all to the decomposition of the business organization and the cutting of value-added chains that thus becomes possible. The reduction in transaction costs may equally enable new forms of cooperation to facilitate decisions, or to transfer enterprises or activities abroad. The application and implementation of norms may become more difficult for network transactions as a whole. Anonymity and encryption technologies may enlarge the possibilities of protection for individual network communication. At the same time, they reduce the potentials for the realization of public interests, which includes, by the way, protection of the individual against invasions of personal privacy. It is obvious that this goes along with risks for an integration of democratic societies controlled by legal norms and their implementation, even if these phenomena empirically seem to have a rather smaller significance and owe their prominence - as in the cases of child pornography - to a heated observation by the classic media, which tends to distract from the fact that those events have their reason in the real and not in the virtual world.

### *a) Increase in significance of international agreements*

With regard to the deterritorialization, it is fair to point at the necessity of international agreements and regimes as - state-related - regulation. Notwithstanding the skepticism that is always found, even long before the times of the Internet, but quite practicable for its communication procedures, there has been, even in sensible fields of the fight against pornography or racist expressions, a range of international law agreements. Take, for example, the Treaty on the Fight Against the Circulation of Obscene Literature from the year 1910 [38], the Convention on the Prevention and Punishment of

---

36 *Trute,* Die Wissenschaft von Verwaltungsrecht, in: Die Verwaltung at book 2, 1999, 9 ff.

37 *A. M. Froomkin*, The Internet as a Source of Regulatory Arbitrage, in: *Kahin/Nesson,* Borders in Cyberspace. Information Policy and the Global Information Infrastructure, 1998, 129 ff.

38 Treaty of 4 May 1910 RGBL 1911, 209, Protocol of 4 May 1949, UNTS 30,3, consolidated version UNTS 47, 159.

Genocide from the year 1948 [39], as well as the International Convention on the Elimination of All Forms of Racial Discrimination from the year 1966 [40]. They are supplemented by international agreements as, for instance, the Convention of the WIPO for the Protection of Copyright in the Internet, as well as regulations of the WTO on the infrastructures of telecommunication. Equally, customary international law may react to certain events. This is supplemented by regulations within international organizations as, for instance, the ITU. It is, however, obvious that the international formulation of a regulation will be achieved with more difficulty, and thus the less it will be related to the technical aspects, common interests and value concepts. The negotiation of international agreements regularly takes a considerable amount of time and, faced with the speed of change in communication processes, it is therefore not the imperative instrument of all rapid international regulation.

### *b)* *Transnational law*

Beyond internationalization, there are indeed regulatory possibilities which are worth examining more precisely in regards to their capabilities. Definite control impulses in national and supranational law for a transnational formation of order exist which, under the keyword of exterritoriality, has always been primarily the subject of competitive attempts. The extraterritorial application of its own law is also available for the regulation of the Internet. An example is the regulation of data protection crossing European borders. As you know, Art. 25 f. EU Data Protection Directive provides a regulation which only allows for data transmission into a third country if there is an adequate level of protection in the recipient country. This quite rigid principle, which is then the subject of much relaxation in Art. 26 EU Data Protection Directive, has sparked off an international discussion on the question of whether the corresponding national regulations must be adjusted to the European standard and how one can ensure that an adequate protection level is reached. Of course, this regulatory strategy is not without problems, as is seen not least in antitrust matters. This applies to its implementation, as well as to the possible conflicts which arise through its extraterritorial application. At the same time, it is obvious that the construction of sufficient national relations, which already have to be demanded sub specie of the international intervention prohibition, may cause difficult problems in the Internet, because the reference to consequences is not always a sufficient criterion. Even this difficulty does not necessarily speak for abandoning the instrument: it only has to be correspondingly restricted [41].

---

39 Dated 9 December 1948, BGBl. 1954 II 729.

40 Dated 7 March 1966, BGBl. 1969 II 961.

41 *Trute*. 21 ff.

### c) *The international coordination of national legal systems*

The international coordination of national legal systems, as it finds its expression downright exemplarily in international private law is a further possible instrument. Its objective is a coordinated implementation of national law in form of a coordinated behavior between several sovereign states. The more flexible instrument of private law may experience a renaissance just for the global networks. It may, however, be doubted whether the problems of order, which will often be problems of public interest, could be solved in this form. Here, a solution of international private law may act as a camouflage for problems which otherwise could arise under the international principle of sovereignty. However, as a result of deregulation and privatization, there may ultimately be an extension of problems concerning the regulation of common interests in social, economic and environmental policy through international private law.[81]

### d) *Self-regulation as an element of a transnational regulatory framework*

Of course, one can observe a formation of regulation which is even more distant than regulation by the state, and which can be circumscribed with self-regulation as compensation for lack of sufficient state regulation. It is precisely against the background of deterritorialization and the intensification of border-crossing communication that the possibilities of self-regulation become visible which, however, give rise to similar problems as they are being discussed in the national realm of law. Serving as reference for the discussion on the Internet is always the formation of the *lex mercatoria,* where one can observe a strong development and professionalization. In this sense, legal scholars recently coined the phrase of a global law without a state[42]. This may appear to be overdrawn in view of its limited effects. Anyway, one may say that self-regulation takes place in functionally defined subsystems which try to compensate for the lack of political regulation. It is characterized by a relatively close relationship to the structures of matter and interest in the relevant field. Thus, it does not attain the independence of state regulation and of professional treatment, hence the distance to the structures of matter and interest which we normally identify with the rule of law and, naturally, it shows deficits in democratic legitimacy.

From the point of view of national and supranational legal systems, it will in future become necessary to circumscribe the conditions of acceptance of those self-regulations by national or supranational legal systems. These conditions have repercussions on the formation of regulations. Above all, they may have effects on the organization of and procedures pertaining to the self-regulation and their implementation. In this manner, deficits of legitimacy could even be made up.

---

42 *Teubner* (Ed.), Global Law Without a State, 1997; same author. Globale Bukowina, *Rechtshistorisches Journal* 15 (1996), 255 ff; see also *Röhl,* ZfRSoz 17 (1996) 1, 33 ff; *Trute,* 30-31.

It is, above all, Internet access providers and host providers who are directly or indirectly pushed to a self-regulation. This can be seen in the protection of minors. In many member states of the European Community, self-regulatory institutions have already been developed, insofar as firms have typically developed codes of conduct and have had them controlled by more or less independent institutions.

It is however necessary, as in all cases of self-regulation, to distinguish the effective self-regulation from the solely symbolical use of this instrument. The recent recommendation of the Council of the European Communities on the promotion of national framework conditions for a comparable level with regard to the protection of minors and the protection of human dignity[43] illustrates the interest in reaching a complementary and European, better still an internationally coordinated standard, independently of a national legal framework. Its elements shall be the representation of participants, the development of codes of conducts (as basic rules within a national self-control system with predetermined minimum contents) and enforcement instruments such as regulations of appeal, effective sanctions and the promotion of cooperation at the level of the Community. The effectiveness of self-regulatory systems shall be promoted by a regular assessment at the national level which, of course, has to be standardized appropriately for all European states.

This form of self-regulation can of course scarcely be effective without a regulatory framework provided by the state. It is correct that the Third Interim Report of the Enquête Commission "The Future of the Media in the Economy and Society - Germany's Way to the Information Society" illustrates that, without support and sanctions and continuous public control, self-regulation can hardly be effective in the long run. Even with regard to the highly sensitive field of the differentiation of freedom of opinion and personal privacy, the regulatory framework will hardly manage without a normative draft made by the state. It has also to be taken into account that, through the strategy of self-regulation, private access providers and host providers adopt an ambivalent role which may be not dissimilar to that of private censorship and control of information. This role has, for example, led to a regulation being formulated in the interest of the freedom of opinion and information in the field of classic media. Thus, significant weight must be attributed to the criteria for the implementation of the self-regulation, and additional transparency becomes necessary. Just because private self-regulation at the expense of third parties is openly directed as an answer not only to problems of implementation, but equally as an alternative to the governmental prohibition of censorship there is a need for a regulatory framework to also be constitutionally tenable.

---

43 Recommendation of the Council dated 24 September 1998 (98/560/EG) ABl EG NR. L 270, 48.

### e) *Shift of responsibility through reference to private possibilities of protection*

Where the duties of governments, sometimes constitutionally based, to protect the interests of citizens are limited due to the transnational character of the impairing processes and its lack of physical attributes, the limited scope of regulatory possibilities by the government and the missing control resources may make it obvious that society needs to enable and promote private self-protection. In the meantime, the law of information and communication technologies knows a multitude of different instruments. These comprise, for instance, the enabling of anonymous communication and the use of pseudonyms in legal relations, as well as encoding technologies which allow the individual to protect himself against observation and investigation via the encoding of information or via filters which filter out certain contents. Here, intelligent technical systems of filtering and admission supervision provide an effective protection of legal values. This strategy, which seems to be pursued by individuals and groups worldwide, indeed finds a legal basis in the constitutional order of the Federal Republic, at least for the protection of minors. This includes a commitment, at least, a constitutionally secured regulatory strategy, which aims at strengthening parents' responsibility through the availability of intelligent protection systems for admission supervision and filtering. This has the further advantage that the control instruments, their sufficient effectiveness being presumed, can be considerably adapted to the parents' standards and thus governmental and private patronage are, however, at first sight excluded. In fact, several rating systems for the assessment of content are already available which allow for the filtering of net contents according to predetermined assessment criteria and thereby contribute - notwithstanding all oversimplification inherent in the filters - to an improvement in admission supervision. With all recognition of the flexibility and decentralization, several questions again arise here which, so far, have not been answered sufficiently. Rating systems cannot be established without assessment which will not, however, be culturally neutral and their criteria will seldom be sufficiently disclosed. Thus the assessment presupposes trusted parties to carry it out, using transparent criteria. It must be visible which contents, based on which criteria, are mediated by whom. This applies all the more if those filter systems become effective not as late as on the level of the users, but already on a previous level, i.e., as early as the filter systems are integrated in the admission software by the providers, or even earlier. Here, the dangers for a free information order are obvious. And here, again, we will therefore scarcely cope without a normative framework.

## IV. Conclusions

The impact of global networks on political institutions and democracy is hard to predict. It depends not least on the design of the respective political-administrative system, on the political culture and traditions. Surely, no different from other innovations in the communication system of society, there will be changes caused or at least supported by the global networks. But they will probably come more slowly than the advocates of a world communication society envisage. As far as the German political-administrative system and the institutions of its democracy are concerned, revolutionary changes cannot be observed or expected, at least no challenges which would not have occurred otherwise. There might be an incremental shift to more transparency, participation, plurality of actors and interests in the political process. There will also be a change in the design of the administration to a more decentralized organization, including networks of public and private actors. And there might be changes in the form of the public, particularly as far as the classic mass media and their relationship to online communication are concerned. Whether and to what extent this will have an impact on political communication, and thus repercussions on the political administrative system, remains an open question for the time being.

One serious challenge is, however, denationalization, which is intensified by global networks, and thus deepens the problems of democracy and governance beyond the nation state that already exist. Again, the nation state will not be abandoned. It remains the central framework for the construction and stabilization of collective identities. Equally, inclusion/exclusion of people remains an important function of territorial limitation. The bundle of rights and duties being linked to citizenship will not easily obsolesce through globalization, even if it might be untied a little bit.[66] Not least, however, the coherence of the constitutional state, democracy and nation state can/will be abandoned for the time being. The institutionalization and implementation of a (legal) framework of regulation, also for denationalized sectors, still remains, despite all changes and adaptations - in the end a task for the nation state. The conception and implementation of international regulations, the use of social resources for the improvement of the state's problem-solving capacity, the coordination of self-regulation with the national and supranational legal order, as well as the distribution of responsibility to public and private actors will also remain an important task of national legal orders,[67] no matter how closely linked to functional self-regulatory or international regimes they may be. The problem of an adequate concept of democracy for denationalized sectors remains unsolved. The impact of global networks on this problem and its solution might at best be called ambivalent.

**References:**


*Benz, A.*, Postparlamentarische Demokratie? In: *M. Greven* (Ed.), Demokratie – eine Kultur des Westens? 1998, 201

*Bernholz,P./ Breyer, F.*, Grundlagen der politischen Ökonomie, vol. 2 Ökonomische Theorie der Politik, 1994

*Buchanan/Tullock,* The Calculus of Consent. Logical Foundation of Constitutional Democracy, 1962

*Dahrendorf,* Anmerkungen zur Globalisierung. In: U.Beck, Perspektiven der Weltgesellschaft, 1998, 41

*Depenheuer*, Informationsordnung durch Informationsmarkt. AfP 1997, 669 ff.

*Froomkin A. M.*, The Internet as Source of Regulatory Arbitrage. In: *Kahin/Nesson,* Borders in Cyberspace. Information Policy and the Global Information Infrastructure, 1998, 129 ff.

*Gerhards, J.*, Politische Öffentlichkeit. Ein system- und akteurstheoretischer Bestimmungsversuch. In: *Neidhardt*, 72

G 8 Goverment Online Publication on Democracy and Online Services, <http://www.statskontort.se/gol-democracy/forward.htm>

GfK Medienforschung, Online-Monitor. Strukturerhebung der Online-Nutzer <http://www.gfk.cube.net/website/mefo/onmowa.htm>

*Hellmann*, Integration durch Öffentlichkeit. Zur Selbstbeobachtung der modernen Gesellschaft. *Berliner Journal für Soziologie*, 1997, 37 ff.

*Herzog D.*, Responsivität. In: *Jarren/Sarcinelli/Saxer* (Ed.), Politische Kommunikation in der demokratischen Gesellschaft, 1998, 298

*Höflich*, Zwischen massenmedialer und technisch vermittelter interpersonaler Kommunikation – der Computer als Hybridmedium und was die Menschen damit machen. In: *K. Beck/G. Vowe* (Ed.), Computernetze – ein Medium öffentlicher Kommunikation? 1997, 85 ff.

*Holtz-Bucha,* Fragmentierung der Gesellschaft durch das Internet? In: *Gellner/v. Korff* , 219 ff

*Jacobson, D.,* New Frontiers: Territory, Social Spaces and the State. *Sociological Forum*, Vol.12 No 1. (1997), 121 ff.

*Kubicek et. al.*, Jahrbuch für Telekommunikation und Gesellschaft, 1999

*Kubicek,* Das Internet auf dem Weg zum Massenmedium? – ein Versuch, Lehren aus der Geschichte alter und anderer neuer Medien zu ziehen. In: *Werle/Lang* (Ed.), Modell Internet?, 1997, 213 ff.

*Leggewie/Bieber*, From Voice to Vote? – Neue Informations- und Kommunikationstechnologien in der komplexen Demokratie. In: *Kubicek* et. al., Multimedia @ Verwaltung, *Jahrbuch Telekommunikation und Gesellschaft* 1999, 257

*Leggewie*, Demokratie auf der Datenautobahn oder: Wie weit geht die Zivilisierung des Cyberspace? In: *Leggewie/Maar* (Ed.), Politik @ Internet, 1998, 15 ff.

*Lenk, K.*, "Electronic Democracy" – Beteiligung an der kommunalen Willensbildung. In: *Kubicek* et. al., 248 ff.

*Marschall,* Das Internet als globaler Raum öffentlicher medialer Kommunikation? In: *Donges/Jarren/Schatz* (Ed.) Globalisierung der Medien?, 1999, 151 ff.

*Müller, Chr.,* Parteien im Internet. In: *Gellner/v. Korff,* 157 ff.

*Neidhardt*, Öffentlichkeit, öffentliche Meinung, soziale Bewegung. In: Neidhardt, Öffentlichkeit, öffentliche Meinungen, soziale Bewegungen, 1994, 7 ff.

*Peters, B.*, Der Sinn von Öffentlichkeit. In: *Neidhardt* (Ed.), Öffentlichkeit, öffentliche Meinung, soziale Bewegungen, KZfSS 1999, 42 ff.

*Rössler, P.*, Wirkungsmodelle: die digitale Herausforderung. In: derselbe (Ed.), Online-Kommunikation, 1998, 17 ff.

*Ruggie, Constructing the World Polity,* 1998

*Ruhrmann/Nieland*, Interaktives Fernsehen, 1997

*Sartori, G.*, Demokratietheorie

*Scharpf,* Versuch über Demokratie im verhandelnden Staat. In : *R. Czada/M. G. Schmidt* (Ed.), Verhandlungsdemokratie, Interessenvermittlung, Regierbarkeit, 1993, 25 ff.

*Scherer, H.*, Partizipation für alle? Die Veränderung des Politikprozesses durch Internet. In*: Rössler* (Ed.), Online-Communication, 1998, 171 ff.

*Schiller, D.,* Parlamente Online: Zum Strukturwandel parlamentarischer Öffentlichkeit im Internet- Zeitalter. In*: W. Gellner/F.v. Korff* (Ed.), Demokratie und Internet, 1998, 127 ff.

*Schmidt, M. G.*, Demokratietheorien, 2nd ed. 1997, 170 ff.

*Stichweh*, Science in the System of World Society, Social Science Information, 35 (1996), 327 ff.

*Stradtmann,* Deutschland auf dem Weg in die elektronische Demokratie? 1998

*Tauss/Kollbeck*, Der vernetzte Politiker. In: *Leggewie/Maar*, Internet&Politik, 1998, 277, 283 ff.

*Trute*, Öffentlich-rechtliche Rahmenbedingungen einer Informationsordnung, VVDStRL 57 (1998), 216 ff.

*Trute,* Die Wissenschaft von Verwaltungsrecht. In: Die Verwaltung at book 2, 1999, 9 ff.

*Werle, R.,* The Impact of Information Networks on the Structure of Political Systems.

*Zittel, Th.,* Über die Demokratie in der vernetzten Gesellschaft. *Aus Politik und Zeitgeschichte* B 42/97, 23 ff.

*Zipfel,* Online-Medien und politische Kommunikation im demokratischen System. In: *L. Hagen* (Ed.), Online-Medien als Quellen politischer Information, 1998, 20 ff.

*Zürn*, Regieren jenseits des Nationalstaates, 1998

*Tommy Tranvik, Michael Thompson and Per Selle*

# Doing Technology (and Democracy) the Pack-Donkey's Way: The Technomorphic Approach to ICT Policy




## Abstract

We propose an anti-reductionist appreciation of technology (and democracy) by constructing the technomorphic model: a model based on insights derived from geomorphology – the study of landscape and landscape-shaping processes – which gives us the opportunity to analyse our technological environment as a „second nature". The technomorphic model avoids the single standpoint views promoted by technological determinism („technology shapes society") and social constructionism („society shapes technology") by setting out a coherent way of integrating these two approaches, showing that they are not as mutually contradictory as much of the literature on technology and social choice has led us to believe. The technomorphic model give rise to „Technology and Policy Characterisation": a method for mapping the democratic properties of technology and technological policy. This method is then applied in evaluating modern information- and communications technology (notably the Internet) and the Norwegian ICT-policy.

## Introduction

„The eye cannot sum up this complex at one view; it is necessary to go around it on all sides". This was the verdict on the new organisation of space represented by the Bauhaus' Dessau building, just outside Berlin (*Geidion* 1982: 497). The Bauhaus building (1926) is a complex of cubes, differing in size, material and location, and so arranged that they „interpenetrate each other so subtly and intimately that the boundaries of the various volumes cannot be sharply picked out. The views from the air show how thorougly each is blended into a unified composition" (ibid: 497). This architectural account is interesting because it casts a shadow over technology analysis: social scientists have not been able to study technical structures with the same eye for nuances that some students of architecture have brought to bear on housing. There may, however, be a way to remedy this shortcoming.

Just as the famous building in Dessau is a complex of cubes that must be viewed from different sides and from above to get a full and clear understanding of its architectonic design, so we need to analyse the mesh of technology and society. We need, somehow, to view the juxtaposed cubes that organise the space of modern everyday life from different sides and from above (and from below, Geidion forgot that!), because the technical and the social interpenetrate each other so subtly and so intimately that the boundaries are hard to discern. Hence, one view of technology and society – a technological determinist view („technology shapes society"), for example, or a social constructionist one („society shapes technology") – does not suffice to grasp the political relevance of technology. We need to analyse the blending of technology and society from more than one perspective; only then can we gain a more complete understanding of „the unified composition" than is presented by any of the traditional theories on technology and society: theories that have, for too long now, been engaged in an ontological tug-o-war: „What is technology – a social or a technical construct?" (ending, of course, with a draw, so that every theory, in a slightly haphazard and ad hoc manner, adds its bit of what was lacking before, while, at the same time denying the validity of the bits that are added by competing theories). This means, to continue the artistic analogy (except that we do not think it is *just* an analogy), that we must try to integrate an impressionistic and expressionistic interpretation of technology.

With impressionism, we point to our everyday perception and experience of technology: the way we go about using these artificial structures, and the way patterns of expectations, actions, power and control change in the process. Expressionism, on the other hand, points to the in-built forces – social as well as technical – that shape the properties of a technology during the innovation and design processes, and that are being represented (or expressed) by that technology. What we need, in other words, is to bend into shape the bridge between technological determinism and social constructionism, and between studies of the effects of a technology once it is here (i. e. impact studies) and the analysis of the conditions for a technology being here in the first place (i. e. design analysis). The way we propose to do this is by taking what we call a *technomorphic approach.* Students of technology, for all their differences, are largely agreed that technology is an artificial landscape, or a „second nature" – an environment that we both live in and alter – and they are certainly addicted to landscape metaphors (see, for instance, *Ellul* 1980; *Hughes* 1987; *Rip* 1998; *Winner* 1983;

1977). Our strategy in this paper is to take this technology-as-landscape idea even more seriously, and to reason that if technology really is a second nature we may have much to learn from the trials and tribulations of those who, for so many years, have struggled so valiantly to understand the natural landscape: the first nature. Geologists, geomorphologists, vulcanologists and other varieties of earth scientist, it is our hunch, are the best guides to the artificial landscape that, as far as determining human behaviour is concerned, is now largely taking over from its natural counterpart. It is by following them, we believe, that we can avoid the „single standpoint" and arrive at an anti-reductionist appreciation of the politics of nuts and bolts. In so doing, we can relate nuts and bolts to democracy – a relationship largely ignored by mainstream political science. Democracy, we argue, should encompass technology because technical structures shape the conditions for social life, and, since democracy is about giving the people that are doing the living the means by which they can decide how this living should be done, this principle must also apply to technology. Democracy-enabling technologies, as opposed to democracy-restricting ones (technologies that are not compatible with the values underpinning democracy), must therefore hold the ability to fulfil the conflicting social and political ambitions entertained by different segments of society. This is, of course, a rather elusive approach to democracy since we do not commit ourselves to one specific model of democracy. Troublesome as this may be, it nevertheless enables us to achieve our aim: to establish an analytical framework for reflecting on the democracy-technology relationship by focusing on some fundamental features shared by all the theoretical and real-life models of democracy.

Rather than speaking of the artificial landscape and its democratic qualities (or lack thereof) in general terms, we will focus on the most high-profile technology policy field of recent years – new information and communications technologies (ICTs) and particularly the Internet – in order to illustrate the usefulness of the technomorphic approach. It is increasingly important to get an anti-reductionist grip on the ICT policy processes because new ICTs – especially, the Internet – have a peculiar technical structure that is not amenable to conventional technology policy. The traditional organisation of industrial and technological policy, so characteristic of the post-1945 era – top-down, centralised and comprehensive programmes – we argue, is in dire straits because digital networks have a bottom-up configuration that is ill-suited to management from the top. Thus, we are going to analyse the policy impact of modern ICTs, leaving the study of the design process itself pretty much untouched. Our modest aim is to tease out the restraints that the Internet, as currently designed, puts on the ICT policy process. To do this we will bring together two theories of technology: one (Cultural Theory) which is a social constructionist theory, the other (technological determinism) which is usually seen as vehemently rejecting constructionism. These theories, we will show, far from being mutually contradictory, are united in their rejection of unconstrained relativism (typified by postmodern constructionism that insists that technology is what we make of it) and their combination gives us our technomorphic model. It also gives us something else: Technology and Policy Characterisation, which is the method we propose for mapping technologies and public policies in order to study the democratic quality of both. Here we will use this method to take a closer look at the Norwegian ICT experience. Those who are expecting a comprehensive treatment of Norwegian ICT policy, however, will be disappointed. Our aim is not to give a detailed account of this particular policy process but to analyse its broad ideological and technological framing: a framing that, in our opinion, is also relevant for understanding the ICT policies of other countries.

Our concern, then, is with how the Norwegian authorities are trying to unite technology with a particular vision of society and democracy, using ICT policy as the intermediary. There is, we will argue, a serious mismatch between the Internet technology and the ideology that currently underpins Norwegian ICT policy: a mismatch that makes that policy neither particularly feasible nor very democratic.

## Impressionism and Expressionism: Strengths and Weaknesses

Schwarz and Thompson (1990: 149) speaks of a "triangular interplay" between *patterns of people* (the different ways in which social relations can be arranged – e.g. hierarchies, ego-focused networks, excluded margins and so on), *patterns of ideas* (the different sets of socially shaped certainties – e.g. that nature is fragile, able to bounce back from everything we throw at it, stable within limits and so on – that differently organized people cleave to) and *patterns of things* (configurations of hardware – e.g. television sets, windmills, nuclear reactors and so on – that work, thanks to the physical properties of the components not being too far out of line with the convictions held by those who have created them and now operate them).[1] In an anti-reductionist theory of technology, each of the three apices makes its distinctive and essential contribution. Like the chicken and the egg in the simpler "two-apex" case, each does something vital that could never be done by the others, singly or in combination. The causal arrows, in other words, point both ways, along each of the three sides of the interplay.

1 This conseptualication of the anti-reductionist challenge is, of course, a long way from actor-network theory's insistance that categories – patterns of things, people and ideas (and the relations between them) – have no relevance because these elements (and the relations between them) are being deconstructed by the actors (humans as well as machines) who make up these categories (*Callon* 1987). The anti-reductionist challenge then evaporates by way of unfettered relativism (society and technology are liquid entities lacking any kind of "hard core"), and is replaced by post-modernist meta-abstractions (for example, that the heterogeneity and complexity of patterns of things, people and ideas allow for the meshing of these phenomena into one super-category – "the organic whole"). The SCOT (Social Construction of Technology) theory (see, for instance, *Bijker* 1995), however, does not address anti-reductionism the ostrich way (that is, by ignoring it): "technological frames", for example, are introduced to denote pools of techno-scientific knowledge that may push technological developments down specific paths. Unfortunately, "technological frames" are not themselves part of the theory; rather, they are uncaused causes that can be brought in to explain things when all else (everything within the theory, that is) fails.Another problem is that the SCOT theory relies heavily on a methodological individualist understanding of "relevant actor groups". In consequence, behaviour and the way institutional biases can lead to the inclusion of certain actors and the exclusion of others from innovation processes, are poorly developed ("relevant" actors often find themselves excluded exactly because they are "relevant". Exclusion is a mechanism employed by certain powerful actors that do not want to be bothered with other actors particular kind of relevance). It is therefore hard to see any consistant anti-reductionist approach emerging from the SCOT theory.

Delete one or more of these causal arrowheads and you have introduced reductionism, and it is by running through the various ways in which you can do this (there are six in all) that we can map the different "single standpoint" theories of technology and, more importantly, rid them of their mutual contradictions by purging them of the particular invalid reductionisms that each is built upon. Here we will do this with just three of them (the most influential three): marxism, technological determinism and social constructionism.

- In marxist theory it is the interplay of things (material) and social relations (the class-based structure of society) that moulds culture (ideas) so as to sustain a particular organisation of social, political and economic life. Technology, marxist theorists tell us, is social relations (in the same way that the chicken is the egg) and the third apex– ideas – is merely a „superstructure" that obligingly positions itself so as to justify and render „natural" the current state of the class-based struggle for control over the means of production. Ideology, in consequence, is an instrument for the alienation and de-skilling of workers, who then become automata in a mechanised production process that is geared to the protection of the interests of the owners of the means of production (*Braverman* 1974).[2]

- Where marxism deletes just one of the causal arrowheads, so as to explain what is going on at one apex (ideas) in terms of what is happening at and between the other two apices (things and people), technological determinism is doubly deterministic. Technological determinism explains what is happening at two apices (people and ideas) in terms of what is going on at the third (things). Technology, it is argued, produces needs and wants where none existed before, creating a culture of mass consumption, and human relations are then rearranged so as to facilitate the cost-effective utilization of that technology (*Ellul* 1964; 1980; *Mumford* 1971; *Winner* 1977). These effects of technology are not primarily a result of our conscious application of technical artifacts, it is reasoned, but are spin-offs of technological path-dependencies. Path-dependence, according to technological determinists, is a process where the initial choice to use a technology requires the subsequent commitment of massive technical, economic and organisational resources in order to build, operate and maintain that technology. As this process of technology implementation gains momentum it becomes irreversible, due to the sheer quantity of resources that have been committed to it, and *entrenchment* is the end-result: the technology has become an indispensable part of society and we cannot imagine life without it (let alone how life was before we made ourselves dependent on it being here). In short, technology has dug itself in in the midst of society (which takes the wind out of the sails of neo-classical economics: the view that a free market does not allow the choice of technology to be restrained by entrenched socio-technical habits).

2 Some feminist theories of technology have the same explanatory structure as marxism. Here, social relations denotes the relationship between the genders, and technology, being a predominantly male domain, stabilises these relationships by imposing a culturally biased view of what men and women are supposed to do: because men enjoy fiddling with greasy, powerful engines, they are equipped to take a job and earn all the money, while women, totally at loss in the face of machines, should stay at home making all the jam (see *Rothschild* 1983).

Entrenched technology (the things apex) thus defines the framework within which politics (the other two apices) take place by shaping and reshaping social life according to its needs. If, for example, nuclear power plants are the main suppliers of energy then the society is deeply committed to nuclear technology in its core functions, and other energy sources that may be more politically desirable are likely to be regarded as non-options because of the amount of re-engineering it would take to effect the switch. Technocrats, in consequence, are at the helm of modern society, because the entrenched nature of technology requires them to be there. High technology, to which we are committed whether we like it or not, simply cannot work properly without competent, centralised steering. The unfortunate result, technological determinism insists, is that technocratic technologies exert an ideological force, impairing citizens', politicians' and technical experts' abilities to envision technological alternatives.

- Social constructionism (see *MacKenzie* & *Wajcman* 1987; *Bijker, Hughes* & *Pinch* 1987; *Jasanoff* et. al. 1995) is almost the reverse of technological determinism, in that it explains what is happening at the things apex in terms of what is going on at and between the other two apices (people and ideas). In this theory, hardware is constructed on the basis of culture and social relations (even if, as many an engineer has complained, that basis requires that the moon is made of green cheese). Influenced both by the „strong programme" in the sociology of science (see, for instance, *Barnes, Bloor* and *Henry* 1996) and the postmodernist insistence that „there are no metanarratives" (*Lyotard* 1979), social constructionists reject the claim (central to both marxist and technological determinist theories) that technology has a substantive factual and technical core. The analytical distinction between technology and society is thus replaced by the notion of a „seamless web", with the borders between the technical and the social being seen as fluid and everywhere subject to interpretation. While marxism and technological determinism are largely focused on the macro-level – the analysis of the role of technology in society – social constructionism is more preoccupied with micro-level analysis: with what is going on in the design of a specific technology. The technology – its nuts and bolts – is then explained in terms of the configuration of actors and interests that take part in (and, in some instances, find themselves excluded from) the design process: interpretive flexibility.

As we can see, these three broad theory traditions are reductionist but, at the same time, each is managing to capture some important aspects of technology that is missed by the others. It would therefore be a great step forward if we could avoid having to choose between them, and this, in effect, is what an anti-reductionist theory of technology enables us to do. It tells us that we will have the „multiple standpoint" understanding – impressionism and expressionism – once we have a triangular framework within which none of the causal arrowheads has been deleted, and this we can do by combining the two theories – technological determinism and social constructionism – that, as we have seen, are virtually the opposites of each other.

In fact, we will be using one particular constructionist theory – Cultural Theory – because it, unlike any of the others, specifies how many viable patterns of ideas and of people there are (and, without that, we would have an unconstrained relativism which, as we have already argued, *would* contradict technological determinism). But why choose this particular combination of theories out of the three that are possible?

Since combining marxism and technological determinism leaves us with two missing arrowheads (ideas to people and ideas to things) and combining marxism and social constructionism gives us all the arrowheads but with two of them (people to things and people to ideas) doubled-up, we have selected the combination that gives us precisely what we are looking for: each arrowhead, once! And, of course, combining all three theories, which is the fourth option, give us redundancy, duplication and overlap way beyond what we need. We should stress that, in not choosing marxism as one of the theories in our combination, we are not ignoring it. All the arrowheads that constitute the marxist scheme are present in our anti-reductionist framework; so we have ended up with it (among the other theories) even though we did not start off from it (and, of course, we have not even mentioned the other three reductionist theories that are implicit in our anti-reductionist framework[3]). In some ways, this round-the-corner way of incorporating the marxist theory of technology is all to the good, because the development of ICTs (especially the Internet), and the way „information workers" are becoming independent agents with ever weaker ties to the businesses that hire them, do not, on the face of it, fit well with the traditional alienation and de-skilling hypothesis. On the other hand, marxists are right in bringing to our attention the social and geographical inequalities in the spread of new ICTs (in Norway, for example, there are at present as many Internet connected people as in India – about 2 million) but tend to entertain a deterministic view on the possibilities of bridging these gaps that may not stand up to scrutiny. Nevertheless, the marxist heritage is valuable because it has provided the first theory that, in any systematic fashion, analyses the inherently political properties of steel and concrete, nuts and bolts. Now, as we move from the „industrial revolution" into the „information revolution", this heritage is being carried further, in more appropriate forms, by technological determinism and social constructionism. What, then, are the strengths that they add to those provided by this marxist heritage?

The strength of technological determinism is that it focuses on *impact analysis:* on how a technical environment is lived by those who find themselves on the receiving end of technological developments. To understand how technology interferes with society, determinists argue, we must study how „real people", as they go about their business, are framed by a technology and how this framing gives rise to entrenched social practices that can be traced back to a technology's inherent properties, whether these properties are socially constructed or not. What technological determinism is saying, then, is that we

---

3 For the record, these are: people explained in terms of things and ideas (*cultural materialism*: see *Harris* 1980), ideas and things explained in terms of people (the „necessity is the mother of invention" school – best exemplified by neo-classical economics – that, for instance, explains the invention of agriculture in terms of population growth: see *Simon* 1981; 1996), and things and people explained in terms of ideas (*intellectualism*: see *Levi-Strauss* 1966).

cannot make sense of technology just by „sterile“ theorising (*Winner* 1991). We also have to dip our toes into the water of real, everyday experiences, trying our best not to have them bitten off by the complex patterns of technology-mediated social practices. The determinist argument, in a sense, is parallel to what the „new institutionalists“ are saying (see, for instance, *March & Olsen* 1989) because entrenched technology emerges as one important type of institution that imposes a social and political order relatively independent of the explicit intentions of calculating actors.[4] But determinists are unwilling to allow that some aspects of technological institutionalism, as experienced at its receiving end, may have been deliberately planned by those who designed the gismos.

Social constructionism, on the other hand, concentrates on design studies. The ambition is to open up the „black box“ of technical innovation and take a look at what is going on inside. Once inside, the determinists' claim – that all the contents are purely technical – is discredited. It is very much a question of social interests (see *Latour & Woolgar* 1986). Technologists, it is argued, do not search for „the one best technical solution“, but struggle to get their socially biased interpretations of what a technology should do to stick with that technology. Conflicts can either be settled through reasoned negotiations (which leads to a mutual understanding of technological designs) or one interest (or alliance of interests) is powerful enough to overrun the opposition. Either way, the impacts of technology on society are decided long before those impacts are experienced and lived by everyday people. In consequence, the constructionists argue, the phenomenological methodology of technological determinism (i. e. the study of how concrete technical designs structure peoples' social experiences and habits) is flawed, since it simply is not possible to pinpoint the exact cause of what is being observed. The determinist thinks it has something to do with the configuration of the technology, but the root-cause is the pattern of social interests that make a particular technical configuration possible in the first place.

We recognise the importance of the constructionist argument: we *do* need to understand how a technology is designed. Nonetheless, constructionists tend to overfocus on contested issues – usually the parts of a technology where uncertainty rules – while little is said about non-decisions (the parts that are not socially contested). In this way, they create an image of innovation processes as ground-breaking and isolated acts of socio-technical ingenuity. However, innovation processes do not somehow unfold within an uncontaminated bubble; they are, to a considerable extent, determined by pre-existing techno-scientific knowledge; by what is technically possible and by what are widely held to be the appropriate ways of dealing with a problem (*Cole* 1992; *Kuhn* 1970). These factors often force technological developments down trajectories (or chreods [meaning „necessary paths“], as they are sometimes called [*Waddington* 1957]), which means that

4 The autonomy of technology promoted by technology determinist readings, is a position where technology is understood as an answer actively looking for a question rather than the other way around. Technology, in other words, is the end and a use is the means. We all know that ICTs, for instance, are important but we struggle to grasp the nature of their significance: what problems do ICTs apply to? Although the answer to such questions may elude us for some time, the answer is often embedded within the technology itself.

a technology evolves into entrenched shapes and forms: forms that are palpably „there“, and not easily moved somewhere else. Even if some constructionist theories (the SCOT [social construction of technology] perspective [see Bijker 1995] and actor-network theory [see *Callon* 1987], for example) do recognise these objections, they pay little attention to the ramifications. Entrenchment, which constructionists tend to overlook (*Woolgar* 1991), exposes the shallowness of the interpretive flexibility argument because technology has the ability to structure behaviour and social relations, sometimes in unanticipated ways, that often become permanent features of social life, resulting, of course, in interpretive inflexibility: technology is not always what we planned it to be and there is not a damn lot we can do about it. Consequently, the most intriguing aspects of a technology are not settled in the laboratory among groups of technologists (or other interested parties) who are supposed to carefully plan its future social effects (this would need a sensationally accurate piece of social forecasting, rendering the social scientist, who is scarcely able to track a technology's effects long after they have happened, obsolete) but by the way technology re-arranges the social conditions for its successful use.

In social constructionism, therefore, technology is largely conceptualised as a non-institutional phenomenon, and a normative social actor vision is promoted (sometimes characterised as „the postmodern condition“ [*Turkle* 1995]), and our criticism of the unbound post-modern constructivism is parallel to March and Olsen's (1989) critique of mainstream non-institutional political theory. Post-modern constructivism is therefore characterised by: (1) *radical contextualism*: „the seamless web“ – technology mirrors its social context; class, culture, economic conditions, ideology and religion all affect technology but are not themselves significantly affected by it, (2) *reductionism*: technology is the aggregated consequences of social actor behaviour, and the possibility that technology in itself defines structures and rules for appropriate behaviour is not entertained or, at best, poorly elaborated, (3) *utilitarianism*: the view that technology stems from calculated self-interest, and the unwillingness to see action as a response to technology-imposed obligations and duties that severely limit the free play of social actor will and calculation, (4) *instrumentalism*: technological decision-making as a means of allocating social or cultural resources is the central concern (e.g. material artifacts as passive „texts“ whose meanings are „prescribed“ by social „narratives“), and scant attention is paid to technologies as „metanarratives“; the way technology-imposed symbols and rituals create meaning which social life is organised around, and (5) *functionalism*: technology as an efficient mechanism for reaching a state of social equilibrium; a view that denies the possibilities of maladaption and sudden sociotechnical change.

What we must do, if we are to build an anti-reductionist theory of technology, is retain technological determinism`s analysis of technologies as institutions that interlock inherent technical properties and social processes. But technological determinism, on its own, is too one-sided, because there are social actors and interests involved in technological processes that may bend the development of a technology in certain directions and not in others. So we also need to understand the social forces that are at work, and how these forces are related to socio-technical institutions. To what extent, we should ask, are material structures deliberately designed to realise institutionalised visions of what a technology should do? It is for these reasons that we turn to Cultural Theory. Cultural Theory brings in what determinism cannot give us: an institutional understanding of plural rationalities that explains why people prefer different types of technological designs and why people think differently about the same technology.

### Expressionism revisited: Cultural Theory

In Cultural Theory, technological design processes are explained in terms of institutions (or, to be rather more precise, in terms of social solidarities that, in varying strengths and patterns of interaction, constitute institutions). Cultural Theory argues that there are five (and only five) distinctive forms of social solidarity (forms of social solidarity are sometimes refered to as „ways of life" or, rather loosely, as „cultures" [*Thompson* 1996a]). Each form of social solidarity is characterized by a mutually supportive coming-together of a particular pattern of social relation and a particular cultural bias (or worldview). By binding yourself into one of these five social solidarities your cognitive properties (your way of assessing the physical and social environment) becomes subject to social construction – peoples` perceptions of what is real are filtered, this way or that, by their solidarities. Rationality, in consequence, becomes plural, because the sort of behaviour that will be viewed as sensible, and morally justifiable, will vary with the convictions as to how the world is and people are that are held by those who are doing the viewing. For example, the rationality of the autonomous, utility-maximising individual – the „economic man" model – far from fitting all humankind, is the rationality that accompanies just one of the solidarities: the *individualist* solidarity, in which ego-focused networks of relationships are supported by the convictions that nature will always bounce back and that humans are irreducibly self-seeking. But, if (to take the convictions that uphold the ranked groups that characterise the *hierarchist* solidarity) humans can be redeemed by firm and nurturing institutions, and nature is robust within certain limits, the individualist behaviour would be highly irrational (criminally irresponsible, even). And both the individualists' behaviour and the hierarchists' will be irrational to the upholders of the *egalitarian* solidarity (characterised by unranked groups) who are convinced that man is caring and sharing and that nature is so fragile as to allow no safe limits. All three of these ways of behaving, in their turn, will be irrational to those – the upholders of the fatalist solidarity (characterised by exclusion from all the other arrangements: ego-focused networks, bounded and ranked groups, unranked groups) – who know that there are no circumstances under which you can trust your fellow humans and that nature, for its part, operates with neither rhyme nor reason. The hermit – the upholder of the fifth, transaction-minimising solidarity – can discern the wrong-headedness of all the four desire-driven solidarities: essentially the stoking-up of ignorance when reason demands that we overcame it (for a full explanation of these solidarities, see *Thompson, Ellis* and *Wildavsky* 1990 and, more specifically, in relation to technology, *Schwarz* and *Thompson* 1990).

Each solidarity, moreover, needs the others to define itself against. Each is a way of organising and, at the same time, a way of disorganising all the others. In consequence, the distinct set of goals, values, and norms that defines each solidarity, and makes it particular, emerges and is stabilized in interaction with the other solidarities. Technological design processes therefore are played out in the crossroads where the solidarities meet and collide (four of them, that is; the hermit floats high above this ignorant fray). And because of this dynamic interplay each design process is unique, much like a classic football Derby: the teams are the same, the ground is the same, the rules are the same and the players may be the same, but no two matches are alike. If we place ourselves in the hermit's position, so as to get a good view of this never-ending struggle (though not, of course, of the hermit's part in it), we can distinguish three „active“ contenders – the hierarchist, the individualist and the egalitarian solidarities – and one „passive“ one – the fatalist solidarity – that seems to perform a sort of cannon-fodder role for the other three:

- *The hierarchists.* Social relations here are structured by prescribed status differences (asymmetry) and by the requirement that those at the higher levels behave appropriately vis-à-vis those at the lower levels (accountability). The rule-obeying bureaucratic model is an example (though, of course, any real bureaucracy will not be fully consistent with this model). Ideally, the hierarchist is committed to large-scale and centralised technologies that are very much in need of expert guidance.

- *The individualists.* Ego-focused personal networks (symmetry but no accountability) characterise social relations here. Personal achievement, not prescribed status differences, is the organising principle, and those on the losing end cannot expect to be looked after like the „deserving poor“ in a hierarchical setting. On the other hand, they do not risk being stigmatized as „deviants“ and are welcome to try again (equality of opportunity). The model here, of course, is the free market (and, again, the reality never quite conforms to this model). The individualist is committed to decentralised (preferably, but not necessarily) and profit-maximizing technologies that are likely to reward the best, brightest, and most daring.

- *The egalitarians.* Equality, not of opportunity but of outcome, is the „bottom line“ in this solidarity. Social relations are arranged so that everyone swaps seats with everyone else (symmetry) and those who begin to introduce inequalities (of status or of outcome) are brought back in line (accountability). Bottom-up grassroots is the model here (but in real life none of these outfits is as organisationally flat as it should be). Egalitarians, therefore, prefer small-scale and emancipating technologies: technologies that, so far as they can judge, are likely to equalise differences.

- *The fatalists.* The members of this solidarity find themselves on the outside of the structured patterns of relationships that characterise the three „active“ solidarities. They are on the sidelines of the classic football Derby: the place where they feel most comfortable. However, like compost in biological systems, this excluded solidarity plays an important role in social and technological processes precisely because it is passive. All three „active“ solidarities compete to mobilise the fatalists in support of their preferred policies: a three-way tug-o-war that gives rise to inherently complex dynamics that are very different from those that are generated by a simple (i. e. two-component) system in which those who are recruited to one position are directly pitted against those who are recruited to the other. And, even when they are not swayed, the fatalists alert those who would mobilise them to the pointlessness of devoting resources to things about which nothing can be done, and technological development, according to the fatalists, is one example of something we cannot do much about.[5]

The significance of technology, according to Cultural Theory, is clear-cut: since technology is so readily and so quickly entrenched, each of the three „active" solidarities, if it is to maintain and strengthen itself vis-à-vis the others, must somehow get its preferred design to stick with a new technology. The trick, therefore, is to get your social construction accepted by the other solidarities as the uncontested and substantive technical core. This trick, as a whole generation of policy analysts (and citizens) now know, can be pulled off by argumentation or arm-twisting or any of the other subtle techniques by which agendas are set, closures achieved and framings accepted. The trouble, of course, is that the trick only works, and only goes on working, if the technological design that the winning solidarity has locked us all into delivers on its promises: „Electricity too cheap to meter" in the case of nuclear power, for instance, „Homes fit for heroes" in the case of Britain's high-rise, system-built housing, not forgetting Margaret Thatcher's „great car culture".

„Marry a technology in haste; repent at leisure", all too often, is the lesson that is learnt by those who, during the whirlwind romance, had been cock-a-hoop at the trick they had pulled on the other solidarities. „If only we had had some way of knowing what it was that we were getting ourselves into", is the lament, and the penitents' woe is only compounded by those who belong to the other solidarities pointing out that they *had* known, and had been telling them that from Day One, only to be met with the suggestion that they go away in jerky movements! Trial marriage, therefore, is the Cultural Theorist's answer. If each solidarity, despite its subsequent lamentations, is still dead-set on tying the technological knot then the only way to prevent all these premature lock-ins – lock-ins that are increasingly resented by those solidarities whose technological preferences have been ignored (and, often enough, regretted by those who caused them as well) – is to somehow ensure that no one solidarity (or pair of solidarities) is ever able to dominate the decision process to the point where it excludes the others. Put another way, the solution is to ensure, through a continuous scrutiny of our democratic institutions, that there is never agreement on a value-free and substantive technical core: that the terrain is always contested (*Schwarz* and *Thompson* 1990 and, more explicitly, *Thompson* 1996b and *Ney* and *Thompson* 1999).

5 The fifth solidarity, the autonomists, will not be included in the analysis since this solidarity defines and stabilises itself by the deliberate avoidance of coercive involvement. In a sense, it floats above the fourfold fray, providing a place of renewal that people (under certain circumstances, for example, writing academic articles about the other four solidarities) withdraw to – to get a perspective on things, to recharge batteries, to figure out some of the great questions of life – before entering again into the zone of social and technological engagement. The Himalayan hermit is the model here even though the real life hermits always have some residual social and technological involvement (indeed, the last of the hundred thousand songs of the famous Tibetan hermit, Milarepa, was inspired by his accidental breaking of the clay bowl in which he cooked the nettles that were his only source of sustenance [*Milarepa* 1977]).

*Flexibility* – a technology's ability to satisfy several interpretations of how life in high-tech society should be lived (the Internet is a good example) – is thus the defining quality of a democratic and socially benign technology. But, and this is the whole justification for our technomorphic approach, it is not quite that simple.

Technological designs, Cultural Theory insists, are not *just* a question of social construction (and it is this insistance that sets it apart from other constructionist theories). A winning design must be physically and technically possible (which, of course, rules out perpetual motion machines for power generation, cold fusion, and moon-buggies with wheels that will give a marvellous purchase on green cheese) and it must prove itself in the functional sense of use (entrenchment).

Unfortunately, these crucial requirements – technical influences and entrenchment – though acknowledged, are not adequately accounted for in Cultural Theory. And this „unfinished business" also has implications for that theory's normative prescriptions: if some social constructions are non-starters then, in the negative sense of there being certain things that you might want to do but cannot, there *is* a technical core, in which case some of the terrain is not contested (or, if it is contested, it should not be). Though Cultural Theorists can claim that this wisdom is built into the fatalist and autonomous solidarities (for which reason these solidarities should somehow be ensured a presence in the decision process) there is more at stake here. The role and effect of hardware (the things apex of the triangular interplay) is under-explored in Cultural Theory, thanks to the emphasis that has been placed on social relations (the people apex) and social constructions (the ideas apex). So Cultural Theory cannot go all the way by itself; it needs a technological determinist underpinning (just as technological determinism needs a Cultural Theory underpinning) if we are to propose a truly anti-reductionist theory of technology.

## From Geomorphology to Technomorphology

We now have all the cubes we need to build a more complete theory of technology and society. Technological determinism draws our attention to the importance of inherent technical factors and entrenchment (i. e. the addictive nature of technology-mediated social practices), while Cultural Theory provides insights about social factors and flexibility (i. e. the way technologies can or cannot be moulded – within the limits of technical restraints – to satisfy social needs and wishes). What we still lack is the architectonic inspiration to juxtapose the cubes so that they interpenetrate each other to form a unified anti-reductionist composition. This inspiration, as we have already hinted, is provided by gemorphology: the study of landscapes and landscape-forming processes in the first nature – the nature that is now being ever more heavily overlaid by the second nature, technology. And geomorphology, it turns out, has already faced, and coped with, its version of the problem we have just found our way to: the integration of technological determinism and social constructionism.

Classical geomorphology was framed by the Huttonian approach (after the pioneer geomorphologist, *James Hutton*, 1726-79) and awesomely elaborated by W. M. Davis after the turn of this century. The jaggernaut of the Davisian system, as it was called, was reductionism. It was believed that an uplift land remained structurally stable while it passed through a series of time-dependent erosional stages (youth, maturity, and old age), characterised by a progressive lowering and levelling of plains towards a predictable and entrenched end-point (*Butzer* 1976). By the 1950s, however, this Davisian system was in serious difficulties. Diastrophic activity (the movements of the Earth's tectonic plates that were responsible for the uplift land being uplifted) and the the effect of climate, both of which had been neglected in the reductionist account, pushed their way to the forefront of geomorphic investigation (*Higgins* 1981). For instance, if the Greater Himalayan Range, thanks to the South Asian plate pushing its way under the Eurasian plate, is rising faster than it is being worn down by the stupendous erosional power of the monsoon rains that its uplifting has brought into existence (*Raymo* and *Ruddiman* 1992) then it does not make much sense to try to locate its position along the youth-to-old-age scale. Indeed, if you try to do that you will have to conclude that these mountains are very youthful and that they are getting younger the older they get!

The Davisian system, not surprisingly, was judged inadequate (not wrong, but far from being entirely right) and today landscape form and landscape evolution are seen as a function of the complex interactions between two types of processes: internal (or *tectonic*) processes (forces emanating from the Earth`s interior and manifested in phenomena such as earthquakes and volcanic activity), and external (or *gradational*) processes (forces shaping the Earth`s surface: soil and wind erosion, human activity, climate impact and so on). The Davisian system, of course, is still there, just as the marxist scheme is still in our combination of technological determinism and Cultural Theory, but geomorphology, having set off reductionist, is now firmly on the anti-reductionist track.

So the first lesson from geomorphology is that landscapes are shaped from the inside as well as from the outside. This means that, just as geomorphology focuses on both tectonic and gradational processes, so technomorphology should consider technical and social processes in the making of technological landscapes. In this second nature, the tectonic forces are inherent in the body of techno-scientific knowledge that must be present to make hardware work. These forces can be analysed in terms of technological determinism, because its main focus is on the entrenched social practices emanating from the technology itself. Gradational forces, on the other hand, are the external social pressures that shape a technology`s properties. Here, Cultural Theory provides an analytical framework for mapping these pressures during the design stages, and explains why flexibility of use is an important and variable quality of technical structures. Therefore, technomorphology – the integration of technological determinism and Cultural Theory under a geomorphic banner - treats this second nature in much the same way that Geidion treats the new architecture of the Bauhaus: as a subtle, multiple-viewpoint-demanding interpenetration of juxtaposed cubes. In this case, we have a tectonic cube (the inherent and irreducible technical properties) and a gradational cube (the social solidarities that are shaping the technology from the outside, as it were). And it is the subtle interpenetration of these two cubes that determines the extent to which a technology becomes entrenched (a major determinant of how we live our lives) and the extent to which it remains flexible (able to be shaped, this way or that, so as to conform to each of the solidarities' criteria for what constitutes a desirable technology).

Within this unified composition (and this, at first sight, is not easily comprehended or accepted) a technology may be high or low on tectonic and gradational influence (the Himalayas, for instance, are very high on both) and high or low on entrenchment and flexibility (characteristics that, in the first landscape, account for the incidence of „relict features“: features that are there because of certain characteristics of a preceding landscape that no longer exists[6]). And the act of constructing the artificial landscape is to be understood as a form of social architecture: a way of building society. And, just like the Bauhaus' Dessau building, if the cubes are juxtaposed in one particular way they cannot be juxtaposed in any of the other ways that might be conceivable. This, of course, is a long way from the „interpretive flexibility“ that is assumed by social constructionism; and, in the other direction, it is a long way from the one single concrete cube that is assumed by technological determinism.

The second lesson from geomorphology is that landscapes are shaped by a complex set of interrelated processes. This means that simple cause-and-effect explanations, the core-business (as we have seen) of most theories of technology and society, cannot get an adequate grasp on the complex reality of the technology-society relationship (in the same way that „which came first?“ explanations cannot say much about the chicken and egg relationship). Determinism analyses technology by contrasting the various tectonic influences (technical properties) during design and entrenchment, or by assessing how the size and ambition of techno-scientific projects result in material structures that are more or less likely to cause social dependency. Here, high-tech technology leads to deep entrenchment, while low-tech technology (including, but not confined to, tacit technology: „community architecture“, for instance, and the context-respecting interventions promoted by „intermediate technologists“) leads to shallow entrenchment. A high-tech and deeply entrenched technology pushes social developments down a one-way street, closing off alternative social futures (democracy-enabling technology), while low-tech and unentrenched technology does not narrow future social developments down to one option (democracy-restricting technology). Cultural Theory, on the other hand, analyses technology in a similarly pairwise way: the contrasted pairings of gradational influences in the design process (social solidarities) and the consequent impacts in terms of flexibility. This implies that technology is flexible or inflexible depending on the number of solidarities included in the design process. Exclusive design processes cause low technological flexibility: technology suited to the needs of only one solidarity (democracy-

---

6 Relicts are, for instance, climatic left-overs from a prior landscape that have effects on the evolution of subsequent landscapes (sometimes relicts may force themselves on landscape evolution long after the processes that initially shaped those relicts [climatic conditions, for example] have ceased to exist). Technologies too progress by including relicts from a prior state of technological development. This is usually referred to as backward compatability: old and new technologies are „wrapped around“ each other and form compounded polygenetic landscapes (for example, the Internet must adjust to the characteristics of the telephone technology. Most notably, modems are needed to convert digital into analog signals and bandwidth is framed by the capacity of twisted pairs of copper wires). The speed and direction of technological development is usually a function of backward compatability: is a new technology destroying „relict features“ so as to escape technological entrapment (Schumpeterian „gales of destruction“) or is its development hampered and guided by the inheritance from an older technology?

restricting technology), while inclusive design processes are more likely to produce high technological flexibility: technology that satisfies some core wishes of all the solidarities (democracy-enabling technology).

None of this, of course, is as simple as it seems at first glance. Unanticipated consequences of new technology and inconsequent anticipations (i. e. intentions driving the design of a technology that are not met when the technology is put to use) can never be eliminated, no matter how hard we try to design democratic decision-making institutions. Accordingly, it is possible that an inclusive design process may produce inflexible technology and that an exclusive one may produce flexible technology. Our point, however, is not to present a fool-proof method for enhancing technological predictability but to provide a humble tool for increasing the possibility of a better match between social needs and wants and technological development or, at the least, for avoiding some of the worst mismatches.

Figure 3, we think, gives some graphic clarification as to why our technomorphic model, at first glance, is not easily comprehended or accepted. Each approach, it shows, considers only one of the two kinds of forces that are shaping technology (technological determinism focuses on the tectonic forces and ignores the gradational ones, and Cultural Theory does the reverse) and each of them considers only one of the two kinds of impact (technological determinism focuses on entrenchment and ignores flexibility, and Cultural Theory does the reverse). On top of that, and this is perhaps more unexpected, each ignores two of the four permutations that *are* available within the limits it has set itself. Technological determinism ignores the deep entrenchment/low-tech technology combination and the shallow entrenchment/high-tech technology combination, and Cultural Theory ignores the flexibility/exclusive combination and the inflexibility/inclusive combination, all of which, as we will see, are quite common.

The reason for this double-blindness, of course, is the reductionism that, in different forms, is built into each of these approaches, and the clinching argument for developing an anti-reductionist theory is that it enables us to replace all this double-blindness with 20:20 vision. And, once we have that 20:20 vision, we can clearly see that technologies can vary in terms of four crucial characteristics, all of which have implications for democracy. Moreover (and, again, this is rather unexpected), once we have that 20:20 vision we can see that some of the democratic implications that *have* been discerned are not entirely correct. In particular, it is not entrenchment *per se* that is antithetical to democracy, but entrenchment in technologies with certain other charactersitics. In other words, things look very different as we go from the various reductionisms to the anti-reductionist framing.

## The Technomorphic Model and Its Method: Technology and Policy Characterisation (TPC)

The four variable characteristics – tectonic and gradational influence, flexibility and entrenchment – are interrelated in complex patterns, and it is their varying degrees of strength in relation to each other that decide the shape and form of a particular technological landscape (a more elaborate model for mapping these complex patterns of interrelations is presented in *Tranvik* 1999).

In this way, technological development is treated as an open-ended process: a process evolving within the „technology and democracy space“ that is defined by these four variables. The infinitude of points within this space means that, just as natural landscape-forming processes are unique events that produce unique landforms, so are tectonic and gradational influences intermeshed, in each technological design process, in slightly different ways. Yet, though each process is unique, some (those that are near to one another in this space) are more alike than others (those that are widely spread). So, by characterising technologies in terms of these four variables, we can put like with like and we can begin to appreciate the different kinds of unlike. For instance, if we take the simple high/low distinctions that are commonly used in the reductionist approaches (see Figure 3), then our anti-reductionist theory gives us the total of 16 kinds of technological landscape, each of which will have its distinctive implications for democracy. And it is this sort of scheme that we are trying to depict (though, of course, we cannot do it justice in only two dimensions) in our Figure 4.

Since the complex pattern of tectonic and gradational interrelations never repeats itself, unique artificial landscapes, each characterised by a particular balance between flexibility and entrenchment, emerge. And, just as natural landscapes in one part of the world have some core properties in common, setting them apart from landscapes evolving under different conditions elsewhere, so technologies that are shaped under the veil of the same chreod (analogue telecommunications, for example, the telegraph and the telephone) are characterised by some core features that distinguish them from other types of technologies. So Figure 4 is just a one-moment-in-time slice out of an evolutionary flux, and if we incorporate a third dimension – time – then we can visualise all the different lines of technological evolution threading their way[7] through this square-sectioned tubular space until they get to its front surface: now[8]. There is, of course, nothing we can do about where our present technologies have come from, but we do have *some* choice about where they will go in the future. Where they are now, however, and where they have come from,

---

7 But not always smoothly. To make maximum sense of all these threads we need to include the discontinous jumps – from one technological path to another – that sometimes occur when gradational forces switch from exclusionary to inclusive or when tectonic forces are suddenly demonstrated to work in ways not imagined before: North Sea oil structures, after Greenpeace's disruption of the Brent Spar disposal, for instance, Uniliver's programme to re-design its Frish lavatory rimblock in the wake of the German Green's campaign against it (*Schwarz* and *Thompson* 1990: 2-4), or *Paul Baran*'s – a Rand Corporation engineer – scheme to reinvent the basic architecture of electronic communication: a scheme that proved digital packet-switched networks (as opposed to old-fashioned analog line-switched networks) to be technically feasible.

8 This is also important because there might be a considerable time-lag between the design of a technology and its impact, so that the technology and the policy, during this phase of development and adjustment, change features (i. e. a value-dislocation on one or more of the four variables in the technomorphic model). Such dynamic and time-dependent alterations can be measured by „Technology and Policy Dislocation Characterisation“ (TPDC): pinpoint the location of the technology and the policy at times Y and Z to find out the speed, direction, and amount of change. „Relict features“ (i. e. backward compatability) can help us to make more precise predictions about the possible furure direction and speed of value-dislocations (what we call „prospective analysis“ [see also endnote 6]).

constitute considerable constraints on that choice. Hence the usefulness of the method for TPC: a way of lessening the likelihood of our committing ourselves to choices (policy) that have been ruled out by the present form of our technological landscape and the various processes that have given it that form.

The „technology and democracy space" of the technomorphic model is arranged by two dimensions. The horizontal dimension (ac) represents, of course, technological determinism, while the vertical dimension (db) represents Cultural Theory. The broken lines represent (very inadequately, because we are trying to depict four dimensions on a two-dimensional sheet of paper) the TPC coordinates employed to pinpoint the relative positions of different technologies within the space according to their values on the two design variables (tectonic and gradational) and the two impact variables (flexibility and entrenchment)[9]. By locating the positions of competing technologies, the technomorphic model gives us the 20:20 vision we need, because it forces us to ask if a technology is compatible with the values and intentions of democracy. And since democracy is itself an open and flexible institution (relatively independent of its real-life models: protective, guardian, participatory, etc.[10]) designed to empower its citizens, openness and flexibility

9 This implies, for instance, that even if a successful technology earns the value „high" on tectonic influences, it does not mean that it was the superior choice. Other technological options, that were the more technically sound choices, may have been available, but, for one reason or the other, did not make it. The characterisation of a technology according to the model is therefore relative to existing technological alternatives (if there are any). This also goes for the values on the three other variables: high or low on gradational, flexibility and entrenchment are relative characterisations: relative to alternative technologies (for example, the Internet compared to the radio).

10 At the heart of Cultural Theory is the idea that each solidarity generates (and is itself sustained by) a distinctive answer to the question „How should we all live together?" These mutually irreducible answers then translate into the different „models of democracy" that have long been familiar to political scientists. Hierarchists favour the „guardian" model (in which a political class, endowed with superior insight and virtue, is given primacy over public affairs on the basis of popular elections every few years); egalitarians reject deference and promote the „participatory" model (in which all concerned have an equal say in public decision making); individualists support the „protective" model (in which the tyranny of the majority is held in check, thereby enabling people to „carry out their plans"); and fatalists know that, whatever they do, the whole system is rigged by those who are not fatalists (see *Hendriks & Zouridis* 1999; *Jensen* 1999). Cultural Theorists (and others) then argue that democracy is an „essentially contested notion", and that only when all the models are present, and in active contention with each other, have you got it. From there they go on to identify the various criteria by which democracy defined in this way (and this, of course, is the definition we are using in this paper) can be measured (this is the unifying theme of the various contributions to *Thompson, Grendstand & Selle* 1999, and is most directly addressed in *Ney & Thompson* 1999). The Cultural Theory approach, however, does not give a complete and comprehensive account of all the different empirical or theoretical models of democracy (for a more elaborate account, see, for instance, *Held* 1996; *Lijphart* 1984) but manages to capture the essential features of the most influential ones. Cultural Theory, therefore, does not define democracy in a traditional sense. Instead, Cultural Theory propose a methodology for analysing the dynamics of democracy: a methodology where democracy itself emerges as a multi-directional process. This clumsy, muddling-through picture of democracy is fitting for us: modern ICTs, it is widely believed, challenge our ideas about what democracy is, and, consequently, force us to re-think institutional arrangements that we have taken for granted over the last 30-40 years. In order to better understand what is at stake here, a multi-directional approach is appropriate because the traditional models of democracy are now mobilised and pitted against each other. Therefore, our use of the term „democracy" denotes the process by which the very essence of democracy is defined: the really important thing is not how different models describe democracy but,

must be the defining characteristics of democracy-enabling technology[11]. Within the „technology and democracy space", there are, in principle, two types of technology that comply with these requirements, i. e. democracy-enabling technology (the upper and middle-right quadrants; high on openness, i. e. inclusive design process, and on flexibility). The other two types of technology (the lowest and middle-left quadrants) are neither open, i. e. exclusive design process, nor flexible, and we call them democracy-restricting technologies. Enabling and restricting, therefore, indicate if technology, to the best of our judgement, is more or less likely to empower the citizens (though, of course, anticipations may be inconsequent and technology may go places we did not expect). Thus, TPC is an instrument for analysing the interlocked relationship between technology and democracy: what technology should we choose to be determined by if we are concerned about the democratic implications of technological developments?

For a crude demonstration of how this can be done, we have, as already indicated, used the TCP coordinates to divide the „technology and democracy space" into four quadrants or main types of technology (see Figure 4). This carving up of the space into just four main types of technology results in too blunt an instrument to be used for a detailed characterisation. The proper way of doing TPC – the way that allows for all possible kinds of combinations of values on the four variables to occur – is by treating the TPC coordinates as Le Corbusier, the famous Belgian architect, treated the non-supporting inner walls of his dwelling houses: as having no fixed positions (what Le Corbusier referred to as „Le Plan Libre") with the exact location of a technology being where the two coordinates intersect. By treating the TCP coordinates as nonsupporting walls, as it were, we get, as we have suggested, a minimum of 16 possible value-combinations. These 16 combinations represent different technology and policy options (not all of which are available to us at any given time, of course), and it is by linking these options to democracy that we can make normative perscriptions about what technologies to choose (if we are concerned for democracy, that is; this linking will also guide us if our goal is to destroy democracy).

---

rather, the way we make democracy work on the basis of these conflicting models. In the end, democracy need not be specified lock, stock and barrel because it is the ambiguity that makes it democratic. Unfortunately, many political scientists insist on a clear, authoritative definition: „if you can't tell me exactly what it looks like, you don't know what it is". We, however, propose a different maxim: „if you know what it looks like, you can't tell me exactly what it is". So, because of the conflict-driven and multi-directional nature of democracy in action, no one stand-alone model can capture the significance of the democracy-technology relationship, and, therefore, it is necessary to treat democracy (and technology) as an open-ended process (see also endnote 11).

11 Democracy-enabling technology is, more precisely, characterised by three intertwined design requirements (also essential for the various models of democracy): (1) *agnostic* – technical structures should be neutral in relation to different social needs and wants; (2) *elastic* – they should facilitate the realisation of conflicting social needs and wants; (3) *reversible* – technical structures should be re-engineerable according to changing evaluations of what we think desirable. Even if most technologies that make up the fabric of modern society may be judged democracy-restricting according to these requirements, it does not mean that our societies are undemocratic but that they are not as democratic as they could have been if we had been aware of this being a problem. Indeed, it is the democratic culture of most high-tech societies that makes us believe that it is worthwhile asking these critical questions and confident that it is possible to rise to this challenge.

Nevertheless, our four-fold scheme, as depicted in Figure 4, is what we need for explaining the logic of our model (and for our sebsequent analysis of Norwegian ICT policy). The Internet, according to our assessment, would end up in the upper quadrant: a relatively high-tech, democracy-enabling technology (inclusive design, high-tech technology, high flexibility and deep entrenchment) that we would be happy to be determined by[12]; while cable- or satellite-television, for instance, ends up in the middle-left quadrant: a relatively high-tech, democracy-restricting technology (high-tech technology and high entrenchment, exclusive design and low flexibility) that we would well-advised to be sceptical about (assuming we value democracy in its various shapes and forms). If we stick to the Internet example, this means that: (1) tremendous resources are being invested in cutting-edge technology (high-tech technology), causing the Internet to become (2) an indispensable part of modern society (high entrenchment), but, at the same time, (3) different groups (social solidarities), with sharply conflicting visions of what the Internet should be, are involved in the technological development (inclusive design), which indicates (4) that the Internet can be put to many different uses (high flexibility)[13].

---

12 This is not to say that the Internet is a perfectly democratic technology or that everything about the Internet is democratic. As will be discussed later, the hierarchical solidarities is at a disadvantage on the Internet, giving the individualist and egalitarian solidarity a disproportional advantage (there is also the question of social exclusion from the net, see next endnote).

13 Many factors help to explain why the Internet is a large-scale, high-tech and entrenched but, at the same time, an inclusive and flexible technology. These factors include, of course, Moore's law and Gilder's laws (or, rather, technical trends) that account for the proliferation of increasing amounts of cheap computing power (that has fuelled the pc-revolution) and the proliferation of increasing amounts of cheap bandwidth (that connect computers to form networks and internetworks). Important as these trends are, there is another reason for our characterisation of the Internet as a democracy-enabling technology (or, more precisely, a host of technologies): its abstractness. By abstractness, we mean the unbundling of hardware and software which makes the physical layout of, for example, a pc independent of the tasks that this pc can perform. If armed with the right software, the pc can solve any problem or carry out any operation that can be expressed as a logical algorithm without re-configuring its physical parts. Pcs are therefore inherently flexible since software can be designed in an infinite number of ways (this is, as we know, not true for physical parts put together to perform a certain task. Even in software, some features may be too cumbersome to re-write from scratch and some of the code is hardwired, i. e. embedded in physical parts). The same goes for the Internet. The Internet is not a physical configuration of moving and spinning wheels and cylinders that must connect to each other according to a centrally executed, predetermined and comprehensive plan if it is to work properly. Although hardware is an important part of the Internet, it is the software (for example, the TCP/IP protocol suit or html, a format for presenting digital information) that makes the Internet tick. The Internet, in other words, is an abstract mega-net from which no physical topology can be discerned. This explains why it makes little sense to try to establish a central administrative, technical or political structure to oversee the network, and why many of these functions are decentralised. There is quite simply no need for collective and authoritative decision-making, because no overall re-engineering is required to accommodate a new type of use, and one type of use will not, in principle, interfere with any other type of use (some tasks may, however, need some level of coordination, for example, the Domain Name System). Decisions about utilization have therefore been trusted to the users which means that they are the driving force of the design process. This is also reflected in the economics of the net, increasing returns to attention (see also endnote 16), which rest on a simple maxim: „plenty is God and rarity is the devil". Increasing returns to attention imply, for example, that shared information is more valuable than monopolised information, and success will come to those that are best at sharing resources because they will attract attention that can be converted into new sharable resources that will attract more attention, and so on (see *Arthur* 1994; *Hagel & Armstrong* 1997) while

Now that we have explained the basic logic of the model, you can check for yourself whether we have done cable- and satellite-television justice by placing them in the middle-left quadrant. The lowest quadrant represents relatively low-tech, democracy-restricting technologies (low values on all four variables). POTS (plain old telephone services) is a candidate here: (1) it is not a particularly sophisticated technology compared to, for example, the Internet (low-tech technology), (2) it is not really open to re-definition (low flexibility), (3) it is dominated by hierarchists at the head-end (exclusive design), and (4) it is under increasing pressure from the Internet (low or, at least, lower on entrenchment than before)[14]. Radio networks would be an example of a technology ending up in the middle-right quadrant: relatively low-tech, democracy-enabling (inclusive design, high flexibility, high-tech technology and low entrenchment[15]).

In essence, the technomorphic model points out that a choice of technology is crucial to democracy because entrenchment (or determinism) is what technological decision-making is about, since we all want to be assured that the technologies we invest our money, time and effort in today will still be around tomorrow. At the same time, we should not be indifferent about what kind of entrenchment we settle for. It is, for instance, better to opt for a relatively low-tech, democracy-enabling technology (the middle left quadrant) than

---

earnings are made from, for instance, advertisement, membership fees, membership profiles (usage and transaction) and transaction commissions. Since the ability to create abundance is the name of the game, the design of the Internet is a dynamic never-ending undertaking. Each time a new user is connected to the Internet, and each time a connected person comes up with a new way to use the network, it changes slightly (or, if you manage to invent a new scheme that triggers increasing returns dynamics, the shape of the network can change considerably). As this happens all the time, closure and stabilisation, the processes by which a technology find its long-lasting shape, is not something that can be expected (although, of course, the crucial technologies underpinning the Internet have stabilised to a greater or lesser extent). Accordingly, the most significant democratic challenge facing the Internet today is the uneven spread of the network (both within countries and globally) and the need to equip people with the know-how for using the Internet on their own terms. And because an important effect of increasing returns dynamics is that „good things will come to those who have and bad things will come to those who have not", a new class of underpriviliged can emerge if nothing is done to address these challenges.

14 There is, however, no doubt that POTS and television have had a positive effect on democracy. Effective nation-wide organisations could scarcely have been thinkable without plain old telephone services, connecting members, raising support and coordinating policies, and television has contributed to the shaping of a national democratic culture. Nevertheless, POTS, for example, occupy a position among low-tech, democracy-restricting technologies because of their entrenched configuration relative to alternative ICTs (i. e. the Internet): the head-end station decides the rules and routines of use in an autocratic, top-down fashion. It is therefore necessary to make an analytical distinction between the technology itself and its impact on society. This is important because we can, within the limits of what it is technically possible to do, exercise control over the design process but not over the way different people decide how to employ a technology once it is here, and they cannot always anticipate the social impact of their own technological choices. Unanticipated consequences of technology, however, are not necessarily a democratic problem as long as the technology producing these surprising effects is not configured in a way that makes it easy for one group to effectively exclude all other groups from the process by which the decisions about how to employ that technology is made (as is the case for POTS and television).

15 The characterisation of these technologies may, of course, change over time as they develop (see also endnote 8). So, our charactication is just a one-moment-in-time snapshot of the position we think they occupy today.

for the high-tech, democracy-restricting alternative (middle-right quadrant) even if the preferred technology may cause us some practical problems that we could have avoided by choosing otherwise. However, most of the technologies that we find today are high-tech but democracy-restricting: technologies that are socially indispensable (we cannot imagine life without them), but there is not a whole lot we can do if we want to do technology our way. All the important decisions about how they can be put to use have already been taken elsewhere. Hence, technological determinism is all around us, everywhere we go (except in most of the academic literature on technology and society). This is the democratic crisis of high technology society (and the theoretical crisis in technology and society studies). But, even if entrenchment proves to be unavoidable for a wide range of technical, social and economic reasons (see *Collingridge* 1980), democracy-enabling technology may still be an option (indeed, the Internet demonstrates this). Thus, TPC argues for a policy of voluntary rather than involuntary technological determinism. The difference is analogous to Bob Dylan's distinction between a song and a poem: "a poem doesn't have to be defined, whereas a song must be defined. It must have a clear definition. I think a song is much more limiting than a poem. A poem is something open-ended and unlimited in scope. A song can't do that, just by the nature of a song" (in *Kaganski* 1998: 63). Like a poem, a policy of voluntary determinism is suited for picking technologies that defy authoritative definition. The chosen technologies have, in their very technical cores, the ability to be, in a sense, whatever the users interpret them to be[16]. Involuntary determinism, however, is likely to bring to the midst of society technologies with song-like qualities: technologies that are limiting and clearly defined, and cannot be otherwise (not without a substantial amount of re-engineering: i. e. writing another song). Therefore, the question of how to pursue democracy-enabling technology is a question of paramount political significance in a high technology society: is a technology suited for sustaining different modes of institutionalised social life? After all, creating a society that is able to facilitate more than one (indeed, more than two or, better still, more than three or, even better, since we should cherish the hermit too, more than four) visions of how life should be lived is what democracy is about.

The technomorphic approach's fourfold scheme enables us to get it both ways, as it were: to propose a consistent way of tracking the different and sometimes conflicting influences involved in technological design processes and, more importantly, to relate those influences

16 Path dependence, the mechanism that causes entrenchment (or lock-in), can be overcome by what is referred to as an optimal perturbation; a small change in one variable of the technological landscape that, within a very short time-frame, changes the face of the whole landscape. Predicting and measuring optimal perturbations is difficult: what variable must change how much to escape from one type of entrenchment to another (and better?) one? On the Internet, however, we know the variable and the exact amount of change needed: human attention and 16 bits per second! (or 16 ones and zeros, the symbols that all digital information is represented by). 16 bits per second is, according to psychologists, the bandwidth of the human consciousness (*Nørretranders* 1997), and the actors that slog it out on the Internet are trying to grab a hold on these 16 bits. Those who manage to do this successfully, whether it is government agencies (the hierarchists), competitive, web-based businesses (the individualists) or non-profit virtual communities (the egalitarians), have caused a lock-in and stand to benefit therefrom. This is the real nature of politics and democracy on the Internet.

to the concrete effects of technology where everyday life (and democracy) is played out. What a pity, then, that most theories of social construction (most notably, the SCOT perspective and actor-network theory) have retreated to the sterile halls of applied science („laboratory studies"), unable or unwilling to get to grips with technology where it is actually going on. The technomorphic approach, however, is able to press forward, while, at the same time, incorporating the valid insights that this non-determinist line of inquiry provides.

There is, of course, much more to the technomorphic approach than is explained here. For example, it suggests a way of speculating about the social impacts of technologies that are still under construction, so that policy makers and others, in the early stages of a design process, can make reccomendations about what can be done to avoid or to promote possible future consequences of a technology („prospective technology analysis" [see Tranvik 1999]), but the above will suffice for our present purpose: to take an empirical peek at Norwegian ICT policy. Can Norwegian ICT policy be located in the upper quadrant of the technomorphic model, which is where we find the technology itself? In other words, is the policy less democracy-enabling than the technology it is supposed to exploit on behalf of democracy, and if so what can be done about it?

**Timberrr!: The ICT Policy is Here**

Since our aim is to keep to the impact side of things – to analyse the extent to which Norwegian ICT policy is informed by the particular features of the Internet technology – we will not use the technomorphic model to discuss how the technology came about in the first place (though, of course, it is important that this be done). Leaving the design question behind, we can go straight on to discuss the match between the present Norwegian ICT policy and the Internet technology. By employing the TPC method we will reason that the policy process and the policy itself are democracy-restricting if valid social and technical concerns are excluded. And if the Internet is more democracy-enabling than ICT policy (e. g. facilitating valid social concerns that are excluded from the policy process) it is by letting technology define public policy that democracy can be enhanced – which is rather strange; we are used to thinking that it is the role of public policy to democratise technology – because then the social solidarities that take part in developing the technology stand a better chance of being recruited to the policy process. If Norwegian ICT policy is indeed less democracy-enabling than the technology, the TPC coordinates will place that policy in the middle-left quadrant (relatively high-tech democracy-restricting policy) or in the lowest quadrant (relatively low-tech democracy-restricting policy) while the Internet technology, of course, has already been located to the upper quadrant (relatively high-tech democracy-enabling technology). The first crucial questions we have to ask are therefore: who framed Norwegian ICT policy, how was it framed, and was the framing „innocent of technological realities"? Let us start at the beginning.

National governments (i. e. hierarchy[17]) did not take a serious interest in the Internet for many years. This is odd, given that the American government established the network prototype (the ARPAnet) that eventually gave rise to the Internet, and that the same government (through its National Science Foundation) was responsible for the Internet's backbone well into the 1990s. However, in the early 1990s, the ICT policy process gained momentum in Norway as well as in other countries. The ICT policy process was triggered by foreign developments: the Clinton/Gore-administration`s vaguely defined „Information Superhighway" initiative and the EU`s Bangemann Report (1994). These documents, in effect, changed the hierarchist position on digital networking from neglect to enthusiasm: a new social order for the next century was to be built on sand (the raw-material used to produce the circuitry of computers and the optical fibres that link them). All of a sudden, the Norwegian government (and other governments in advanced industrial countries) found itself face-down in paperwork hammering out „ICT strategies for the 21th century", mainly by copying the American/EU initiatives and adding a local twist (see The Norwegian IT Way: Bit by Bit, 1996)[18].

Framed in a hierarchical setting, it was quite natural that the „Information Superhighway", like the physical transport network it evoked, cried out for centralised and competent planning. However, much of the money needed to actually build this network was to be provided by the market, although the Norwegian government was ready to shoulder a greater financial burden than most other governments. It was also unclear exactly what kind of network the „Information Superhighway" was supposed to be: how, in detail, it should be built; what type of infrastructure technology was necessary (traditional copper wires, fibre optics, coaxial cable, wireless or a combination of these?); how should private and public actors work together to accomplish the task? The „Information Superhighway" metaphor was suited, clearly, more for ideological than for practical purposes: it was a device for trying to come to grips with the new realities of an emerging technological paradigm. But, before long, the flaw in the „Information Superhighway" ideology became apparent: bad timing. Why should anyone invest in a build-it-from-scratch system when a digital network (the Internet), stretching its octopussy tentacles around the globe, was already in place? Gradually, the Norwegian and other Western governments realised that the „Information Superhighway" was already here; indeed had been for years. But, to the hierarchist's eyes, it was in a deplorable state, because no-one was ultimately responsible for building, maintaining and policing it: no „officer-in-charge", no „chain-of-command". In short, there was no-one to hold accountable if the whole shebang did not run properly.

This problem of accountability, so central to the hierarchist's view of things, has arisen because the Internet was (and still is) built according to the pack-donkey's way of

---

17 Here, the four social solidarities of cultural theory are used as ideal types: not totally in harmony with empirical reality but, nevertheless, reflecting important defining aspects of, for example, government authorities' way of thinking and organising.

18 Extensive information about the Norwegian ICT-policy and concrete ICT-projects is available at <http://odin.dep.no> and at <http://forvaltningsnettet.dep.no> Information about county and municipal network services and web-projects is available at <http://www.ks.kommorg.no/html/informasjonsteknologi/html>

meandering along: a do-it-on-the-fly enterprise, following the zigzag electronic paths of least resistance, where multiple nodes of uncoordinated intelligence – not one huge brain – are responsible for the entire construction (for a more eloquent – and tremendously more negative – presentation of „the pack-donkey's way", see *Le Corbusier* 1987). This means that the Internet differs from other types of ICT (for example, the television and telephone networks) because it does not have a head-end station where the responsibilities for financing, building and maintaining the network rest. Hence, there is no central hub responsible for the filtering of contents and the monitoring and directing of traffic. All these tasks are distributed: it is the actors who, in one way or the other, use the Internet that take care of these things – usually without consciously coordinating their efforts. The Internet is therefore a „clumsy pack-donkey" system: it works exactly because no-one in particular is formally or de facto in charge of making it work – the socio-technical properties that qualify the Internet for a place among the rare examples of relatively high-tech, democracy-enabling technologies. The „Information Superhighway", however, was shaped by the „straight line": a comprehensive high-tech program that, like traditional technology and industry policy undertakings, needed centralised and top-down guidance. Accordingly, in its early stages, Norwegian ICT policy can be characterised as middle-left quadrant (relatively high-tech democracy-restricting policy). The problem, of course, is that, even if the hierarchist's obsession with expert control is well adapted to the „Information Superhighway", it is at a loss in the face of the considerably more anarchic world of the Internet[19]. Unfortunately – and this is our reason for the, at first sight, rather harsh verdict on the „Information Superhighway" – the „clumsy pack-donkey" Internet system is well suited for the technological commitments of the other social solidarities:

- The individualists take to the Internet because its instant, asynchronous communications seem tailor-made for personal networking, and because the Internet`s global reach promises an expanding market, largely free (thanks to the Internet's hierarchy-outsmarting features) from regulatory authorities, that is likely to reward the best and brightest (*Dyson* et al. 1994; *Kelly* 1998). The quintessence of cyber-individualism is represented by the entrepreneurs of call-back services: minute companies, like Telegroup and USA Global Link, that, in the early 1990s, decided to rent some switches and telephone-lines and go into the high-risk international tele-market, taking on the gigantic national tele-monopolists around the world with great creativity and success.

---

19 Consider, for example, the problems that traditional tv-rating companies (for instance, Nielsen Media Research) face when they try to establish a measurement standard for how many people are visiting different websites (these numbers are used by buyers and sellers of ads to pin down the price of ad banners). The hierarchical, broadcast-structure of television makes measuring audiences a piece of cake: the companies pull data from a randomly selected panel of, let's say, 5,000 households and project the viewing habits of all tv-watching households. This they can do because contents are selected at the tv-networks head-end station. The distributed, narrowcast-structure of the Internet, however, puts the viewer in command of content-selection, which means that it becomes much harder to project peoples' online habits since there may be as many „channels" as there are „viewers". Suddenly, the centralised control and manipulation of information seems to crumble, and consumer-centric measurement-tools, tailor-made for the Internet, are needed. The credo is: „Customise or Die".

- The fatalists are, quite naturally, the individualists' targeted customers: the ones likely to enjoy „infotainment“ (and pornography), and to pay anyone for saving them the trouble of having to search for the material themselves. Even if the fatalists seldom figure in the headlines, they play a very important role in Internet developments: the Internet will go where the fatalists can be swayed to go. The fatalists' interest lies in calming down rapid technological change by getting behind the technologies that they feel are most likely to cause path-dependency and entrenchment, because they detest the bother of learning to use a new technology every fortnight.
- The egalitarians, on the other hand, perceive this free-floating system of zigzag electronic paths as a technology that is likely to equalise differences, since it is designed to circumvent gates and gate-keepers: the mechanisms that, according to the egalitarians, introduce inequalities among people (*Rheingold* 1993). Among the first, and undoubtedly the most influential, cyber-egalitarians are the people behind The WELL (Whole Earth 'Lectronic Link): the San Francisco Bay-Area based cyber-community, that went online in 1985 (for an account of The WELL history, see *Hafner* 1997)[20].

It is because the Internet facilitates the concerns of these three solidarities that we consider it to be more open, flexible and democracy-enabling than the ideology underpinning the early ICT policy.

## Doing ICT-Policy The Pack-Donkey's Way

The paradox of the early ICT-policy process in Norway (and in other countries) is therefore that the social solidarity (hierarchy) least comfortable with, and least knowledgeable about, digital networking is responsible for the planning of such an ambitious endeavour while the other solidarities, which have used digital networks for years and know everything about the technology (especially the cyber-enthusiastic individualists and egalitarians), have been kept pretty much on the side-lines[21]. This, as we have argued, makes the ICT policy less

20 It might even be argued that the Internet is suited for the autonomists because hyper-texts and hyper-links facilitate surfing the Web, never settling anywhere, and, as a result, avoiding coercive involvement.

21 This paradox is further emphasised by the Internet's business model, „coopetition“ (or „c-commerce“ as some call it), in which hierarchical solutions are hard to spot. In reality, „coopetition“ is a blend of egalitarian „sharing and caring“ and individualist cut-throat competition. According to the Internet business magazine „Business 2.0“ (February 1999), „coopetition“ was developed by the „Sleaze Squeeze“ industry (online adult entertainment). For example, if you set up your own website (let's say, academic.sex.com) and put up a banner ad link to Sex.com (and 10 other adult entertainment sites), you earn a few pennies for every click-through. To make the relationship mutually satisfying, Sex.com (and all the other sites) will include a link to your website. Do not, however, expect a free lunch: among (and, partly, within) webs of interlocked sites, the survival-of-the-fittest is law. At closer examination, this is not as nasty as it sounds because the success of academic.sex.com depends on the network you are hyper-linked into, and your own success feeds new value to this network (remember the increasing returns to attention dynamics?). In short, the success (or failure) of the network facilitates the success (or failure) of individual sites (this may, however, cause controversy. So-called

democratic than the technology itself and the side-lining of these social solidarities has important implications: first, because the opinions of these actors carry weight. This is not to say that their words on this matter are politically superior, but only that government planners would be well advised to listen to their informed opinions before taking action. Second, the constructive engagement of the other solidarities will lend greater democratic legitimacy to a more pratically feasible ICT policy. Consider, for example, the furious debate over censorship and encryption (i. e. Western governments' attempts to combat Internet-porn and the proliferation of high-end encryption to Internet-users). This debate demonstrates that government measures, even if introduced to curb real problems (the availability of child pornography on the Internet and the use of high-end encryption by criminals [see, for instance, *Miller* 1996; *Seemann* 1996; *Denning* 1994]), have not taken due consideration of other rightful concerns – free speech and privacy – that many people think are so important that law-enforcement must take second place.

An inclusive policy process, where the social solidarities that are heavily involved in technological developments are also involved in public policy framing, would have brought to light technical constrains on Internet law-enforcement, and might, as a result, have inclined the government to propose measures that promised to handle the problems in a more appropriate manner (filtering technology instead of censorship laws, for example). It might also have led to governments reviewing their somewhat anacronistic position on encryption and law-enforcement[22] so as to better promote something they are equally concerned with – e-commerce – which depends on high-end encryption being available so that business transactions are protected from crackers and peeking competitors (an alternative to government control, is presented by the "Online Privacy Alliance" at http://www.privacyalliance.org. This is, by and large, the approach of the German

---

deep-linking, the pratice of pointing hyperlinks deep into another site – bypassing ad banners and other revenue sources – is, by some service providers, considered infringement: hyperlinks must be pointed to the front page). Die-hard egalitarians (like the website Password Universe) are, of course, trying to undercut „coopetition" by publicising the passwords of pay sites. Nonetheless, the logic of „coopetition" seems to regulate the relations between businesses and netzien organisations (for example, the British consumer group „Campaign for Unmetered Telecommunications" [CUT]). The global Internet industry is, in the absence of effective state regulations, increasingly governed by what can be conceptualised as „netzien compliance"; a consumer-centric policy of voluntarily adopted standards for business-to-business and business-to-customer conduct (mirroring the grassroots-oriented technology standardisation process. For an account of this process and the organisations involved, see *Lerdell* 1998). The reason for this growing netzien power is simple: Internet businesses are extremely concerned about what customers think and want, because of the ease by which they can surf from one site to the next. „Netzien compliance" is therefore a strategy for cultivating long-term consumer trust and loyalty. „Prosumption" (e. g. the merger of consumers and producers into one figure) is another compelling reason for this strategy. Since Internet users often partake in developing online-products, it may be the business with the smartest and most loyal „prosumers" that wins.

22 Encryption has traditionally been the perogative of the state. Particularly during the Cold War, the state authorities considered encryption to be of great strategic importance – the side that was able to convey messages without having the content exposed to „the enemy" would enjoy a significant advantage. After the end of the Cold War, the need for a state-monopoly on encryption-tools seems less urgent, and the Internet makes the proliferation of high-end encryption to ordinary citizens easy. Nevertheless, most countries have been reluctant to change their Cold War encryption-policies.

government). This might have satisfied the market-oriented individualists and gone some way to allaying the "Big Brother" fears of the egalitarians[23], leaving the government with responsibility for hammering out a legislative framework for supporting e-commerce, instead of taking heavy-handed care of the means by which market actors (and others) settle deals. From a government point of view, this solution is not perfect, of course, but better than the alternative that promises (1) that the Internet will be safe only for criminals (high-end encryption being available for those who want it badly enough), thereby causing (2) the law-abiding citizen to feel exposed to the „dark forces" still at large somewhere on the Net, which may result in (3) few, other than those equipped with high-end encryption (by definition, criminals), using the Internet for serious purposes: something that would lead to (4) the distinctly depressing conclusion that the policy of cleaning up the Internet has failed spectacularly (and it has!). Finally, this would amount to (5) a strengthening of the broad-based opinion that the government should stay away from the Internet altogether, and thereby (6) prompting even more resistance against government measures the next time around (and it did!). In other words, an inclusive policy process will leave everyone better off (even those included to begin with).

So, to summarise: the distributed bottom-up structure of the Internet does not fit the technological commitment of the typical top-down approach of the hierarchical solidarity very well. Nevertheless, from the outset, the ICT policy has been framed by the hierarchical way of doing things – the centralised mode of bureaucratic planning as embodied by the „Information Superhighway" policy – where all the ills of the Internet: pornography, encryption, privacy, fraud, etc., were to be curbed by making people accountable to state authority. The essence of the „Information Superhighway" was to capture and redefine digital networking technology by pulling it from the upper quadrant of the technomorphic model (relatively high-tech, democracy-enabling technology) to the middle-left one (relatively high-tech, democracy-restricting technology). It is not, of course, hierarchy in itself that is democracy-restricting. Rather, it is the capture of the ICT policy by hierarchical concerns, and the parallel exclusion of other rightful concerns, that make us arrive at this conclusion. But the policy of cutting off the Internet's life-support – by getting people to use the never-existing „Information Superhighway" instead – failed. In Norway, the government authorities seem to have realised this around 1997. By then, the writing on the wall was clear for all to see: hierarchy, thanks to the inherent properties of the technology, could not do the ICT policy all by itself. Thus, the question is: how well does the shaping of the post-1997 ICT policy measure up to these requirements? Has the policy, framed in the middle-left quadrant, been pushed into the upper quadrant where digital networking technology is located?

---

23 High-end encryption is also handy for the person (an egalitarian) who wants to send a politically incorrect message to his or her kindred spirits but does not want anyone else, particularly not the government, to pick up the „deviant" opinion.

## How The Pack-Donkey's Way Becomes A Straight Line

Those who do slalom know that a crooked line is much more challenging than a straight one. The pack-donkey's winding course, therefore, is more difficult to go down than Le Corbusier (op. cit.) makes out, because you need to do much more brain-work – many crucial decisions will have to be made and each of them, as any slalomer can tell you, may prove to be decisive (well, disastrous, in our experience) – than you need to when racing down a slope without making a single turn. A policy process informed by the pack-donkey's winding course, where the three „active" solidarities (within the limits identified by the technology) enlighten one other on the possible roads ahead, is the challenging, slalom-like policy of voluntary determinism, as defined by the upper quadrant of the technomorphic model. Has Norwegian ICT policy moved towards this position over the last couple of years so as to effect a better match between policy and technology? Put another way, has the ICT policy experienced a value dislocation on the gradational and the flexibility variables in our technomorphic model (from low to high on both)?

On the face of things, the post-1997 policy-development seems encouraging: changes have occured over the last two years. What is less encouraging, is that the changes have come about the hard, technocratic way: by painstakingly piling up technical evidence, report by report, and putting the individual pieces of information together to form a „comprehensive picture". Nevertheless, this learning process has, it seems, resulted in a shift of strategy. Two developments are striking here.

First, and as has already been mentioned, the Internet has moved to the centre-stage of Norwegian ICT policy, while in 1996 (when the first major ICT-policy document [The Norwegian IT-way: Bit by Bit] was published) the Internet was treated as one intriguing but not really important example of what was in store for us when the government-sponsored „Information Superhighway" got under way. Now, the „Information Superhighway" has evolved into a set of losely coordinated web-based projects: for instance, the „Administrative Public Service Network" (APSN), a project still in progress, that includes independent vendors and consultants, county and municipal authorities. The aim, of course, is the electronification of a wide range of local public service functions but, as is the situation on the Internet, the process of electronification is decentralised: choice of services to go online, technical solutions, implementation, standards for quality-of-service and, ultimately, financing, are questions that are left for the individual county or municipal authority to answer. A new web-based project; „Electronic Government" (initiated February 1999), is supposed to do the same on the central government level as the APSN-project does on the county and municipal level, using pretty much the same kind of decentralised strategy. By opting for the do-it-yourself-as-you-go-along-dammit! approach, government authorities are being encouraged to get onto the pack-donkey bandwagon, as defined by the upper quadrant of the technomorphic model: public web-projects are to be planned and implemented by those who know the topology of the local, institutional environment. The success of the ICT policy, like that of the Internet, is therefore dependent upon the aggregation of largely uncoordinated, local performances[24]. This is a far cry from the

24 It should be added that the delegation of responsibility for web-initiatives to the regional and municipal

„Information Superhighway" ambitions and reflects, on the face of it, a rather substantial change in ICT philosophy and an admission that the „Information Superhighway" could not be implemented as planned in an Internet environment.

What seems to have been going on since the early days of 1996 is that the policy of centralised, heavy-handed steering proved, even to the die-hard hierarchists of government departments, to be undo-able. The „Information Superhighway", therefore, never made much of a real-life impact but served as a cognitive and ideological tool for framing the early thinking about ICT policy[25]. Perhaps the most spectacular evidence of this failure was the closing down of the ICT department – The Department of National Coordination and Planning was its official name – in 1998; a decision which suggests that the indicated value-reorientation on the gradational and the flexibility variables (from low to high on both) has indeed occured.

The second shift is in policy rethoric. In the government's „The Norwegian IT-Way" document, the significance of ICTs for democracy is mentioned only in passing and the importance of web-based businesses is, at best, haphazardly analysed. However, the role that ICTs may play in promoting economic growth, employment and regional development in traditional industries is elaborated at length[26]. Hence, the hierarchy-doped structures of corporatist interests saw an early opportunity to impose their mark on this new and exciting policy arena. The relative neglect of „web-onomics" is excusable, since the high-risk web-entrepreneurs at that time hardly understood the new market themselves (and, as a consequence, made no money). But the failure to consider the democratic implications of new ICTs is rather strange in view of the fact that the Norwegian Parliament, in 1994, approved an information policy for the central government level stating that the aim was to enhance greater „democratic participation", and that administrative decisions should, in principle, spring out of a „symmetrical dialogue" between the citizen and government institutions (Proposition to Parliament, no. 1, 1994-95). The bandwidth of digital

---

level of government, at least partly, is inspired by a long political tradition of local autonomy. At the central level of government, the fragmentation of web-authority seems to have been aided by a fight between different government agencies over who should be in charge of the various projects. But, on the other hand, it is hardly likely that these problems of control and authority would have arisen had it not been for the distributed structure of the Internet itself (no one has, for example, suggested that the Norwegian municipalities should own and operate their own telephone and television networks).

25 One exception in this respect is the NIN (National Information Network) supported by the government. NIN, according to government agencies, is supposed to increase quality of life, enable growth in various industries and facilitate greater public participation in public matters, and it encompasses a vast number of network initiatives, for example, a tele-medical network, national road traffic information network, EDI, electronic marine navigation, national environment information network, information network for the oil sector, etc.

26 These possible rewards are further elaborated in a White Paper on „ICT Knowledge in a Regional Perspective" (No. 38, 1997-98) and an ICT strategy document for industry, 1998-2001. The perspectives here seem to be informed, to a substantial extent, by the EU's White Paper on „Growth, Competitiveness, Employment: The Challenges and Ways Forward Into the 21st Century" (1994), while the Clinton/Gore initiative seems to have influenced the earlier documents dealing with the „Information Superhighway", for example, „The IT-based Infrastructure in Norway – Status and Challenges" (1994).

networking systems, be it the elusive „Information Superhighway" or the Internet, made such a hybrid of egalitarian deliberation and open-access individualist decision-making technically feasible. Nevertheless, little emphasis was initially put on these questions.

Despite these early shortcomings, it has, over the last couple of years, been fashionable to elaborate on the ramifications of the Internet for democracy. This change in ICT rethoric is particularly striking when one looks at the main concerns of the central government's administrative policy. Here, the three „active" solidarities end up with about equal influence (see Proposition to Parliament, no. 1, 1998-1999), and the government seems to have learned how to race down a winding slope:

- Hierarchists are assured that government involvement and accountability are central in achieving a smoothly running and flexible public sector. The pace of public sector use of ICTs is not going to be set by market developments alone, but will, in principle, be decided by government agencies.
- Individualists will be happy to see the emphasis on market involvement in the implementation of ICT projects in the public sector (for example, by extensive out-sourcing of certain support services) and the commitment to individualised, two-way public informatisation.
- Egalitarians may take comfort in the government's plan to adapt its routines to the needs and wishes of the citizens by developing ICT-services for facilitating participatory-oriented administrative systems and so-called „collaborative learning processes".

Of course, this type of political accounting does not only have up-sides. In a policy process based on checks-and-balances of interests, the down-sides too must, in principle, be equally divided between the solidarities. With the administrative policy, there seems, at first glance, to be a nice balance of down-sides: the hierarchists give up their self-proclaimed monopoly on a valid interpretation of ICTs and democracy, the individualists agree to some government intervention even if the Internet promises a free-floating market, and the egalitarians must get used to the fact that important decisions will still be made at the crossroads between goverment and market. These developments seems to strengthen what we suggested above: Norwegian ICT policy is being dislocated from the middle-left quadrant of our technomorphic model towards the upper one. The trouble, however, is that it is not as simple as that; we need to take a second look at how these promises are followed up in practice.

After having taken that second look, the suggested dislocation of ICT policy within the „technology and democracy space" is largely confined to web-projects and to the public administrative policy, while other important ICT policy areas are still dominated by the hierarchist way of doing things, partially in alliance with the individualists. The already mentioned ASPN-project and „Electronic Government" are examples of this alliance. Here, market actors are allowed a greater say in the planning, implementation and maintenance of public service networks, while bottom-up, grassroots inputs are supposed to adapt to the solutions chosen by the market and condoned by local or central authorities. It is therefore tempting to say that the rather decentralised nature of these projects is an effect of web-based industry becoming more closely integrated into the ICT policy process than before and convincing the government that a more low-key and market-oriented approach is better suited to technological realities. The egalitarians' concerns, though given space in some policy-documents, seem to amount to little more than „stolen rethoric“: the deceptive use of egalitarian arguments to lend the policy an air of democratic inclusiveness. The neglect of egalitarian arguments, it may be argued, is an unanticipated consequence that regularly occurs as the policy moves from the drawing-board to practical implementation and does not reflect initial intentions. Maybe so, but our point is simply that – whatever the cause might be – the end-result is insensitivity towards significant social concerns.

Market and government – the „unholy alliance“ as far as the egalitarians are concerned – are also heavily represented in the newly-formed „Joint Forum for E-Commerce“, even though it is supposed to decide on issues on which the egalitarians have particularly strong views: for example, consumer rights and privacy[27]. Furthermore, the ICT education policy is tailor-made for the needs of traditional or web-based industries, and it goes without saying that the ICT industrial policy is shaped by more of the same concerns. However, on one important issue, the IT-Fornebu project (a plan to locate the most significant ICT-related research and development activities in one place: the now superceded Oslo Airport), the individualists are, as things are going at the moment, completely by-passed. According to a majority in Parliament (the right-wing Progress Party and the Labour Party), IT-Fornebu needs centralised planning and bureaucratic solutions if it is to get off the ground. For example, the responsibility for the project is to be allocated to one small group of investors – who, by and large, know little about the ICT-business – and, as things start moving, the „real“ ICT companies are supposed to follow suit. The plan has been met with much head-shaking and bewilderment. It is claimed to be old-fashioned, market-averse, and not in line with the Internet's potential to decentralise research, development and production facilities. In short, money down the drain. Whether these complaints are correct (as we believe they are) or not, is not so important here. The point is that a policy process based on the exclusion of those the technology is inherently benign towards, spells trouble, because democracy, as well as technological reality, has been suspended.

This means that, despite some promising changes in policy, the straight line is still preferred over the pack-donkey's way: the practical policy is still mostly based on a hierarchist understanding of democracy and technology: the belief that all types of technology programs need to be framed in a top-down and centralised fashion if they are to promote economic growth, employment and good (i. e. deferential) citizenship. The irony is that

27 Grassroots-based consumer organisations, for sure, will wish to have a say in this process, and consumer rights and privacy have traditionally been regulated in favour of the citizens. In the wake of the Internet, however, there is a stronger pressure from industry to relax on consumer and privacy legislation to facilitate the capture of usage and transaction profiles needed to customise net services (steps in this direction are outlined in a White Paper on „Electronic Commerce and Business Administration“ [No. 41, 1998-99]). This upsets the levelling-crazy egalitarians because such measures will, in their minds, expose people to market dynamics: forces that introduce inequalities among people. „Netzien compliance“ (see endnote 17) may prove to be a workable compromise because the individual user may, according to this scheme, oversee the utilization of his/her own usage and transaction profiles.

digital networks, resting in the upper quadrant of the model, already promise a democratic and productive technology but the policy itself, because it is locked-in by a limited vision of what technology and democracy should be, is both democracy-restricting and innocent of technological realities. But, as we have argued, democracy and technology *can* be brought back into the process, if we are aware of the mismatches and of what we can and cannot do about them. This, we hasten to add, does not imply that hierarchy can play no constructive role vis-à-vis the Internet and other modern ICT. Providing marginalised groups (the elderly, low-income groups, ethnic minorities, etc.) with access to the Internet, facilitating ICT-education, crafting a legislative framework for e-commerce, and promoting policies for bridging the technological gaps between North and South and West and East, are issues where hierarchy can and indeed must be centre-stage.

## The Technomorphic Approach: What's Hot (And What's Not)?

The hottest thing about the technomorphic approach is that it analyses technology as a man-made second nature by proposing an anti-reductionist approach to technology. Artificial landscapes, this approach suggests, are, in principle, shaped by the same sorts of forces as shape natural landscapes – forces emanating from within (i. e. the hard-core technical and scientific knowledge that makes the gismos work) and forces pushing themselves in the from the outside (i. e. the social actors that take part in, or find themselves excluded from, technological processes). By using technomorphology it is possible to map these influences during the design stages and to make the vital connection to the impact of technology on society, thanks to the realisation that artificial landscapes, like natural landscapes, evolve into shapes and forms that are more or less flexible and entrenched. What is not so hot, is that the technomorphic approach is based on already established theory: geomorphology, technological determinism and Cultural Theory („old wine, new bottles", the cynic would say), but that is also why it is anti-reductionist (and that *is* hot!).

In this essay, we have only done technomorphology and „Technology and Policy Characterisation" half-way. We have analysed the broad ideological and technological framing of Norwegian ICT policy in order to understand the mismatches between the ideological bias of the policy and the technological bias of these new ICTs, particularly the most important one: the Internet. We have not, however, made any attempt to analyse the compelling social and technical factors shaping the peculiar technological bias of the Internet (this we will leave for another day). Nevertheless, the analysis shows that ICT policy and the technology, while moving in the same direction, are doing so at different paces: the policy is held back by the „Information Superhighway"-thinking of the middle-left quadrant of the technomorphic model (relatively high-tech, democracy-restricting policy) while digital networking technology is, at an accelerating pace, pulled to the upper quadrant (relatively high-tech, democracy-enabling technology). Our conclusions are therefore: (1) that the bottom-up and distributed configuration of important ICTs (notably, the Internet) cries out for the inclusion of individualists and egalitarians in the policy process: the solidarities best equipped to formulate a technically feasible ICT policy (an ICT policy that is only modestly informed by technological realities, has, in the long run, little chance of success) and (2) that, if a technological policy is to command democratic legitimacy, it must be open to inputs from the people that the policy is supposed to apply to. If not, the cyber-literate individualists and egalitarians are unlikely to comply with government policy, and they already harbour the technical means to undermine the efforts of the state. In both these respects, and despite some encouraging changes in strategy, the Norwegian ICT policy has some distance to go.

## References


*Arthur, Brian W.* (1994): Increasing Returns and Path Dependence in the Economy. Ann Arbor: University of Michigan Press.

*Barnes, Barry, David Bloor & John Henry* (1996): Scientific Knowledge: a Sociological Analysis. London: Athlone.

*Bijker, Wiebe E.* (1995): Of Bicycles, Bakelites and Bulbs. Towards a Theory of Sociotechnical Change. Cambridge, MA: The MIT Press.

*Bijker, Wiebe E., Thomas P. Hughes & Trevor J. Pinch* (eds.) (1987): The Social Construction of Technological Systems. New Directions in the Sociology and History of Technology. Cambridge, MA and London: The MIT Press.

*Braverman, Harry* (1974): Labor and Monopoly Capital. The Degradation of Work in the Twentieth Century. New York: Monthly Review Press.

Business 2.0, February 1999.

*Butzer, Karl W.* (1976): Geomorphology From the Earth. New York: Harper & Row Publishers.

*Callon, Michel* (1987): „Society in the Making: The Study of Technology as a Tool for Sociological Analysis". In: *Wiebe E. Bijker, Thomas P. Hughes & Trevor J. Pinch* (eds.) op.cit.

*Cole, Stephen* (1992): Making Science: Between Nature and Society. Cambridge, MA: The Harvard University Press.

*Collingridge, David* (1980): The Social Control of Technology. London: Frances Pinter.

*Denning, Dorothy E.* (1994): Encryption and Law Enforcement. Available at http://guru.cosc.georgetown.edu/~denning/crypto/Future.html

*Dyson, Esther, George Gilder, George Keyworth & Alvin Toffler* (1994): Cyberspace and the American Dream: A Magna Carta for the Knowledge Age. Release 1.2, The Progress and Freedom Foundation, Washington, D.C. Available at http://www.townhall.com/pff/position.html

*Ellul, Jacques* (1980): The Technological System. Translated by Joachim Neugroschel. New York: Continuum.

*Ellul, Jacques* (1964): The Technological Society. Translated by John Wilkinson. New York: Vintage Books.

*Geidion, Sigfreid* (1982) Space, Time and Architecture. The Growth of a New Tradition. Fifth edition. Cambridge, MA: Harvard University Press.

*Hafner, Katie* (1997): „The World's Most Influential Online Community (And It's Not AOL)". In: *Wired* 5.05.

*Hagel, John & Arthur G. Armstrong* (1997): Net Gain. Expanding Markets Through Virtual Communities. Boston, Mass.: Harvard Business School Press.

*Harris, Marvin* (1980): Cultural Materialism: The Struggle for a Science of Culture. New York: Vintage Books.

*Held, David* (1996): Models of Democracy. Cambridge: Polity Press.

*Higgins, Charles G.* (1981): „Theories of Landscape Development. A Perspective". In: *Wilton N. Melhorn & Ronald C. Flemal* (eds.): Theories of Landform Development. London: George Allen and Unwin.

*Hughes, Thomas P.* (1987): „The Evolution of Large Technological Systems". In: *Wiebe E. Bijker, Thomas P. Hughes & Trevor J. Pinch* (eds.): The Social Construction of Technological Systems. New Directions in the Sociology and History of Technology. Cambridge, MA and London: The MIT Press.

*Jasanoff, Sheila, Gerald E. Markle, James C. Patersen & Trevor J. Pinch* (eds.) (1995): Handbook in Science and Technology Studies. Thousand Oaks, London & New Delhi: Sage Publications.

*Jensen, Lotte* (1999): „Images of Democracy in Danish Social Housing". In: Michael Thompson, Gunnar Grendstand & Per Selle (eds.): Cultural Theory as Political Science. London: Routledge.

*Kelly, Kevin* (1998): New Rules for the New Economy. 10 Radical Strategies for a Connected World. New York: Viking Penguin.

*Kaganski, Serge* (1998): „An Interview With Bob Dylan". In: *MOJO*, February 1998.

*Kuhn, Thomas S.* (1970): The Structure of Scientific Revolutions. Chicago: University of Chicago Press.

*Latour, Bruno & Steve Woolgar* (1986): Laboratory Life: The Construction of Scientific Facts. Princeton, NJ: Princeton University Press.

*Le Corbusier* (1987): The City of Tomorrow And Its Planning. Translated by Frederick Etchells. New York: Dover Publications.

*Lerdell, David* (1998): Organising the Internet. The Evolvement of Order. Paper presented at the SCANCOR conference „Samples of the Future", Stanford University, 20-22 September 1998.

*Lèvi-Strauss, Claude* (1966): The Savage Mind. Chicago: Chicago University Press.

*Lijphart, Arend* (1984): Democracies: Patterns of Majoritarian and Consensus Government in Twenty-One Countries. New Haven, Conn.: Yale University Press.

*Lyotard, J-F* (1979): La Condition Postmoderne: Rapport sur le Savoir. Paris: Les Editions de Minuit.

*MacKenzie, Donald & Judy Wajcman* (eds.) (1987): The Social Shaping of Technology. How the Refrigerator Got Its Hum. Milton Keynes: Open University Press.

*March, James G. & Johan P. Olsen* (1989): Rediscovering Institutions. The Organisational Basis of Politics. New York & London: The Free Press & Collier Macmillan Publishers.

*Milarepa* (1977): The Hundred Thousand Songs of Milarepa. Translated by Garma C. C. Chang (2 volumes). Boulder, Colorado & London: Shambhala Publications.

*Miller, Steven E.* (1996): Civilizing Cyberspace: Policy, Power, and the Information Superhighway. New York: ACM Press.

*Mumford, Lewis* (1971): The Pentagon of Power. London: Secker & Warburg.

*Ney, Stephen & Michael Thompson* (1999): „Consulting the Frogs". In Michael Thompson, Gunnar Grendstad & Per Selle (eds.): Cultural Theory as Political Science. London: Routledge.

*Nørretranders, Tor* (1997) Stedet som ikke er. Fremtidens nærvær, netvær og Internet. Copenhagen: Aschehoug.

*Raymo, M. E. & W. F. Ruddiman* (1992): „Tectonic Forcing of Late Cenozoic Climate". In: *Nature*, 359, 117-122.

*Rheingold, Howard* (1993): The Virtual Community: Homesteading on the Electronic Frontier. Reading, MA: Addison-Wesley.

*Rothschild, Joan* (ed.) (1983): Machina Ex Dea. Feminist Perspectives on Technology. New York: Pergamon Press.

*Seemann, Luke* (1996): Keys to Secret Drawers: The Clipper Chip and Key Escrow Encryption. Available at http://www.stardot.com/~lukeseem/j202/essay.html

*Schwarz, Michiel & Michael Thompson* (1990): Divided We Stand. Redefining Politics, Technology and Social Choice. Philadelphia: University of Pennsylvania Press.

*Simon, Julian* (1996): The Ultimate Resource 2. Princeton, NJ: Princeton University Press.

*Simon, Julian* (1981): The Ultimate Resource. Oxford: Martin Robinson.

*Thompson, Michael* (1999): Global Networks and Local Cultures: What Are The Mismatches And What Can Be Done About Them? Paper presented at the Global Networks and Local Values Symposium 1, 18.-21.02 1999 in Dresden/Germany.

*Thompson, Michael, Gunnar Grendstad & Per Selle* (eds.) (1999): Cultural Theory as Political Science. London: Routledge.

*Thompson, Michael* (1996a): Inherent Relationality. An Anti-Reductionist Approach to Institutions. Report No. 9608, The Norwegian Research Centre in Organisation and Management, University of Bergen.

*Thompson, Michael* (1996b): Social Complexity and the Design Process. A discussion paper prepared for The Design Council. London: The Musgrave Institute.

*Thompson, Michael, Richard Ellis & Aaron Wildavsky* (1990): Cultural Theory. Boulder, Colo.: Westview Press.

*Tranvik, Tommy* (1999): Technomorphology: Explaining Railway Accidents And The Rest Of Technology. Paper submitted for the workshop: Plural Rationality and Policy Analysis, the ECPR Joint Sessions of Workshops, Mannheim/Germany, 27.-31.03 1999.

*Turkle, Sherry* (1995): Life on the Screen. Identity in the Age of the Internet. New York: Simon & Schuster.

*Waddington, C.H.* (1957): The Strategy of the Genes. New York: George Allen and Unwin.

*Winner, Langdon* (1991): Upon Opening the Black Box and Finding It Empty. Working paper no. 44. University of Oslo: Centre for Technology and Human Values.

*Winner, Langdon* (1977): Autonomous Technology. Technics-out-of-control as a Theme in Political Thought. Cambridge, MA: The MIT Press.

*Woolgar, Steve* (1991): „The Turn to Technology in Social Studies of Science". In: *Science, Technology and Human Values*, vol. 16, pp 20-50.

**Official documents**

Electronic Commerce and Business Administration. White Paper, no. 41, 1998-99. Prepared by The Norwegian Department for Trade and Industry.

Europe and the Global Information Society (the Bangemann-report). Prepared for the European Council's meeting on Korfu, 24.-25.06 1994.

Growth, Competitiveness, Employment: The Challenges and Ways Forward Into the 21st Century. White Paper for the European Union, 1994.

ICT Strategy Document for Industry, 1998-2001. Prepared by the Norwegian Department for Trade and Industry.

ICT Knowledge in a Regional Perspective. White Paper, no. 38, 1997-98. Prepared by the Norwegian Department for Trade and Industry.

The IT-Based Information Infrastructure in Norway – Status and Challenges. Report prepared by The Inter-Departemental Workgroup for the Planning and Monitoring of Public Sector Use of Information Technology, 1994.

The Norwegian IT-Way: Bit by Bit. The overall ICT strategy document. Prepared by the Social Democratic Cabinet, 1996.

Proposition to Parliament, no. 1, 1998-99

Proposition to Parliament, no. 1, 1994-95.

## Figures

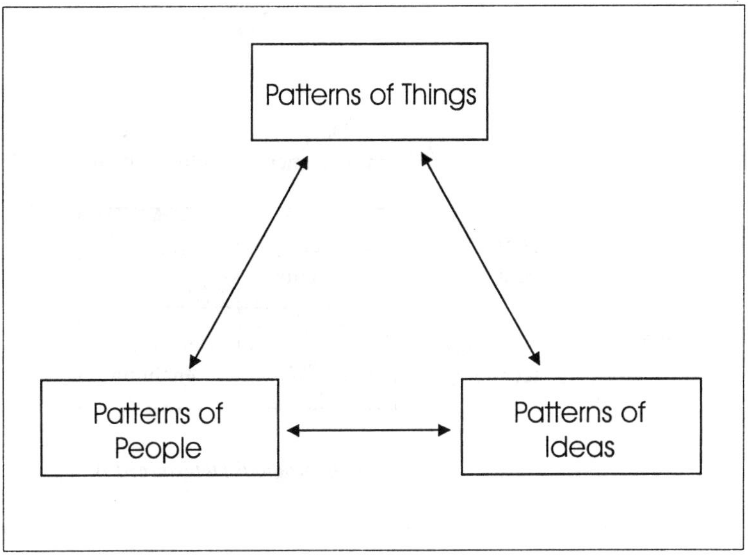


*Figure 1: The Triangular (and Anti-Reductionist) Interplay*

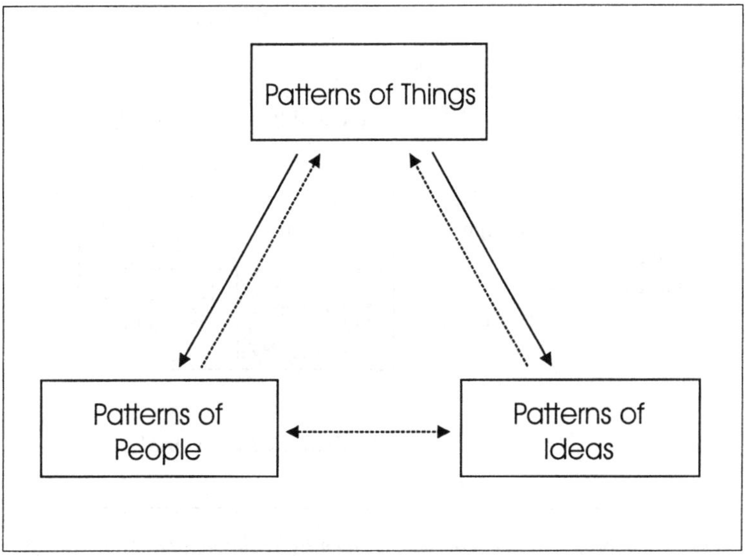


*Figure 2: The Requisite Combination (The solid arrows depict technological determinism. The broken arrows social constructionism)*

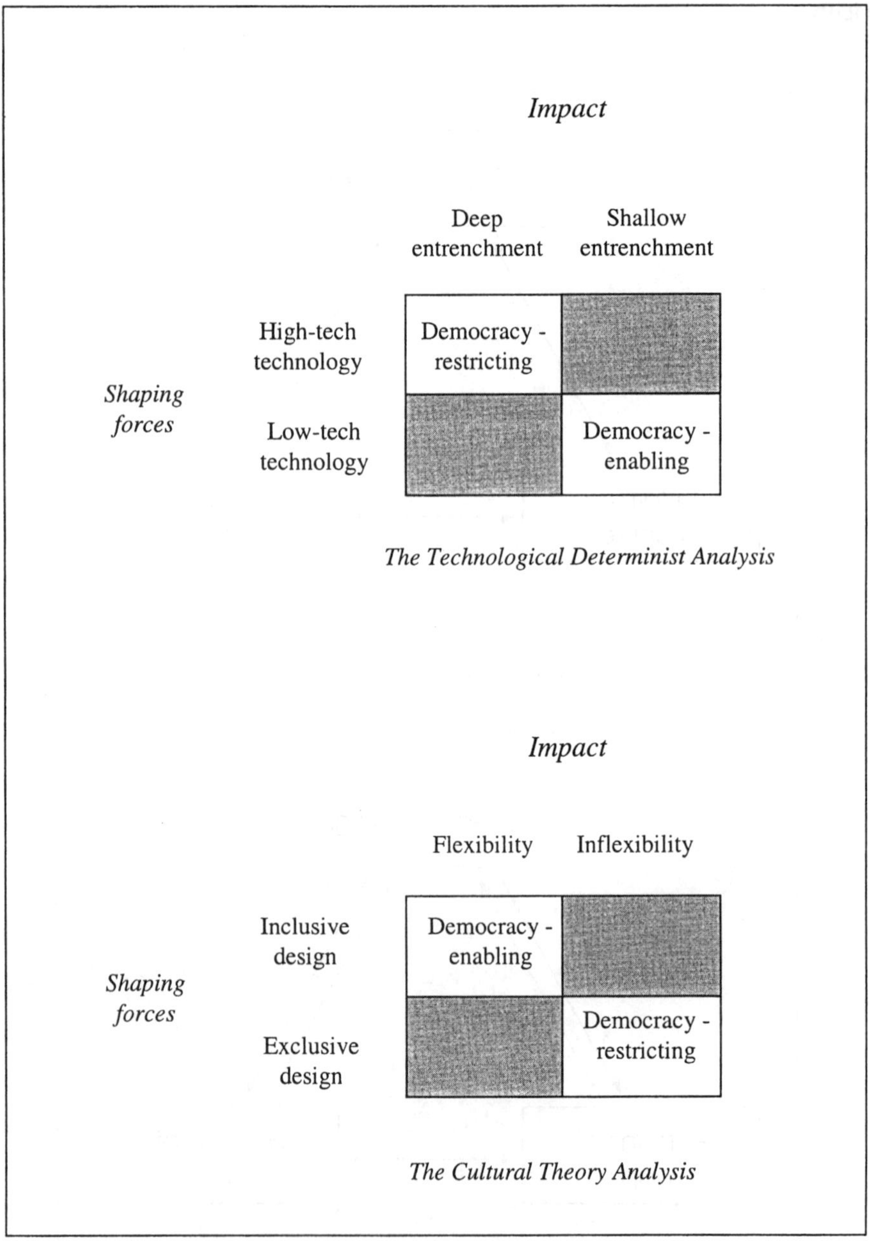


*Figure 3: Technology and Democracy, as seen by Technological Determinism and by Cultural Theory*

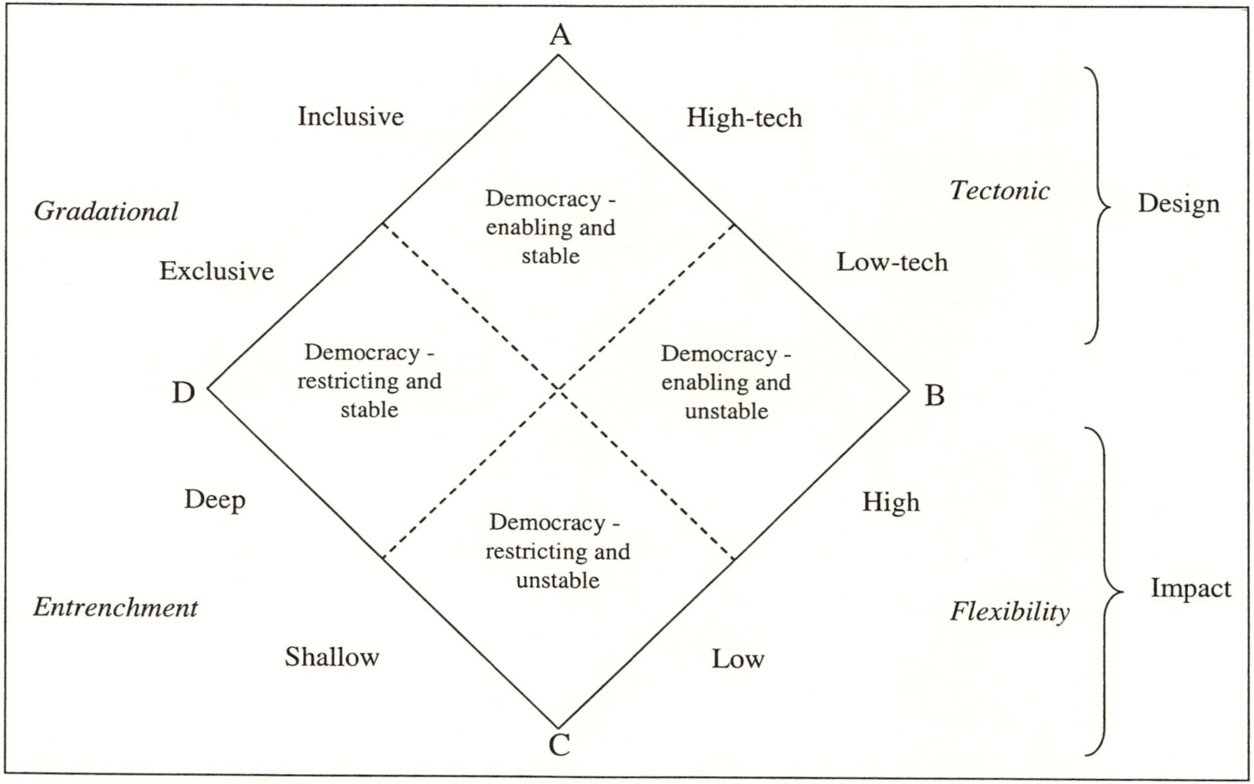


*Figure 4: The Technomorphic Model (The vertical dimension [ac] depicts technological determinist analysis and the horizontal dimension [db] Cultural Theory analysis).*

*Jack Goldsmith*

# The Internet, Conflicts of Regulation, and International Harmonization



A standard set of assumptions underlies the debate on the jurisdictional difficulties presented by regulation of the Internet. Internet protocol addresses do not do not necessarily correlate with physical location. This means that persons communicating and transacting via the Internet often do not know each other's physical location and usually cannot control the geographical flow of content. In addition, information mediated by many Internet services can appear simultaneously in almost every nation in the world. Finally, information transmitted on the Internet can easily flow across national borders without detection.

These assumptions have led many to conclude that Internet regulation creates a jurisdictional quagmire[1]. It is generally accepted that a nation can regulate a transaction that has local effects. But if Internet transactions have effects in every nation, then every nation can regulate the transaction. Since nations differ in their regulatory commitments, many Internet transactions will be subject to inconsistent regulations. And most unilateral national regulations of the Internet – and especially the most demanding and restrictive ones – will affect the regulatory efforts of other nations and the Internet activities of parties on other jurisdictions.

---

1 See, for example, *David Post* and *David Johnson*, Law and Borders – The Rise of Law in Cyberspace, 48 *Stan. L. Rev.* 1367 (1996).

To make the problem concrete, consider an example drawn from the Bavarian Justice Ministry's 1995 threat to prosecute CompuServe for carrying on-line discussions involving persons from around the globe that violated German antipornography laws[2]. CompuServe initially blocked access to these discussion groups in Germany. Because CompuServe could not control the geographical flow of the information on the discussion group, its response to the Bavarian regulation had the effect of blocking access to these discussion groups for all CompuServe users worldwide. Faced with multiple regulatory regimes in the many places where it did business, CompuServe bowed to the most restrictive. The consequence was that the Bavarian regulation interrupted the flow and availability of the discussion groups for CompuServe clients everywhere in the world. Any other nation attempting to enforce restrictive anti-pornography laws against CompuServe would presumably have a similar effect.

These types of jurisdictional difficulties appear to be implicated by unilateral national (or regional) regulations of privacy, Internet gambling, data collection, consumer protection, intellectual property, and so on. How are we to think about and resolve the conflicts of laws that arise when nations unilaterally apply regulations embodying "local values" to Internet transactions on global networks? My answer has two parts. I first try to show why the jurisdictional clashes presented by the Internet are not as severe, and certainly not as novel, as the conventional wisdom sketched above would suggest. Once we have a more realistic conception of the nature of the jurisdictional conflicts presented by the Internet, I sketch the possibilities for resolving, or at least minimizing, these conflicts through international harmonization techniques.

## I. Understanding the Jurisdictional Quagmire of the Internet

The claim that unilateral national regulation of the Internet invariably leads to multiple and conflicting regulation of the Internet is, for several reasons, exaggerated.

It is true that a nation can, in theory, apply its laws to a transnational transaction that has local effects. It does not follow, however, that every nation where an Internet information flow appears can regulate that information flow. To understand why, it is necessary to distinguish between a nation's *prescriptive* jurisdiction and its *enforcement* jurisdiction. Prescriptive jurisdiction is a nation's power to make its laws applicable to particular transactions[3]. A nation can apply its regulations to an Internet communication that produces harmful local effects. This is prescriptive jurisdiction. But the force of this law – whether or not the regulation is effective – depends on the nation's ability to induce or compel compliance with the law. This is enforcement jurisdiction[4]. The true scope and power of a nation's regulation is measured by its enforcement jurisdiction, not its prescriptive jurisdiction.

---

2 The details of the example have been simplified for illustrative purposes.

3 Restatement (Third) of the Foreign Relations Law of the United States, sec. 401 (1987).

4 Id.

For the most part, a nation can exercise enforcement jurisdiction only against persons or entities with a presence or assets within its territory[5]. The vast majority of content providers on the Internet have no presence or assets in the jurisdictions that wish to regulate their information flows. (Here and through this essay, I use the term "content provider" as a generic term to refer all persons transmitting information on the Internet, including e-commerce buyers and sellers, porn purveyors and consumers, chat room participants, web page owners, and the like.) The vast majority of Internet content providers need worry only about the regulations of the nation in which they are physically located. Their activities are *not* subject to multiple regulation, at least not directly so. As a practical matter, the entities potentially subject to multiple Internet regulations are users, systems operators (especially Internet access providers), and transaction facilitators (such as banks and credit card companies) with a presence in more than one regulating jurisdiction. The potential multiple regulatory exposure of these entities is non-trivial; but the scope of this exposure is far narrower than is commonly thought, and mirrors the multiple regulatory exposure faced by persons and firms in "real space.".

Of course, offshore content providers can still feel the effects of local regulations indirectly. Even though a nation's enforcement jurisdiction does not extend to such offshore content providers, the nation can regulate content from offshore indirectly by regulating local persons and entities. For example, it can penalize in-state end-users who obtain or use the foreign content[6]. Or it can regulate in-state hardware and software through which Internet transmissions are received[7]. Or it can regulate Internet access providers and other local firms that facilitate the local transmission of the digital goods[8]. Or it can regulate local financial intermediaries – banks, credit card companies, and the like – that facilitate Internet transaction[9]. In these and many other ways, unilateral national regulations directed at local persons and firms raise the costs of transmission to the offshore content provider, and thereby regulate the flow of the foreign- provided content.

---

5 There are exceptions to this point. A nation can enforce its laws against persons abroad over whom it can obtain personal jurisdiction and enforce a default judgment abroad. It can also extradite persons from other countries. For reasons that I have outlined elsewhere, these forms of enforcement jurisdiction are not likely to have relevance when the issue is unilateral regulation of Internet transactions. See *Jack L. Goldsmith*, Against Cyberanarchy, 65 *U. Chic. L. Rev.* 1199, 1216-1222 (1998).

6 As, for example, many consumers of child pornography have discovered.

7 See *James Boyle*, Foucault in Cyberspace: Surveillance, Sovereignty, and Hardwired Censors, 66 *U. Cin. L. Rev.* 177 (1998); *Lawrence Lessig*, Reading the Constitution in Cyberspace, 45 *Emory L J* 869 (1996).

8 For example, pending Internet gambling legislation authorizes federal and state officials to order Internet service providers to shut down illegal Internet gambling sites under threat of penalty. See *John T. Fojut*, Legislative Update, Ace in the Hole: Regulation of Internet Service Providers Saves the Internet Gambling Prohibition Act of 1997, 8 *DePaul-LCA J. Art & Ent. L.* 155 (1997).

9 For example, credit card companies have recently been sued in connection with their facilitation of on-line gambling. See *Matt Beer*, Wages of the Web, *San Francisco Examiner*, August 17, 1998.

A clearer picture about the possibility of multiple and conflicting Internet regulations thus looks like this. Most Internet content providers will not be subject to any regulation other than the one in the territory in which they have presence. The Internet-related entities that need be concerned about multiple, potentially-conflicting regulatory requirements are persons and firms with a multi-jurisdictional presence. This is just as it is in "real space." Also as in "real space," local regulation of such persons and firms can indirectly affect the availability and cost of Internet transactions in other countries. Such indirect regulation is the way in which unilateral regulation has extraterritorial consequences.

Three features of this picture should be highlighted before addressing harmonization issues. I will use the simplified CompuServe example to illustrate.

*First*, unilateral national regulation of the harmful local effects of Internet information flows is, from a jurisdictional perspective[10], perfectly legitimate. It is clearly consistent with international law for Germany to regulate within its borders the local harms caused by offshore Internet activity. It is also fair for Germany to do so. For German citizens such regulation is a cost (or, depending on each citizens' perspective, a benefit) of citizenship. For foreign companies like CompuServe that engage in local business, the German regulation is a cost of doing business in Germany. CompuServe reaps financial and other benefits from its presence in Germany. Without this presence German enforcement threats would be empty. CompuServe need not remain in Germany; it can close its shop there if German regulations are too burdensome. Its decision to stay in Germany and comply with German regulations reflects the company's judgment that the benefits of doing business outweigh its costs.

*Second*, the extraterritorial spillover effects of unilateral national regulation of Internet transactions are both inevitable and legitimate. Anyone familiar with the ancient discipline of conflicts of law (or private international law) realizes that there are *always* spillover effects from unilateral regulation of transnational transactions. For example: When reinsurance agents in England design contracts that are legal in England but that cause anti-competitive effects in the United States, the application of U.S. antitrust laws to the English reinsurers raises the costs of their activities in England and affects the reinsurance market worldwide[11]. If English rather than U.S. regulation governed the situation, U.S. insurance companies and U.S. regulatory interests would be harmed and

10 This is an important caveat. I am talking throughout this essay about regulation of the Internet from the perspective of jurisdiction and choice of law. This is an issue wholly distinct from the merits of any particular regulation of the Internet – for example, whether particular national regulations of the Internet promote democracy, or are efficient, or are good or bad for humanity. Resolution of these substantive regulatory issues turn on contested normative judgments and difficult context-specific, cost-benefit analyses that have little to do with jurisdictional issues. But resolution of these issues also turns on how we understand the jurisdictional confusions that arise when national regulation, which has traditionally been understood primarily in geographical terms, applies to a phenomenon that appears to resist geographical orientation. This jurisdictional puzzle is my focus here.

11 See Hartford Fire Ins Co. v. California, 509 U.S. 764 (1993).

the worldwide reinsurance market would be affected[12]. This example shows that spillovers are present whenever one nation regulates transnational conduct differently than another, regardless of which nation's regulation applies. These spillovers are inevitable as long as we wish to maintain both national (as opposed to international) lawmaking and transnational activity. And under current conceptions of international law and territorial sovereignty, such spillovers are perfectly legitimate in the absence of some international law to the contrary.

These points apply with equal force to unilateral regulation of the Internet. Consider again the CompuServe example. Germany bans certain forms of pornography within its borders. If the medium of the porn were paper, there could be no jurisdictional objection to a German prohibition on the porn's entry at the border or to German punishment of those later discovered to have smuggled it in. From the German perspective it makes no difference whether the porn enters the nation via the Internet or the postal service. The rational for the regulation is the same in both contexts: preventing local harms. The German regulation of the Internet affects the cost and availability of pornography in other countries. But if Germany did not regulate the transnational Internet activity, it would suffer local harms from extraterritorial conduct. There is no legal or moral principle that requires Germany to yield local control over its territory in order to accommodate the users of the Internet in other countries. Nor does any such principle require Germany to absorb the local costs of foreign Internet activity because of the costs that German regulation might have on such activity[13]. In the absence of some international law to the contrary, Germany can regulate the local harm of transnational Internet activity even if this regulation produces spillover effects.

*Third*, the extraterritorial effects caused by a unilateral Internet regulation are premised to a great degree on the architectural assumption that content providers and Internet service providers cannot control the real-space geographical flow of Internet content. This claim is largely false, and increasingly so. Content flow can today be regulated geographically through a variety of means ranging from conditioning access to content on geographical identification, to centralized filtered servers, to mandated end-user filtering, to the imposition of severe penalties for uploading or downloading certain information. The question is not whether the architecture of the Internet permits geographical content discrimination; the question is the cost of geographical content discrimination and the desired degree of effectiveness. The intense demand by Internet users, content providers, service providers, and regulating jurisdictions to reduce such spillovers is driving the development of technologies that lower the costs of discrimination and increase its effectiveness. The adequacy of these developments will

---

12 The same analysis applies to the European Commission's recent imposition of strict conditions on an FTC-approved merger between Boeing and McDonnell Douglas. The application of European competition law raised the cost of the predominantly-U.S. merger, and inevitably had spillover consequences on the aircraft production market in other countries. Similarly, the non- application of European law would have resulted in harm to European interests.

13 These points have special force in the CompuServe case because foreign persons indirectly affected by the German regulation remain free to choose among dozens of Internet access services that are unaffected by the German regulation.

depend on yet-unanswered empirical and technological issues. The point for now is that as content providers and systems operators are increasingly able to control the geographical flow of information, they (like purveyors of information via other communication media) can keep information out of the regulating jurisdiction, thereby reducing regulatory spillover effects and multi-jurisdictional regulatory exposure.

In sum, the unilateral application national regulations to Internet activity can be expected to produce spillover effects and regulatory conflict. The negative spillovers and regulatory conflicts caused by such regulation are narrower than is often claimed. But they are non-trivial; they impose significant costs on Internet activity. How, if at all, should nations think about resolving or minimizing these conflicts?

## II. How to think about Resolving or Minimizing Regulatory Conflict

There are three basic responses to the spillovers and conflicts caused by unilateral Internet regulation: (1) private ordering; (2) various harmonization strategies; and (3) muddling through and learning to live with regulatory conflict. Private ordering plays an important role in Internet communities but cannot come close to an adequate response to the many Internet regulation difficulties. Harmonization comes in many stripes and can, in some contexts, alleviate regulatory conflicts. But harmonization is rarely an effective or comprehensive response to conflicts among regulations that reflect important local values. This means that in many Internet contexts (as in many real-space contexts), we will have to learn to live with regulatory conflict, alleviating them on a piecemeal basis and at the margins when possible.

### 1. Private Ordering

One response to conflicts of national regulations is to let Internet participants regulate their own transactions and communications. This option has intuitive appeal because the conflicts of national regulations often seem to cause severe spillover harms, and because the Internet has been conceptualized as a separate place than can regulate itself.

The problem is that the Internet is not a separate place, and Internet users do not form a self-contained group removed from our world[14]. Internet users are no more removed or self- enclosed than participants in other trans-jurisdictional communication mediums, such as telephone users or postal users or carrier-pigeon users. They are in real space in front of a screen using a keyboard and scanner to communicate with someone else, often in a different territorial jurisdiction. And these real-space communications cause real-world harms. For example: Internet gambling can decrease in-state gambling revenues and cause family strife; a book uploaded on the Internet can violate an author's copyright; a chatroom participant can defame someone outside the chatroom; terrorists can promulgate bomb-making or kidnapping tips; merchants can conspire to fix prices

---

14 See *Lawrence Lessig*, The Zones of Cyberspace, 48 *Stan. L. Rev.* 1403 (1996).

by e-mail; a corporation can issue a fraudulent security; a pornographer can sell kiddie porn; and so on. It is these and many other real-space costs – costs that Internet communities have not effectively internalized – that national regulatory regimes worry about and aim to regulate[15].

Pointing out the harmful real-world effects of Internet transactions is not, by itself, an argument for national (or international) regulation of the Internet in any particular context. It is simply an argument for more realism about the possibility and efficacy and even legitimacy of private ordering of various Internet activities. The best argument for private ordering is an efficiency argument that says the third-party harms of unilateral national regulation are more severe than the third-party harms of private ordering. This calculus requires difficult and controversial valuations that most Internet regulation skeptics have not begun to consider. Such an analysis would also need to focus on particular regulatory contexts rather than on Internet regulation per se. It is very unlikely that such an analysis would lead to the conclusion that self- regulation is cost-effective in all contexts. Indeed, the normative arguments for self-regulation of issues like privacy, consumer protection, gambling, data collection, and pornography are not likely to be any more powerful in the Internet than in the non-Internet contexts.

## 2. Harmonization Strategies

When regulatory conflict and regulatory spillover occur with respect to "real-space" transnational transactions, nations have responded with a variety of international harmonization strategies. Sometimes harmonization takes the "hard" form of treaties that either establish a uniform international standard, or an international anti-discrimination regime, or an international choice-of-law regime. Other times harmonization takes "softer" forms like information sharing among enforcement agencies or informally-agreed-upon regulatory targets.

Various harmonization strategies are being employed to address the challenges of regulating the Internet. Consider a few examples. Several recent treaties and related multinational edicts that have strengthened digital content owners' right to control the distribution and presentation of their property online[16]. These harmonization efforts

15 Critics of Internet regulation tend to ignore or attenuate the real-world harms of Internet activity. They do not consider these effects because they take it as an article of faith that Internet participants form a self-contained group that can internalize the costs of its activity. But this assumption is simply false. Internet participants are no more self-contained than telephone users, members of the Catholic Church, corporations, and other private groups with activities that transcend jurisdictional borders.

16 In December 1996, the World Intellectual Property Organization ("WIPO") reached agreement on a treaty that significantly extended international copyright protection for digital property. WIPO Copyright Treaty, adopted Dec 20, 1996, WIPO Pub No 226(E) (WIPO 1997). Within a year, the European Commission issued a draft directive to bring European law into line with these international obligations. See Draft EC Directive Provides Strong Online Copyright Protection. The United States has enacted similar legislation. See WIPO Copyright Treaties Implementation Act; Digital Millennium Copyright Act of 1998. (May 6, 1998).

grow out of an international copyright regime that is over one hundred years old[17]. The G8 economic powers have recently begun to coordinate regulatory efforts concerning Internet-related crimes in five areas: pedophilia and sexual exploitation; drug-trafficking; money-laundering; electronic fraud, such as theft of credit-card numbers, and computerized piracy; and industrial and state espionage[18]. These initiatives mirror similar efforts to redress similar regulatory leakage problems in real-space contexts such as environmental policy, banking and insurance supervision, and antitrust regulation[19]. Several international organizations have drafted model laws and guidelines to facilitate Internet commerce and related digital certification issues[20]. There are scores of other international efforts in a variety of Internet-related contexts.

Harmonization strategies such as these are clearly an important response to the jurisdictional difficulties of Internet regulation[21]. If successful, these strategies can reduce or even eliminate the costs of regulatory conflict. But harmonization is not a panacea. Harmonization usually comes at the cost of local values and national difference, and whether the gains from harmonization outweigh these costs is usually difficult to determine. Moreover, harmonization is often not easy to achieve. And many harmonizations efforts reflect coercion by powerful nations rather than truly fair or efficient regulatory improvements. It is very difficult to generalize about when harmonization is appropriate and what form harmonization should take. Here are some notes that may help us to understand the problem:

---

17 The digital protection treaty signed in Geneva operates as a protocol to the Berne Convention for the Protection of Literary and Artistic Works, a treaty regime that began in 1886. See Berne Convention for the Protection of Literary and Artistic Works (WIPO 1970).

18 See *Clifford Krauss*, 8 Countries Join in an Effort To Catch Computer Criminals, *NY Times* A12 (Dec 11, 1997).

19 See *Anne-Marie Slaughter*, The Real New World Order, *Foreign Affairs* 183, 18992 (Sep/Oct 1997).

20 For example, in February 1997, the United Nations Commission on International Trade Law ("UNCITRAL") began to draft model international digital signature legislation. See Report of the Working Group on Electronic Commerce, Thirty-First Session (New York, Feb 12-28, 1997). See also UNCITRAL Working Group on Electronic Commerce, Planning Of Future Work on Electronic Commerce: Digital Signatures, Certification Authorities and Related Legal Issues A/CN.9/WG.IV/WP.71 (Dec 31, 1996). Similarly, in November 1997, the International Chamber of Commerce issued the General Usage for International Digitally Ensured Commerce ("GUIDEC"), a set of guidelines for ensuring trustworthy digital transactions over the Internet. And the Organisation for Economic Co-operation and Development ("OECD") recently adopted principles to guide countries in formulating their own policies and legislation relating to the use of cryptography. See OECD Cryptography Policy: The Guidelines and the Issues, Unclassified OCDE/GD(97)204 (1997).

21 They are also important for resolving the related problem — hinted at above but not developed in this draft — of regulation evasion. Regulation evasion appears to be a particular problem posed by the Internet, for nations cannot enforce regulations directly against offshore content providers, and because the Internet makes it relatively easy for content providers to shift the source (or apparent source) of content offshore. A good example is on-line gambling. The regulation evasion problem, like the problem of regulatory conflict and the problem of spillovers from unilateral regulation, is real but usually exaggerated. Harmonization strategies can help to eliminate or minimize regulation evasion by ensuring that the same regulatory standards apply everywhere.

*First*, we should keep in mind that there are good reasons for regulatory difference among nations. Nations have different regulatory commitments because of, among other things, differences in endowment, technological capacities, and preferences[22]. A primary virtue of decentralized lawmaking by nation-states (as opposed to uniform international rules) is that it allows populations to implement policies that reflect these differences. This in a nutshell is the theory that informs, among other things, the concept of national sovereignty, the European principle of subsidiarity, and the American conception of federalism. In addition to these "substantive" differences among nations, there is "procedural" value in having decisions made at the smallest possible political unit[23]. These substantive and procedural values are diminished by international harmonization. They are costs to be weighed in the balance when considering the virtues of harmonization.

*Second*, when regulatory difference reflects important local values, harmonization is very difficult to achieve because of (among other things) domestic political opposition. This is why almost all international regulatory regimes are littered with (usually ill-defined) mandatory or local public policy exceptions[24]. This fact should give harmonization's champions pause when addressing national differences concerning privacy, free speech, consumer protection, competition policy, and the like.

*Third*, the WTO – at least as currently conceived – is probably not the ideal forum for resolving conflicts of regulatory difference implicated by the Internet. The WTO and its predecessors have largely succeeded in lowering express trade barriers because the first generation of anti-discrimination principles they have employed – national treatment and most- favored nation – rest on well accepted economic theory and are relatively easy to enforce. As the WTO has moved into the more contested non-tariff trade barrier contexts (such as health and environmental regulation), its work has become much more controversial. It is likely to become more and more difficult to harmonize social regulations through the rubric of free trade. Many provisions of the WTO scheme recognize this point explicitly[25].

*Fourth*, harmonization of Internet-related regulations will likely to be easiest to achieve in two contexts. First, we can expect relatively robust harmonization in those contexts—like many aspects of criminal law enforcement—where nations'

---

22 See *David Leebron*, Lying Down With Procrustes: An Analysis of Harmonization Claims, in 1 Bhagwati and Hudec, Fair Trade and Harmonization: Prerequisites for Free Trade? 67-70 (1996). I am indebted to Leebron's excellent analysis of the virtues and vices of harmonization.

23 Id. at 71-75.

24 This is true, to give but a few examples, of the Rome Convention on the Law Applicable to Contractual Relations, all of the Hague Conference treaties, and the New York Convention on the Enforcement of Arbitral Awards.

25 To take one example, the General Agreement on Trade Services creates an exception for national regulations designed to prevent deceptive practices and protect privacy in data collection and dissemination. See GATS, Article XIV.

interests converge and the gains from cooperation are high. Second, harmonization is easiest to enforce in coordination situations — such as the communication protocols that define the Internet – where every nation has an incentive to adhere the adopted standard. The particular standards adopted of course have distributional consequences, which usually mean that powerful nations determine their content[26]; but after the standard is adopted, all nations have incentives to adhere to it. This type of coordination situations, it must be admitted, is not likely to be present when contested social values are in issue.

*Fifth*, we are likely to see soft harmonization of contested national regulatory regimes before we see hard harmonization. With issues like privacy, consumer protection, and free speech, the most feasible approach for harmonization in the short run is through informal means such as informal enforcement agreements, targeted goals, a softening of unilateral extraterritorial enforcement on a case-by-case basis, and information sharing. These soft strategies can help to reduce regulatory difference, and can lead to harder harmonization agreements.

*Sixth*, it is hard to overstate the extent to which regulatory conflict related to the Internet might be reduced through technological innovation. The central difference between transnational transactions via the Internet and transnational transactions through other means is that it is much more costly to control information flows geographically over the Internet. Firms in real space minimize multiple regulatory exposure by directing business away from in restrictive jurisdictions. As discussed above, this is relatively costly to do under the current architectural structure of the Internet. This appears to be changing; conditioned access to content, geographical identification, and more sophisticated filtering devices permit much greater geographical discrimination today than a few years ago. Technological predictions are precarious (especially by me); the only point here is that as Internet content providers can discriminate the flow of their content with greater precision and at less cost, their regulatory exposure, and thus the nature of regulatory conflict, will come to look just as it does in real space.

*Seventh,* beyond these relatively banal thoughts, it is difficult to make generalizations about the likelihood and desirability of harmonizing regulations pertaining to the Internet. Global arguments for and against regulatory harmonization will not do. In each regulatory context, the costs and benefits of harmonization must be carefully considered, and if harmonization is normatively desirable, the best and most feasible form for achieving harmonization must be chosen. All of these issues are contested. Progress is likely to be achieved slowly and in narrow rather than broad contexts.

---

26 On this problem see *Stephen Krasner*, Global Communications and National Power: Life on the Pareto Frontier, 43 *World Pol.* 336 (1991).

## 3. Learning to live with Conflict

Scholars who study conflicts of law are used to regulatory conflict. They do not see it as the unalloyed evil that other scholars do because they realize that it is often normatively preferable to harmonization and that it is in any event often inevitable. With this thought in mind, it is important to remember that unilateral national regulations of Internet activity will not, as many once feared, destroy the Internet. They will raise the cost of Internet transactions and lower their speed, at least until technology eliminates or changes the nature of the problem. But there is nothing sacrosanct about Internet speed or expense. Increasing Internet speed and lowering the costs of Internet transactions are values to be weighed in the mix.

*Wolf Osthaus*

# Local Values, Global Networks and the Return of Private Law

– On the function of Civil Law and Private International Law in Cyberspace –

The second half of this century may, at least in the western legal hemisphere, be referred to as the era of public law. Whilst in the civil world of the 19th and early 20th century, legal relations between private persons were still in the foreground, public legal relations between the state and its citizens started to increase. But this direct regulation by the state is restricted by the fact that its authority is primarily limited to its territory[1]. The increasing globalization of phenomena in need of regulation, accelerated by global datanets – mostly by the internet[2] – leads to an increasing separation between problem level and regulation level and thereby erodes the base of the present system of national regulation[3]. Being on the threshold of the new millennium these developments could lead to a "return of private law"[4].

Private law can also be used where, in the course of increasing globalization, local values should be preserved. The differences in the basic attitudes of previously more insular societies about what deserves special protection, which value is due priority before another, are in danger of being increasingly leveled. By this the solidarity of individual societies might also eventually be endangered. It is not always necessary, out of principal, to counteract this. But in some ways, there will certainly be the need to preserve inherent values and protect oneself against the imposition of foreign values and standards. The aptitude of private law for this task is the subject of the present survey. Firstly, the limitations of other possible forms of regulation – public law on national and international level as well as self regulation – and possible advantages of regulation by private law will be shown (A.). Reflections will then follow about which mechanisms private law provides to the State for value-preserving regulations (B.). However, it is only the established system of international co-ordination of national private legal systems that marks any real advantage of these regulations as opposed to public law regulations – how does this system work and also, does it maintain its function in Cyberspace (C.)? Lastly, possible problems of regulation by private law will have to be considered (D.).

---

1 An exception showing extra-territorial regulation is, for example, personal jurisdiction - but the state here often meets difficulties of enforcement when there are no treaties granting legal assistance.

2 For this reason in the following, regulations concerning the internet should be considered as a matter of priority that are of the utmost practical relevance.

3 Cf. for instance: *Joel Reidenberg*, "Governing Networks and Rule-Making in Cyberspace", *Emory Law Journal* 45 (1996), pp. 911 (913 et seq.).

4 This prognosis – but without the relation to globalisation and the internet – was made in 1991: *Ernst-Joachim Mestmäcker*, "Die Wiederkehr der bürgerlichen Gesellschaft und ihres Rechts" in: id., Recht in der offenen Gesellschaft (Baden-Baden 1993), pp. 60 et seq.

## A. The different models of regulation and their limitations

The necessity to think about civil regulation for the protection of local values arises solely as a consequence of the restricted suitability of other models of regulation.

### 1. Public law regulation by individual states

The traditional form of public-law regulation by individual States is weakened in its effectiveness by the strongly increased mobility of private protagonists. By global datanets, legally relevant activities can be transferred to another territory; even those who transfer their whole existence to another territory are, due to the possibilities of modern communication, not compelled to leave anything behind. But it is also possible to escape regulation by specific out-sourcing of the linking elements that are relevant for the application of the rules – one could call this virtual migration[5]. Protagonists, who really take advantage of these new possibilities, might thereby as a consequence indicate where there is a deficit of regulation. Especially by the lightning-quick transfer of problematic data it is possible to escape into spheres that are not, or at least only partially regulated, without restricting the range of internet-activities. Nevertheless, it is necessary to distinguish between small and therefore flexible protagonists, individual persons or small businesses, and the remarkably slower big enterprises - *Peter Swire* has characterized this distinction as the one between 'mice' and 'elephants'[6]. Big enterprises, doing business in several states, are not easily able to evade unpleasant regulations, but rather see themselves facing a multitude of – often contradictory – regulations. Therefore there is a danger of over-regulation threatening the large economic opportunities provided by global datanets[7].

Both effects can also amount to a danger for specifically local values meaning particularly the specifically local evaluation of values. As regards the 'mice', the attempt to protect local values by national regulation simply does not work because of the possibilities for regulation avoidance provided by their flexibility. In contrast, the 'elephants' run the risk of having to submit to the dictates of reigning standards during their network activities[8], be it the strongest standard or one that is applicable in a particularly economically important region, from which the 'elephant' does not want to withdraw. Thus they often loose the possibility of taking local specialties into account.

5 Cf.: *Christoph Engel*, "The Internet and nation-state", in: *Christoph Engel / Kenneth H. Keller* (eds.): Understanding the Impact of Global Networks on Local Social, Political and Cultural Values (Baden-Baden 2000), p. 213 (241).

6 *Peter Swire*, "Of Elephants, Mice, and Privacy: International Choice of Law and the Internet", *The International Lawyer* 32 (1998), pp. 991 (993, 1015 et seq.).

7 *Swire*, [n. 6], pp. 993, 1019 et seq.; *Matthew Burnstein*, "A Global Network in a Compartmentalised Legal Environment", in: *K. Boele-Woelki / C. Kessedjian* (eds.), Internet, Which Court Decides? Which Law Applies? Quel tribunal décide? Quel droit s'applique? (The Hague/London/Boston 1998), pp. 23 (26 et seq.).

8 In particular this fear exists in the relation of the USA to the EU in the area of data protection, cf. for instance *Swire*, [n. 6], pp. 991 et seq.

To a restricted amount countermeasures are available against both effects – lack of regulation on the one side and over-regulation on the other side. The 'elephants' could avoid at least some regulations by withdrawing from the affected area completely. However, the price would be the surrender of a market with its possibilities of winnings; here profit orientated firms will simply have to carry out an economic benefit analysis. Because of their size and economic importance, the 'elephants' might possibly be able to influence the outcome of the regulation[9]. In times of increasing locational competition, the threat of withdrawal of economic activities might be sufficient for this.

Furthermore the 'elephants', who mostly have good legal counsel could try to transfer the problematic activities to individual subsidiary companies in other states and thereby evade responsibility. The individual States though, in order to get hold of the 'mice' that are trying to escape their reach, instead of attempting to catch the individual originator still have the possibility of grabbing the provider or also the user of problematic contents[10]. That's what happened in the first CompuServe decision, where the director of the German division *Felix Somm* was found guilty[11], and is also common practice when it comes to the 'consumption' of child pornography by criminally sanctioning the mere possession of such material. However, such an infringement of one's liberty is rather problematic; because the repercussion on the real intruder, and therefore the suitability of the measure, is quite questionable.

## 2. The limited chances of international harmonization

The chance for successful regulation at the international level rests on co-operation between the states. Here, the different levels of problem and regulation come together again. International co-operation regarding implementation and enforcement of the rules are possible by agreements about responsibility for regulation or by harmonization of the regulations as such. Harmonization of the law is regarded by some as the only solution to meet the challenges of global nets[12]. But the danger that some states would refrain from co-operation is always existent. This depends to a great extent on the subject of the proposed regulation. The chances for co-operation are smaller the more controversial attitudes towards the aim of regulation are. Only in case of consensus

9 *Swire*, [n. 6], p. 1019.

10 *Jack Goldsmith*, "Against Cyberanarchy", *The University of Chicago Law Review* 65 (1998), p. 1199.

11 Amtsgericht München of 28th May 1998, published (inter alia) in: Multimedia und Recht 1998, pp. 429 et seq. (commented by Sieber, pp. 438 et seq.). In the meanwhile the judgement was overruled by the decision of the Landgericht München of 17th November 1999.

12 For the area of E-commerce: *Assafa Endeshaw*, "The Proper Law for Electronic Commerce", *Information & Communications Technology Law* 7 (1998), pp. 5 (10 et seq.); *Coen Drion / Joost Linnemann*, "Aansprakelijkheidskwesties en andere uitdagingen van het Internet aan de nationale rechtsorde", *Nederlandse Juristenblad* 1996, p. 1734 (1740). *Willem Calkoen* uses drastic words in his plea for harmonisation: "The issue is rapidly becoming one of whether we choose to have laws or live in a lawless society." (in "Harmonisation of Laws and the Internet", *International Business Lawyer*, April 1998, pp. 146 et seq.).

could international co-operation be achieved quickly and fairly comprehensively. Symptomatic of this are the five fields for which the G8-States are planning co-ordinated measures of regulation: pedophilia and sexual exploitation, drug dealing, money laundering, computer fraud and espionage aimed at states and economic enterprises[13]. Here, without exception, values are concerned that are of equal renown in the industrial countries and where the need for regulation is obvious. But already, participation of developing countries, without whom there would be further possibilities for avoidance, is not certain in all respects. Even in the above mentioned areas, successful regulation is considered to be considerably less important by these states – if not even harmful to their economic development. Consequently, probably only a small readiness for cost intensive engagement might exist. And even if there is a basic readiness for co-operation, the danger still exists that some individual states will want to make their contribution part of an agreement in order to gain political or economic advantages by combining it with other questions. But a single state who denies co-operation can, by too low standards of protection, create a regulation-leak that mobile intruders will use, or it may unilaterally implement particularly strict rules, so that less agile protagonists become subject to over-regulation.

## 3. Alternative regulation with participation of private subjects

The reduced potential of regulation of the individual states and the competition between systems promoted by mobility, signifies - from the point of view of individuals - a multiplicity of possibilities. The "opportunities of the citizen in the fight for his rights are increasing"[14]. The advantage lies in the fact that subjects of private law – be it citizens as natural persons or enterprises as legal entities – may themselves exert a greater influence on the regulation of various areas of their life and work. This might possibly be valid to a particular degree in the sphere of the internet. For regulation with the participation of citizens one additional distinction has to be drawn: the extreme form is the purely private order that completely manages without the participation of the state (and has to do so). But the complete exclusion of states leads to several concerns (a). A middle way is provided by the second possibility, which also relies on subjects of private law as protagonists, but whose actions are ruled by the national private-law system and the national system for the settlement of disputes (b). This attempt shall be further examined in the following parts.

13 *Goldsmith*, Cyberanarchy [n. 10], p. 1231; *Engel*, Internet [n. 5], p. 258 et seq.

14 *Manfred Streit*, "Systemwettbewerb im europäischen Intergrationsprozeß", in *Ulrich Immenga* et al. (eds.), Festschrift für Ernst-Joachim Mestmäcker zum 70. Geburtstag (Baden-Baden 1996), p. 521 (521).

*a) The opportunities and dangers of self regulation*

Private ordering of the internet in the form of self regulation by the users is what lies behind the widespread claim for inherent rules for 'Cyberspace' independent of national borders. 'Cyberlaw', '*lex informatica*'[15] or 'common law of the internet'[16] are propagated, always using the much-cited *lex mercatoria* in international business as an example[17]. Here, the somehow careless use of 'law' and 'lex' might lead to misunderstandings. In any event, both expressions always symbolize non-governmental rules – like the *lex mercatoria* – that evolved as self regulation of the participants. This was inevitable because their area of validity does not match that of national territories. Such self regulation as long as it is not declared 'real' law by enactment or by a court, is, at best 'soft law'.

Initially the problem arises, how such 'soft law' can establish any validity between the parties at all. In contractual relations this can be negotiated - either expressly or even by implication. But even here the question arises, if such a referral to extra-legal rules can exclude the validity of compulsory, i.e. not-changeable by *intra parties* understanding, rules of national law, that serve the protection of third persons or even only paternalism[18]. This would depend on whether a choice of law may indicate non-governmental regulation at all, or whether such an agreement may only be understood as a negotiation between the parties concerning material matters by making reference to set of various rules. In German law Art. 4 II EGBGB, that only refers to the choice of the 'law of a State'[19], provides a clear answer: mandatory rules of national law that would be applicable can not be avoided by reference to non-governmental rules.

It is considerably more difficult to construct the validity of 'Cyberlaw' in relation to infringements outside existing legal relations. These could only be caught by self regulation if all users had in advance – possibly before each logging in[20] – declared their willingness that potential infringements should fall under these rules. But even if all (!) internet accesses were constructed in such a way, it would still be questionable if such a general 'choice of law', that is focused on future events, could really be acknowledged. Another problem, besides its vagueness, is the difference between internet users. Other than in international trade between merchants, that structurally are all on the same level, internet users with completely different horizons, different experiences and therefore different needs of protection are present: ranging from the global entrepreneur to the

---

15 *Reidenberg* [n. 3], p. 929; *Aron Mefford*, "Lex informatica: Foundations of Law on the Internet" (1997) <http://www.law.indiana.edu/glsj/vol5/no1/mefford.html> (01.08.1999).

16 *Burnstein*, Global Network [n. 7], p. 28.

17 Cf.: *Matthew Burnstein*, "Conflicts on the Net: Choice of Law in Transnational Cyberspace", *Vanderbilt Journal of Transnational Law* 29 (1996), pp. 75 (108 et seq.); id., Global Network [n. 7], p. 28; *David Johnson / David Post*, "Law and Borders – The Rise of Law in Cyberspace", *Stanford Law Review* 48 (1996), pp. 1367 et seq. (especially pp. 1387 et seq.).

18 *Goldsmith*, Cyberanarchy [n. 10], p. 1200.

19 Cf.: *Christian von Bar*, Internationales Privatrecht II – Besonderer Teil (München 1991), No. 425.

20 *Burnstein* (Global Network [n. 7], pp. 31 et seq.) suggests such a negotiation. Following the expression shrink-wrap he calls for "click-wrap-contracts".

simple consumer and even minors. For the two last mentioned groups one would hardly be able to assume that by a simple 'click' of a Login-Button that they would choose, for all possible situations on the net, an unknown non-governmental regulation and thereby give up existing protection. Such desire would first of all require legal capacity (not given for minors) and apart from that, understanding of the consequences of this decision - which can not always be expected even from adult consumers.

Apart from this problem, if self regulation could completely take the place of governmental rules, when one considers its contentious aims, this also gives reason to doubt the suitability of self regulation. In particular, protection of minorities or weaker entities is in danger of being neglected in a self regulatory system, where protagonists participate according to their strength[21]. Initially the internet with a homogeneous group of users might have been shaped by idealistic ideas. At this time one could maybe expect that new users would be influenced so much by this attitude, that they would also comply with this idealistic regulation[22]. But such a mould requires intensive contact and an homogenous, unanimous group. However, such an "Internet Community" already belongs far in the past and would be mere illusion today, solely because of the internet's terrific rate of growth. In particular, the increasing commercialization of the net is leading to a supremacy of hard monetary interests. Because of the market power that stands behinds such concerns, they have the best opportunities in the process of self regulation and do not leave much space for idealistic values and the protection of minorities and weaker entities[23]. The protection of local values quite often does not signify anything else than the recognition of differing ideas of small, not majority-able groups and protection of them. "Cyberlaw" arising from self regulation promises only small benefits in this prospect today and for the future.

Additionally, the fact that the strongest are exerting the biggest influence in the process of self regulation leads one to the additional fear that "Cyberlaw" will mainly use US-American law as well as US-American interests and values for its orientation. On the European side this leads to the fear of "Americanization by the backdoor" [24] that is not in the least promoted by American lawyers to create a competitive advantage in the consultancy market[25].

The dangers of unsatisfying self regulation as regards content could only be banned if the national state could at least take indirect influence on the arrangement of the content. That would require that the state were plausibly able to threaten intervention with its own regulations, or at least could offer benefits if the aims of regulatory intentions were achieved. The possibilities of the individual state is – as always when it comes to the

21 *Goldsmith*, Cyberanarchy [n. 10], p. 1200.

22 This idea hides behind the concept of "Netiquette".

23 Also sceptical: *Mefford* [n. 15], under I.

24 Very clear is: *Peter Mankowski*, "Wider ein transnationales Cyberlaw", Archiv für Presserecht 1999, p. 138 (140). A warning of American hegemony in the area of internet law is also expressed by: *François Dessemontet*, "Internet, la propriété intellectuelle et le droit international privé" in: *Boele-Woelki/Kessedjian* [n. 7], p. 47 (47).

25 *Mankowski*, Cyberlaw [n 24], p. 140.

regulation if the internet – extremely restricted by their limited jurisdiction. Usually it can only reach the internet users residing within its own territory. Towards others the threat of its own regulation is rather a blunt sword. A credible alternative regulation could only be promised by the Community of States in the form of harmonized law, but this is – as already mentioned – hard to achieve.

Non-participation of states in self regulation also represents a disadvantage to the participants. For the enforcement of non-governmental rules they cannot solely rely on the national apparatus of power with its territorially restricted authority. Generally in international trade, apart from the validity of the *lex mercatoria* in case of litigation, resort to a court of arbitration is agreed, whereby the way to national courts is denied to the parties. If, due to the lack of such an agreement, the case comes before a national court anyway, non-governmental rules of conduct do not achieve legal status but could, if at all, be taken into account as customs on the factual basis. In order for litigation to be negotiated in arbitration at all, agreement between *all* possible parties has to be made in advance, as it is commonly held in international trade. In principal such an agreement could also be considered for litigation arising from internet-activities[26]. For the arbitration clause to be effective, the decisive factor is that it is also recognized by the national courts and thus they do not accept litigation that has been brought before them for decision. They will obviously have high requirements regarding this agreement in order to guarantee sufficient protection for structurally weaker persons. Parties need to have sufficient understanding about the meaning and the reach of such a negotiation, especially as the agreement generally has to be made before it is really foreseeable to which conflicts it will apply[27]. Here too, doubts are justified in relation to groups of weaker persons such as consumers and in particular, minors.

For the enforcement of some arbitration awards, especially when they are focused on performance, the co-operation of other states might be necessary[28]. Only they are in possession of the authority to enforce against the person or the assets. Courts of arbitration may exert such powers only if the authority has contractually been agreed beforehand, or, if the enforcement has correspondingly been assured; both things cannot be achieved for all internet users in the same way[29]. In order to effectively enforce an arbitrated settlement with the help of the state, willingness to recognize the arbitration court's decisions without extensive verification and to enforce them towards objects and persons within their territory has to exist on the side of the states. For border crossing cases, international agreements are needed for the recognition and enforcement of

---

26 *Goldsmith*, Cyberanarchy [n. 10], pp. 1214, 1246 et seq.

27 Also: *Mefford* [n. 15], under III B., who would also refer to conflict of laws. – Compare further to the limitations of choice of applicable law here under pp. 224 et seq.

28 Also: *Mefford* [n. 15], under III D. Examples for mechanisms for self enforcement of rules by network-participants (sometimes without resort to arbitration) are to be found in: *Reidenberg* [n. 3], p. 920.

29 One may ask for a deposit for security, but that can hardly be expected of private persons, or by corresponding agreements opening access to internet specific values such as domain-names or the saving of IP addresses on routes is opened.

arbitration awards[30]. The New York Convention on the Recognition and Enforcement of Arbitral Awards dating from 10.06.1958 is principally applicable to all awards of arbitration. However, many states affirmed the reservation in Art. I § 3 Phrase 2, whereby the Convention is only applicable to commercial causes.

In conclusion self regulation can only be used really efficiently in some areas. The biggest opportunities lie in economic transactions between similarly strong partners, as for example between enterprises. But in vast regulatory areas, participation of the state is inevitable – and in any event, it is worthwhile to many usergroups. In particular, the protection of local values can not be achieved without the state.

*b) Combination of "civil society" and a national private legal system*

The failure of a purely public legal order as well as a purely private order suggests that one should look for another mediating solution, whereby private persons are integrated into the regulations, but the state is not totally excluded. It is found in the combination of a *civil society* and a national private legal system. To use civil law and the private protagonists for the process of regulation has a special flair to it, especially in relation to the originally global questions of the internet. The civil society, by its basic idea is not only individualistic but also universal; the citizen becomes cosmopolitan in a society, that as a consequence of basic civic principles of freedom and equality, is intended in its nature for cosmopolitan society[31]. These are the best premises by which to meet the global challenges of the internet.

First of all here the subjects of private law are also the central protagonists, who within the scope of their private autonomy are free to shape their legal relations. But the private persons don't stand alone here: their relations are underpinned by a national system of private law that provides optional law in case of incomplete agreements and additionally withdraws some questions of compulsory law from autonomous formation by private entities. Thereby uninvolved third persons are granted necessary protection and at the same time, in case of structural imbalance, procedural fairness between the parties in the settlement process and if needed, substantial fairness of the settlement result is also guaranteed. Furthermore the state provides an institutionalized system for the resolution of conflicts, that also in international cases is able to co-ordinate the participating laws and institutions. Thus the state does not appear to be an involved protagonist, but rather stays in the background as guardian and at the same time assists with the enforcement of private rights. The actual protagonists are subjects of private law, as they need to take action in order to obtain the protection of their given rights. This can be an advantage insofar as the individual protagonist will fight more determinedly for the enforcement of his rights than a national agency would do whilst looking after the interests of the public at large[32].

---

30 Cf.: *Goldsmith*, Cyberanarchy [n. 10], pp. 1246 et seq.

31 *Mestmäcker* [n. 4], p. 63.

32 *Christoph Engel,* "Zivilrecht als Fortsetzung des Wirtschaftsrechts mit anderen Mitteln", *Juristenzeitung* 1995, p. 213 (215).

In order to be able to evaluate the opportunities for the protection of local values in private law, it is first of all necessary to make oneself clear about the mechanisms of private law for the protection of values (see B.). Afterwards one comes to the actual advantages of private law in the range of global datanets: the established system for international co-ordination of national private legal systems (see C.).

## B. The protection of values in private law

How then does the protection of local values work in private law and how may the state – despite his servile role – take advantage of these mechanisms of regulation?

First of all, it can restrict or extend the rights and authorities of the private protagonists. On the one hand there is the possibility of assigning actual subjective rights that belong to a subject of private law with regard to all – such as an absolute right like property – or only with regard to certain persons. Less broader is the second, more seldom used possibility, to guarantee instead of subjective rights only the authority to claim one's rights. This may happen in relation to the subjective rights of third persons, which is particularly recommendable if the holder of the right himself doesn't have sufficient incentive or no real possibility to claim his rights. Rights of actions can also refer to collective or diffuse interests, i.e. those not belonging to individual persons. The perception of a right of action will, in both cases, generally be left to associations of interests. Actions of associations are of particular renown in competition law, some systems make use of it in environmental law[33], and they are now also provided for in consumer protection law. Art. 11 II of the EU-directive on distance selling[34] demands the implementation of a right of action for associations concerned with consumer protection[35].

Regulation of the internet by institutions of civil law, be they in existence or to be created, must always take inter-private legal relationships as the starting point wherefrom the private protagonists should commence their actions. For one, this could be contractual relationships, like for instance the relationship between user and service provider. Contracts can also be found between the different suppliers of the internet forming components (routers, datalines etc.) up to the content provider and his access provider to the internet. Besides these direct contractual relationships, legal relations may also arise outside of contractual agreements on the basis of legal orders. This, for instance, is the case in tort law. Such an approach via legal relations then also allows a

33 For instance in the Netherlands; following Art. 18 of the non-ratified Lugano Convention on Civil Liability for damage resulting form activities dangerous to the environment of 1993 of the Council of Europe claims of associations in relation to environmental damages shall be implemented throughout Europe.

34 Directive 97/7/EC of 20th May 1997, O.J. EC 1997 No. L 144 pp. 19 et seq.

35 The current draft of the German statute regulating distance-selling (as at June 1999 - <http://www.bmj.bund.de/download/fernag.pdf>), that will enact the directive in Germany, provides for association based claims in consumer protection affairs by virtue of the new § 22 AGB-Gesetz, that despite its position shall be applicable to all consumer protection provisions.

differentiation between the various mechanisms that are provided by private law for the protection of local values. Here one can differentiate as to whether the values that need to be protected are endangered by actions forming a private legal relationship – these mainly take part within contract (see under 1.) - or by other actions that are not directly connected to private law (see under 2.).

## 1. Protection against actions in private legal relations

The protective task of private law is obvious where values might be threatened by actions within private-law relations like, for instance, the conclusion of a contract. Here, one can further differentiate, if the values infringed by the action are actually inherent to private law (a), or values that are without direct connection to private law (b).

### *a) Values inherent to private law*

Private law is based in all its parts on certain moral concepts that might vary considerably upon their local background. The possible differences of moral concepts in the field of family law and law of succession are quite remarkable. But modern communication techniques might only lead to a rise in the quantity of possible conflicts, as to the quality, no new challenges are thereby created for private law and its conflict of laws rules. Therefore they should not be of further interest at this point.

A clear foundation of values can also be found in other rules of private law referring to interpersonal actions. The private legal systems of the western hemisphere are based centrally on the guarantee of property, be it physical or intellectual. In particular the latter section has to face new dangers in the form of the new communication technologies. But also within civil law transactions in a free market, one meets numerous values that – often in mutual weighing up – are actually protected by private law. On the one side, these are values like freedom of contract, competition or even creation of trust (for instance by rules for the protection of the creditor), that assure a free market. On the other side, certain groups are protected that have structural disadvantages - like consumers and minors. These values can be found as ideas in all western private legal systems, but one meets clearly differing evaluations. Especially when it comes to the need of consumer protection, one meets an astonishing variety of evaluations.

These values that are inherent in private law are mainly protected by the private legal system itself. For this, rights of disposition can be appointed to the individual person (like with physical or intellectual property), that entitle him to defense against infringements. In order to also prevent value-adverse agreements between the parties, law makes use of compulsory rules – for instance for the protection of minors and consumers. Public law only applies in a supplementary and reinforcing way in extremely serious cases, especially in the economic sphere, and also occasionally with the threat of punishment (for instance the protection of physical and intellectual property).

### b) *Protection of other values*

Other values are not immediately related to private law and are therefore not actual objects of its regulations. Values like data protection, personal honor or the ban on hard pornography are mainly protected by the rules of public law, including criminal law. But these values can also be infringed by actions in the form of private law so that here there are also attempts to regulate. In these cases the rather unproblematic hull of private law transactions is filled up with value-adverse content. A sales contract can have forbidden pornographic material as subject matter, which is delivered in a physical form or is downloaded as file via internet; a text with insulting content can be printed against payment or made public as a file; access to databanks with protected data can be opened.

In order to punish such value infringements outside of the actual regulation-sphere of private law, the private law not only refers to general clauses that provide an entry to public-law value decisions in the form of prohibitory enactments[36], but also moral concepts of the society in form of "common decency"[37]. As a consequence for the infringement of a negative statute or public morals, civil law sanctions are pronounced, for contracts it is usually a pronouncement that it is void. Moreover, when it comes to forbidden or immoral performance, suing for the pecuniary benefits of performance can be excluded for the party who acted in a forbidden or immoral way[38]. When it comes to less serious infringements, like for instance gambling, civil law contents itself with denying its help as it only grants incomplete claims that either do not give right of action or do not even form a duty to perform at all, but only form a possible legal basis if a duty has already been performed[39].

## 2. Protection of values against endangerment outside of private law

If on the other hand values outside of private-law relations are endangered, upon first glance, this is not the business of private law. Here, the initial conduct gearing regulation is the duty of public law. However, this does not mean that private law is left completely outside. With tort law, private law is in possession of an instrument to legally register actions with harmful consequences to other persons. Thus, for instance, an insult that shall be prevented mainly by the threat of criminal sanction, also leads to private-law consequences in tort. This is made possible, as private law guarantees

---

36 In German law the infringement of statutes forbidding conduct according to § 134 BGB, in French law Art. 1131 Code civil, in Anglo American law the matter is one of "public policy"; compare hereto: *Konrad Zweigert / Hein Kötz,* Einführung in die Rechtsvergleichung (3rd ed., Tübingen 1996), § 28.

37 In German law "die guten Sitten", § 138 BGB; in French law the correlative is "les bonnes moeurs". In common law, as a consequence of its case law structure a similarly formalised counterpart is missing, but the idea of "common decency" is analogous.

38 In German law, for instance: § 817 BGB.

39 So in German law regarding gambling – § 762 BGB – and still for marriage-broking - § 656 BGB.

subjective rights to the individual person that are then protected by tort law. In this way, infringements are pursuable for the individual, independent from any governmental activities.

This in particular happens to values that are inherent to the private-legal system, physical and intellectual property being the frontrunners, but also, individually appointed rights of disposition exist in relation to trade-marks and other rights to identity. Outside of these obviously civil-law objects, other values are also protected by the granting of individual rights. In relation to the dangers of global datanets in particular, rights of personality are especially important: honor is protected against insults from others; personal data is subjected to rights of disposition that exclude others from non consensual access and use; by relying on the protected private sphere one can take action against unwanted external attacks ( e.g. email-spamming, commercial mails or the confrontation with obscene content). Even the right to the custody, care and control of parents or other guardians may be used in order to prevent others from having an influence on children, especially by material liable to corrupt the young.

The decisive factor is the barrier of unlawfulness for whose assessment public-law prohibitions can again be the decisive factor, but also applicable are general rules of conduct about which infringements of foreign legal goods are allowed or are not allowed[40]. Sometimes fault of the intruder is also necessary. If these requirements for not allowed action are met, the injured party may claim from the intruder elimination of the arisen infringements, compensation for material and immaterial damages and – if the threat is sufficiently concrete – omission from future infringements[41].

## C. The international co-ordination of private legal orders

The demonstrated mechanisms of protection in national legal systems provide help in the internet only in cases where the participants of the respective contractual or tortuous legal relations are resident within the scope of the same legal order. As soon as a border-crossing data-transfer takes place – and be it only by servers, that are located abroad – a national private legal system initially has to face the same limits as public law.

Nevertheless, national private legal systems are much better co-ordinated in comparison to public law ones. By the conflict of laws rules of private international law for the determination of the applicable law and the rules of the international law of civil procedure for the authority to adjudicate on national jurisdictions as well as for the recognition and enforcement of foreign judgements, border-crossing private legal actions can also be resolved. In contrast to public international law, here the application of foreign legislation as well as the recognition and enforcement of foreign judgements is no peculiarity, rather it is an everyday process in civil courts. This established system

40 The so-called "Verkehrspflichten" or "Verkehrsschutzpflichten" in German law.

41 The right to forbearance in German law can be constructed by analogy with the property right rules in § 1004 BGB.

for the co-ordination of national private legal systems and consequent jurisdictions is the standard by which one can work in the new, necessarily globalized world of Cyberspace. It should now briefly be demonstrated here, how this co-ordination works, if the co-ordination system can also surmount the new challenges of global datanets and lastly, if due to this system there really can be a demonstrable advantage to public law. The description is based on the European perspective, but occasionally the US-American perspective will be referred to for comparison. For co-ordination, one can distinguish between three questions, three forms of *jurisdiction*: Private International Law answers the question about the applicable law (*prescriptive jurisdiction* – see 1.), the international law of civil procedure deals on the one side with the (international) jurisdiction of national courts to adjudicate an action (*adjudicative jurisdiction* – see 2.) and on the other side, the authority to enforce a judgement (*enforcement jurisdiction* – see 3).

## 1. Applicable law

It is the duty of private international law (PIL) to determine which law is applicable. Generally PIL is – in contrast to the first impression given by its name – *national* law. Conflict of laws rules that are truly international and established by treaty are rare. To the areas in question here, it is important to mention the Rome Convention on the Law Applicable to Contractual Obligations of the 19th June 1980[42], that is in force amongst the EU-members.

Furthermore in the field of private law there is a standardized substantive law. Especially important, particularly to many sales of goods via internet[43], is the Convention on Contracts for the International Sale of Goods (CISG) of the United Nations.

But standardization of law is, one should be clear about this fact, generally in antipathy to specific local legal developments and local values[44]. It is therefore only worthwhile, where the internationality of the factual matrix is so compelling that a relinquishment of standardization would signify great damage that would be more serious than the loss of legislation that features local peculiarities. Besides international commercial trade, this is for instance, also valid for law concerning checks and bills of exchange, which consequently was standardized at an early stage[45]. Also for E-commerce that is by its

42 The current version is 2nd draft from Funchal from 18th May 1992.

43 The respective transaction has to be within the factual, spatial and personal area of application that is defined in Art. 1-6 CISG. An important exception here is the exclusion of all consumer sales in Art. 2 lit. a).

44 The opposite is only true, when states come together in order to better protect mutual local values by standardising the law. Hereto one might include the legal standardisation by directives within the EU in the area of consumer and data protection.

45 Compare the two Geneva conventions in international law concerning Bills of Exchange from the 7th June 1930 and Cheques from the 19th March 1931.

nature international, an international standardized law on certain questions will develop, for instance in the areas of electronic signatures, the electronic conclusion of contracts or electronic payments[46].

But before the genesis of a standardized law in the above mentioned areas comes about, or in areas legal and geographic where no standardized law exists, there is still the necessity of determining the applicable law by the relevant conflict of laws rules. International law contains few provisions about the requirements of conflict of laws rules. The application of legal rules (generally this, of course, refers to the application of domestic legislation by courts or authorities of the state), is only not allowed if the factual matrix has absolutely no relation to the state[47]. There is then no legitimate interest to regulate, usually no interest to regulation at all, so that the restriction is only of limited importance.

The decision about the applicable law is therefore orientated toward the ordering duty of PIL[48]. The aim is to achieve a possibly conflictless co-ordination of the national legislation focused on a possibly standardized determination of the applicable law. In order to achieve this, one seeks to establish the legislation with the strongest connection to the decisive state of facts. The determination of this strongest connection becomes more and more difficult in a increasingly internationally linked and therefore more complex world[49]. The reason for this is the traditional concept of PIL, that looks for objective criteria in determining the applicable law and in order to locate the legal relationship in question by looking for its 'seat'[50]. To locate the legal relationship - according to kind – various criteria may apply: the location of an already carried out or to be carried out action, the site of a physical object, the residence of a person. Also applicable are fictitious local connections by formalized criteria such as legal residence or nationality. The sense of conflict of law rules, that are orientated upon geographic criteria becomes questionable when considering areas of performance like the internet or other datanets, that are, to a far reaching extent, removed from local references[51].

---

46 Also: *Engel*, Internet [n. 4], p. 255.

47 *Jan Kropholler*, Internationales Privatrecht (3rd ed., Tübingen 1997), § 8 I 1.; *Goldsmith*, Cyberanarchy [n. 10], pp. 1207 et seq.

48 For individual duties of order and the concept of justice in Private International Law compare: *Kropholler* [n. 47], §§ 4-7.

49 That applies not only for 'Cyberspace' factual status, but also – perhaps to a lesser extent – also for 'Realspace' actions: *Goldsmith*, Cyberanarchy [n. 10], p. 1208.

50 Therefore the law applicable to the cause is not only called the lex causae, but also (particularly in American usage) the lex locus.

51 *Johnson/Post* [n. 17], pp. 1374 et seq.; *Burnstein*, Conflicts [n. 17], pp. 81 et seq.

But skepticism should not be exaggerated, because behind actions within 'Cyberspace' stand actions in the real universe, real persons are participating who make use of technology provided by the real world[52]. The problem therefore does not consist of a missing local connection, but rather in the determination of the location (at least *ad hoc*), but particularly within the local variety that may result from the place of the participating users and the used technical instruments. But this is not a phenomenon restricted to Cyberspace, it can also manifest itself in the real world that is increasingly determined by international contacts and great physical mobility[53]. As a consequence of the increasing number of points of connection, it may be that to one case more than one law is applicable - possibly also often various jurisdictions in different courts. This depends on how one deals with a bigger choice of justifiable connections. One could think of alternative or cumulative connections, a right to choose for the plaintiff; a comparison of what is more favorable in the interest of the party that has been acknowledged protection or simply the priority of the respective national law of the deciding court. However, one need not fear that the variety of applicable laws would become too big, as not every local connection is evaluated in the same way[54]. Besides the places where the data is put onto the net by users machines or was retrieved therefrom, no additional connection, for instance from the transfer of data through a state, could result. The selection of the relevant local connection (very rarely maybe also two of these connections) demands evaluation and is thus no longer just a factual question, but also a normative and therefore a legal question. But for these cases the law – and particularly the conflict of laws rules that are used to complex constellations that are not easily subsumed – is well equipped. In some areas that are especially relevant to the internet, it should briefly be demonstrated, that the conflict of laws rules are able to adopt to the new challenges.

### a) *International Contractual law of obligations, consumer protection and rules of interference*

The area that is most important for E-commerce is PIL in the area of contracts. As already mentioned, this has been standardized in the European Union by the Rome Convention on the Law Applicable to Contractual Obligations of 1980[55].

Principally the choice of the applicable law by the parties has priority (Art. 3). They are thereby given the possibility of pre-emptively avoiding the previously mentioned

52 *Herbert Kronke*, "Applicable Law in Torts and Contracts in Cyberspace", in: *Boele-Woelki/Kessedjian* [n. 7], pp. 65 (65 et seq.); *Rufus Pichler*, "Internationale Gerichtszuständigkeit im Online-Bereich" in: *M. Immenhauser / J. Wichtermann* (eds.), Jahrbuch Junger Zivilrechtswissenschaftler 1998: Vernetzte Welt - globales Recht (Stuttgart et al. 1999), pp. 229 (232 et seq.); Goldsmith, Cyberanarchy [n. 10], p. 1200.

53 *Goldsmith*, Cyberanarchy [n. 10], pp. 1234 et seq.

54 *Goldsmith*, Cyberanarchy [n. 10], p. 1234.

55 See supra p. 222 and n. 42.

problems regarding the applicable law[56]. Choice of law is only restricted where the law recognizes special interests of protection, for instance towards third persons or structurally weaker parties. Their position should not be attacked by the parties by denying them use of legislation that is favorable to them. As a guideline one could say that the autonomy of a party, such as in choice of applicable law, can only exist where in the substantive law private regulations altering the legislative position are also possible. For instance the liberty to choose legislation is restricted in the relation of enterprises and consumers, because due to structural imbalances, free agreements on the applicable law cannot readily be expected. Art. 5 of the Rome Convention subsequently claims that for certain contracts about consumer protection even though there has been agreement on choice of law, the provisions on consumer protection of the native country of the consumer will continue to be applicable. The presupposition is that the contractual partner of the consumer in the native country of the consumer took action by advertising, an expressive offer or even acceptation of an order, so that the consumer could rely on the continuance of the existing protection he knows. If this also applies to consumer sales via the internet depends on whether one would want to consider the provision of offers in the internet that could be raised from abroad, as advertising or offers made there. What speaks in favor for this is that the offers are easily accessible from the place of residence of the consumer and that he quite often is not able to know, if he has "virtually" crossed any borders (other than reading a foreign newspaper or watching foreign TV channels). What undoubtedly speaks against this are the economic interests of the providers. They are not technically able to restrict the scope of their content effectively[57], and suddenly see themselves having to face a myriad of national consumer protection rules. But confrontation with foreign law is not unusual in international business. An American mail order business, that sends a printed catalogue to Germany in the traditional way, also has to take into account German consumer protection rules. Similarly he who advertises in the internet knows the international reach of his offer and will often also use it for the acquirement of new markets. He can, however protect himself, by restricting his offer expressly to customers only within a specified area and by not accepting any orders from outside this area[58]. But this becomes problematic if the location of the consumer is not recognizable to the provider. This is only guaranteed, as long as the goods are delivered "offline". For Online-deliveries, for instance of digitized documents, music files or software, the delivery address within the net is not a reliable indicator of the location of the consumer[59]: an e-mail under "meyer200@hotmail.com" can be subscribed to by everybody world-wide. Here, the provider could protect himself by asking the customer about his country of origin when he makes his order and possibly excluding delivery to customers in certain states. If the customer gives false information, although he had been correctly informed about the

56 For the requirements for an express or conclusive choice of law on the internet: *Peter Mankowski*, "Das Internet im Internationalen Vertrags- und Deliktsrecht", *Rabels Zeitschrift für ausländisches und internationales Privatrecht* 63 (1999), pp. 203 (209 et seq.).

57 *Burnstein*, Global Network [n. 7], p. 24; *Mankowski*, Internet [n. 56], pp. 243 et seq.

58 *Mankowski*, Internet [n. 56], pp. 244 et seq.

59 *Goldsmith*, Cyberanarchy [n. 10], pp. 1204 et seq.

relevance of the information, he no longer deserves protection. Thus there is no need any longer to enforce the rules protecting him[60]. Although it is not technically possible to exclude certain groups of people – for instance by state grouping – this is made possible by private law – at least as a fiction. Thereby providers can prevent the application of regulations not expressly wanted.

Possibly one would also consider it as being sufficient, if the consumer has been sufficiently instructed (and has possibly confirmed this, too), that he has 'virtually' crossed the borders of his country of origin and may therefore no longer rely on the well-known protection of his own country. The European Union decided in favor of a more intense form of consumer protection, as detailed in the previously mentioned directive on distance selling[61]. According to Art. 12 II, in consumer sales that have arisen from telecommunications technology like telephone, fax or even the internet, the protection-rules provided by the directive are not influenced in the case of the parties choosing to use the law of a third country. This additional conflict of laws rule is principally necessary because a choice of law also excludes the compulsory provisions of the outvoted law; they are replaced by the compulsory provisions of the chosen law. A choice of law is not influenced by the compulsory factual rules of the law applicable by objective criteria, but only by mandatory conflict of laws rules[62], as for instance enforced in the consumer protection rule in Art. 5 Rome Convention or in Art. 12 II of the distance selling directive.

This separation between compulsory substantive law and mandatory conflict of laws rules seems to contradict Art. 7 of the Rome Convention, which in paragraph 2 provides for the continuation of compulsory laws of the state of jurisdiction, without consideration of the law applied to the contract. But the term "compulsory law" might be misleading because here, in a more narrow sense, only such *rules of interference* are meant, which, as a consequence of their absolute nature, always dominate. In civil law, generally, the only rules that are considered to be absolute are those that reflect public law rules of behavior (e.g. the prohibition against price-fixing)[63]. These submissions should of course encompass all actions carried out within the territory without taking into account that the parties had maybe chosen another law. This is also true, if to the private-law questions foreign private law applies, not as a consequence of choice of law, but as a consequence of objective conflict of laws rules.

These objective conflict of laws rules in the international law of contract, which are always referred to if no choice of law has taken place, are hardly endangered by global datanets in their application as they are principally attached not to related actions, but to person related criteria. Thus within the EU for instance, the location of the seller is the principal decisive factor (as provider of the performance characteristic of the contract,

60 *Mankowski*, Internet [n. 56], pp. 249 et seq.

61 See supra p. 218 and n. 34.

62 *von Bar*, IPR II [n. 19], No. 420 et seq.

63 Cf.: *von Bar*, IPR II [n. 19], No. 452 et seq. - In purely civil law subject matter, the provision only becomes relevant in the area of tenancy agreements and purchase of a flat.

compare Art. 4 Rome Convention). Also the proposition of the EU-Commission for guidelines on E-commerce[64] provides in its Art. 3 I, the establishment of the principle of origin[65]. Though to consumer contracts, insofar as a choice of law is missing, Art. 5 III Rome Convention provides that the law at the usual place of residence of the consumer is applicable.

### b) *International tort law*

The person-related connections, such as location, residence or location of a contractual party raise fewer difficulties than the action-related connections in the internet. An action within the internet can consist of a mouse-click in State A, that triggers a calculation or save-process in State B, possibly also a data-transfer in State C, whereby the data is transmitted via the States D, E and F etc. The consequences of the action can eventually, due to the global access possibilities to the contents of the World Wide Web, be world wide. This is the problem in the sphere of tort law, where traditionally the connection is action-related to the *locus delicti commissi* - the location where the tort has been committed. The constituent action in the internet is not easy to locate: it definitely lies where a computer has been used to achieve access to the internet, but there is also a place where a process of calculation or saving has occurred, particularly in this context, a place where the *Uploading*, has been triggered[66]. But the determination of the *lex loci delicti* becomes much more difficult by the fact that in most legal systems not only the place of performance, but also the place where the factual (which is therefore also considered to be part of the tort-action) effect happens. Theoretically, by the potentially world-wide reach of internet-activities, every legal system could become applicable. As a consequence for the potential tortfeasor, the applicable law, and thus the yardstick by which his conduct is measured, can no longer be foreseen.

But here too it is apt to note that not all local connections have the same importance. *Defamation* via internet can in fact be received world wide, but the strongest connection, apart from the place where the statement has been put onto the net, will be the place where the victim of the defamation resides. To obtain this result, it is always necessary to start in one's mind with the immediately affected object of legal protection, and not from the developing consequential damages. Sometimes it will also be necessary to consider the localization of certain objects of legal protection. For example, personal honor is still generally regarded as an object of legal protection in any and every place as it only arises from people's relation to other people and their opinions. With such an understanding the effect of defamation potentially happens globally - where it had actually happened by the retrieval of defaming content, will probably be

64 Document KOM (98) 586 of the 18th November 1998; Text and considerations in O.J. EC 1999 No. C 30, pp. 4 et seq.

65 Cf.: *Arthur Waldenberger*, "Electronic Commerce: der Richtlinienvorschlag der EG-Kommission", *Europäische Zeitschrift für Wirtschaftsrecht* 1999, pp. 296 (298 et seq.).

66 *Pichler* [n. 52], p. 247; more detailed is: *Mankowski*, Internet [n. 56], pp. 257 et seq.

hard to establish. A solution could only exist in disconnecting honor from interpersonal relationships and see it as a value, inherent to the bearer and can thereby also be connected to his place of residence.

### c) *Conclusions*

It appears then that the challenges created by global datanets can generally be managed by conflict of laws rules. Sometimes a rethinking of out-dated concepts is necessary, but the further development of law due to a fast changing world is nothing unusual. The process of adaptation will be a lot easier if one uses the more flexible Anglo-American system and not a fixed connection system of Continental-European design. Here a more open approach, at least during the application of the norm by the judge would help. The tendency toward this can already be ascertained[67]. The open approach allows one to orientate to the case and to consider the special features of the internet. This way is, in any event, preferable to an untimely capitulation by holding onto a purely schematic, but well established connection like the location of the plaintiff or the defendant[68]. At a later time it might be possible to draw generally valid abstract norms out of the experiences.

In the meanwhile, one has to avert the danger that a variety of possible connection points are used to 'return to home', i.e. to drive towards the application of one's own law. This may happen by convenience, but also in a desire for the protection of (supposed) national interests. Here, in particular, the USA wide 'governmental interest approach' could undergo an undesired renaissance[69]. A consequence would be the accumulation of inconsistent regulations which would also appear in the area of public law. Regulations in this field are permitted as soon as the regulable conduct has domestic consequences. The perception of this right of regulation inevitably leads to spillover effects that cannot be dealt with by international law and therefore have to be accepted[70]. In contrast to private law, the state stands alone when it comes to public-law regulation and the enforcement of its claims. Instead, private law can rely on international co-operation. This achievement becomes endangered however when the single state uses the increase of potential connecting points provided by global data-transfer for extensive extension of its regulatory competence in private law. Only

67 In the international contractual law of the Rome Convention primarily only the link creating the strongest connection is established, which is put into concrete form by a series of legal assumptions (Art.4). Symptomatic is also the tendency to "loosen" the scene of the originating occurrence in international tort law (compare *Kropholler* [n. 47], § 53 V), that is also based on American preparatory work (laid down by: *J.H. Morris*, "The Proper Law of a Tort", *Harvard Law review* 64 (1950/51), pp. 881 et seq.).

68 But this, for instance is claim by: *Burnstein*, Global Network [n. 7], pp. 27 et seq.

69 The statement of the founder of this theory *Brainerd Currie*, is characteristic: "We would be better off without choice-of-law rules.", cited by: *Christian von Bar*, Internationales Privatrecht I – Allgemeine Lehren (München 1987), No. 503.

70 Cf.: *Goldsmith*, "The Internet, Conflicts of Regulation, and International Harmonization", in this volume, sub I.

confidence in the sensible dealing of each state with its competencies in regulation, decisions and enforcement leads to a readiness to apply foreign law, to leave the judgement of an action to a foreign court and eventually, if necessary, to accept the foreign court's decision and to enforce it.

## 2. Adjudicative jurisdiction

The question of adjudicative jurisdiction is of great importance for the litigating parties. Proximity to the court has great influence on the costs of litigation. Because of the *lex-fori* rules that are applied to procedural law, whereby only the law of the home-state of the court is applied, the domestic party has a clear advantage due to their better knowledge of the procedural law. Of particular importance can be the fact that every court applies its own national PIL. If the appropriate conflict of laws rules differ, the plaintiff may choose between different responsible courts and thereby influence the law applicable to the case and possibly the result of the decision (so-called *forum shopping*).

Generally, legal action has to be taken at the place of residence, meaning the location of the defendant (principal of *actor sequitur forum rei*). This principal is universally recognized, but there are exceptions, and these vary between the European and United States systems.

The Brussels Convention on Jurisdiction and the Enforcement of Judgements in Civil and Commercial Matters of 1968/96[71],

that is in force within the area of the European Union, works with a strictly formalized system of legal fori. Besides the general legal forum at the place of the defendant, it also establishes some exceptional, i.e. additional legal fori that can be of particular relevance to claims in consequence of activities on the internet. Especially important is the tort forum, Art. 5 No. 3 Brussels Convention, whereby in a tortuous matter, action may also be taken at 'the court of the place where the harm occurred'. Despite this formulation, that appears to only focus on the results of the effect, one needs to understand this sentence according to the principle of ubiquity in International tort law. Accordingly, in the case of distance torts, action can be taken at the place where the tortuous act originated as well as at the place where its effects were felt[72]. As with the determination of the applicable law, the place where the effect occurred consequently provides more problems than the place where the tortuous act originated due to the global effects of many internet activities. But here also it is true that by sensible adaptation of some

71 The newest version is the fourth one from 26th November 1996 (O.J. EC 1997 No. C 15, pp. 1 et seq.), which came into power on 1st January 1999. For the other European states that are not EU members the almost identical Lugano-Convention of 16th September 1988 applies.

72 Thus the rule corresponds to § 32 of the German civil procedural law, which seems to refer to the exact opposite ('where the action started'), but can also be interpreted in the sense of the ubiquity principle – to determine the places of both action and effect on the internet. Compare: *Birgit Bachmann*, "Der Gerichtsstand der unerlaubten Handlung im Internet", *Praxis des Internationalen Privat- und Verfahrensrechts* 1998, pp. 179 (182 et seq.).

concepts, the usefulness of the basic system can be retained. There is one further argument to be mentioned when it comes to the question of jurisdictional competence: one cannot count on the actual retrieval of the harmful information, because the plaintiff, who is the one to choose the court, will not always be able to obtain information about the retrievals. In Germany for instance the surrendering of this information is strictly forbidden for providers of telecommunication services[73].

An important consequence of an extraordinary jurisdiction is the possibility to force the defendant to submit himself to legal assessment in another country. Service of originating documentation abroad is not easy, but here international agreements have been concluded that makes this possible at least in wide parts of the world[74]. If proper service of writ has taken place and the rules of procedure have been followed, judgement by default may be given in the event of the defendant not appearing, this can also be recognized and enforced abroad[75]. Thus sufficient incentive exists for the foreign plaintiff to face the trial, or, if he declines due to costs (particularly those associated with a lost trial), to accept the outstanding debt and meet it.

In the sphere of contractual litigation, the Brussels Convention provides a special legal forum at the place of performance (Art. 5 No. 1 1. Alt); if an additional legal forum apart from the location of the performer is justified depends, therefore, on whether he is already, by contractual agreement, obliged to carry out performance in another country. Of additional importance in the contractual sphere are the special rules applicable to consumer affairs in Art. 13 ff. They open an additional legal forum at the place of residence of the consumer in the case of contracts that do not serve the professional or commercial activities of a person. Restrictive provisions are also existent here: for instance, prior to the conclusion of the contract an express offer or an advertisement in the state of origin of the consumer has to be expressed, and that the consumer on his behalf must have taken all actions necessary to conclude of the contract in this state (Art. 13 I No. 3 together with Art. 14 Brussels Convention). For the classification of advertisements or offers in the internet, the considerations that have been taken in relation to the applicable law also apply[76]. At least as long as it is not quite clear to the consumer, that he has (virtually) left his home country, the protection of his home legal forum should be granted to him[77].

---

73 § 6 III 1 Teledienstedatenschutzgesetz.; cf.: Bachmann [n. 72], p. 186.

74 The most important international treaty in this area is the Hague treaty covering foreign service of legal and extra-legal documents in the areas of civil law and business matters from the 15.11.1965, that inter alia is valid concerning Germany-USA.

75 Compare Art. 27 No. 2 Brussels Convention, whereby a decision will only not be recognised when the defendant was not properly served with the originating documentation and therefore took no part in subsequent proceedings.

76 See supra p. 225 et seq.

77 In the near future, transfer of the independently ratified Brussels Convention to the EU legal machinery is planned. That is possible owing to the Amsterdam Treaty which created the possibility for legal co-operation in civil matters. According to the suggestion of the commission from 14.07.1999, inter alia, the courts responsible for contractual matters shall be precisely defined. Also, the courts responsible for consumer protection shall have their jurisdiction extended to cover all

Generally the Brussels Convention also allows for express agreement of a legal forum between the parties (Art. 17). But this freedom principally requires a written agreement (except for differing habits resulting from continuous business practice or deviating customs in international trade) that is hard to achieve on the internet. Additionally, freedom of choice in consumer protection affairs is restricted to the time after litigation has commenced, or the change must be favorable to the consumer (Art. 15).

US-American law, that previously also for *adjudicative jurisdiction* paid strict attention to the necessity of possible enforcement and therefore only accepted jurisdiction for judgements if the person *(jurisdiction in personam)* or at least some of their assets (*jurisdiction in rem*) were in the country, nowadays shows broader understanding about international jurisdiction. So it should be sufficient, that the defendant had 'minimum-contacts' with the state of jurisdiction and that the authority has to comply with the requirements of 'fair play and substantial justice'[78]. These quite open phrasings could – rather than the formalized rules of the Brussels Convention – lead to an extensive widening of international jurisdiction, because owing to the ubiquitous working of the internet, each action has domestic connection. A responsible way of dealing with such open criteria is therefore important. If one's own regulatory and jurisdictional competence is enlarged too much, one's decisions may loose international acceptance and therefore international enforceability[79]. For enforcement of a judgement in another state, prior recognition is necessary (hereto see 3 directly). For this one of the necessary prerequisites is that the deciding court had international jurisdiction from the point of view of the recognizing state. A decision that is based on a jurisdiction that had been broadened too far, would thus only be of use if domestic enforcement is possible.

## 3. Recognition and enforcement

The most relevant difference between public and private law might be found in the area of recognition and enforcement of foreign judgements. Whereas co-operation is the rule in private law, it still is an exception in public law. *Prima facie*, every decision of a state's institution, be that a court or other official authority, has no effect beyond its borders. But in the field of civil law, the willingness of states to officially recognize and give effect to decisions of other states is much greater than in the field of public law (and especially criminal law) decisions. The willingness to recognize decisions in civil actions is based on the fiction of equality of private legal systems and civil courts in all parts of the world[80]. This is only a fiction – also in the sphere of civil law - but it, quite

---

consumer affairs. This last suggestion could symbolise an additional hurdle for E-commerce and that is why the commission is planning a hearing this Autumn to attempt to find a balance between consumer protection and E-commerce.

78 The leading cases from the U.S. Supreme Court about the "minimum-contacts-doctrine" are: International Shoe Co. v. Washington, 326 U.S. 310 (1945) and World-Wide-Volkswagen Corp. v. Woodson, 444 U.S. 286 (1980).

79 See also: *Goldsmith*; Cyberanarchy [n. 10], p. 1219.

80 *Reinhold Geimer*, Internationales Zivilprozessrecht (3rd ed., Köln 1997), No. 37 and 2751.

correctly, is missing in public law where the state itself actually appears as protagonist and legal subject. Here, equality of the legal system, for instance when requirements of the state's constitution, protection of freedom etc. are concerned, needs to be determined in every single case. With recognition and enforcement in civil procedures, the recognizing state solely helps the private person who has obtained a judgement that has to be recognized and enforced in another country. In public law however, the recognizing state would become the henchman of a foreign state authority, that at the same time is party to the legal relationship in question.

Of course international agreements on legal and administrative assistance also exist in the field of administrative law, in particular in criminal law. The sometimes very close co-operation of friendly countries should not be underestimated. But this is generally restricted to particular legal areas and introducing new areas often requires lengthy negotiations. However a single hole appearing as a consequence of lack of co-operation on behalf of one state can make the efforts towards regulation obsolete. In the sphere of global nets for instance, a provider of forbidden material could escape to another country. The net of existing treaties on legal co-operation is quite confusing[81], procedures are often complicated and lengthy and consequently there often is a lack of practical experience on how to handle them.

With decisions in civil cases recognition is the rule, the denial of recognition however is an exception that requires explanation. It can principally only be denied because of serious formal mistakes in the original judgement (for instance lack of international competence of the adjudicating court, denial of legal hearing, with default judgements lack of proper writ etc.). Controls regarding the content of the decision are generally absent[82]. A rejection of recognition by reasons regarding the content is only exceptionally possible if there had been an infringement of the domestic *ordre public.* This hurdle to common understanding is very high. Recognition of the judgement, i.e. the reflection of the effects of the judgement on the recognizing state would have to be incompatible to its elementary values. For this a sufficient relation between the effects of the judgement and the recognizing state has to exist: the closer this relation is, the smaller are the requirements for *ordre-public* adversity (so-called 'Relativity of the *ordre public*'). Nevertheless, they remain considerable.

A further possibility is part-recognition, particularly of judgements that are focused on monetary performance. This plays an important role in the field of the often exorbitant *punitive damages*, that are awarded by US-American courts with the express aim of penalty and prevention in cases of tortuous act. As this function is alien to German civil law – as it is with other continental-European civil legal systems – these judgements are recognized in Germany only up to an amount necessary for compensation[83]. Thus the

---

81 Compare only the nomination for Europe by *Wolfgang Schomburg*, "Internationale vertragliche Rechtshilfe in Strafsachen", *Neue Juristische Wochenschrift* 1996, pp. 3328 et seq.

82 Art. 29 Brussels Convention forbids any verification of the matter.

83 Cf. the decision of the German Bundesgerichtshof of the 4th June 1992, BGHZ 118, pp. 312 (334 et seq.) – see also: *Geimer* [n. 80], No. 2974 with references to the many comments on that decision (n. 272).

intended control of conduct, that is made possible by US-American Civil law, is with no effect in international cases owing to the lack of enforcement.

It may not be the essential point that it is legally impossible for a state to deny recognition of a foreign civil law judgement because of high requirements applied to *ordre-public* infringements. The much more relevant point could be, that it openly need to pronounce that it puts a value that it claimed to be in the scope of *ordre public* over the aims pursued in the original decision. Said differently: a compulsion exists to clearly and *actively* come clean. In the area of public law, a *passive* bystanders position in negotiations for international agreements on co-operation is sufficient to not have to enforce unpopular decisions in one's own country. From these two possibilities, the active decision against the recognition of a judgement is probably more perceptible and will trigger stronger protest in the international community of states and in the public in general. If a court refuses recognition of a judgement obtained abroad, seeking the banning of an appeal to commit murder that is published in the internet by referring to freedom of speech, the decision would create a lot of waves in the international arena. In any event, it would probably not have a great influence that this decision of non-recognition is taken by a court and therefore of the (hopefully) independent "third authority". In the international arena, this decision of a national authority will be attributed to the respective state[84].

Indignation will be greater, however, the more global the acceptance of a certain value is. With the protection of a human life or with the fight against child pornography for example, the expectation of co-operation will be very high and not meeting these expectations will create correspondingly high waves. In some cases, where a strongly ambivalent attitude towards the value exists, a split echo will be the consequence. On the other side, non-recognition of a very radical judgement from a ideologically isolated country, that is not compatible with the reigning ideas of freedom would, to the majority, meet understanding - if not even applause. Thus, eventually, the community of states gains indirect influence on the enforceability of values; the more acceptable to a majority a value is, the more approval its enforcement meets in the international sphere. Generally speaking, moderate moral concepts find easier acceptance than more radical opinions. One might therein even see an opportunity for the moderation of radical ideologies and a further understanding and recognition between cultures.

84 One thinks of the sometimes severe international reactions to the first CompuServe judgement of the Amtsgericht München (see supra n. 11) or the Iranian reaction to the "Mykonos Judgement" of the Kammergericht Berlin, to which Iran responded to the therein implied reproach that the Iranian state supports terrorism, with the suspension of diplomatic relations with the National Republic of Germany.

## D. Problems of regulating by private law

The existing international co-ordination of civil legal procedures can really be of help in meeting the challenges of global datanets. The individual actors will increasingly make use of this as soon as they realize that the state is not able to provide the desired protection. However, the picture should not be drawn too optimistically. Regulation by private law systems also meets considerable practical problems, that in individual cases could lead to the "fight for right" getting lost.

The most important restriction depends – like so often – on money: the private law system depends on the participation of the protagonists which to them represents a financial burden. Until they possibly obtain a judgement in their favor and enforce it, they have to make considerable advance payments. Here also the effectivity of the participating judicial systems plays a role – even in highly developed countries (e.g. Italy) in the course of the procedure barely supportable delays with considerable expenses may arise. The costs furthermore multiply with every additional instance and even more with every additionally necessary recognition in another state[85]. Whether or not the means used will eventually bear fruit, generally remains uncertain[86]. Cost risks may, in individual cases, have an prohibitive effect such that the holder of a right abstains from pursuit of his rights[87]. Here possibly instruments like legal action instituted by an association or a *class action* following American models may help[88]. Opposingly, the cost risk may also lead to the position that a defendant gives in to a claim even though there was no legal duty to perform. In particular, costly kinds of procedure, like for instance the US-American *pre-trial discovery,* include a high potential for blackmail[89]. This serves neither justice nor the law.

One further problem might exist in the identification and location of the defendant[90]. One cannot sue a domain-name or an IP-address. It will be important here to create the necessary rights to information in order not to let the pursuit of rights fail due to such basic information deficits. It is therefore quite pleasing that the EU Directive on distance

---

85 According to an investigation carried out by the EU-Commission the costs for lawyers and courts for the enforcement of a judgement worth 4.000 Marks, even within the common market, amounts to 5.000 Marks; Enquete-Commission "Future of the Media in the Economy and Society – Germany's way in the Information-Society: Fifth report on Consumer Protection in the Information-Society (*Bundestags-Drucksache* 13/11003), p. 26 (with further references).

86 Here, the national costs associated with litigation are important. The German solution, that all costs follow the event, is advantageous providing one wins. But a victory in court is never sure. The American system, by which everyone carries their own costs, has the danger that the party has to split his award with his lawyers – this is not always compensated for by the high levels of compensation for pain and suffering, structured settlements or punitive damages. Therefore lawyers find themselves hunting cases and are content with being remunerated only by a share of the amount awarded (contingency fee).

87 *Henry Perritt*, "Will the Judgement-Proof Own Cyberspace?", *The International Lawyer* 32 (1998), pp. 1121 (1123, 1132).

88 *Engel*, Zivilrecht [n. 32], p. 216.

89 The Americans speak here of the "nuisance-value" of discovery.

90 *Mankowski*, Internet [n. 56], pp. 284 et seq.

selling[91] expressly states that the consumer, even before the conclusion of a contract, needs to be informed about the (real) identity of his contracting partner (Art. 4 I lit. a). But even if the defendant has been identified, enforcement of the judgement can still fail as a consequence of the high mobility of persons and capital. That, at least, is a given fact for the "mice"[92]. It could be of interest here to think about new means of coercion, like for instance the withdrawal of a domain-name, or the withdrawal of the IP-addresses from the domain servers and routers[93]. These means of coercion are especially suitable for the specific performance of conduct, but compensation for suffered damage cannot be directly obtained by this means[94]. In some cases the exerted pressure might already be sufficient to obtain fulfillment of an obligation to pay.

Lastly one has to fear that clever intruders know how to play around with private law and its international co-ordination. Virtual migration, where the protagonist adapts to the requirements of a legal rule by changes that are as small as possible so that he no longer falls within its scope has already been mentioned at the beginning[95]. This can, for one, happen on the level of substantive law where the intruder tries to escape from the target group of the regulation. This generally is much more difficult than trying to evade the points of connection in the field of the conflict of laws rules which decide as to the applicability of national rules. Here a sharp eye is necessary on the side of the legislator, but especially on the side of the courts. An open formulation of the factual requirements quite often allows for interpretation that prevents circumvention. But beyond the borders of interpretation the court can, if intention of circumvention (the *fraus legis)*, can clearly be recognized, fabricate the existence of a obligatory constituent fact and thus nevertheless enforce the legal rule concerned[96].

## E. Closing remarks

The system of private law thus provides some clear advantages as opposed to public law and self-regulation. Here the individual citizen gets an opportunity to protect himself by personal commitment if the state is no longer able to fulfil its duty of protection. However, in some places, owing to the nature of Cyberspace, private law is stretched to its limits. It can therefore only be a useful component in the attempt to regulate, but not a full replacement. Eventually only a mixture of direct national regulation in the forms of public law, international harmonization, self regulation and – last, but not least – private law systems will be able to effectively meet the new challenges.

---

91 Supra n. 34.

92 *Swire* [n. 6], p. 1024.

93 *Perritt*; Judgement-Proof [n. 87], pp. 1123, 1132 et seq., 1139 et seq.

94 *Perritt*, ibid.. pp. 1132 et seq.

95 See supra p. 211.

96 Compare the different forms of evasion and possibilities of correction: *von Bar*, IPR I [n. 69], No. 574 et seq.

*Klaus W. Grewlich*

# Conflict and good Governance in "Cyberspace"

## Multi-level and Multi-actor Constitutionalisation



The wealth of "*Cyberspace*",[1] i.e. the economic and social benefits of electronic content, multimedia services and information infrastructures are particularly dependent upon state-of-the-art, seamless, networked communications infrastructures *(global communications networks),* adequate national and regional (de)regulation and ultimately international good governance, guaranteeing both free access to markets and the vindication of vital public interest objectives.

The market-driven transition to "Cyberspace", the planetary artefact of the global information society, requires governmental, as well as business and user action: Users must identify their needs and enter interactive learning processes. Enterprises may take

1 "Cyberspace" may be described as the invisible, intangible world of electronic information and processes stored at multiple interconnected sites, with controlled access and manifold possibilities for interaction; *Grewlich Klaus W.*, Governance in "Cyberspace" – Access and public interest in global communications, Den Haag/London/Boston 1999 , 1ff.

advantage of many new economic opportunities. Governments must formulate or adjust framework policies to guarantee effective competition in global markets and at the same time to safeguard the public interest. Law is the necessary companion of free market forces[2]. Market forces not only have to be released; they also must be contained by rules!

To produce additional wealth, free markets should effectively support the convergence potential of industries and services, the diffusion of new services, as well as efficient pricing structures, employment creation and productivity growth. Failing or inefficient markets, high prices and insufficient competition would delay or distort the transition to the age of "Cyberspace", i.e. dilute the benefits of global information networks, multimedia and cyber commerce. Good governance, i.e. a judicious framework of equitable non-interventionist "principles" is required to allow for wealth creation in the digital environment.

## 1. Potential Conflicts – Competing Cyber Policies

Countries and regions attach particular importance to the success of future-oriented industries operating in their areas of influence. This applies notably to the communications and media services industries and, thus, to the key industries of "Cyberspace": *firstly* because high quality jobs are created by the growing demand for technology, information and communication services and for technical as well as artistic software; *secondly,* because modern information and communications have a rejuvenating effect on traditional economic sectors, i.e. are significant for the overall economy, and *thirdly,* because of the importance of media and "information power", i.e. the perception that "stars and stories allow to colonize the imaginations of audiences everywhere"[3].

### 1.1. New "comparative advantages"

"Global communication networks" and "multimedia"[4] play an important part in the rivalry between states to enhance a country's or region's socio-economic conditions and image as a "place to do business", to attract communications and multimedia players with global reach. Given the mobility and global accessibility of capital, technology and

2 *Gerber David J.*, Constitutionalizing the Economy: German Neo-liberalism , Competition Law and the "New Europe", 42 *American Journal of Comparative Law* 25 (1994).

3 See, for instance, *Puttnam David*, The Undeclared War – The Struggle for Control of the World's Film Industry, London 1997; *Nye Joseph S.*, *William A. Owens*, America's Information Edge, 75 *Foreign Affairs* 20-36 (1996).

4 *Grewlich Klaus W.*, Konflikt und Ordnung in der globalen Kommunikation – Wettstreit der Staaten und Wettbewerb der Unternehmen (Conflict and Order in Global Communications – Rivalry among States and Competition between Enterprises), Baden-Baden 1999.

human resources in the age of globalisation,[5] "arbitrary" *comparative advantages* may be created not only by the traditional judicious mixtures of incentives and disincentives that may distort international investment flows[6], but also by proactive national or regional liberalisation and de(re)regulation. In a multilateral free trade system driven by competition[7], where the process of "constitutionalizing the economy" has not yet really begun, one of the new phenomena that are not yet fully understood is the *instrumentalisation* of market philosophy and of unilateral liberalisation policies in order to achieve competitive advantages[8].

Thus, we observe not only competition between enterprises/global business alliances. There are new forms of "competition" between governments of different states pertaining to political "visions" and (de-regulatory) "frameworks". The new World Trade Organisation (WTO) regime forbids restrictive protection once liberalisation has been agreed, but it does not appear to hinder some states in their efforts to liberalise and deregulate more than others in order to attract direct investment. This rivalry of deregulatory policies in terms of "systems competition" is different from traditional straightforward protectionism in terms of tariffs, quotas and non-tariff barriers (NTBs).

The instruments used for achieving success in the international technology race and innovations competition have become more subtle. What we recognise today are "policy mixes" combining *first,* political vision; *second,* blends of deregulation and re-regulation; *third, a small amount of* seed money for (basic) R&D and certain strategic applications; and, *fourth,* targeted trade policies in terms of "opening foreign markets"[9].

To the extent that such "policy mixes" lead to conflicts, they would normally become the subject of the international diplomatic and legal process and might also be addressed by business fora and possibly other stakeholders. Two questions must be clarified: *First,* what is the importance of the problem in the field of "Cyber" commerce? *Second;* what principles and procedures may be applied to deal with the issues resulting from competing "Cyber" policies?

---

5 *Porter Michael*, Nationale Wettbewerbsvorteile – Erfolgreich konkurrieren auf dem Weltmarkt, München 1991.

6 *Grewlich Klaus W.*, Direct Investment in the OECD Countries, Alphen aan den Rijn 1978, (50f.; 100f.).

7 *Trebilcock Michael J.*, *Robert Howse*, The Regulation of International Trade, London/New York 1995.

8 *Grewlich Klaus W.*, Wettstreit im Regulierungsrecht der Kommunikation – Auswirkungen auf Unternehmen und Geschäftsallianzen, *Kommunikation & Recht* (K&R) December 1998, 523ff.

9 The question of whether such judicious policy mixes are intentional in all details or emerge (as "collective rationales") because of a number of other circumstances in the globalising economies may be left open.

## 1.2. "Cyber" commerce – Comparative analysis of key policies

In April 1997, the European Commission published "A European Initiative in Electronic Commerce". One of the objectives of this policy document is the "vigorous growth of electronic commerce in Europe" and the strengthening of "Europe's competitiveness in global markets"[10]. In the same month, Japan's Ministry of International Trade and Industry released a draft policy paper "Towards the Age of the Digital Economy – For Rapid Growth in the Japanese Economy in the Twenty-First Century". This paper postulates that increased investment in information technology will invigorate and transform the Japanese Economy[11]. In July 1997, US President Clinton issued the "Framework for Electronic Commerce". That policy paper assumes that "commerce on the Internet could total tens of billions of dollars by the end of the century"(!), with sales estimated at US$ 200 million in 1995 [12]. Thus, the Japanese paper postulates the rapid and prosperous progress towards the age of the digital economy by contrast with the long period of stagnation after the bursting of the "economic bubble". The US policy statement refers to the Global Information Infrastructure (GII), while the European document positions itself in the wider framework of the development towards the Information Society[13].

These papers contain strategic statements from the leading industrialised countries regarding the Internet and "Cyber" commerce. Their main focus are economic and business related issues that need a common political stance, progress or adjustments in the international legal framework.

---

10 Available online at <http://www.ispo.cec.be/ecommerce/initial.html>.

11 Available online at <http://www.glocom.ac.jp/news/MITI-doc.html>.

12 Available on line at <http://www.whitehouse.gov/WH/New/Commerce/>.

13 EU, Commission of the European Communities, Europe and the global information society, Recommendations to the European Council, Brussels, 26.05.1994; EU, Commission of the European Communities, Green Paper on the Convergence of the Telecommunications, Media and Information Technology Sectors, and the Implications of Regulation – Towards an Information Society approach, COM(97)632, 03.12.1997; EU, Commission of the European Communities, Communication from the Commission to the Council, the European Parliament, the Economic and Social Committee and the Committee of the Regions, Globalisation and the Information Society – The Need for Strengthened International Coordination, COM (1998) 50 fin. 4.2.1998; EU, Commission of the European Communities, Green Paper Living and Working in the Information Society, COM(96) 389 fin., 24.07.1996; EU, Commission of the European Communities, Communication from the Commission to the Council, the European Parliament, the Economic and Social Committee and the Committee of the Regions on "Europe at the Forefront of the Global Information Society: Rolling Action Plan", COM(96) 607 fin., 27.11.1996; EU, Commission of the European Communities, Communication from the Commission to the Council, the European Parliament the Economic and Social Committee and the Committee of the Regions, Cohesion and the Information Society, COM(97) 7 fin. 22.01.97; EU, Commission of the European Communities, Building the European Information Society for all of us, Final policy report of the high-level expert group (Employment & Social Affairs) , Brussels 1997.

A comparative analysis of the EU, US and Japanese policy statements leads to the distinction of three areas[14]:

- fundamental principles where there is broad agreement, and issues where there is basically a common approach;
- issues where there are divergences, but agreements seem within reach;
- potentially conflictual issues where positions seem to diverge widely and the views are potentially irreconcilable.

As the Japanese statement is far less detailed, the following analysis mainly deals with the US and EU policy documents.

### *1.2.1. Areas of broad agreement*

In terms of scope and substance, there are considerable areas of agreement between the US policy document ("Framework") and the European statement ("Initiative"). The commonality of views found its expression in the "Bonn Ministerial Declaration of 8 July 1997 on Global Information Networks – Realising the Potential"[15] where, in addition to European ministers, the US and Japan were also present, and later in the "Joint EU-US Statement on Electronic Commerce" of 5 December 1997 [16]. It is also reflected in the results of the OECD "Ottawa Conference on Electronic Commerce" (7-9 October 1988)[17].

Both the US and the European Union express in their respective policy statements[18] their determination to seek – in addition to the implementation of the WTO's Basic Telecommunications Agreement[19] – effective implementation of the "Information

---

14 See also *Maxwell Elliot*, The Internet and Electronic Commerce – A Tale of Three Cities, Institute for Information Studies, The emerging Internet, Queenstown/USA 1998 109-128, *Vittet-Philippe Patrick*, Towards a Common Framework for Global Electronic Commerce – A comparative analysis of US, EU and Japanese E-Commerce Policies, (European Commission DG XIII) Brussels 6.10.1997; *Murase Emily M.*, Electronic Commerce over the Internet – a Comparison of Policy Directions in the U.S., Europe and Japan, Institute for Communications Research, 27 May 1997.

15 Available with "theme paper" at <http://www2.echo.lu/bonn/themepaper.html>.

16 Available at <http://www.qlinks.net/comdocs/eu-us.htm>.

17 OECD Ministerial Conference "A Borderless World: Realising the Potential of Global Electronic Commerce", Conference Conclusions, Ottawa 7-9 October 1998, OECD Document SG/EC(98)14/REV6, 26.10.1998; OECD, Ministerial Conference – A Borderless World: Realising the Potential of Global Electronic Commerce, Ottawa 7-9 October 1998, Paris 1998; OECD Ministerial Conference "A Borderless World: Realising the Potential of Global Electronic Commerce", A Global Action Plan for Electronic Commerce Prepared by Business with Recommendations from Governments, 7-9 October 1998, Ottawa, Canada, OECD Document SG/EC(98)11/REV2, 5 October 1998.

18 U.S. "Framework" <http://www.whitehouse.gov/WH/New/Commerce/> at 16; European "Initiative" <http://www.ispo.cec.be/ecommerce/initial.html>. at 26.

19 This Agreement takes the form of a Protocol to be attached to the General Agreement on Trade and Services (GATS), and is officially designated as the Fourth Protocol to the GATS. (The Second Protocol deals with Financial Services); World Trade Organisation (WTO), Agreement of the

Technology Agreement" (ITA)[20] concluded by the members of the WTO in March 1997, which is designed to remove tariffs on almost all types of information technology, and to find effective ways for streamlining requirements to demonstrate product conformity. These include "Mutual Recognition Agreements on Conformity Assessment" (MRAs) that can eliminate the need for a single product to be certified by different standards laboratories across national borders. Various other fora such as the "International Organisation of Standardisation" (ISO) will be used for international discussions on telecommunications-related Internet issues and for removing barriers that inhibit the export of information technology.

Thus, in order to promote a favourable telecommunications-based Cyberbusiness environment, basic agreement exists on three key lines of action: *first,* ensuring open *access* to the global marketplace (Infrastructure, technology and services); *second,* creating a favourable regulatory framework; and, *third,* harmonising commercial laws for electronic commerce[21].

In the Atlantic relationship, this basic understanding must be placed in the context of the transatlantic economic network which has grown particularly strongly over the years, and which is underpinned by particularly strong trade and investment interdependence. Moreover, the EU-US relationship developed further with the adoption of the "New Transatlantic Agenda" (NTA) at the EU-US summit of December 1995 and the accompanying EU-US Joint Action Plan. The documents contained a joint commitment, not only to strengthen and consolidate the multilateral trading system, but also to create a "Transatlantic Marketplace", by progressively eliminating the remaining barriers that hinder the flow of goods, services and capital between the European Union and the United States.

---

Implementation of the Ministerial Declaration on Trade in Information and Technology Products (March 26, 1997), 36 I.L.M. 366ff. (1997); see also the results of the "Second World Telecommunications Forum 16-18 March 1998", ITU-Documentation, Geneva 1998.

20 WTO, Agreement on the Implementation of the Ministerial Declaration on Trade in Information Technology Products, Text of the Agreement in 36 I.LM 377ff. (1997).

21 As to the latter, reference is made to the work under way in UNCITRAL, other international bodies (e.g. UNIDROIT and the International Chamber of Commerce (ICC)), academic and private groups and bar associations as to the establishment of rules and norms that validate and recognize contracts formed through electronic means, set default rules for contract formation and governance of electronic contract performance, define the characteristics of a valid electronic writing and an "original document", provide for the acceptability of electronic signatures for legal and commercial purposes and clarifies the admission of computer evidence for arbitration proceedings and courts. The drafting of such rules for global electronic commerce should be governed by the following principles:

- parties should be free to order the contractual relationship between themselves as they see fit;
- rules should be forward-looking and technology-neutral (i.e. rules should not require or assume a particular technology),
- new rules should be adopted only as necessary;
- consistent international rules for electronic signatures and authentication procedures as well as dispute resolution mechanisms for global commercial transactions should be promoted.

Both sides, the European Union and the United States, advocate free trade and interconnectivity. European efforts to eliminate a considerable number of impediments, ranging from traditional tariff and non-tariff barriers to differences in the legal systems that are due to the absence or limitations of internationally agreed rules and disciplines, should also be seen in relation with trade policy initiatives to improve access to foreign markets[22].

Specifically as far as telecommunications services is concerned, the US remains concerned about full implementation of the "GATS schedules" and particularly the Basic Telecommunications Agreement, full liberalisation in the EU internal market and, notably, the market power of former telecommunications organisations, while the European Union opposes the hurdles that US legislation presents for those non-US and foreign-owned firms that wish to invest in radio telecommunications infrastructure and to provide mobile and satellite services.

Another point of concern for the European Union is the perceived high degree of autonomy and discretion that the US Federal Communications Commission exercises in regulating this sector, including reciprocity-based licensing procedures for foreign enterprises[23].

### *1.2.2. Areas of relative divergence*

The presentations of policy orientations, as contained in the strategic documents for electronic commerce, i.e. "Initiative", "Framework" and "Digital Economy" issued by the European Union, the US and Japan, show a number of divergences that, however, do not seem to be insuperable. Part of this group of relative divergence that calls for constructive discussion are the issues pertaining to tax policy, tariffs and standardisation.

(i) Electronic commerce and other global network-based activities in "Cyberspace" are regarded by many national tax administrations as having the potential for creating new streams of funds. The US has already experienced attempts at state and local level to raise revenues by taxing Internet-related activities. Proposals for Internet *taxes* at the national level, such as a "bit tax"[24], are not welcomed by the European Commission[25].

---

22 EU, COMMISSION OF THE EUROPEAN COMMUNITIES, Communication, "The Global Challenge of International Trade – A Market Access Strategy for the European Union" COM(96)53 fin., 14.02 1996.

23 EU, COMMISSION OF THE EUROPEAN COMMUNITIES, Report on United States Barriers 1997, Brussels July 1997 (42f.).

24 Interim Report of the High Level Group of Experts on the Social Aspects of the Information Society, <http://www.ispo.cec.be/hleg/hleg.html>.

25 EUROPEAN COMMISSION, A European Initiative in Electronic Commerce, Communication from the Commission to the Council, the European Parliament, the Economic and Social Committee and the Committee of the Regions, COM(19) 157 fin. 16.041997; available online <http://www..ispo.cec.be/ecommerce/initial.html> at 19.

The European Commission is of the opinion that a "bit tax" is not appropriate since VAT already applies to these transactions. The territorial concepts which underlie direct taxation systems, i.e. "residence" and the "source" of income need to be examined in the light of commercial and technological developments. European Commission and EU member states have recently started an analysis of the impact and consequences of electronic commerce on customs and indirect taxation. The US Treasury Department has issued a policy paper aimed at developing a federal taxation policy framework[26]. There are several initiatives in the US Congress for freezing new state and local taxes related to Internet and electronic commerce[27]. The US "Framework" recommends that the Internet be treated as a tariff-free environment whenever it is used to deliver products or services, together with a ban on new Internet taxes. The Japanese "Digital Economy" report reflects similiar concerns about the application of value-added taxes given the uncertain location of buyers and sellers.

On taxes, the US position is close to that of the European Commission. Both agree that "taxes on electronic commerce should be clear, consistent, neutral and non-discriminatory"[28]. Like the EU "Initiative", the US "Framework" stresses that "the taxation of commerce on the Internet should be consistent with established principles of international taxation, should avoid inconsistent national tax jurisdiction and double taxation, and should be simple to administer and easy to understand."[29] Both the US and the European Commission declare their commitment to the work of the OECD in this field ("OECD Committee on Fiscal Affairs")[30].

The 1998 OECD "Ottawa Conference on Electronic Commerce"[31] welcomed a report "Electronic Commerce: Taxation Framework Conditions"[32] which sets out the taxation principles that should apply to electronic commerce, outlines the agreed conditions for a taxation framework, and endorses the proposals on how to take forward the work contained within it. The broad taxation principle which should apply to electronic commerce is that taxation should seek to be neutral and equitable between forms of electronic commerce, and also between conventional and electronic forms of commerce.

---

26 U.S. DEPARTMENT OF TREASURY/Office of Tax policy, Selected Tax Policy Implications of Global Electronic Commerce, Washington November 1996.

27 e.g. "Internet Tax Freedom Act", introduced by Representative *Christopher Cox* on 13 March 1997 (H.R. 1054).

28 Joint EU-US Statement on Electronic Commerce, 5 December 1997; <http://www.qlinks.net/comdocs/eu-us.htm>.

29 <http://www.whitehouse.gov/WH/New/Commerce/> at 5.

30 OECD, Dismantling the Barriers to Global Electronic Commerce, available at <http://www.oecd.org/dsti/sti/it/ec/prod/DISMANTL.HTM>; in addition see OECD, Electronic Commerce – The Challenges to Tax Authorities and Taxpayers, available at <http://www.oecd.org/daf/fa/TURKU18.PDF>.

31 OECD Ministerial Conference "A Borderless World: Realising the Potential of Global Electronic Commerce", Conference Conclusions, Ottawa 7-9 October 1998, OECD Document SG/EC(98)14/REV6, 26.10.1998 (7).

32 OECD, Electronic Commerce: Taxation Framework Conditions, OECD/Fiscal Affairs, 3 October 1998.

Business decisions should be motivated by economic considerations, rather than tax considerations. Taxpayers in similiar situations carrying out similiar transactions should be subject to similiar levels of taxation.

(ii) As regards *tariffs and customs*, however, the US "Framework" document goes further than the "Initiative" paper of the European Commission, which did not deal with this issue. The US paper, backed by the authority of the President of the United States, calls for the Internet to be declared "a tariff-free environment whenever it is used to deliver products or services". The US Administration's intent to act quickly "before nations impose tariffs, and vested interests form to protect these tariffs" is shared by a number of countries. But President Clinton's announcement[33] to turn the Internet, i.e. electronic commerce[34], "within twelve months into a free-trade zone" has been seen as a controversial initiative.

Diplomatically, the problem was solved to some extent in the WTO: On the occasion of the Second WTO Ministerial Conference, held in Geneva between 18-20 May 1998, ministers declared that WTO members will continue their current practice of not imposing customs duties on electronic transmisssions, and established a work programme in the WTO on electronic commerce. The objective is that the Third Ministerial Conference will review the extension of this declaration, as well as any recommendation for action[35]. This result is, of course, far from a " free-trade zone for the Internet".

(iii) The US "Framework" paper states the well-known general philosophy on *standardisation*: Premature standardisation can lock-in outdated technology; standards may be employed as de facto non-tariff trade barriers; the marketplace, not governments should determine technical standards. The US paper warns: "The US considers it unwise and unnecessary for governments to mandate standards in electronic commerce."

The Japanese "Digital Economy" report sees a need for governmental action, noting that market-based standards may possibly impede the workings of the marketplace. Important is the "flexible application of the process of public standardisation". The Japanese report also stresses the importance of guaranteeing the openness of different types of interfaces. This consideration leads to the contentious issue of compulsory licensing.

---

33 see Newsletter U.S. Embassy in Bonn 9.7.1998.

34 *Vittet-Philippe Patrick,* Towards a Common Framework for Global Electronic Commerce – A comparative analysis of US, EU and Japanese E-Commerce Policies, (European Commission DG XIII) Brussels 6.10.1997; *Grewlich Klaus W.*, Atlantische Kommunikationsallianzen – Der Wettstreit im Cyberspace, *Internationale Politik* 1998 25-32 (at 26).

35 WTO Second Ministerial Conference, Declaration on Global Electronic Commerce, adopted on 20 May 1998, *WTO - FOCUS* (Newsletter) No. 31/June 1998 (7): "Ministers, Recognizing that global electronic commerce is growing and creating new opportunities for trade, Declare that: ... Without prejudice to the outcome of the work programme or the rights and obligations of Members under the WTO Agreement, we also declare that Members will continue their current practice of not imposing customs duties on electronic transmissions...".

The European "Initiative" paper shows that, as a matter of fact, an agreement already exists pertaining to the "emergence of industry collaboration" to ensure "de facto interoperability in a competitive environment".

It is, however, in the area of standards that the harmony exemplified in the adoption of the Internet Protocol (IP) is in danger of breaking down! Enterprises engaged in "cut-throat competition" with each other will try to influence the rules of the game and the content of critical standards. Governments in the amazing race of "technological visions" and "commercial advocacy" may, even in a borderless electronic world, be tempted to retrograde into old thinking i.e. discriminating in favour of entities perceived as "national champions".

### *1.2.3. Areas of potential conflict: Content, Encryption, Data Protection*

(i) The issues pertaining to *illegal and harmful content* are not dealt with extensively in the European Commission's "Initiative" paper, but these were previously addressed by the European Union[36]. This issue is central to the debate on electronic commerce in the United States, particularly after the US Supreme Court decision on the "Communications Decency Act" (CDA)[37].

In the centre of the policy statements on "content" lie the political tensions between the objective of increased access to a vast continuum of information made possible by the Internet and the desire to prevent dissemination of material alleged to be harmful, particularly to those users (e.g. children) who are perceived as being vulnerable.

The US "Framework" argues in favour of the free flow of information in the Internet and against the censorship of electronic commerce. Users should be empowered to control the content with the help of rating and filtering systems[38], combined with appropriate

---

36 EUROPEAN PARLIAMENT Resolution of 24 April 1997 on the COMMISSION communication on illegal and harmful content on the Internet (available online at <http://www2.echo.lu/legal/en/internet/communic..html>), EUROPEAN PARLIAMENT Resolution of 24 October 1997 on the Commission Green Paper on the protection of minors and human dignity in audiovisual and information services, COM (96) 483; see also COMMISSION OF THE EUROPEAN COMMUNITIES, Communication to the European Parliament, the Council, the Economic and Social Committee and the Committee of the Regions, Action Plan on Promoting Safe Use of the Internet, COM(97)582 (available online at <http://www2.echo.lu/ legal/en/internet/actplan.html>).

37 US Supreme Court, *Reno v. Aclu*, 117 S.Ct. 2329 (1997); see also American Civil Liberties Union et. al. v. Janet Reno, Att. General of the United States, US District Court for the Eastern District of Pensylvania, Civ. Act. 96-963." Just as the strength of the Internet is chaos, so the strength of our liberty depends upon the chaos and the cacophony of the unfettered speech the First Amendment protects."

38 A debate is, however, increasingly unfolding over the double-edged nature of technological filtering and rating systems: Supporters argue that such systems may, for instance, improve the control that parents have over the exposure of their children to harmful material (assuming the price of the technology is acceptable and not only "privileged families" use the technology). Opponents, on the other hand, argue that these systems may possibly be used by a number of governments to enforce oppressive information policies; see for instance *Harmon Amy*, Rules for Filtering Web Content Cause Dispute, available online at <http://www.nytimes.com/library/cyber/week/

forms of (industry) self-regulation. The "Framework" recognizes that the issues pertaining to content, notably advertising and the protection of consumers from fraudulent information, but also decency and of course "quotas for content", must be seen in the international context[39].

Like the "Framework", the Japanese "Digital Economy"[40] proposes addressing the issues of illegal and harmful content by "user-controlled refusal and selection mechanisms" rather than governmental control.

The European "Action Plan on Promoting Safe Use of the Internet"[41] underlines that harmful content[42] comprises more than child pornography. Illegal relates to a wide variety of issues that governmental institutions or self-regulatory mechanisms may have to deal with:

- National security (instructions on bomb-making, illegal drug production, terrorist activities);
- Protection of minors (abusive forms of marketing, violence, pornography);
- Protection of human dignity (incitement to racial hatred or racial discrimination);
- Economic security (fraud, instructions on pirating, credit card misuse);
- Information security (malicious hacking);
- Protection of privacy (unauthorized communication of personal data, electronic harassment);
- Protection of reputation (libel, unlawful comparative advertising);
- Intellectual property (unauthorised distribution of copyrighted works, e.g. software or music).

The European Union anticipates its own research funding and the development of filtering mechanisms.

The need for an adequate harmonisation of legal frameworks is evident as court battles are being fought implying such questions as the mandatory use of national language, or prohibition of "hate speech". At present, the international debate concentrates primarily on "adult content". In the future, there might be much more conflict surrounding

---

01998filter.html>.

39 <http://www.whitehouse.gov/WH/New/Commerce/> at 18.

40 Towards the Age of Digital Economy, Issue: Dealing with Illegal and Harmful Contents <http://www.glocom.ac.jp/news/MITI-doc.html> at 2.

41 COMMISSION OF THE EUROPEAN COMMUNITIES, Communication to the European Parliament, the Council, the Economic and Social Committee and the Committee of the Regions, Action Plan on Promoting Safe Use of the Internet, COM(97)582 (available online at <http://www2.echo.lu/legal/en/internet/actplan.html>) at 1f.

42 Harmful content means both content which is allowed but whose distribution is restricted, and content which may offend certain users, although its publication is not restricted because of the principle of freedom of expression that is subject to legal restraints in a number of countries, but protected to some extent in the United States by the First Amendment.

commercial questions such as advertising of professional services through global information networks.

(ii) The US "Framework" statement includes a potentially conflictual trade policy issue of a different nature: i.e. possible barriers to free circulation of content, in particular "*content quotas*". These are central concerns for the United States in the traditional media and even more in the new digital environment. The US paper amalgamates audiovisual issues (such as quantitative limits to advertising) with the Internet and electronic commerce. Complex negotiations, both bilaterally and in the WTO framework are likely to develop. At present, the WTO/GATS framework on basic telecommunications reached on 15 February 1997 does not cover broadcasting and it only applies to "basic" telecommunications (transport) services. Thus, it does not cover "content services" which may be transmitted through telecommunications services! The GATS commitment on basic telecommunications services, as undertaken by the European Union, expressly excludes the economic activity of content provision which requires telecommunications services for its transport; such content provisions being subject to the specific commitments undertaken by the European Union in other relevant sectors, such as "financial services". On audiovisual/broadcasting services, the European Union has not undertaken any GATS commitment[43].

(iii) The US "Framework" states that the US Administration, in promoting the robust security needed for electronic commerce, will take steps that will enable people to place trust in encryption und the provision of safeguards. Market-driven standards, public key management infrastructure services and key-recoverable encryption products are to be promoted in partnership with industry. The "Framework" indicates that the US government will work internationally to promote the development of market-driven key management infrastructures with key recovery.

The export controls for commercial encryption products, as practised by the United States, have provoked criticism from US industry but particularly also from foreign trade partners[44].

The United States, the European Union and Japan are in favour of continuing the pertinent work on cryptographic policy underway in the OECD[45].

(iv) The same technologies that have facilitated the emergence and use of the Internet have made gathering (profiling) and manipulation of *personal data* easy. To some extent, such data collection activity is considered by experts as a "must" for being successful in the expanding business field of electronic commerce. Within the US government, the Federal Trade Commission (FTC) has played a key role in scrutinizing

---

43 Commission of the European Communities, Green Paper on the Convergence of the Telecommunications, Media and Information Technology Sectors, and the Implications of Regulation – Towards an Information Society Approach, 3 December 1997 at 37.

44 National Research Coucil, US National Academy of Sciences (*Dam Kenneth W., Herbert S. Lin*, ed.), Cryptography's Role in Securing the Information Society, (Washington: National Academy Press 1996).

45 OECD, Guidelines on Cryptographic Policy, Paris 1997.

self-regulatory proposals as well as proposals for governmental action to guarantee online privacy.[46] The US "Framework" supports private sector efforts "to implement meaningful, consumer-friendly, self-regulatory privacy regimes"[47].

The Japanese "Digital Economy" report, in addition to legal regulations, also relies on voluntary efforts, as well as on increased privacy options for consumers in harmony with consumer education and the creation of a general awareness of privacy issues[48]. The policy direction suggests: "While policy measures should be based on those which promote voluntary action by the private sector, including the provision of guidelines for the protection of personal data, legal regulations should be examined depending on the types of industry and business. Both the US "Framework" and the Japanese "Digital Economy" refer to the work currently being conducted in the OECD[49].

The European Union has enacted a broad directive on the protection of personal data[50]. The European "Initiative" suggests a number of specific measures to supplement the "Privacy Directive" and to address privacy in the context of electronic commerce.

The European Privacy Directive has been identified as a possible source of conflict between the United States and Europe. The Directive, in the extreme, is perceived as barring the transfer of personal data to countries that – from the European point of view – do not extend "*adequate*" privacy protection to citizens from the European Union. In those cases where servers are located outside the European Union in third countries and personal data is transferred for processing, the respective third country must ensure an adequate level of protection. Where the EU Commission finds that a third country does not ensure an "adequate" level of protection, member states are bound to take appropriate measures. The problem here is that the critical notion of "adequacy" is not defined, nor does the Directive contain criteria that could be helpful for judging what in fact "adequate level of protection" means[51]. Some countries, in addition, express concern about potential extraterritorial effects of the European Privacy Directive.

Thus, based on reality or perception, divergences and sources of possible conflicts exist that may need both case-by-case treatment and solutions in terms of the system of governance.

---

46 U.S. Federal Trade Commission (FTC), Hearings and Reports on privacy issues, available online at <http://www.ftc.gov>.

47 U.S. National Information Infrastructure Taskforce/Information Policy Committee, Options for Promoting Privacy on the National Information Infrastructure, draft for public comment. April 1997, available online at <http://www.iitf.nist.gov/ipc/privacy.htm>.

48 Towards the Age of the Digital Economy, Issue: Protecting Personal Data and Privacy, <http://www.glocom.ac.jp/news/MITI-doc.html> (2).

49 See OECD, Implementing the OECD Privacy Guidelines in the Electronic Environment: Focus on the Internet, <www.oecd.org/dsti/sti//it/secur/prod/reg97-6e.htm>.

50 EU, Directive of the European Parliament and of the Council of 24 October 1995 on the protection of individuals with regard to the processing of personal data and on the free movement of such data (95/46/EC; OJ L 281/31, 23.11.1995.

51 For an assessment see *Perrit Henry H., Margaret J.Stewart*, False Alarm?, 51 *Federal Communications law Journal* (1999), 811ff.

## 2. Governance

The notion of *governance* appears to have been originally developed in corporate law. "Corporate governance" issues encompass the entire functioning and distribution of powers within the large corporation[52]. Ever since the formation of the first joint stock company, a continuing debate about the structure of corporate governance has been waged. Today, this debate relates to the controls, both legal and institutional, that are or should be exercised over corporate management, the role of shareholders (including institutional shareholders), the board structure, the regulatory framework including issues pertaining, for instance, to codes of conduct (including e.g. takeovers and mergers)[53].

Close to this use of the term "governance" in corporate law is the notion of "Internet governance" pertaining, for instance, to the question of "domain names" and complex power relationships in a decentralised network structure, where some essential technical and economic elements still need a certain amount of central control, and relevant contracts, international law and conventions must be respected[54].

In an even wider sense, the notion of *governance* could in future become relevant for international relations, as well as public international and European law. In European law and politics, *governance* may describe the constitutional problematique of powers being exercised by a multitude of actors at different levels of authority and action. The core of the question is: how to coordinate, in applying the principle of subsidiarity,[55] the legal (substantive law) and political action of, *firstly,* national governments, their provinces and regions; *secondly,* European institutions and of different arrangements at the European level, whether based on EC treaties and binding secondary European Law or on additional competences and tasks leading to a European political union (Maastricht and Amsterdam treaties); and, *thirdly,* possible self-regulatory schemes (e.g. voluntary agreements) of industry, labour and public interest and civil society groups.

### 2.1. Governance and cooperative international law

In scholarly discussions pertaining to public international law on economic issues and European law, the notion of *governance* appeared only recently. We are at an early stage of "brainstorming". While the notion of *governance* in the international area is to be

---

52 See *Wymeersch Eddy*, The Corporate Governance Discussion in some European States, in *Prentice D.D., P.R. Holland*, Contemporary Issues in Corporate Governance, Oxford 1993 (3).

53 *Prentice D.D.*, Some Aspects of the Corporate Governance Debate, in *Prentice D.D., P.R. Holland*, Contemporary Issues in Corporate Governance, Oxford 1993 (25ff.).

54 See OECD, Internet Domain Names: Allocation Policies, OECD Document GD(97)207, Paris 1997; see also Chapter Seven.

55 The principle of subsidiarity is enshrined in Article 3 b (2) EC Treaty: "In areas which do not fall within its exclusive competence, the Community shall take action, in accordance with the principle of subsidiarity, only if and in so far as the objectives of the proposed action cannot be sufficiently achieved by the Member States and can therefore, by reason of the scale or effects of the proposed action, be better achieved by the Community." (emphasis added).

distinguished from government and from intergovernmental organisations in terms of powers and institutions, it is yet comparatively close to the function of "multilateral organisation"[56]. The latter is concerned with the task of how to organise orderly (and ideally peaceful), international political and economic relations effectively, based on the respect of agreed rules and principles, i.e. the rule of law and justice. *Governance* in international relations might also be translated by the idea of effective rule-based partnerships instead of domination by certain countries, institutions and people! The postulated "new multilateralism"[57] namely comprises: mandatory cooperative solutions of transborder issues; the rule of law in international relations on the basis of an increasing amount of normative solutions in terms of treaties and conventions and dispute settlement mechanisms; and the strengthening of various forms of "international organisation", particularly of the Bretton Woods system[58] and the United Nations framework.

However, participation in global *governance* is not necessarily limited to public institutions. New actors with a political will and transborder reach, such as multinational or transnational enterprises[59], internationally organised public interest and civil society groups, and various non-governmental organisations (NGOs) enter the field. These internationally linked, non-governmental actors increasingly assume influence and responsibilities – complementary to, or in cooperation with, established public actors of the international legal community[60]. Modern communication technologies, notably the Internet, play an important role in the internal opinion-making and the external action of these new entities. These actors are not the subjects of international law like states or international organisations. However, they may become (necessary) partners in a system of *governance*. Does this eventually advocate an enlargement of the international society as a legal community[61]?

States as primary actors in international relations and many traditional international lawyers define them as quasi-monolithic units, identifiable mainly by their public

---

56 See The Commission on Global Governance (Ed.), Our Global Neighbourhood, Oxford, London 19995; the subtitle of the journal "Global Governance" published by the United Nations University reads "A Review of Multilateralism and International Organisations".

57 *Nuscheler Franz*, Eine neue Weltpolitik – Multilateralismus statt Pax Americana, *Internationale Politik* 1998, 10-16 (10).

58 To a large extent, international economic interdependence and globalisation can be attributed to the success of the institutions put in place just after World War II, called the "Bretton Woods System", including the International Monetary Fund (IMF) and the GATT/WTO; see *Jackson John H., William J. Davey, Alan O. Sykes*, Legal Problems of International Economic Relations - Cases, Materials and Texts, 3d ed. St.Paul/Minn. 1995.

59 *Grewlich Klaus W.*, Transnational Enterprises in a New International System, Alphen aan den Rijn 1980

60 *Rosenau James, Ernst-Otto Czempiel* (ed.), Governance without Government, Cambridge 1992

61 *Mosler Hermann*, The International Society as a Legal Community, Alphen aan den Rijn: 1980; *Mosler Hermann*, Die Erweiterung des Kreises der Völkerrechtssubjekte, *Berichte der Deutschen Gesellschaft für Völkerrecht* 4 (1961) 39-83; see also *McDougal Myres*, International Law, Power and Policy - A Contemporary Conception, 82 *Hague Recueil* 137 (1953).

international and constitutional law functional characteristics. The underlying domestic, political power structures are not taken into account[62]. These structures, however, represent the activities of political, economic and societal pressure groups, including lobbying. Their achievements may eventually lead to democratic majorities. On that basis, certain political, economic and cultural forces are represented by the states. This situation, i.e. that a multiplicity of sub-state actors that determine or attempt to determine state policy at the domestic level are not considered in the power balance of international relations, may change in the future. The capacity of information technology, i.e. its use, may nationally and internationally revolutionize the way political interaction occurs[63]. Individuals using communications technology operating in both domestic and transborder civil society may become powerful in the international system and thus have a chance of gaining bargaining strength in domestic matters, as may be observed for instance in the activities of several environmentalist groups. As such, international civil society groups become influential as a matter of fact, political state behaviour, in turn, is determined not only by "objective interests of sovereign entities" and the balance of power, whether or not mediated by international institutions, but also by the political weight and bargaining power of civil society entities. This raises, of course, from the point of view of public international and constitutional law, the problem of legitimation[64].

While, for the recognizable future, states remain the privileged international actors endowed with genuine, not derived, powers[65] and with the monopoly of physical force (police and military forces), the (voluntary) contribution of non-governmental actors may be needed to achieve certain public policy objectives. Notwithstanding the states' superior powers, in systems of *governance* states would position themselves in a network of partnership relations with other entities. The "procedural principles and rules" that are part of *governance* would coordinate in some way some of the actors having an influence on the development towards "Cyberspace", i.e., states and international organisations, multintional enterprises and business confederations, certain civil society groups and NGOs.

"Substantive principles and rules," and possibly a regime of competences, may be part of *governance*. But *governance* does not necessarily require a fully fledged regime prescribing a complete set of substantive rules and powers for the different actors. Some basic institutional and procedural arrangements may be sufficient to start an evolutionary process.

---

62 In this context see *Slaughter Anne-Marie*, Liberal International Relations Theory and International Economic Law, 10 *Am.U.J. Int'l L & Policy* 717, (721ff.) (1995).

63 *Bollier David*, The Global Advance of Electronic Commerce – Reinventing Markets, Management, and National Sovereignty, Queenstown (Aspen Institute) 1998.

64 Pertaining to the development and creation of law: "Normative Kraft des Faktischen", *Jellinek Georg*, Allgemeine Staatslehre, 3rd ed., Bad Homburg 1966, (337f.). However, this qualitative jump in the public international law character of international non-governmental actors has at present not yet been reached.

65 *Kelsen Hans*, Reine Rechtslehre, 2nd ed., Wien 1983 (333ff.).

*Governance* in "Cyberspace", because of the multitude of rules and principles and the wide constituency that is affected, may possibly assume some sort of "umbrella function" covering both the normative principles, agreements and arrangements pertaining to the subjects of public international law and the principles and self-regulatory schemes that would respectively apply to business, civil society and other non-governmental entities.

In this construct that juxtaposes different entities and prinicipIes of different legal quality, such as binding public international law, "soft law," self-regulatory arrangements, and non-binding self-policing measures of moral importance, public international law, as such, might in the long term originate, but also be affected by, a law creation process: Gradually, the scheme of *governance* that was originally designed to achieve some sort of workable decentralised coordination, could also develop stronger normative principles in fields that initially were not part of the body of international law and, in parallel, generate rational procedures adjusted to new circumstances.

### 2.2. *Taking governance seriously – Principles for action: Open markets, cooperation, quality of regulation; private sector responsibilities*

(i) *Open markets*: The central "policy principle" for the transition to "*Cyberspace*" is the existence of open markets to allow free national and transborder competition for the benefit of the consumer. This policy principle is decisive for the worldwide, rapid growth in production and use of new services and the take-up of innovative technologies.

The establishment and use of global information infrastructures should be left to competitive market forces. To the extent that "governmental industrial or innovation policies and programs" exist that are designed to promote national or regional "competitiveness" by introducing and enhancing high-tech information infrastructures, such programs should be phased out.

Core policy principles, calling on governments to ensure an appropriate framework aimed at stimulating private investment in, and usage of, global information networks for the benefits of all citizens were agreed, for instance, at the G7 Brussels Conference in February 1995. These principles are: promoting dynamic competition; encouraging private investment; defining an adaptable regulatory framework; providing open access to networks; ensuring universal provision of, and access to, services; promoting equality of opportunity to the citizen, promoting diversity of content, including cultural and linguistic diversity; recognizing the necessity of world-wide cooperation with particular attention to less-developed countries.

A number of political activities and international events such as the "1997 Ministerial Conference on Global Information Networks" in Bonn[66] and the 1998 OECD Ministerial Conference "Borderless World: Realising the Potential of Global Electronic Commerce"

66 Ministerial Conference Bonn 6-8 July 1997 ("Global Information Networks").

in Ottawa[67] have contributed to refining these principles. Besides fundamental policy questions, the latter events notably also addressed legal issues such as specific responsibilities of the different actors, security and confidentiality, authentication and integrity of messages, data protection, intellectual property rights, the facilitation of trading in multimedia content and taxation. This conference and spezialised follow-up meetings should contribute to paving the way for rapid growth and effective and fair use of global information networks, electronic commerce and other "Cyber" content.

The "Ministerial Declaration" ensuing from the Bonn Conference as well as a collateral "Industrial Declaration" put forward by the private sector contained key principles for further progress such as, for instance: regulation should be as light-handed and flexible as possible; legal rules applicable to global information networks should be consistent across borders; telecommunications markets should be opened up rapidly to effective competition; market forces must be allowed to rapidly develop open technical standards; discriminatory tax costs should not be imposed on the use of these networks; a high level of intellectual property rights protection is necessary for the creation, storage and distribution of "Cyber" content.

In the framework of the OECD Ottawa Conference, business proposed a set of fundamental principles "to shape the policies that govern electronic commerce, if the promises of electronic commerce are to be fulfilled"[68]. This list, whose main thrust is to guarantee open markets for electronic commerce, notably comprises the following principles:

- The development of electronic commerce should be led primarily by the private sector in response to market forces;
- Government intervention, when required, should promote a stable, international legal environment, allow a rational allocation of scarce resources and protect general interest. Such intervention should be no more than is essential and should be clear, transparent, objective, non-discriminatory, proportional, flexible and technology-neutral;
- Mechanisms for private sector input and involvement in policy making should be promoted and widely used in all countries and international fora;
- Regulation of the underlying telecommunications infrastructure, where necessary, should reduce impediments to competition, enabling new services and new entrants to compete globally in an open and fair market;
- A high level of trust should be pursued by mutual agreement, education, further technologcal innovations to enhance security and reliability, the adoption of adequate dispute resolution mechanisms, and private sector self-regulation.

67 Conference Conclusions, OECD Document SG/EC(98)14REV6, 26 October 1998, Paris 1998.

68 OECD Ministerial Conference "A Borderless World: Realising the Potential of Global Electronic Commerce", A Global Action Plan for Electronic Commerce Prepared by Business with Recommendations from Governments, 7-9 October 1998, Ottawa, Canada, OECD Document SG/EC(98)11/REV2, 5 October 1998, (9).

Business should make available to users the means to exercise choice with respect to privacy, confidentiality, content control and, under appropriate circumstances, anonymity.

When attempting to contribute to establishing more detailed elements for governance in "Cyberspace", it remains to be seen to what extent the newly created "Global Business Dialogue for Electronic Commerce" (GBD), a private business initiative, will encounter the sort of divergencies of interests and "frictions" that are similar to governmental competition in "Cyber" policies, or whether business will, to some extent, be "clearersighted" than governments, overcome territorial fragmentation and vindicate the "global interest" (without establishing global trusts and cartels!).

Open markets, liberalisation and competition and most other of the "G7" and "Bonn Conference" principles" have become overall, guiding principles for the leading industrial nations in their national strategies and action programmes dealing with global information networks. The OECD's Ottawa conference confirmed this development. Thus, governments appear to vigorously pursue procompetitive and deregulatory policies. I would advance here, however, two *caveats: First*, the more important telecommunications, information services, electronic commerce and global information networks become to national societies and economies, the less likely it is that some governments would relinquish all controls; *second*, on the flipside, the procompetitive withdrawal of controls, i.e. liberalisation and deregulation, will only work *if,* at the same time, the web of international cooperation becomes more solid and (in conformity with the principle of "subsidiarity") some authority is transferred to efficient international entities. This is a major aspect of *"governance"* in "Cyberspace". Another aspect are the synergies that would be created by "industry-led, market-driven, self-regulatory" participation[69], and active contributions by international organisations, labour, consumer and public interest groups and other stakeholders[70]. As far as governmental authority is concerned, it is a myth to assume that there can be free global markets without an adequate international framework entrusted with effective enforcement powers as, for instance, in the case of the WTO!

(ii) *Cooperation:* On the one hand, a basic international G7 and OECD consensus pertaining to key strategies for the regulation and deregulation of global communcations exists. But, on the other hand, not all countries of the world are versed in these understandings and, in practice, the various implementation strategies do, as experience tells us, not only lead to harmony but also produce discrepancies and conflict. Thus, *international cooperation* designed to reduce tension, prevent conflict and foster opportunities provided by the digital environment is fundamental, both as a principle of policy and as a basic element of international law.

---

69 Agreement reached in the meeting of the "Global Business Dialogue" (GBD) on 25 September 1998 in New York.

70 OECD, Ottawa Conference of Electronic Commerce, News Release Paris 13 October 1998, <http://www.oecd.org/news-and-events/release/nw98-95a.htm>.

Systems analysis may support and elucidate the pertinence of the "principle of co-operation". We need to be aware that in the age of interdependence and "globalisation" (in terms of communications technologies and transport, trade, financial flows and capital movements), it is not possible for one person, organization, country or region to derive lasting benefits from advanced technologies without the cooperation of others.

The international law of the past, which intended to define the areas of sovereignty of different states, was simply a law of international coexistence. It is increasingly being superseded by a more highly developed law of international cooperation.[71] But this is a slow advancement. The public, international law-making process requires patience, persistence and focus. Governments and regions need effective transnational legal frameworks to relate to each other and to be able to establish sustained cooperation. Many have recognized this need for change in political attitudes. Less enlightened policy makers, on the other hand, may at some stage advocate once again for a recourse to "power politics" in order to achieve (or protect against) new forms of perceived dominance (e.g. "electronic imperialism").

A more enlightened international law of cooperation, however, asks countries to cooperate at the bilateral, regional and global levels in an ever-increasing number of fields. Where this is not possible, it states that, when anyone adopts new measures, the interests of third parties should be taken into account and the negative consequences be minimized. This spirit, which is the very basis of the "Bretton Woods system"[72] including GATT/WTO and other successful international organizations such as the OECD, is vital for more than just trade policies. It may contribute to matching global technological progress on political, cultural and even moral levels in the transition to "Cyberspace".

A number of international agreements and arrangements have been concluded that are of importance as a basis for international cooperation in the digital environment. The "Ministerial Declaration on Trade in Information Technology Products" agreed upon in Singapore on 13 December 1996 provides for the enhancement of trade in information technology products. Follow-up negotiations have produced the result that tariffs on IT products will gradually be reduced to zero by 1 January 2000. This agreement[73] covers approximately 90% of world trade in IT products. The "WTO Agreement on Basic Telecommunications Services" concluded in Geneva on 15 February 1997 provides for important liberalisation measures[74]. The WIPO Diplomatic Conference held in Geneva from 2-20 December 1996 adopted two treaties in the field of copyright and neighbouring rights.[75]

---

71 *Friedmann Wolfgang*, The Changing Dimensions of International Law, 62 Colum. L. Rev. 1147, at 1150 (1962); *Wolfrum Rüdiger*, International Law of Cooperation, in: *Bernhard Rudolf* (Ed.), Encyclopedia of Public International Law, Instalment 9 (1986) ; *Verloren van Themaat P.*, The Changing Structure of International Economic Law, The Hague 1981; see Chapter Two 1.

72 *Jackson/Davey*, Legal Problems of International Economic Relations, 2nd ed. St.Paul, Minn 1986 (251ff.).

73 World Trade Orgnisation (WTO), Agreement of the Implementation of the Ministerial Declaration on Trade in Information and Technology Products (March 26, 1997), 36 I.L.M. 375 (1997)

74 World Trade Organisation (WTO), Agreement on Telecommunications Services (Fourth Protocol

As the transnational nature of global networks reduces the effectiveness of purely national or regional regulatory initiatives, there is a correlating powerful reason for enhanced international cooperation to vitalize the process of liberalisation, deregulation and fair competition. This does not necessarily lead to overregulation. Enlightened international cooperation concentrating sharply on bottleneck problems would alleviate concerns about the danger of a coming regulatory "global Leviathan"[76]. The objective rather is that regulators agree internationally on light-handed regulation and undertake as soon as possible not to regulate at all, or agree on "phasing-out schemes to advance deregulation".

As regulatory self-restraint prevails and deregulation advances internationally, competition law and the pertinent instruments of the WTO would have to ensure fairness and neutrality in terms of a "level playing field". However, as competition law is, at present, predominantly national or regional, elements of a "world competition order", including schemes for dealing with mergers, would gradually have to be developed, starting from existing bilateral and multilateral cooperation arrangements and agreements[77]. An important building block of a "world competition order" is the principle of "positive comity"[78]. Traditional comity is about avoiding conflicts over

---

to General Agreement on Trade in Services), done at Geneva, February 15, 1997, 36 I.L.M. 354 (1997) (with introductory note by Laura B. SHERMAN); see also the assessment contained in ITU, World Telecommunication Development Report – Trade in Telecommunications - World Telecommunication Indicators, Geneva: ITU 1997 (98ff.) – The new agreement ("Fourth Protocol") covers all communications services both public and private that envolve end-to-end transmission of customer supplied information, including voice telephony, data transmission, telex, telegraph, faximile, private leased lines and circuit services (i.e. the sale or lease of different transmission capacities), fixed and mobile satellite systems and services, cellular telephony, mobile data services, paging, and personal communications systems. The new agreements do not formally encompass on-line data processing, on-line data base storage, and retrieval, electronic data interchange, e-mail or voice mail. Such values added services are to a considerable extent already included in the "schedules" that are in force as a result of the Uruguay Round; see *Bronckers Marco* C.E.J., *Pierre Larouche*, Telecommunications Services and the World Trade Organisation, in 31 *Journal of World Trade Law* 5-48 (1997); *Grewlich Klaus W.*, Konflikt und Ordnung in der globalen Kommunikation – Wettstreit der Staaten und Wettbewerb der Unternehmen, (*Law and Economic of International Telecommunications* Vol. 33) Baden-Baden 1997 (195ff.); *Barth Dietrich*, Die Liberalisierung der Telekommunikationsdienstleistungen in der Welthandelsorganisation, in Arch PT 2/97 112ff..

75 WIPO Copyright Treaty, WIPO Doc. CRNR/DC/94 and WIPO Performances and Phonogramm Treaty, WIPO Doc. CRNR/DC/95; see Chapter Eight.

76 *Hobbes Thomas*, Leviathan, 1651.

77 *Fox Eleanor*, Trade, Competition Law and the Agenda for the WTO – Forging the Links of Competition and Trade, 4 *Pacific Rim Law & Policy Journal* (1995), 1-36; see "Draft International Antitrust Code as a GATT-MTO Plurilateral Trade Agreement" ("Munich Code"), in 64 *Antitrust and Trade Regulations Report*, Special Supplement August 19, 1993 (No. 1628); detailed analysis in *Grewlich Klaus W.*, Konflikt und Ordnung in der globalen Kommunikation – Wettstreit der Staaten und Wettbewerb der Unternehmen, (Law and Economics of International Telecommunications Vol. 33) Baden-Baden 1997 (229ff.); *Drexl Josef*, Perspektiven eines Weltkartellrechts, Bonn 1998 (26ff.).

78 *Kiriaziz Georgios*, Positive Comity in EU/US Cooperation in Competition Matters, EC Competition Policy Newsletter 1998/3 11-14 (12).

enforcement activities. Conflict avoidance is achieved by closely cooperating with a partner and clearly stating one's important interests at various stages of proceedings. "Active" or "positive comity" provides that an authority initiates an investigation to respond to a request by another authority. This is the product of increased awareness that, in certain circumstances, a cooperative approach may be more successful.

For the communications infrastructure, regulations have been developed to create a framework within which market forces can play. Now the emphasis shifts from the infrastructure to the creation and transmission of information *content*. The WIPO treaties on copyright are important steps on this road. A number of the emerging national "Cyber legislations" are meant to deal with issues where the incongruence between national territory and the potential global reach of actors in global information networks becomes particularly prominent. To reduce the adverse effects of such discrepancies, an international concertation with some substantive "rules of the road", a multilateral coordination scheme based on and helping to further evolve critical elements of an international framework of "principles", becomes imperative.

In addition, there still remain a number of basic principles of public interest such as security and privacy, and the protection of minors that have to be effectively enforced, in agreement with constitutional law and basic public international law principles.

Thus, clear policy direction must be given, in order to take advantage of the achieved level of international *cooperation* and to vigourosly progress "tous azimuths" in this spirit, whether this concerns:

- the next GATS review round in the WTO, where multimedia products will play a particular role;
- the next ITU meetings after the 1998 Plenipotentiary;
- the WIPO efforts towards an IPR treaty for the protection of databases;
- the arrangements pertaining to Internet domain names;
- peering schemes for the sharing of traffic;
- settlements of accounts;
- the IP-standard family;
- shared public/private efforts, tied to schemes of cooperative self-regulation for the protection of minors; or
- arrangements on information and communications security following a solution of the inter-governmental issues pertaining to the export of encryption keys and "lawful access or non-access".

(iii) *Quality of regulation:* In North America, in Europe, but also in other regions and countries, the Internet is to a large extent an unregulated phenomenon, but supported by a regulated infrastructure (telecommunications). Internet users are even less regulated than Internet service providers as the Internet, for some time, was foremost a medium of speech and association, the invisible "new frontier", the "innovative and cultural" space" of the "Internet communities". This was a "space, where governments and lawyers should stay out" and; and if some security of behaviour was felt desirable, it was to be achieved through self-regulation, such as the "netiquette". But, now, as commercial interests ("electronic commerce") in global information networks that may develop under circumstances of "convergence" of computer networks, telecommunications and the audiovisual become more pronounced, as different attempts at "appropriation" of the invisible "global commons" may be observed, the "public domain" seems to be shrinking and market actors, who may even come closer to monopoly positions, may be distinguished.

Running on global information networks, tomorrow's knowledge economy may unleash a storm of individual activities and competition, as both capital costs of entry into the market and the difficulty of establishing recognition and trust on the part of the consumer in a transparent information market evaporate. An opposing view argues that the expected reduction of information costs is just as likely to spawn massive enterprises that leverage the capacity of global informations networks to enhance "intranets", product branding and discriminatory distribution channels, in order to achieve unassailable market dominance in a world characterised by information acceleration and information overload. The scenario to emerge in reality will hinge on the path of regulation and de-regulation, and on whether both suppliers and consumers manage to develop organisations that assure inexpensive and accurate sharing of information about quality and prices in "Cyberspace".

In parallel to "open-access regulation" there is "public-interest regulation". There now are calls on governments, regulators and lawyers to protect personal and economic freedom, to legally guarantee and, as necessary, enforce the "public interest" (notably: human dignity, decency, privacy, data protection and the existence of a "public domain" matching the needs of democratic societies).

Regulatory responses must be given also at a more operational level pertaining to daily activities, i.e. at the different levels of the multimedia value chain and at the various stages of business activity – from the establishment of a business to the promotion and provision of electronic commerce activities through the conclusion of contracts, to the making of electronic payments. Here again, some "de-ideologisation" may be needed: Neither regulation nor a weakening the state is an objective in itself! The test for any regulation should always be: What does the respective regulatory measure do to the advantage of the individual, the citizen or the consumer? Seriously following the "state-of-the-art methods" for ensuring "quality of regulation" and asking the latter question carefully may sometimes lead to the conclusion that "the best regulation" is not to regulate at all or not at the time being, to allow for trial and error and to preserve and increase areas of freedom and free choice. Governments should live up to the challenges of the information society and global networks, but focus on bottlenecks and exercise "regulatory self-restraint", allowing for timely "phasing-out" of regulation ("sunset clauses").

This is even more important, as globalisation implies (because of its very nature) the "internationalisation" of rule-making, thus forcing governments to question long-standing administrative law and regulatory traditions. The quality of regulatory decisions in one government becomes a matter of concern to other states that are exposed to cross-border effects, or linked by agreements and arrangements for regulatory harmonisation, mutual recognition or coordination schemes for administrative law[79].

(iv) The private sector should, as often as possible, take the initiative to ensure compatibility between standards at appropriate interfaces. This is a major aspect of "self-regulation" to guarantee access to networks and markets.

Global networks particularly need international standards. Seamless interoperability is essential. In the "global information society" different forms of information content, services, network and equipment must be able to interoperate without unnecessary restrictions. Standardisation should be voluntary, industry-led and market driven. It should continue to be based on open procedures, though there is a need for greater representation of consumer, user and local community needs. The needed standardisation is primarily the task of international cooperation within the *private sector* (manufacturers, network operators, service providers) using standardisation facilities such as ISO fora or the Internet Protocol (IP) mechanism.

There is a decentralised power structure in the Internet. But, as a pure anarchy, global networks could not function. The definition of protocols, for instance, must be coordinated. Technical compatibility of networks must be ensured, otherwise content would not be able to pass seamlessly between different networks. Participants in the Internet communicate on the basis of a common protocol, the "open standard TCP/IP". This protocol is first written, then freely distributed to any individual or entity who wants to use it. Revisions of the protocol take account of the experience of the users. Business and other stakeholders should ensure that effective self-regulation pertaining to open standards is maintained and no restrictions on free competition and access occur. This is important, in order to avoid circumstances where public institutions would feel obliged to interfere on the basis of their regulatory powers and authority.

A tidal wave may be observed in dealing with issues related to the new digital environment and "convergence" in the broader context of "good governance": The global movement towards liberalised markets in communications is mirrored in international and regional organisations' efforts[80] that are designed to shape a

---

79 Common principles may be derived from comparative national administrative law including the administrative law of international organisations, notably the EU; see for instance *Schwartz Bernard, H.W.R. Wade*, Legal Control of Government – Administrative Law in Britain and the United States, Oxford 1972 (26ff.); see also the material contained in *Mosler Hermann* (Ed.), Liability of the State for Illegal Conduct of its Organs, Köln, Berlin et al. 1967.; *Mosler Hermann* (Ed.), Judicial Protection against the Executive, Köln, Berlin 1970.

80 Notably "World Trade Organisation" (WTO) for pertaining to agreements on basic telecommunications, tariff reduction concerning information technology products and a so-called "tariff-free zone" for electronically delivered products, as well as possibly extending binding multilateral trade rules to the new area of electronic trade; the "United Nations Conference on

compatible framework for industry development and regulation. These organisations are encouraging national governments to perform changes in attitudes, policies and regulation that will bring their communication structures closer to common regional and international frameworks. Pertinent organisations deal with action items such as compatibility and standardisation (e.g. the International Telecommunications Union (ITU)), issues of comparative practices and performances and consensus-building in view of forthcoming international negotiations (e.g. the OECD and the TU) and common policy and legal platforms for national communications development (e.g. the World Trade Organisation(WTO))[81] and the World Intellectual Property Organisation (WIPO). Apart from regulation designed to create or to guarantee competition und to secure access to markets (e.g. open network provision/access (ONP/ONA), interconnection and access to "essential facilities"), there are "public interest/ordre public" objectives to be achieved (e.g. privacy, human dignity, security), consumer protection must be realised (e.g. fair trading, prevention of fraud, dealing with breach of contract) or vital framework conditions must become operational (e.g. for cryptography, trademarks and copyright, "Cyber-cash"). Such efforts undertaken by national governments and their intergovernmental organisations may be complemented, stimulated even substituted (as a matter of "subsidiarity") by international business fora, such as the "Transatlantic Business Dialogue" (TABD), the "Global Business Dialogue" (GBD) and grass root undertakings of broad based transborder/civil society groups.

---

Internationational Trade Law" (UNCITRAL) for the updating of commercial law and for the recognition of the digital signature; the "World Intellectual Property Organisation" (WIPO) for IPR aspects of the new digital environment; the "Organisation for Economic Cooperation and Development" (OECD) for comparative practices and performances and consensus-building, particularly in view of forthcoming international negotiations; the "International Organisation for Standardisation" (ISO) and the "International Electrotechnical Commission " (IEC) for setting standards in various areas of information technology; the "World Bank" for communications infrastructure and advice to developing countries, - the "United Nations Conference on Trade and Development" also has the objective of helping developing countries joining the global markt place; the "Bank for International Settlements" (BIS) for the analysis of the impact of electronic financial transactions, including electronic banking and electronic payments; the "World Customs Organisation" (WCO) for adjusting and simplifying customs clearance procedures; the "World Wide Web Consortium" (W3C), a self-regulatory mechanism for Internet standards and technical protocols; the European Union (EU), notably the European Commission is working on all aspects of the global information society; other international organisations active on different aspects comprise the "International Telecommunications Union" (ITU), the "United Nations Educational, Scientific and Cultural Organisation" (UNESCO) and the regional United Nations Commissions, notably the "UN-Economic Commission for Europe" (UN-ECE); and the Council of Europe.

80 *Héritier Adrienne*, After liberalization – Public-interest Services in the Utilities, *Preprints aus der Max-Planck-Projektgruppe Recht der Gemeinschaftsgüter*, Bonn 1998/5.

81 World Trade Organisation (WTO) – Agreement on Telecommunications Services (Fourth Protocol to the General Agreement on Trade in Services), Geneva, February 15, 1997, 36 *I.L.M.* 354 (1997).

## 3. Facilitating change towards "constitutionalisation"

In the management of change towards the global information society, where a wide constituency and a multitude of rules and principles are affected, an even more developed legal expositum of governance may emerge.

(i) A first step leads to multi-level constitutionalism. This concept refers to a multi-level organization of public authority and responsibilities that does not necessarily imply statehood at each level. Rather, each level of this system of governance may have "original" legitimacy, as far as it is democratically founded on the will of the constituency affected by its policies[82].

The next step would combine the multi-level analysis with multi-actor analysis[83]. A constitutionalized international law[84] would then possibly assume some sort of "umbrella function" for elements of both a public law order and a "private law" order, covering normative principles, agreements and arrangements pertaining to the subjects of public international law but also to principles and self-regulatory schemes that would respectively apply to business, civil society and other non-governmental entities. A new, genuinely multilateral public international law, both in terms of substantive principles, institutions, levels of authority and procedures might first cover and comprise and, later on, integrate both the traditional public international law community and the newly emerging internationally active non-governmental business, labour and other civil society actors. This is a major operational aspect of the development towards "constitutionalisation".

In actively participating in this transition to "constitutionalisation" today's increasingly networked legislators, regulators, diplomats, business and civil society entities need a common mental framework, in terms of shared essentials of "governance" (and a vision of "constitutionalisation") including normative principles, to safeguard both competition and public policy objectives, at a scale congruent to "Cyberspace". The required effort should reflect that, in harmony with the principle of "subsidiarity", regulatory and self-regulatory action pertaining to electronic commerce may have to take place at different levels of competence, i.e. regional, multiregional or global (multi-level analysis) and imply not only states but also economic actors and civil society entities (multi-actor analysis).

---

82 See in this context *Pernice Ingolf*, Multilevel Constitutionalism and the Treaty of Amsterdam – European Constitution-Making Revisited?, 36 *Common Market Law Review* (1999), 703 (709).

83 *Grewlich Klaus W.*, Governance in "Cyberspace" – Access and Public Interest in Global Communications, Den Haag/London/Boston 1999 , (Chapter Ten).

84 *Petersmann Ernst-U.*, How to Constitutionalise International Law and Foreign Policy for the Benefit of Civil Society?, *Michigan Journal of International Law* 20 (1999); *Schloemann Hannes L., Stefan Ohlhoff*, "Constitutionalization" and Dispute Settlement in the WTO – National Security as an Issue of Competence, 93 *American Journal of International Law* 424 (1999).

(ii) "Cyberspace" is neither a metaphysical "cyber nirvana,"[85] nor an irresistible blind destiny that mankind has to suffer at the beginning of the millenium. The "transformative power" of global networks is man-made, not a result of technological determinism, and can thus be adjusted by human intervention.

The greatest economic happiness for the greatest number as a result of free competition is a legitimate objective. And the liberal creed relies on full competition and framework laws to ensure that competition works. But policy and law, including de(re)regulatory law and practice designed to guarantee access to global networks, are substantially more than mere facilitators and auxiliary instruments for technological and economic advancement.

According to this line of thinking, governance would not remain forever a pragmatic minimalist "default solution" that could, in the worst case, even prevent the development of an ambitious European and International law. On the contrary, global governance could enable and facilitate the development not only towards a mature and genuinely universal "international law of cooperation"[86], but even more ambitiously a "constitutionalisation" of public international law and international relations that would match the planetary nature of "Cyberspace".

What is envisaged is more than "cooperation" and "governance", but much less than an irrealistic full supranational solution or a "world state". In the search for establishing adequate trade-offs between freedom and public interest in global communications (such as relating to national, business and personal security, consumer protection, protection of minors and human dignity, privacy and data protection and, on the other hand, the economic rationale of electronic commerce) many trade-offs and balancing solutions must be envisaged and decisions must be made to safeguard fundamental values and to reach policy objectives. But: neither the core elements of human rights, democracy and the rule of law, nor that of the "basic integrity of the market mechanism" are negotiable! The fundamental creed of the humanistic (judeo-christian) liberalism, which notably underlies the EC Treaty is that, in principle, there is no opposition between free markets and fundamental (constitutional) rights and values, if the framework for competition is "constitutionally" protected. Economic freedom and fundamental values/human rights would then mutually reinforce each other. Public interest considerations, transformed into specific "ordre public" interventions would be expedient only in well-defined, exceptional cases, but do not legitimate horizontal measures hindering or paralysing the play of market forces[87].

85 The notions of "virtual" and "metaphysical" are sometimes confused; *Esterbauer Reinhold*, Gott im Cyberspace? – Zu religiösen Aspekten neuer Medien, in *Kolb Anton* (ed.), Cyberethik – Verantwortung in der digital vernetzten Welt, Stuttgart 1998.

86 *Friedmann Wolfgang*, The Changing Structure of International Law, New York 1964; *Bourquin Maurice*, Pouvoir Scientifique et Droit International, 70 *Hague Recueil* 331 (1947) (359f.).

87 Referring to "ordoliberal" thought (Freiburger Schule) *Gerber David J.*, Constitutionalizing the Economy: German Neo-Liberalism, Competition Law and the "New Europe", *42 The Am. Journal. of Comparative Law* 25 (1994); in the thinking of *Eucken* and of other members of the "ordo-liberal school" human rights, the rule of law and the "invisible hand" (free markets) are intimately

Whatever the use of global information networks may promise, whatever the benefits of the transition to the age of "Cyberspace" may be, whatever innovative international arrangements may be required to fully take advantage of the potential of the information society - law must act as the necessary companion of competition and legal practice and public policy must remain faithful to the rule of law[88], respect human rights and fundamental principles as contained in written or unwritten constitutions and live up to international agreements and arrangements, thus supporting the evolution of a truly *universal and constitutionalised* "public international law of cooperation".

---

intertwined; see *Eucken W.*, Grundsätze der Wirtschaftspolitik (Principles of Economic Policy), Introduction by *Ernst-Joachim Mestmäcker*, 6th ed., Tübingen 1990; see also *Böhm Franz*, Wettbewerb and Monopolkampf, Berlin 1933.

88 One of Adam Smith's basic convictions is that the "rule of law" protects economic actors and society against arbitrary state interventionism.: see *Hayek Friedrich von*, The Constitution of Liberty, Chicago/Ill. 1960), (German edition: Die Verfassung der Freiheit, Tübingen 1983, 285f.).

# List of Symposium Participants

| | |
|---|---|
| **Prof. Dr. Jeffrey B. Abramson**<br>Louis Stulberg Professor of Law & Politics<br>Brandeis University<br>Waltham, MA, USA | **Jacques Arlandis**<br>Directeur Scientifique/IDATE<br>Editor Communications & Strategies<br>Montpellier; France |
| **Privatdozent Dr. Herbert Burkert**<br>Senior Researcher, German National Research Centre for Information Technology, St.Augustin, Germany;<br>Assistant Professor for Information and Communication Law, St.Gallen; Switzerland | **Prof. Dr. Kenneth Dam**<br>Max Pam Professor of American and Foreign Law<br>University of Chicago<br>Chicago, IL, USA;<br>Member of the Steering Committee |
| **Prof. Dr. Paul A. David**<br>Senior Research Fellow<br>All Souls College<br>Oxford University, Oxford, UK<br>Professor of Economics and History<br>Stanford University,Stanford, CA, USA;<br>Member of the Steering Committee | **Prof. Dr. Christoph Engel**<br>Head of the Max Planck Projektgroup on the Law of Common Goods, Bonn; Germany<br>Co-Chairman of the Steering Committee |
| **Robert Gellman**<br>Privacy and Information Policy Consultant<br>Washington, DC, USA | **Prof. Dr. Jack Goldsmith**<br>Associate Professor of Law,<br>University of Chicago<br>Chicago, IL, USA |
| **Prof. Dr. Dr. Klaus W. Grewlich**<br>College of Europe, Bruges;<br>Universities of Freiburg and Bonn;<br>Center for European Integration Studies, Bonn;<br>Member of the Steering Committee | **Prof. Dr. Bernd Holznagel**<br>Westfälische Wilhelms-University, Münster, Institute for Information Telecommunication and Media Law, Germany<br>Member of the Steering Committee |
| **Prof. Dr. Michael Hutter**<br>Professor of Economics, chair for economic theory, Witten/Herdecke University;<br>Founding Director of the Institute for Economy and Culture, Witten/Herdecke University; Germany<br>Member of the Steering Committee | **Prof. Dr. Kenneth H. Keller**<br>Charles M. Denny, Jr. Professor of Science, Technology and Public Policy University of Minnesota<br>Minneapolis, MN, USA<br>Co-Chairman of the Steering Committee |

| | |
|---|---|
| **Prof. Dr. Kenneth Keniston**<br>Andrew W. Mellon Professor of Human Development<br>Massachusetts Institute of Technology;<br>Cambridge. MA, USA;<br>Member of the Steering Committee | **Wolf Osthaus**<br>Max Planck Projectgroup<br>on the Law of Common Goods, Bonn;<br>Germany |
| **Prof. Dr. Henry H. Perritt, Jr.**<br>Dean & Professor of Law<br>Chicago-Kent College of Law,<br>Illinois Institute of Technology;<br>Chicago; USA;<br>Member of the Steering Committee | **Prof. Dr. Per Selle**<br>LOS-centre, Bergen, Norway |
| **Dr. Robert Spinrad**<br>Vice President, Technology Strategy (ret.)<br>Xerox Corporation<br>Palo Alto Research Center<br>Palo Alto, CA, USA;<br>Member of the Steering Committee | **Prof. Michael Thompson**<br>LOS-centre, Bergen, Norway;<br>Director of The Musgrave Institute,<br>London, UK |
| **Tommy Tranvik**<br>LOS-centre, Bergen, Norway | **Prof. Dr. Hans-Heinrich Trute**<br>University of Technology, Dresden,<br>Department of Law; Germany |
| **Dr. Raymund Werle**<br>Max Planck Institute for the Study of Societies, Cologne; Germany<br>Member of the Steering Committee | **Prof. Dr. Joachim Wieland**<br>Bielefeld University, Faculty of Law;<br>Germany |
| **Prof. Dr. Martina Zitterbart**<br>Operating Systems and Computer Networks, Technical University,<br>Braunschweig; Germany<br>Member of the Steering Committee | |